AUSTRIA

DRIVE 8
pp86–95

Brunico

Merano Bressanone

Bolzano

DRIVE 9
pp96–103

DRIVE 12
pp122–129

Villach

Tarvisio

DRIVE 10
pp104–113

ENTINO-
TO ADIGE

Trento

Rovereto

Belluno

Feltre

Vittorio Veneto

Bassano
del Grappa

Treviso

FRIULI-VENEZIA

GIULIA

Pordenone

Udine

Gorizia

SLOVENIA

Monfalcone

Trieste

Golfo
di Trieste

VENETO

Vicenza

Verona

Padova
(Padua)

Mestre

Venezia
(Venice)

DRIVE 11
pp114–121

Golfo
di Venice

CROATIA

Rovigo

Rovinj

Pula

S482 S434

DRIVE 13
pp130–139

Ferrara

Modena

LIA-ROMAGNA

Bologna

Imola Ravenna

Faenza

Forlì

Cesena

Mar
Adriatico

DRIVE 24
pp236–245

Rimini

SAN
MARINO

Pesaro

Urbino

Fano

Ancona

0 kilometres   70

0 miles   70

Firenze
(Florence)

DRIVE 16
pp160–169

DRIVE 17
pp170–177

OSCANA

Arezzo

Siena

Città di
Castello

DRIVE 23
pp226–235

Gúbbio

Jesi

DRIVE 25
pp246–255

Macerata

Civitanova
Marche

MARCHE

DRIVE 19
pp188–195

DRIVE 21
pp206–215

Perugia

Foligno

UMBRIA

DRIVE 20
pp196–205

San Benedetto
del Tronto

Ascoli Piceno

Spoleto

Terni

Teramo

Viterbo

Narni

DRIVE 22
pp216–225

Rieti

Pescara

ABRUZZO

L'Aquila

Chieti

LAZIO

Civitavecchia

Vatican City Roma
(Rome)

EYEWITNESS TRAVEL

BACK ROADS

NORTHERN AND CENTRAL ITALY

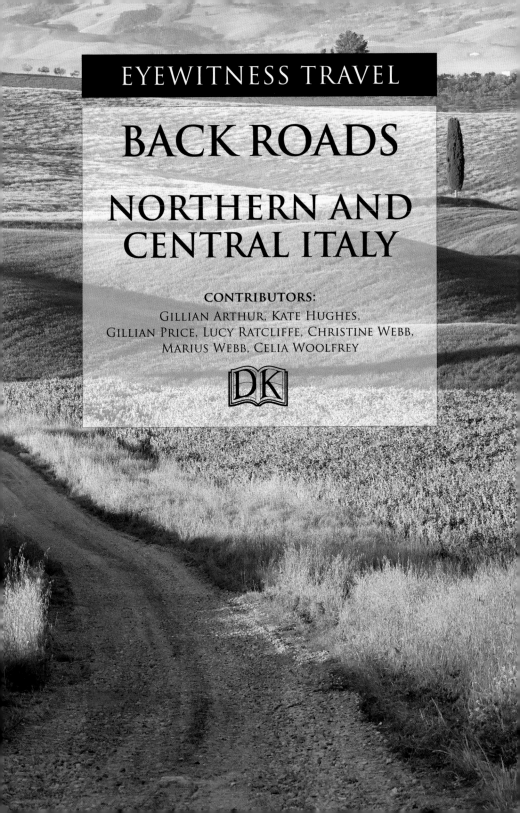

EYEWITNESS TRAVEL

BACK ROADS

NORTHERN AND CENTRAL ITALY

CONTRIBUTORS:
GILLIAN ARTHUR, KATE HUGHES,
GILLIAN PRICE, LUCY RATCLIFFE, CHRISTINE WEBB,
MARIUS WEBB, CELIA WOOLFREY

DK

DK | Penguin Random House

MANAGING EDITOR Madhavi Singh

EDITORIAL MANAGER
Sheeba Bhatnagar

DESIGN MANAGER Kavita Saha

DEPUTY DESIGN MANAGER
Mathew Kurien

PROJECT EDITORS Sandhya Iyer,
Shikha Kulkarni

PICTURE RESEARCH MANAGER
Taiyaba Khatoon

PICTURE RESEARCHER
Sumita Khatwani

SENIOR DTP DESIGNER
Azeem Siddiqui

SENIOR CARTOGRAPHIC
MANAGER Uma Bhattacharya

CARTOGRAPHY Zafar-ul-Islam Khan

ILLUSTRATOR
Arun Pottirayil

Colour reproduction by Media Development
Printing Ltd, UK

Printed and bound in China

17 18 19 20 10 9 8 7 6 5 4 3 2 1

First published in the UK in 2012 by
Dorling Kindersley Limited, 80 Strand,
London WC2R 0RL
A Penguin Random House Company

Reprinted with revisions 2015, 2018
Copyright 2012, 2018 © Dorling
Kindersley Limited, London

ISBN 978 0 2413 0657 4

Front cover: Cypress tree by a narrow road winding
through corn fields near Ville di Corsano

MIX
From responsible
sources
FSC
www.fsc.org FSC™ C018179

CONTENTS

Above Pretty Riomaggiore, built over the Rio Major

e harbour at

Above Fresco at Varese's Sacro Monte

Above Le Balze sandstone landscape near Piantravigne

Above View across Prato della Valle in Padua

Below Typical blue and white road signs near Lake Como

Below The winding road up to Santuario della Madonna del Ghisallo

NESSO 23
SORMANO 5
CAGLIO 5
REZZAGO 2

About this Book

The 25 drives in this book capture the diversity of Northern and Central Italy, from the snow-capped mountain ranges on the borders with France and Austria to the hill towns of Tuscany and Umbria; from the dramatic coastline of the Ligurian Cinque Terre to the lakes of Lombardy and the Veneto. A modern, industrialized nation with its finger on the commercial and cultural pulse of Europe, Italy is also a country where traditional values are maintained, and the pace of life outside of its cities is still refreshingly slow.

Our drives embrace the region's world-famous art towns, but rather than being treated as isolated spots on a weekend break, they are included in tours that encourage a wider exploration of the history, culture and landscape that gave rise to them. Other drives go right off the beaten track – to enchanting villages, remote mountain outposts, hidden rocky coves and rarely visited archaeological sites – allowing visitors to explore facets of Northern and Central Italy that many never experience.

Getting Started

The guide begins with all the practical information you need to plan and get the most out of a driving holiday in Northern and Central Italy: how to get there; tips on bringing your own vehicle or hiring one; details of the documentation required; and motoring advice, from the quirks of Italian driving and road signage to where you can buy petrol and what to do if your car breaks down. Health, money and communications are also covered and there is an overview of dining and accommodation options. A language section at the back lists essential words and phrases, including key driving-related vocabulary.

The Drives

The main touring section of the guide is divided into leisurely drives, ranging in duration from one to seven days. Most of the tours are on paved roads, and where they are not, they are on good-quality unmetalled roads, which should pose no problems for a standard vehicle. The drives encompass every area of Northern and Central Italy. To help visitors choose and plan a trip, each drive begins with a list of highlights

and a clearly mapped itinerary. There is advice on the best time of year to do the drive, road conditions, market days and major festival dates. The drive pages contain detailed descriptions of each sight and activity, linked by clear driving instructions. Side panels offer information on places to stay and eat. Tinted boxes feature suggestions for extra activities and background information. These might include details of a local festival or speciality; tips for a wine-tasting tour; or where to go hiking. The flexible nature of the tours means that some can be linked together to create a longer driving holiday, or simply dipped into to plan day trips while based in one particular region. Each drive also features a mapped town or countryside walking tour, designed to take no more than three hours at a leisurely pace with stops on the way.

Using the Sheet Map

A pull-out road map of the entire region is supplied at the back of the guide. This map contains all the information you need to drive around the country and navigate between the different tours. All motorways, major roads, ferry ports and airports – both domestic and international – are clearly identified. There is also a comprehensive index, allowing you to locate sights quickly and easily. The map is further supplemented by a handy distance chart, to enable you to gauge the distances between the major cities. All of these features make the pull-out map an excellent addition to the individual drive-itinerary maps within the book.

Top left Manarola, a Cinque Terre town in Liguria **Top right** Fishing boats moored at Lazise, on the eastern shore of Lake Garda **Centre left** Grey-stone houses in the medieval heart of Abbadia San Salvatore **Centre right** The rolling Tuscan landscape near Montisi **Below left** Fiat 500, Greve in Chianti **Below right** A fresco in the Neo-Classical Villa Melzi, Bellagio

Above Driving in the Upper Tiber region of northern Umbria

Introducing Northern and Central Italy

The culture, cuisine, traditions and landscape of Northern and Central Italy are best appreciated close up, and there is no better way to home in on this endlessly fascinating part of the world than to slow down, leave the busy *autostrada* and explore the countryside by its back roads. Follow one road to a vineyard and meet a prize-winning winemaker; pull over on another to let a shepherd pass with his flock; or take a third to experience the genuine hospitality of a B&B owner proudly introducing you to regional specialities at the breakfast table. In Northern and Central Italy – whether driving through the Alpine peaks of the Alto-Adige, over the rolling hillsides of Le Langhe or along the Adriatic coast in Le Marche – the visitor will never be far from beautiful towns rich in culture and history, evocative landscapes and gourmet delights. Travelling the back roads reveals how, beneath the contemporary surface, a world that many thought had ceased to exist half a century ago is alive and well, and as alluring as ever.

When to Go

Each drive includes a recommendation for the ideal time to make the trip. This may be because the scenery is at its best or rivers are at their highest and most spectacular, or perhaps because the azaleas or apple blossom are in bloom. There might be a local festival taking place, or it could be that a certain food is in season. The weather, of course, is also a factor. The northern half of Italy has a varied climate falling into three distinct geographical zones: in the north, expect cold, Alpine winters and warm, wet summers; in the vast central Po valley, summers are hot and humid and winters damp, foggy and freezing; Tuscany, Umbria and Le Marche enjoy a more clement climate, with long, hot summers and relatively mild winters. In general, the best times to visit Northern and Central Italy are spring and autumn, ideally between April and June or September and October, when the climate should be mild without being too hot, and the whole region is generally much less crowded than in high summer.

Times to Avoid

As far as possible, roads and airports should be avoided at the beginning of August and in the days just before and after Ferragosto (15 August), the national summer holiday. The start of school holidays also sees a great surge in traffic levels. Schools break up for summer in mid-June and resume in mid-September. The Easter holidays usually begin on the Thursday before Easter and end on the Monday or Tuesday afterwards. Summer weekends and days around public holidays can also be very busy on the roads.

Festivals

Festivals and fairs take place all over Italy throughout the year. As well as the Easter and Christmas festivities, every town and village has a patron saint, and each one marks its saint's day with special celebrations. Spring and autumn are the best times for *sagras*, festivals devoted to local foods. Mushroom, sausage, olive oil, chestnut and wine *sagras* are common in autumn, while spring *sagras* are often devoted to seasonal fruits like strawberries or cherries. *Carnevale* sees masked and fancy-dress parades in many towns and villages, most spectacularly in Venice and Ivrea. Ferragosto is marked by free outdoor concerts, dancing and often fireworks.

Public Holidays

New Year's Day (1 Jan)
Epiphany (6 Jan)
Easter Sunday and Monday
Liberation Day (25 Apr)
Labour Day (1 May)
Republic Day (2 Jun)
Ferragosto (15 Aug)
All Souls' Day (1 Nov)
Immaculate Conception of the Blessed Virgin Mary (8 Dec)
Christmas Day (25 Dec)
Santo Stefano (26 Dec)

Left The pretty resort village of Limone sul Garda, on the shores of Lake Garda

Above The springtime ritual of Calendimaggio, celebrated in Assisi

Getting There

The increasing availability of low-cost flights has revolutionized travel to and within Italy. Provincial airports across the country are now open to international flights from other European cities, both major and provincial. Arriving at a small airport – where queues for immigration and baggage are short, and where a hire car can easily be collected (often at a discounted rate through the airline company) – generally makes for the best start to a driving holiday in Italy. Travellers from outside Europe may find it cheaper to fly via London or another European hub to take advantage of the many low-cost flights on offer.

Above Motorway through Val Isarco, Trentino Alto Adige

Arriving by Air

From the UK and Ireland, the scheduled airlines – **British Airways**, **Alitalia** and **Aer Lingus** – fly to airports throughout Northern and Central Italy, including Milan, Turin, Bologna, Verona, Venice and Pisa. London and Dublin offer the greatest choice but there are also flights from Edinburgh, Manchester, Birmingham and Bristol. Low-cost carriers including **Jet2**, **flybe**, **Ryanair** and **easyJet** fly from provincial airports all over the UK and Ireland to small airports across Northern and Central Italy.

Delta, Alitalia and **American Airlines** offer daily flights from New York, Los Angeles, Chicago, Miami and Atlanta to Rome and Milan; one short stopover greatly extends the network. Many European carriers fly to Italy (via their capitals) from major US and Canadian cities – for instance, **Lufthansa** (via Frankfurt), **KLM** (via Amsterdam) and British Airways (via London).

Air New Zealand offers the best deals from New Zealand to Italy but **Malaysia Airlines**, **Thai Airways**, British Airways, **Qantas** and **Emirates** are all

good alternatives; they also fly from Australia. From South Africa, KLM and Lufthansa are often the best options.

If you are heading for any of the more southerly areas covered by this guide – for instance Umbria or Le Marche – it's worth noting that Rome's Fiumicino is a closer inter-continental option than Milan's twin airports of Linate and Malpensa. Even if you're heading further north, it may still make sense to fly into Rome if the Italian airline **Meridiana** can offer a competitively priced way of taking you on to your destination.

It's also worth bearing in mind that air companies frequently offer a range of discounted tour packages and "air passes", which allow you to fly to multiple destinations within a designated area, with varying degrees of flexibility.

Italian Airports

Italy's system of naming its airports can be confusing to the uninitiated. Airports are named not only after the nearest major city, and perhaps the nearest village as well, but usually after a famous Italian too. For example,

Verona airport is known as Verona-Villafranca but also as Valerio Catullo. Note that on road signs, an airport may be referred to by any of its names, or a combination – including by the airport's international code (for example, MXP for Malpensa or VBS for Brescia-Montichiari).

Arriving by Rail

Countless direct services (including many sleepers) link Italy with the major European cities. Connections from Paris (and, via **Eurostar**, from London) run to Turin, Milan, Venice, Bologna, Florence and Pisa.

Rail services also operate from German, Swiss and other northern-European cities to Milan, Turin, Venice and Verona, and there are direct services from Vienna, Spain and the south of France.

Low-cost airlines have forced the train companies to be a little more competitive. Special discount fares are often available online. As the trains can be extremely busy during peak periods (Friday and Sunday evenings, the Christmas and Easter holidays and during July and August), it is advisable to make reservations if you intend to travel at those times.

There are direct motorail train services to Livorno in Tuscany and Alessandria in Piemonte from 's-Hertegenbosch (convenient for the Hook of Holland ferry port) in the Netherlands. Three German railway stations – Hamburg, Dusseldorf and Neu-Isenburg – are boarding points for motorail services to Alessandria and Bolzano. There is no direct motorail connection from France, although you can travel to Nice via motorail then drive across the Italian border.

Arriving by Road

Most roads into Italy from the rest of Europe involve Alpine crossings by tunnel or mountain pass. The exceptions are the approach from Slovenia in the northeast (on the A4 motorway) and the route along the French Riviera that enters Italy as the A10 motorway at Ventimiglia.

The most popular route from Geneva and southeast France is via the Mont Blanc tunnel and A5 motorway, entering Italy close to Aosta and Turin. Another busy approach (from Switzerland) uses the St Bernard Pass and Tunnel. The main route from Austria and southern Germany crosses the Brenner Pass and goes down to Verona on the A22 motorway via Trento and the Adige valley. Most motorways are toll roads – you pay as you exit them.

Travellers from the UK could take a car to one of the French Channel ports by ferry or on the **Eurotunnel** rail shuttle. Once there, the drive to Genova in the north of Italy takes

around 12 hours (a journey of some 1,900 km/1,200 miles). The **AA** and **Michelin** both offer reliable route planners on *www.theaa.com* and *www.viamichelin.co.uk*.

Arriving by Sea

A well-developed network of ferries links Northern and Central Italy with neighbouring Mediterranean countries such as France, Spain, Croatia, Greece and Tunisia. **Minoan Lines** and **Anek** run large ferries with cabins and vehicle decks from several ports in Greece to Venice, the northwest's busiest port, most months of the year. A grand way to travel, the Istrian peninsula and the Dalmatian coast are linked to Venice through the summer by fast catamarans and ferries run by operators such as **Venezia Lines**, and **Atlas**. Venice is also a key port for state-of-the-art cruise ships bound for the Mediterranean. Companies stopping here include **P&O Cruises** and **MSC Crociere**.

Both ferries and cruise ships dock at Venezia Terminal Passeggeri, a large terminal near Tronchetto that spreads along the lagoon and canalside from the Stazione Marittima basin to Santa Marta and San Basilio.

Genoa's Stazione Marittima is the northwest's main ferry hub, with links to Corsica, Tunis and Barcelona. Ferries from Corsica also arrive at Vado. Several companies operate these services, including **Tirrenia** and **Grimaldi**.

Far left Malpensa airport, Milan **Left** MV Crystal Serenity navigating the lagoon on departure from Venice **Below** High-speed train in Milano Centrale station

Practical Information

There is relatively little red tape involved in visiting Italy, especially for nationals of other European Union countries. Once you are there, the systems work reasonably well, even if at times they can be rather bureaucratic. Things tend to be more efficiently run in the north of the country than in the south, but it is still advisable to sort out your paperwork before leaving home. If you find yourself needing to visit a bank, the police or a doctor, make sure you have a photo ID, a good book and plenty of patience.

Above The green neon sign of an Italian pharmacy

Passports and Visas

European Union (EU) nationals can enter Italy and stay indefinitely with a valid passport or identity card. Citizens of the United States, Canada, Australia, New Zealand and some other countries (for example, Brunei and Barbados) can stay for up to three months on production of a passport, but will need to apply for a visa at their local Italian embassy in advance if they wish to stay longer. Citizens of some countries (for example, Bahrain and Bolivia) will need a visa from the outset – for details, visit the website of the Italian Ministry of Foreign Affairs (*www.vistoperitalia.esteri.it/home/en*).

Travel Safety Advice

Visitors can get up-to-date travel safety information from the Foreign and Commonwealth Office in the UK, the State Department in the US and the Department of Foreign Affairs and Trade in Australia.

Travel Insurance

All travellers should consider getting travel insurance. A policy will usually cover you for loss or theft of luggage and other property (such as passports and money), and for personal accident, repatriation in case of severe illness, third-party damage

and delayed or cancelled flights. Check that the per-article limit covers your most valuable items. You will need to take out special cover if you are intending to take part in sports, or in any activities that are considered hazardous, including skiing, wind-surfing and mountaineering. Most insurance policies also include legal cover up to a specified amount, as do comprehensive motor policies.

Health

As a member of the European Union, Italy has reciprocal health agreements with the other member states. All EU nationals are therefore entitled to the same treatment as Italian nationals – at the same price – in Italy's public healthcare system. To be eligible you must produce a European Health Insurance Card (in the UK, forms are available at most post offices or you can apply online at the website of the **UK Department of Health**). The card is free and is valid for five years. In holiday areas there may be a *guardia medica* – a kind of minor ailments and emergencies clinic – designed to deal with the sort of accidents that befall tourists; all non-residents will be asked to pay a flat fee, usually around €15. Otherwise, visiting the *pronto soccorso* (accident and emergency) department

of a local hospital is often the quickest way to get reliable treatment – but be aware that this can cost you around €30 a visit plus prescription charges. If you are taking prescription medi-cines, it is a good idea to bring the packaging with you in case you run out. Many pharmacists will be happy to sell you a replacement for drugs such as anti-inflammatories, antibiotics and blood pressure medications without requiring a prescription. Pharmacies are also a good source of advice on minor ailments. They are signalled by a green cross, and if the one you go to is closed, there will be a notice on display telling you where to find the nearest open one.

If you are involved in an accident, call 112 or 118 or go to the *pronto soccorso* department of the nearest hospital. If you are in a major town or city, it may be possible to find an English-speaking doctor – or, at least, someone who can translate for you.

Medicare Australia has a reciprocal agreement with Italy. All other non-EU citizens should make sure that the terms of their health insurance policies cover all eventualities.

No inoculations are required for Italy, but mosquito repellent is useful in the summer months. In recent years, there has been a

Left US passports **Middle** Recent legislation is slowly making the area more accessible for Disabled Travellers **Right** The *carabinieri*, a military police force

marked increase in jellyfish numbers in the Mediterranean. None are particularly dangerous, but a sting is painful and can leave weals on the skin for days. To relieve the pain and swelling, wash the wound with sea water (never fresh water, which will react with the sting and worsen the pain) and put a bag of ice on it for five or ten minutes before disinfecting it. In severe cases, seek medical attention.

Personal Security

Random violence is generally less prevalent in Italian society than in many northern European countries. Drinking to excess is simply not a cultural norm, and Italy suffers less from alcohol abuse than anywhere else in the Western world. As a result, drunken violence is mercifully rare. Petty crime, however, is just as rife as in any European country, particularly in inner-city and tourist areas. Take care in stations, markets, on public transport and around busy tourist sights; keep an especially close eye on your mobile phone and camera. Make sure you leave bags or valuables out of sight when you park your car, especially if you have foreign plates. You will always look like a tourist to those with a trained eye, but try not to be an easy target; look as if you know where you're going, and keep

your valuables in zip or button-down pockets. Unless you speak good Italian, it is better to report a crime in person rather than phoning. If you are going to claim for stolen goods on your insurance, you will need a crime report. There are two crime-fighting forces in Italy, the rivalry between which is legendary. The *carabinieri*, the military branch, have stations in just about every village; the civil police, *polizia di Stato*, have a station, known as the *questura*, in most sizeable towns. Either can furnish you with a crime report, but English is not always spoken.

Disabled Travellers

Italy can be quite challenging for the mobility-impaired. Archaeological sights and castles can be inaccessible by their nature, and even museums and galleries are frequently stepped, with non-existent or poorly maintained lifts. On-street parking and uneven pavements can make villages and towns hard work for those using sticks or wheelchairs, and for the sight-impaired too. Recent legislation is beginning to make a difference in some areas: spacious, specially adapted toilets are on the increase in bars and restaurants, as are modified bedrooms in hotels; but you should come to Italy aware that it won't always be free-wheeling.

DIRECTORY

CONSULATES
Australian Consulate General
3rd Floor, Via Borgogna 2, 20122 Milan; 0277 6741; www.italy.embassy.gov.au

British Consulate General
Via San Paolo 7, 20121 Milan; 0272 3001; www.gov.uk/government/world/organisations/british-embassy-rome

Canadian Consulate General
Piazza Cavour 3; 02 62694238

New Zealand Consulate General
Via Terraggio 17, 20123 Milan; 02 721 70001; www.nzembassy.com

United States Consulate General
Via Principe Amedeo 2/10, 20121 Milan; 0229 0351; milan.usconsulate.gov

TRAVEL SAFETY ADVICE
Australia
www.dfat.gov.au; smartraveller.gov.au

United Kingdom
www.gov.uk/foreign-travel-advice

United States of America
www.travel.state.gov

HEALTH
Medicare Australia
www.humanservices.gov.au/customer/dhs/medicare

UK Department of Health
www.dh.gov.uk

Below far left Pedestrian crossing signal **Below left** Ambulance **Below middle** Police woman giving directions **Below right** Herbal pharmacy **Below** Police officer directing traffic

The Telephone System

In Italy, the city phone code is an integral part of every number and always has to be dialled. So in calling Italy from abroad, the initial zero of the city code must be retained.

Italy has more mobile phones per head of population than anywhere in Europe except Finland. European mobiles will work in Italy, but Americans will need a tri-band phone. Coverage is generally good, although it can be patchy near some of the higher mountain ranges. Check with your provider for roaming options and international booster packages, which greatly reduce the cost of phone and data charges while you're abroad. Roaming charges for visitors from certain countries were banned in the EU in 2017. Check with your operator.

Logo seen on Italian public phones

In the past, you could only use an Italian SIM card if you had a *codice fiscale* (Italian tax code). However, several reliable service providers now offer pre-registered Italian SIM cards for unlocked European-standard GSM phones, giving you an Italian mobile number and reduced-rate calls. Alternatively, international SIM cards work well in Italy – again, as long as you have an unlocked European-standard GSM phone. The main phone operators in Italy are TIM, Vodafone, Wind and 3.

Public phone booths are becoming something of a rarity, and the few left only accept coins. Some of the public phones found at airports or stations do accept credit cards, but prices are often incredibly expensive.

A good alternative to public phone booths are the numerous call centres (usually found around the stations of larger towns) from which local migrant workers often phone home. The international rates are competitive, you pay when you've finished and you don't have to contend with the noise of passing traffic.

Internet

With the increasing availability of high-speed internet (ADSL) and Wi-Fi, most hotels and many cafés have somewhere you can access the web; travellers with their own laptop will probably need a plug adaptor. Public libraries also provide half-hour and one-hour slots, which you may need to book in advance.

Post

The Italian postal system – **Poste Italiane** – is somewhat erratic. It can be marvellously efficient, but also, at times, appallingly slow. If your package is urgent, avoid sending it registered, as registered mail tends to be amassed at the collection point before being sent on. Instead, use the postal system's courier service, *Posta Celere*, or, for international deliveries, *Pacco Celere Internazionale*, which is cheaper and more widely available outside major cities than international operators like DHL, UPS and Fedex. Stamps *(francobolli)* are sold at post offices, tobacconists and at most shops that sell postcards.

Above Popular Italian newspapers

Banks and Money

Italy is one of the many European countries whose currency is the euro. The euro is split into 100 cents. There are seven euro notes (€5, €10, €20, €50, €100, €200 and €500) and eight euro coins (€2, €1; and 1, 2, 5, 10, 20 and 50 cents).

The easiest way of drawing cash is to use a debit or credit card at a Bancomat (ATM) machine. Most cards have a maximum daily withdrawal limit (typically €250). It is essential to inform your bank that you will be using your card abroad, as many banks will block transactions they regard as "unusual".

Many banks charge high rates of interest (typically 2.5 per cent) for withdrawals and transactions made abroad. Debit or credit cards with a PIN are increasingly accepted at larger shops, hotels, restaurants and petrol stations, but some smaller establishments (including some restaurants) will not accept cards, and in general Italians still prefer to use cash.

Travellers' cheques have now been largely replaced by so-called Cash Passports – prepaid currency cards that are loaded before travelling and can be used in shops and ATMs abroad. They are available from **Thomas Cook**, **Travelex** and various banks.

Left Regional bank of the Südtirol **Middle** Public telephone **Right** Sign for a post office

Banking hours in Italy are quite restricted, so its best to acquire some local currency before you arrive. If you want to take cash euros, you might get a better rate of exchange by using online currency operators.

Once you have arrived, the best exchange rate for cash will usually be obtained at an Italian bank, but check the commission fees as they can vary widely. Bureaux de change can be found in most towns and offer the convenience of long opening hours, but they tend to charge higher commission rates. Rates in hotels and exchange booths are rarely competitive.

Tourist Information

Most Italian towns have either an APT (Azienda di Promozione Turistica) or EPT (Enti Provinciali per il Turismo) information office. These can vary enormously in the level of service they offer, but will at least provide maps, travel guides and information on local events.

Opening Hours

Most shops open Monday to Saturday 9am–1pm and 4–7pm, but many remain closed on Monday morning and Saturday afternoon. State-run museums tend to open Tuesday to

Saturday 9am–1 or 2pm; the same goes for privately owned museums, but they may also open for several hours in the afternoon. Sunday opening is generally mornings only. Many large museums now open throughout the day year-round, with late-night openings in summer (till 10pm or later Tuesday to Saturday and till 8pm Sunday). Most archaeological sites open daily, from 9am until dusk.

Time and Electricity

Like most of Europe, Italy is one hour ahead of Greenwich Mean Time (GMT), year-round. Italian voltage is 220 volts. Plugs have either two or three round pins, which can vary in diameter; a travel plug often comes in handy.

Smoking

Smoking was banned in bars, restaurants and public buildings in 2005, though many places have an outdoor terrace where it is permitted. The situation is different in hotels; make sure that you request a no-smoking room if you don't want it smelling of the last occupant's favourite brand.

Below far left Walking-trail information boards, Pietrarubbia **Below left** "Open" sign **Below middle** The Torrazzo (clocktower) in Crema **Below** Post box

Driving in Italy

Driving is one of the best ways of exploring Northern and Central Italy – particularly for getting away from the crowds and reaching the more remote areas and sights. For long distances, Italy has a comprehensive motorway system, easily accessed from the rest of Europe. The condition of minor roads may vary in quality, but most are passable with care. Mountainous terrain can make for an exhilarating drive along twisty, hairpin roads, but be sure to take them at a relaxed pace.

Above Sign showing the Italian speed limits for main and secondary roads

Insurance and Breakdown Cover

In Italy it is compulsory for drivers to have third-party motor insurance. Check with your insurance provider that you are fully covered to drive abroad; in some cases, drivers will only be covered for basic Road Traffic Accident insurance – not for theft, or for the legal costs that can ensue in the event of an accident. UK drivers can arrange full breakdown cover while abroad – some companies even offer a package that includes a 24-hour English-language helpline.

What to Take

If you are driving your own car, you should carry your vehicle insurance policy with you – ideally with a statement of cover in Italian, usually provided by your insurer. The insurer should also provide a European Accident Statement form. Additionally, you will need to carry with you the vehicle registration document and a valid driving licence, and you should also have spare bulbs, a warning triangle and a high-visibility jacket (to be worn if your car breaks down and you have to leave the vehicle). The headlights of right-hand-drive cars will need to be adjusted for

left-hand driving, to ensure that the hot-spot of the beam lights up the edge of the road and does not dazzle oncoming drivers. EU drivers must display a country sticker on their car (unless the numberplate includes their country's euro-symbol).

Road Systems

Italy was the first country in the world to build a motorway: the Autostrada dei Laghi, which runs from Milan to Varese, and was opened in 1924. Nationwide, there are now more than 6,000 km (3,700 miles) of *autostrade*, built by both state and private companies, with several new roads planned. The privately built motorways are toll roads; non-toll roads are managed by ANAS (Azienda Nazionale Autonoma delle Strade Statali). On a toll road, you pick up a ticket when you join the motorway and pay as you exit. Tolls can be paid in cash, by credit card (Visa, MasterCard, American Express or Diners Club), or with a prepaid "ViaCard", available from motorway service stations and toll-booth operators. As you approach a toll station, make sure you get into the correct lane: for payment in cash, follow the white signs; for credit card

and ViaCard, look for the blue signs. A white sign with only banknotes and coins indicates a self-service lane; a white sign with a hand holding the bank notes indicates that there will be an operator. Avoid the yellow Telepass lanes; these are for drivers with an on-board device that registers tolls and deducts them from their bank account.

Italian motorways are designated with the letter "A" followed by a numeral – for instance A8, for the Autostrada dei Laghi. Some motorways are also part of the pan-European system, whose roads are designated with an "E" followed by a numeral. Therefore an Italian motorway can have two numbers: say A11 and E45. On signage, these are indicated in white on a green background.

Secondary roads are known as *strada statale* (SS), *strada provinciale* (SP) or *strada comunale* (SC) – the latter sort is usually very small, and maintained by the local town council. SR (rare) signifies a *strada regionale*. Although the road numbering system is comprehensive, it is not widely used in Italy; you will see the numbers on milestones at the side of the road, but they are not always given on signposts. It is useful to know the

Left Roadside mirror near Radda in Chianti **Right** Automatic lanes at a motorway toll station

next place of any size on your route, as it is the town or village name rather than a number that will probably be referred to on the sign. Note that some roads may just be named, and may not use a number at all.

The privately run motorways have their own website, *www.autostrade.it*, where you can get live traffic reports by clicking on a map.

Speed Limits and Fines

On motorways, the speed limit for cars and motorcycles over 150 cc is 130 kmph (80 mph); on main roads it is 110 kmph (70 mph); on secondary roads, 90 kmph (55 mph); and in built-up areas, 50 kmph (30 mph). Speed limits are lower if you are towing *(see p21)*, or if you have held a licence for under three years, in which case you must not exceed 90 kmph (55 mph) on main roads or 100 kmph (62 mph) on motorways. Limits are also lower if there is fog or heavy rain.

Some drivers disregard the motorway speed limit, but the use of speed cameras is becoming more widespread. If you incur a fine while you are driving a rental car, the rental company will deduct the money from your credit card when the fine arrives; speed fines can range from around €150 to €250. Tourists who are stopped by

the police for speeding may be asked to pay 25 per cent of the total fine on the spot; a receipt will be issued. The use of mobile phones in cars (except hands-free) is prohibited. Seat belts, if fitted, are compulsory for both front- and rear-seat passengers, although somewhat alarmingly, many Italians do not use seat belts, even when driving on motorways. Never drink and drive – the alcohol limit is 0.05 per cent.

Driving with Children

Children under 1.5 m (4 ft 11 in) and 36 kg (79 lbs) must be transported in an appropriate restraint system: up to 18 kg (40 lbs) in a baby seat, and above that in a booster seat. If you are renting a car, baby and booster seats can be hired when you book. Remember to check that there is no airbag fitted if you intend to put a child in the front passenger seat. Service stations are tolerably frequent on motorways, but although toys and sweets are prominently displayed in their bars, children are not well catered for; baby-changing facilities are virtually non-existent, and there is unlikely to be anywhere for older kids to let off steam safely. Some car rental companies hire out portable DVD players, which might make long journeys less stressful.

DIRECTORY

COMMON ROAD SIGNS

Centro
Town or city centre

Incrocio
Crossroads

Lavori in corso
Roadworks ahead

Parcheggio
Car park

Rallentare
Slow down

Senso unico
One way

Senso vietato
No entry

Sosta vietata
No parking

Strada a doppia corsia
Dual carriageway

Strada panoramica
Scenic route

Tutte le direzioni
All directions

Uscita
Exit

Below far left Hiking-route signs, Val di Planol **Below left** Road climbing through a tunnel to the village of Pieve **Below middle** Parking sign **Below right** Drive through the spa town of Pré-Saint-Didier in the Valle d'Aosta **Below** Road signage for Citerna

Left Motorway in Milan **Right** The precipitous road out of Elva, in the Valle Maira

Rules of the Road

Remember: always drive on the right. Most visitors from a country with left-hand traffic get used to right-hand driving pretty quickly, but roundabouts and crossroads can be disorientating at first, as can turning from a one-way street onto a road with two-way traffic – especially if that road is empty.

On motorways, Italian drivers can be aggressive. Some of them believe the inside lane is only for lorries, don't like being overtaken and rarely use the rear-view mirror. They concentrate on the cars in front of them and those to the side, and if they see a space ahead of them, they will fill it. The best advice is to let them pass. If a car flashes its headlights it is telling you to get out of the way, and it is best not to argue.

Unless road signs indicate otherwise, you should give way to vehicles joining your road from the right. Outside built-up areas, use dipped headlights at all times or risk a hefty fine. Surprisingly, in a country where football victories and weddings are celebrated by convoys of cars sounding their klaxons, you should only use the horn in emergencies. The British **Foreign and Commonwealth Office** offers detailed advice on safe Italian road travel in the "Travel Advice by Country" section of its website.

Buying Petrol

Petrol *(benzina)* stations are frequent; most open from early morning until lunchtime, then from 3pm till around 7pm. Outside those hours you will often find an automatic pump that accepts either credit/debit cards or banknotes, although these are less common in rural areas. Petrol stations on motorways tend to be open 24 hours a day. Unleaded *(senza piombo)* petrol is universally available, as are diesel *(gasolio)* and LPG *(PLG)*. If you are driving near Switzerland, it's worth noting that petrol prices there are about two-thirds of what they are in Italy, so it might be worth a trip over the border to fill up – many Italians will be doing just that. If you decide to follow suit, don't forget that you will need your passport and, where applicable, an appropriate visa.

Road Conditions

Italy's motorways often flow freely, although rush hours and summer holidays can see the kind of long tailbacks common to most of Europe. The busiest times are weekends in July, and the beginning and end of August. Travel of any kind on either side of the national summer holiday, Ferragosto (15 August), should be avoided at all costs. Sunday is usually a good day to travel if you have a long distance to cover, as the lorry drivers are safely at home eating lunch with their families.

Road maintenance is a major issue. Italian roads have a lot to contend with, from freezing winters in the mountains to landslide-inducing rainstorms and baking hot, tarmac-melting summers. "White roads", known as *strade bianche*, have only a gravel surface, though these are still marked on road maps.

Mountain Roads

Reaching some of Italy's most spectacular viewpoints and mountain passes inevitably involves tackling hairpin bends (the Stelvio Pass in Trentino-Alto Adige has 48 of them in succession!) and some steep, narrow roads with sheer drops, such as those on the route through the valleys of the Ortles mountain range. In spring, road surfaces may have been eroded by heavy winter snow, snow-melt and frost, and it can take some time for repairs to be undertaken, especially off the beaten track.

Unless you are used to driving in snow and ice, it is safer to avoid mountainous areas in winter conditions, especially on unfamiliar roads. In certain areas, snow chains will be

Left Petrol pumps near Lake Garda, Lombardy **Right** Road signs near Costigliole d'Asti

recommended in mid-winter, and it would be foolish to ignore such advice. For advance weather warnings that might affect your journey, always check one of the Italian weather websites, such as *www.meteo.it* or *www.ilmeteo.it*.

Taking a Break

Service stations on Italian motorways are less frequent than in the UK and other parts of Europe, and they can be pretty basic, with little more than a toilet and a bar where you can get a coffee and a heated-up pastry or a toasted sandwich. Service stations with fast-food restaurants are on the increase – in particular the Autogrill chain, which offers decent sandwiches and usually has a small supermarket where you can pick up basic supplies and even some local specialities. On the back roads, however, you are more likely to find a pretty village with a bar where you can have a good coffee or snack at a fair price, so if you are getting tired, consider leaving the motorway and taking a break in the nearest town or village. Well-priced set-lunch deals aimed at local workers (*pranzo di lavoro*) are worth looking out for; service will be fast, and you can get a simple, well-cooked three-course meal for under €20.

Breakdown and Accidents

In the event of an accident or breakdown, switch on your hazard warning lights and place a warning triangle 50 m (164 ft) behind your car. If you break down and do not have pan-European breakdown cover, you will need to call the **ACI** – the Italian Automobile Club. This organization offers free tows to anyone driving in Italy with foreign number plates. If you are in a hire car, call the rental company and follow their advice; the ACI should still offer a free tow, as long as you can produce your rental contract and flight tickets. If you do have pan-European cover, your provider will contact the nearest garage and make arrangements for you.

If you are unfortunate enough to be involved in an accident, depending on its severity, call one of the emergency services listed in the Directory. If there is any damage to a vehicle or to passengers, it is obligatory to call the police. You will then need to fill out a European Accident Statement (*see p16*) and take the contact details and vehicle registration number of any other cars involved. If you have a camera, it is a good idea to take photos of the accident from all angles before any of the vehicles are moved.

Below far left Mountain road in the Dolomites **Below left** Symbol of Agip, a petrol company **Below middle** Road through the Val d'Orcia, Tuscany **Below** Road signs near Lake Como

Parking

Parking in an Italian town or city can demand a great deal of time and patience. When kerb-space is limited, drivers tend to park anywhere and everywhere: on pavements, at bus stops, even blocking private entrances. The anarchy of Italian parking notwithstanding, it is unwise to follow suit; parking attendants are on the rise, as are *zone di rimozione* (tow-away zones).

In cities and villages alike, double parking is common, triple parking becoming more so. Towns and villages popular with tourists usually have paying car parks just outside the centre, and many places now operate a zoned parking scheme, with the type of zone indicated by the colour of the lines on the side of the road. Blue-zone parking spaces have a maximum stay of between one and two hours, and cost around €1 an hour (though they can be free at lunchtime, after 8pm and on Sundays). White-zone areas are free. Yellow-zone areas are for residents only. For zones where there is a time-limit but no parking fee, Italian cars (including rental cars) come equipped with a *disco orario* (mini clock dial) that you set with your time of arrival and display in the window; if you do not have one, you may be able to get one from the local tourist office.

When parking, do not leave any valuables in your car – and certainly nothing visible. Virtually all Italian cars have removable car radios, which Italian drivers invariably take with them when they park. Secure, indoor, city car parks are expensive, but hotels can offer guest discounts.

Disabled drivers displaying the blue disabled badge can park in designated disabled spaces.

Restricted Traffic and Congestion Charges

The centres of many Italian towns and historic villages are closed to non-resident traffic. These so-called Zona a Traffico Limitato (restricted traffic zones) are usually indicated by signs displaying the letters "ZTL" in black on a yellow background. Many of these zones are monitored by cameras, and fines are issued to those who enter without authorization. Other towns impose traffic restrictions on certain days, or at certain times of day – Bergamo, for instance, does this in its historic centre, Città Alta. Make sure you read the signs: *lavorativo* or *feriale* means Monday to Saturday, and is marked by two crossed hammers; *festivi* indicates Sundays and public holidays, and is marked by a Christian cross. If your hotel is within a restricted area, you will need a police permit to enter with your car (they will need to know your registration number).

The city of Milan has introduced a congestion-charge scheme (Area C) in an attempt to reduce traffic volumes and pollution. Other towns – among them Genoa and Turin – are discussing following suit.

Car Hire

All the major international car rental companies – such as **Avis**, **Budget**, **Hertz** and **Europcar** – operate in Italy. It is worth comparing rates online before you decide which to use, as well as investigating any deals offered by your airline; low-cost airlines are particularly competitive in this area. You could compare the deals you have found yourself with those of a reliable car-rental broker such as **Holiday Autos** or **AutoEurope**.

Above Street mirror on a narrow road in Amiata

To rent a car in Italy you need to be over 20, and to have held a full licence for at least one year. Be sure that your rental agreement includes collision-damage waiver (CDW) and theft protection, as well as unlimited mileage. Child seats need to be booked in advance. With the rise in inner-city congestion, automatic cars are becoming more widely available.

When you collect the vehicle you will need to produce your passport, driving licence and credit card (from which an impression will be taken as a security deposit). Cars are usually supplied with a full tank of petrol, and it is wise to return them refilled, as if not, you will be charged at an inflated rate for filling the tank.

Motorbikes and Scooters

Italy is the land of the Vespa, and 10 per cent of the population has a motorbike or scooter. Two-wheel transport makes sense for navigating the labyrinth of streets that forms the centre of many cities, and you will usually find somewhere (free) to park, even in the busiest metropolis.

Away from the city, Italy is an exhilarating country to traverse by bike, with roads twisting up and down mountains and along dramatic coastlines, unmade "white" roads to

Left An Italian camp site in summer **Right** Terminillo Road, a typical, winding mountain drive

explore and a landscape that changes constantly. Note that if you are on a motorbike or scooter, a helmet is compulsory for both driver and pillion – a rule enforced with increasing frequency. A driving licence or motorbike driving licence is required for all vehicles over 49cc. Motorcycles must use dipped head-lights at all times during the day.

Caravans and Motorhomes/RVs

In recent years, motorhomes have become very popular in Italy. Local councils have established designated camper parks near many popular tour-ist areas, and larger camp sites nearly always accept campers and caravans. Camper van or mobile home rental is becoming increasingly common. Prices are usually around €1,000 for a four-berth vehicle for a week in high season, with unlimited mileage – companies to try include **Italy Motorhome Hire** and **Comocaravan**.

In peak season, you will need to book places in advance at camp sites. In quieter areas, free camping is on the increase, but it is illegal. To avoid offending local sensibilities (or ruining other people's views), ask advice from the local traffic police (*vigili*) before parking up for the night.

The speed limit for driving with a caravan or trailer is 50 kmph (30 mph) in built-up areas; 70 kmph (45 mph) on secondary and main roads; and 80 kmph (50 mph) on motorways.

Maps and Sat Nav Devices

The best maps for long journeys and overall planning are the *AA Road Atlas Italy* (1:250,000) and Touring Club Italiano's *Atlante Stradale d'Italia* (also 1:250,000). Regional maps from Touring Club Italiano (1:200,000) are invaluable for local exploring, but even they will not plot every country lane and unsurfaced track. Touring Club does, however, occasionally produce maps of small areas of particular interest – such as national parks – at 1:50,000 scale. These are rarely sold in shops, but available at park offices.

Satellite navigation devices such as TomTom or Garmin now come with good maps that cover Italy. Some car rental firms offer these devices as an extra if you book in advance. If you are intending to use a sat nav application on your mobile phone, check that the software has on-board mapping rather than relying on the mobile network to download maps as you go, or you'll incur call charges (with accompanying roaming charges) whenever you use the maps.

DIRECTORY

CAR HIRE
AutoEurope
www.autoeurope.com

Avis
www.avis.com

Budget
www.budget.co.uk

Europcar
www.europcar.com

Hertz
www.hertz.com

Holiday Autos
www.holidayautos.co.uk

CAMPER VAN HIRE
Comocaravan
www.comocaravan.it

Italy Motorhome Hire
www.italy-motorhome-hire.com

Below far left Road signage, Chianti **Below left** Camper van near Lake Como **Below middle** Tourist information map in Valli di Comacchio **Below middle right** Iconic Italian scooter **Below** Getting about in Parco di San Bartolo

Where to Stay

Italy has some of the most memorable places to stay in Europe, ranging from grand hotels oozing *belle époque* glamour to boutique hotels on the cutting edge of contemporary design. Both the *agriturismo* scheme – which allowed the owners of farms, vineyards and country estates to convert historic barns, villas and palaces into rooms and apartments – and the vibrant bed-and-breakfast scene have made it easier for visitors to avoid the impersonality of service found in so many traditional hotels and *pensioni*.

Above Hotel Splendid, Baveno, on the shores of Lake Maggiore

B&Bs

Since legislation came into force in 2001 allowing ordinary people to offer bed-and-breakfast in their homes, hundreds of B&Bs have opened in Italy. The best of these can offer excellent value for money as well as the opportunity to experience exceptional Italian hospitality, whether the setting is a couple of rooms in a simple city apartment or a glamorous suite in a historic palace. The **BB Planet** website is a useful online resource.

   The rules state that a B&B should have no more than five rooms and that the owners must live on the premises (although not all B&Bs fully adhere to these rules). In the best-run places, breakfasts can be fantastic affairs, with home-made jams and cakes, fresh croissants and fruit; at the other end of the spectrum, you might be handed a cellophane-packed croissant and a juice box the night before.

   If you are looking for a B&B on spec, ask if there are any staff on the premises and if not, how to contact the owner should the need arise. Also check if breakfast is served in the B&B, or whether they have an arrangement with a local café. Occasionally, B&Bs may allow you free use of the kitchen.

Boutique Hotels

The international trend for boutique hotels has found fertile ground in Italy – not surprisingly, given the plethora of historic buildings as well as the Italian sense of food, hospitality, lifestyle and design. Some boutique hotels are run by hospitality-trade professionals, others by passionate newcomers, often from the worlds of architecture and design. Visitors will find plenty of boutique hotels recommended in this guide, but websites such as **i-escape** and **Mr & Mrs Smith** are also well worth a browse.

Hotels

Italian hotels are given an official rating of between 1 and 5 stars (though the 7-star Town House Galleria has recently opened in Milan: *www.sevenstarsgalleria.com*). Note that the number of stars awarded to a hotel is based solely on a checklist of facilities and services, such as how many rooms have a telephone or ensuite bathroom, the presence or absence of a restaurant on site, and whether there is 24-hour room service. This means that the star rating is no guide to the subtler, more subjective charms of hotels, such as cleanliness, the style of decor

or the friendliness or helpfulness of staff. If such things are important to you, then the accommodation recommendations made in this guide should help you to find the kind of place you are looking for.

Agriturismi

The *agriturismo* scheme began in the 1980s to enable farmers and landowners to boost falling revenues by renting out converted farm buildings to tourists. They can range from cool, state-of-the-art country hotels to simple down-to-earth self-catering apartments. Some serve food for guests made from home-grown produce, others have full-blown restaurants. Many offer activities such as horse riding, and some have developed into little country resorts, with swimming pools, tennis courts and mountain bikes to rent.

Booking

It is wise to book well in advance if you are travelling in July and August, or around Easter and the various springtime public holidays. Hotels in coastal and lake resorts often close between October and Easter. Reservations can often be made online, though not all sites belonging

Left Alpine Hotel, Courmayeur, in the Valle d'Aosta **Right** Stylish bedroom in the Hotel Greif, Bolzano

to individual hotels are secure, which may be a little unsettling if credit card details are requested as a guarantee. You can mimimize risk by booking over the phone or by using a hotel-booking site with a secure website such as **Trip Advisor** or i-escape.

Facilities and Prices

Double rooms in Italian hotels usually have a double bed *(letto matrimoniale)*, so if you prefer twin beds *(due letti)*, it is wise to request that when you book. Single rooms are rare, and you will often end up having to pay for a single use of a double. Bathrooms, even in 4-star hotels, do not always have bathtubs. Many B&Bs have rooms without an ensuite bathroom, but frequently there will be a bathroom across the corridor for your sole use. In the cheapest hotels, bathrooms are likely to be shared.

In hotels, rates are quoted per room; in B&Bs, per person. The more expensive B&Bs will usually cost about as much as a 2- or 3-star hotel, but tend to offer better value in terms of service and surroundings. You will often find rooms at a reduced rate on the web, either on the hotel's own website or on one of the many sites brokering bargain hotel deals. Weekend rates in city hotels are often great value.

Camping

Camping is becoming increasingly popular in Italy, and there are plenty of sites both on the coast and in the mountains. They are usually open from April to September, though some sites stay open year-round in the south and in Sicily. For the tentless, sites often have bungalows, sleeping up to six, and there is normally space for caravans and camper vans.

Self-catering

If you want to focus on a single region, consider renting a villa or rural house for a week or two. There are lovely places throughout Northern and Central Italy, ranging from simple rustic retreats and seaside apartments to palatial places with pools, maids, chefs and masseurs. The widest choice can be found in Tuscany and Umbria, but Lake Como and the Veneto are also popular villa destinations, with many properties in exquisitely restored country houses. The **Italy by Italy** websites both have useful self-catering sections.

Below far left A relaxing guest lounge **Below left** Spa at the Hotel Victoria, Turin **Below middle** Doorway of a B&B in Castelmuzio **Below** Hotel Ristorante Locanda San Vigilio, on the eastern shore of Lake Garda

PRICE CATEGORIES

The following price bands are based on a standard double room in high season, including tax and service:

inexpensive – under €100
moderate – €100–€200
expensive – over €200

Where to Eat

One of the great pleasures of travelling in Northern and Central Italy is exploring the rich culinary and wine-making traditions of each region. Every drive in this guide provides the opportunity to sample regional specialities, whether it be the *pesto* and fish dishes of Liguria, the truffles, hams and salamis of Umbria or the cheeses, dumplings and smoked sausages of the Alto-Adige. Below is a basic guide to the typical kinds of eating places you will find in Italy, from simple pizzerias to sophisticated gourmet haunts.

Practical Information

Perhaps the most typical Italian breakfast is a croissant *(cornetto)* and coffee at a bar. The coffee comes in a staggering variety of modes, from short and sharp *(un caffè)* to long and milky *(latte macchiato)*. An espresso diluted with hot water to make it resemble American filter coffee is an *Americano*; an espresso with a blob of frothy milk is a *caffè macchiato*. Italians wouldn't dream of having a frothy cappucino at any time of day other than breakfast. In summer, there is usually iced coffee – *caffè freddo*.

The main meal is lunch, normally served in restaurants from noon until 2pm, though in summer resorts you'll find a few restaurants that keep their kitchens open right through to dinner, which is usually served from 7:30–10:30pm. Most restaurants are closed one day a week and display their *giorno di chiusura* (closed day) in the window, although in the summer, many open seven days a week.

Meals begin with an *antipasto*, or starter, followed by the *primo*, or first course – most commonly pasta, risotto or, in winter, a *minestra* (hearty soup). The *secondo* is the meat and fish course, with the *contorno* (vegetables or salad) usually served on a separate dish alongside. Finally, there is the *dolce*, or dessert. House wines can vary in quality, but a *quarto* (quarter), *mezzo* (half) or 1-litre *caraffa* (carafe) will always be at the very least drinkable.

In cities and major towns, credit cards are widely accepted – less so in smaller places and in the country, where it is advisable to carry cash. Tax and service must be included in the bill by law, and a small cover charge *(coperto)* is usually added. Tipping is becoming more common; 10 per cent is usual in smarter or more touristy places.

Italians rarely dress down, so dressing fairly smartly will generally fit the bill. Men – like women – will be expected to wear tops during meals, even at beachside places. Only in the most exclusive restaurants is dress formal, and men required to wear a tie and jacket. Children are welcome in restaurants, even late at night.

Ristoranti, Trattorie, Osterie

These are the three main types of restaurants in Italy, and until some years ago they were quite distinct. A *ristorante* was a "proper" restaurant, with linen tablecloths and waiters in uniform. A *trattoria* was usually a more basic, homely sort of place; the menu was often scrawled on a blackboard, and there were sheets of newsprint to cover the tables and on which to write the bill. An *osteria* was an unpretentious country or city hostelry, offering a few cold cuts of meat with some cheese, and maybe a simple pasta dish to accompany a glass of the local wine. However, that has all changed, and these days the choice of name for an establishment depends more on the tradition the place identifies with than price, decor or ambience. *Ristorante* is now a neutral, generic term that could apply to anything from a Michelin-starred gem to a seaside joint where mass-catering is the order of the day; and although there are *trattorie* and *osterie* that have existed for half a century, today the terms might as easily apply to the best restaurant in town. *"Trattoria"* often implies an interest in reviving and reinventing traditional dishes; whereas *"osteria"* tends to suggest an emphasis on sourcing the very best primary ingredients and wines, as promoted, for instance, by the Slow Food movement.

Above Menu for a pizza restaurant in Riva del Garda, near Lake Garda

Left Restaurant table in the Parco Naturale del Monte San Bartolo **Right** Caffè degli Specchi on Piazza dell Unita d'Italia, Trieste

Pizzerias

Pizzerias are found throughout Italy, but contrary to popular myth, it is only too easy to find doughy, substandard pizza. You have more chance of striking gold if you go to a pizzeria with a wood-burning oven *(forno a legna)*, from which the pizzas should emerge bubbling, scorched and blistered. Pizzerias are almost always informal places, and pizza is usually only served in the evening (as it takes hours to get the oven hot enough). The classic accompaniment to pizza is a cold draught beer.

Cafés and Bars

At one end of the spectrum are grand cafés with chandelier-lit interiors and terraces fringing some of the most spectacular piazzas in Italy; at the other, modest local bars with 1980s colour schemes, steaming coffee machines and dusty plastic flowers. These unpretentious neighbourhood bars often have standing-room only and are places to come for breakfast, a quick toasted sandwich or a swift shot of coffee. Some have a few tables outside for a more leisurely breakfast or aperitif, though you should find time at least once on your trip to dawdle over a Campari soda and olives in a traditional pavement café watching life pass by.

Picnics

There is no better excuse for sampling local produce than a picnic. With that end in view, you will need to find a delicatessen *(alimentari)* where you can buy delicacies such as rosemary-spiked hams, mature gorgonzola, speck and olives; a bakery *(il forno)*; and a greengrocer *(fruttivendolo)* or market *(mercato)* packed with seasonal fruits and vegetables. Along with stall upon stall of the freshest fruit and vegetables, weekly markets also bring together local smallholders offering such things as home-cured cheeses and salamis. There are often stalls with specialities from the south of Italy too – capers, sun-dried tomatoes, mozzarella di bufala and spicy salami – which add an exotic touch. Less romantically, Italian supermarkets, including chains like Esselunga and Coop, stock very good-quality fresh produce as well as freshly baked bread.

Mountain regions often have picnic areas with massive outside grills – a great way of sampling a Chiavenna steak or a freshly caught red mullet. Around the lakes you will find free beaches *(spiaggia pubblica)* where you can settle on a grassy patch by the lakeside and enjoy your carefully chosen delights.

DIRECTORY

PRICE CATEGORIES

The following price bands are based on a three-course meal for one, including a half-bottle of house wine, cover charge, tax and service:

inexpensive – under €25
moderate – €25–€45
expensive – over €45

Below far left Black truffles at the Sansepolcro market **Below left** Fruits on a Bolzano market stall **Below middle** Al fresco dining in Orvieto **Below middle right** Subterranean wine vault, Canonica a Cerreto, Chianti **Below** Display at a bakery and bar in San Casciano dei Bagni

THE
DRIVES

In the Shadow of the Alps

Turin to Castello di Rivoli

Highlights

- **Royal Turin**
  Admire the sweeping boulevards, elegant hunting lodges and pleasure palaces of this aristocratic city

- **Gourmet Piedmont**
  Taste the region's famous mushrooms and truffles and sample the rich, French-influenced cuisine

- **Strategic mountain passes**
  Walk in the footsteps of some of history's greatest armies – Hannibal, Augustus and Napoleon all marched through the Alps near Aosta

- **Paradise park**
  Explore Italy's first national park, the Parco Nazionale del Gran Paradiso, and see ibex, chamois, marmots and magnificent golden eagles

Spectacular view of the valley from the Col de l'Iseran

In the Shadow of the Alps

The rolling hillsides around Turin produce some of the world's most delectable wines and prized gourmet delicacies, such as white truffle and various kinds of cheese. Encircled by palaces and former hunting lodges and set against the amphitheatre of the snow-capped Alps, Turin is well-endowed with beautiful architecture and cutting-edge design. The tour then passes through the dramatic landscape of the Valle d'Aosta and the Gran Paradiso – the highest mountain entirely within Italy – to the spectacular Monte Bianco (Mont Blanc), Europe's loftiest peak, and to the towns at her feet.

Above Driving cows along the winding road from La Thuile to Col du Mont Cenis, *see p36*

0 kilometres 20

0 miles 20

ACTIVITIES

Ride up to the top of Turin's iconic Mole Antonelliana to view the towering mountains backing the city

Discover a wilderness paradise in Italy's first national park, the Gran Paradiso

Hike in the mountains and then take a chairlift or cable car from Courmayeur or La Thuile up to the highest peaks in Europe

Take the healthy waters in the thermal spa town of Pré-Saint-Didier

Follow in the footsteps of Hannibal and his elephants on the border between Italy and France

Below Stunning green farmland in the Valle d'Aosta, *see pp34–5*

Above Remains of an aqueduct, part of the remarkable Roman ruins at Susa, *see p37*

KEY

🚍 Drive route

PLAN YOUR DRIVE

Start/finish: Turin to Castello di Rivoli.

Number of days: 3–4, allowing half a day to explore Turin.

Distance: 470 km (292 miles).

Road conditions: Generally well paved and signposted, but there is steep terrain in the Valle d'Aosta, which is often snowbound in winter; drivers are required to have winter tyres fitted and carry snow chains Oct–Jun.

When to go: Roads in the Alps are very dangerous in the winter. Stretches of the route between Pré-Saint-Didier and Col du Mont Cenis are closed during the winter months, when there is high snowfall. The best time to do this drive is between June and October.

Opening times: Shops tend to open Mon–Sat 9am–1pm and 4–7:30 or 8pm. Some shops are shut on Mon mornings or Wed afternoons, but city supermarkets often stay open for the siesta. Churches and museums are usually open 8 or 9am–noon and 4–7 or 8pm. Many museums are closed on Mondays.

Main market days: Turin: Porta Palazzo, Mon–Fri mornings and all day Sat; Aosta: Piazza Cavalieri di Vittorio Veneto, Tue.

Shopping: Gourmet produce such as nougat, mushrooms and truffles, cheese made from mountain milk and, of course, wine. Other good buys include textiles in Biella and cuckoo clocks in Aosta and the mountain areas.

Major festivals: Turin: Cultural heritage week, Apr; Turin book fair, mid-May; Classical music festival, Sep; Slow Food fair, Oct (biannually); Luci d'Artista illuminations, Nov–Jan.

DAY TRIP OPTIONS

Those interested in **architecture** will find a host of **buildings** to explore in Turin with the works of Baroque architect Juvarra, and impressive **museums** and **churches**. **Outdoor enthusiasts** can take the **mountain air** in historic Aosta. See the fantastic **castle** at Fénis and enjoy the natural glory of the **Parco Nazionale del Gran Paradiso**. For full details, *see p37*.

VISITING TURIN

Parking
Parking is difficult and it is best to use an underground car park – try the ones at Piazza Vittorio Veneto or Piazza Castello.

Visitor Information
Piazza Castello/Via Garibaldi, 10100; 011 535 181; www.turismotorino.org

Cable car to Basilica di Superga
Departs every hour from Sassi station in the Piazza Modena (Tram No.15).

WHERE TO STAY IN TURIN

Hotel Victoria *expensive*
Close to Via Roma and Piazza San Carlo, this resembles an English country house and has a garden for al fresco meals.
Via Nino Costa 4, 10123; 011 561 1909; www.hotelvictoria-torino.com

Des Artistes *moderate*
Centrally located near the Piazza Vittorio Veneto, this "boho chic" hotel has just 22 pleasant and well-appointed rooms and offers good, professional service.
Via Principe Amedeo 21, 10123; 011 812 4416; www.desartisteshotel.it

Le Meridien Art + Tech *expensive*
Away from the centre in Lingotto (the old Fiat factory designed by Renzo Piano), this hotel has minimalist airy rooms, glass walls and large bathrooms.
Via Nizza 230, 10126; 011 664 2000; www.starwoodhotels.com/lemeridien

Below (clockwise from top left) The grand Piazza San Carlo; the Roman Palatine Gate; former bedroom in the Palazzo Madama; exterior of the Palazzo Madama in the Piazza Castello; dome of the Chiesa di San Lorenzo

① Palazzina di Caccia di Stupinigi
Piazza Principe Amedeo 7, Torino; 10042
Set in huge grounds with roaming deer, this palatial, Rococo-style hunting lodge belonged to the Savoys – a rich family from the Swiss Alps who went on to rule Italy. Its **Museo di Storia, Arte e Ammobiliamento** (Museum of History, Art and Interior Design) *(closed Mon)* displays exquisite frescoes, chandeliers and marquetry. The Saletta degli Specchi (Hall of Mirrors) holds a marble bath owned by Napoleon's sister, Paolina Borghese.
🚗 *Head northeast on the SS23/Viale Torino. Follow Corso Unione Sovietica to "centro". Park under Piazza Vittorio.*

② Turin
Torino, Piedmont; 10100
With the Alps as a glorious backdrop, Turin (Torino) has squares, castles, palaces and boulevards fit for a king. Indeed, it was the first capital of the Kingdom of Italy (1861). Today, it is the country's design and contemporary art capital. And, for a taste of the dolce vita, Turin is a gourmet paradise and the birthplace of Italian cinema.

A three-hour walking tour
From Piazza Vittorio Veneto, walk up the Via Po to the town centre. Turn right into Via Montebello to reach the unmissable **Mole Antonelliana** ①. Topped by a 167-m (550-ft) spire, this edifice is a symbol of the city and home to the excellent **Museo Nazionale del Cinema** *(closed Tue)*. The Italian film industry was born in Turin, which was also the film production capital of the world (1906–16). The museum re-creates the story of cinema with props and classic film clips, including the car chase in *The Italian Job*. Take the glass lift to the viewing platform on the spire for fabulous views of the city and the Alps. Next, turn right and then left into the wide Corso San Maurizio and left into the Giardino Reale. Continue through the park to the far corner and the Baroque **Palazzo Reale** ② *(closed Mon)*, once the official Savoy residence. The opulent interior is graced with chinoiserie, gold, velvet and tapestries. Next door is the

Madonna and child, Palazzo Madama

Above Elegant colonnaded walkway along Via Roma, Turin

Piazza Castello, site of the Palazzo Madama, which houses the **Museo Civica d'Arte Antica** ③ *(closed Tue)*. Highlights here include Roman foundations in the basement, architect Filippo Juvarra's sinuous staircase and atrium, and *The Portrait of a Man* by Antonello da Messina (1476). Two of Turin's most atmospheric cafés are in the piazza – Mulassano and Baratti & Milano. On the western corner of the piazza is the **Chiesa di San Lorenzo** ④ *(open daily)*. The interior of this church is a Baroque fantasy of marble, stucco and gilding. It also has a replica of the Sindone di Torino (Turin Shroud), believed to be the sheet in which Christ's body was wrapped. Walk west from the piazza to the **Quadrilatero** ⑤ – the gridded area that recalls the old Roman settlement. The cobbled streets are full of bars, cafés, markets and churches. Return to Piazza Castello and walk down Via Roma and, near Piazza San Carlo, turn right into Via Accademia delle Scienze and the **Museo Egizio** ⑥ *(Egyptian Museum: Closes early Mon)*. The collection includes papyri, a black statue of Ramses II (13th century BC), sarcophagi and the tomb of Kha and Merit (c.1430 BC), complete with vases of food and unguents for the afterlife.

🚗 *From Piazza Vittorio Veneto, cross Ponte Vittorio Emanuele I and follow brown signs for Superga. Turn left on to Corso Casale, right at Strada Comunale di Superga, left at Piazzale Alberto Geisser and on to Superga.*

❸ Basilica di Superga
Torino, Piedmont; 10020
Spectacularly perched on a hill and visible for miles around, this grand

mausoleum *(closed Wed)* bears the tombs of over 62 members of the Savoy family and has a cloister with an Italian style garden. Duke Vittorio Amedeo engaged Juvarra to build the basilica in 1717 after defeating an invading French army in 1706. The funicular ride from Sassi station (just below) up to the basilica is always popular with children. A large plaque in the grounds commemorates the tragic loss of the Grande Torino football team, whose plane crashed into the hillside in 1949.

🚗 *Head west to pick up SS11 then SP45. Take SS593 and after Alice Castello take SR143 to Biella.*

EAT AND DRINK IN TURIN

L'Osteria del Corso *inexpensive*
Simple, good family-run fish place. Great value lunch buffet. *Corso Regina Margherita 252/b, 10144; 011 480 665; closed Sun*

C'era Una Volta *moderate*
Welcoming restaurant offering regional specialities and an excellent *menu degustazione*. *Corso Vittorio Emanuele II 41, 10125; 011 655 498; www.ristoranteceraunavolta.it*

Ristorante del Cambio *expensive*
Turin's most famous restaurant serves authentic *bollito misto* – a mix of cooked meats. Booking essential. *Piazza Carignano 2, 10123; 011 546 690; www.delcambio.it; closed Mon & Sun eve*

Above The Basilica di Superga, built to commemorate the liberation of Turin from the French

Eat and Drink: inexpensive, under €25; moderate, €25–€45; expensive, over €45

Above The fortress Il Melograno, Issogne, originally built in 1480

④ Biella
Biella, Piedmont; 13900

At the heart of "Textile Valley", Biella is famous as a major centre for high-quality wool and yarn production, and Italian designer names such as Zegna and Loro Piana have close links with the town. More than 50 factory outlets line the industrial approach roads – many of which are on the SS230 – look for *spaccio* on signs, meaning "outlets". There are also outlets in Biella *(see right)*. The town has a compact, attractive centre and highlights include the Renaissance basilica and cloister of **St Sebastian**, with lovely frescoes inside. A funicular goes up to the beautiful medieval village of Piazzo.

🚗 *Head southwest, then take the SS338/Via Ivrea and turn right on the SS419. Fork right on SP73, then the SP72 to the SS26 before turning off on to the SR4 to Issogne.*

⑤ Issogne
Aosta, Valle d'Aosta; 11020

The Valle d'Aosta is full of castles and medieval forts. Many were fortresses, while others were more palatial, such as **Il Melograno** *(closed Wed)*. More château than fort, it is named for the fountain in the courtyard, which has a pomegranate tree *(il melograno)* of iron. Restored over the years, the palace has frescoes of 15th-century street life, along with period furniture and artifacts. Nearby, the village Champdepraz (just north on the A5) is the access point for the **Parco Naturale del Mont Avic** *(Apr–Sep: open daily; Oct–Mar: closed Mon; www.montavic. it)*, whose lakes and marshes and Alpine

bogs are home to many flower species, which attract clouds of butterflies.

🚗 *Go north, signposted Champdepraz, turn right at SR6, left at SS26 towards Aosta and follow signs to Fénis.*

Piedmontese fare
Local cuisine matches robust flavours with French flair, reflecting the area's relationship with the House of Savoy. The woods, especially near Alba, are truffle- and mushroom-rich and any dish with *salsa di tartufi bianchi* will be delicious. *Bagna cauda* is a warm dip made with oil, anchovies, garlic and cream. Blue gorgonzola is the best-known cheese – *dolce* (creamy) or *piccante* (crumbly). Look for soft cheeses, too, such as *caprino* (goat), *fontina* (cow), and *raschera* (a combination of cow's and either goat's or sheep's milk). Fondue *(fonduta)* is often made with *fontina* – delicious with Alba's white truffles.

---

⑥ Fénis
Aosta, Valle d'Aosta; 11020

The most famous and spectacular of all the castles in the Valle d'Aosta is the **Castello di Fénis** *(Apr–Sep, open daily; Oct–Mar: open Tue–Sun)*. Set on a grassy knoll, backed by a chestnut forest, it is every inch a fairytale medieval castle, bristling with towers and turrets, keeps and crenellations. Its origins date to the 13th century, but what is visible today is largely the 1340 creation of Aimone de Challant, who belonged to a noble family linked to the Savoys. The castle has a pentagonal layout and the keep is enclosed by a double perimeter wall, with watchtowers linked by a walkway. The inner

Above The remarkably well-preserved Castello di Fénis, watching over the Valle d'Aosta

courtyard has a semi-circular staircase and wooden balcony, decorated with exquisite frescoes of St George killing the dragon and a group of wise men and prophets holding scrolls. There is also a small museum of local furniture inside.

🚗 *Take the SR13, then turn left on to the SS26 west to Aosta. There is a car park at Piazza Arco d'Augusto.*

⑦ Aosta
Aosta, Valle d'Aosta; 11100
Named after Emperor Augustus, Aosta was once a mini-Rome in the centre of its own valley; today it is the regional capital. The triumphal Arco d'Augusto now sits on a traffic island and from it runs the Roman Via Sant' Anselmo, a pedestrian precinct. To the right, outside the city walls, is an impressive series of ancient church buildings around the **Collegiata di Sant'Orso** *(open daily)*, dedicated to the patron saint of Aosta. Sant' Orso itself has a Gothic (15th-century) façade, a 12th-century Romanesque bell tower and an elegant cloister. At the end of the Via Sant'Anselmo, where all kinds of souvenirs can be purchased – from cuckoo clocks to local gourmet delights – is the Porta Praetoria, the two thick, arched walls forming the impressive stone entrance to the city. Inside, on the right, lie the remains of a Roman theatre. Just to the north, accessed through the Convento di San Giuseppe, is the **Amphitheatre** *(open daily)*. In the old town, the Duomo in Piazza Giovanni XXIII dates from the 12th century and contains some of the best Christian art treasures from the area in the **Museo del Tesoro** *(open daily)*. Next to the Duomo is the Roman Forum with a supporting arcade *(cryptoporticus)*.

🚗 *Leave Aosta on the SS26 and bear left on to the SR47 heading south to Cogne.*

⑧ Cogne
Aosta, Valle d'Aosta; 11012
This is an excellent base for exploring Italy's first national park, the beautiful **Parco Nazionale del Gran Paradiso**. Originally a Savoy hunting reserve, 21 sq km (5,200 acres) were donated by King Vittorio Emanuele III in 1929 to form the present park. Today, it is home to the endangered ibex, as well as to numerous chamois, marmots, ptarmigans and golden eagles. Maps of the footpaths and routes are available from the visitor information centre *(Via Bourgeois 34, 11012; 0165 740 40)*. A path meanders south to Valnontey, where the **Giardino Alpino Paradisia** *(1st Sat Jun–1st Sat Sep: open daily)* has a fine collection of more than 1,000 species of Alpine flora. The best time to see these is from late-June to mid-July.

🚗 *Head northwest on SR47, then turn left on to the SS26. This road becomes the Avenue du Géant (Champex) leading into Courmayeur.*

Above left Near the Parco Nazionale del Gran Paradiso, Cogne **Above** Bikes – a favourite way to explore Aosta's national park

EAT AND DRINK

AOSTA

Vecchio Ristoro *expensive*
This Michelin-starred restaurant is centrally located and combines rustic charm with an elegant dining experience. The chef, Alfio Fascendini, is a master of innovation and seasonal specialities such as wild mushrooms. *Via Tourneuve 4, 11100; 0165 33 238; www.ristorantevecchioristoro.it; closed Sun, Mon lunch & Jun*

COGNE

Lou Ressignon
moderate
Well-established family-run inn specializing in authentic Valdostano specialities. At weekends, music complements feasting. Also has rooms. *Rue des Mines 22, 11012; 0165 74 034; www.louressignon.it; closed Mon eve & Tue in low season*

Bar a Fromage *moderate*
Splendid little restaurant with a warm, intimate atmosphere where cheese is definitely king. Visitors can also buy some excellent produce in the shop. *Rue Grand Paradis 21, 11012; 0165 74 96 96; reduced hours in low season*

SHOPPING IN BIELLA

While there are many outlets just outside town, within Biella itself is **Fratelli Cerruti** *(Via Cernaia 40; closed Sun)*, selling discounted men and women's classic clothes, and cashmere specialist **Piacenza** *(Via talia 32; closed Mon)*

Far left Glorious Romanesque fresco in Aosta's cathedral **Left** A *salumeria* (delicatessen) full of treats on Via Sant'Anselmo, Aosta

Above Climbers traversing an icy path in the mountains, Courmayeur **Above right** Museo Alpino Duca degli Abruzzi, Courmayeur

VISITING COURMAYEUR

Parking
There is a large car park by the cable car to Plan Checrouit, on the southern edge of town.

Visitor Information
Piazzale Monte Bianco 8, 11100; 0165 842 060; www.regione.vda.it/turismo

WHERE TO STAY

COURMAYEUR

Hotel Auberge de la Maison moderate
Warm and welcoming, this homely mountain hotel and restaurant is rustically decorated. There are 33 individually designed rooms, together with a sauna, solarium and Turkish baths. The restaurant is noted for its excellent food and service.
Via Passerin d'Entreves 16, 11013 (4 km/ 7 miles north of Courmayeur); 0165 869 811; www.aubergemaison.it

Grand Hotel Royal e Golf expensive
Set on the main street of Courmayeur, this prestigious hotel is noted for its charm and good service. There is a small wellness centre with swimming pool and solarium and splendid views of Monte Bianco. There is also a very pleasant restaurant.
Via Roma 87, 11013; 0165 831 611; www.hotelroyalegolf.com

⑨ Courmayeur
Aosta, Valle d'Aosta; 11100
In the majestic shadow of Monte Bianco (Mont Blanc), Courmayeur is a popular year-round resort and a joy to explore. The main hub, Via Roma, is traffic free and full of designer shops and gourmet gems. The **Museo Alpino Duca degli Abruzzi** (Piazza Abbé Henry 2; 0165 842 064; closed Wed morning) tells tales of dramatic mountain rescues. Just north of Courmayeur at Entrèves, a cable car leads to Punta Helbronner – at 3,462 m (11,360 ft), the views are literally breathtaking.
🚗 Take the SS26 to Pré-Saint-Didier.

⑩ Pré-Saint-Didier
Aosta, Valle d'Aosta; 07021
At just over 1,000 m (3,280 ft) high, the picturesque town Pré-Saint-Didier is famous for its warm thermal waters. The spring is at a constant 36°C (98°F) at the point where the River Thuile forces its way through the narrow gorge into the Dora Valley. There is a well-known spa in the town, **Terme Pré-Saint-Didier** (0165 867 272; open daily). The waters are said to have detoxifying, toning and anti-inflammatory properties.

Nearby **La Thuile** (reached via the SS26) was once a mining area and is now a picturesque skiing and hiking town, and more of a family resort than chic Courmayeur. In summer chairlifts allow access to heights of 2,400 m (7,900 ft) for some spectacular walking and trekking.
🚗 Take the SS26, entering France on the D1090. Turn on to the D84, then take D902 past Val d'Isère, followed by the D1006 to Col du Mont Cenis (use the Fréjus tunnel in winter).

⑪ Col du Mont Cenis
Lanslebourg-Mont-Cenis, 73480; France
Col du Mont Cenis (Cenisio in Italian) is a 2,084-m (6,831-ft) high mountain pass in the Alps on the French-Italian border. It was an important invasion route and Napoleon I built a road there in 1810. It is also believed by some to have been Hannibal's pass when he marched his army and elephants over the Alps against Rome during the Second Punic War (218–203 BC). The picturesque Lac du Mont Cenis is frozen usually until the end of May. The **Jardin Alpin** (open daily) has more than 120 flower species.
🚗 Take the D1006 south. Enter Italy on the SS25, then take the SS24 to Exilles.

⑫ Exilles
Torino, Piedmont; 10050
Overlooking the Valle di Susa, the little medieval town Exilles is spectacularly located and dominated by a splendid fort. **Exilles Fort** (Via degli Alpini; 0122 58270; closed Mon) is not only one of the oldest monuments in the valley, but also a great example of military architecture. A fort has kept watch over this passage between

Right Lac du Mont Cenis on a key invasion route in Italian history **Far right** The Italian skiing village of La Thuile

Where to Stay: inexpensive, under €100; moderate, €100–200; expensive, over €200

France and Italy since the 12th century, although what is visible today is mainly from the 19th century. It is said that from 1681–87, the "Man in the Iron Mask", a prisoner whose face and identity remain a mystery to this day, was incarcerated within these walls. Many have theorized as to his identity, most famously Alexandre Dumas, who postulated that he was Louis XIV's identical twin. Highlights include the Knights' Courtyard and the Staircase of Paradise leading to the Prison Courtyard. The fort's museum charts its long history and the story of Italy's Alpine troops. From the roof there are splendid views of the upper Valle di Susa.

🚗 *Head back northeast on the SS24.*

⑬ Susa

Torino, Piedmont; 10059
Known in Roman times as Segusium, Susa is a pretty mountain town with much evidence of its earlier existence. In the old town, at Piazza Savoia, the Porta Savoia gateway dates originally from the 4th century AD, although it was reconstructed in the Middle Ages. There is also a **Roman amphitheatre** *(open daily)*, aqueduct arches and the remains of some Roman baths. The remarkably well-preserved marble triumphal Arco di Augusto (Arch of Augustus) was built in the 1st century BC by Gallic chieftain Cottius to commemorate the alliance with the ruling Romans. In the medieval historic centre, the Romanesque **Cattedrale di San Giusto** *(open daily)*, dating from the 12th century, has lovely frescoes and a fine campanile. The town is noted, too, for its shops full of gourmet delights.

🚗 *Head north, turn right on to SS25, signposted Avigliana, then Rivoli. Follow signs to car park at Castello.*

⑭ Castello di Rivoli

Rivoli, Piedmont; 10098
Set on a hill with splendid views, this castle was one of the Savoys' country residences. It is an imposing Baroque building bearing the classical French trademark style of master architect Filippo Juvarra. Inside, the **Museo d'Arte Contemporanea** *(closed Mon)* has works by Gilbert and George and Jeff Koons, while Maurizio Cattelan's stuffed horse is suspended from the ceiling – making a dramatic and inspiring contrast between modern and ancient. The museum often has excellent temporary exhibitions and there is a good café, as well as the highly acclaimed cuboid Combal.zero restaurant.

Above left The honeycomb façade of the 4th-century Porta Savoia, Susa **Above** The fort of Exilles, strategically located in the Valle di Susa **Below** In the Museo d'Arte Contemporanea, Castello di Rivoli

EAT AND DRINK

SUSA

Zizi
This shop offers free tastings and low-price local alcoholic beverages. Established in 1945, it draws customers from all over the area. *Corso Inghilterra 52, 10059; 0122 622 717; www.zizi-susa.com; closed Sun*

CASTELLO DI RIVOLI

Combal.zero *expensive*
Michelin-starred restaurant in the Museo d'Arte Contemporanea, featuring classic Piedmont dishes, but with very creative twists – a variant of molecular gastronomy – under the expert eye of chef Davide Scabin. This is where traditional meets ultra-modern. *Museo d'Arte Contemporanea, Piazza Mafalda di Savoia, 10098; 011 956 5225; www.combal.org; closed Mon & Sun*

DAY TRIP OPTIONS
For visitors based in Turin, the first trip makes a good day out, while for those based in Aosta, the amazing mountain scenery is easy to explore.

Baroque architecture tour
In Turin ❷, see the beauty of the work of the great Baroque architect Filippo Juvarra (1678–1736) in the façade and staircase of the Palazzo Madama, as well as the other architectural and historical sights of the city. Then head out to the grand hunting lodge Palazzina di Caccia di Stupinigi ❶ and the magnificent Castello di Rivoli ⑭ – filled with thought-provoking modern art.

Head south on the SS23 to Stupinigi. Then take the E70 north (Tangenziale Sud) turning left on to the SP7 to Castello.

Art and castles in paradise
Based in Aosta ❼, take a trip to the fairytale castle in Fénis ❻ . Next, head to Cogne ❽ to visit the Parco Nazionale del Gran Paradiso for an invigorating walk among breath-taking scenery.

Aosta is located on the SS26. For Fénis, take the SS26 and SR13. To reach Cogne, take the SS26 and then the SR47.

Eat and Drink: inexpensive, under €25; moderate, €25–€45; expensive, over €45

DRICE **2**

In the Land of the Truffle

Barbaresco to Cuneo

Highlights

- **Kings of wine**
  Taste the nectar of the gods made from the Barolo and Barbaresco vineyards in the Langhe region

- **Gourmet delights**
  Linger over your meal in Bra, the home of Slow Food, and savour the famous white truffle of Alba

- **Mountain rides**
  Zig-zag up the mountain pass from Sampeyre for spectacular views

- **Valley pastures**
  Stroll along the lush, wooded Valle Maira to the sound of sheep bells

- **Timeless Saluzzo**
  Take a tour of mellow Saluzzo's historic core, through frescoed Renaissance houses and palazzi

View of the wine-making town of La Morra

In the Land of the Truffle

Piedmont's attractions are diverse. The vine-braided hills of the Langhe yield velvety and elegant wines such as Barolo and Barbaresco – among Italy's most celebrated – while in the oak woods around Alba, keen-nosed hounds sniff out valuable musky white truffles. Villages in the area are dotted with fine restaurants (Bra was the birthplace of the Slow Food movement), which make the most of the bounty of hazelnut and chestnut groves, fruit orchards and mountain pastures. Castles and churches perch on hills; Occitan, the ancient Romance language of troubadors, is still spoken in the Alpine valleys; and the dramatic mountain scenery is never less than enthralling.

KEY

Drive route

ACTIVITIES

Follow a wine trail in the Langhe wine region at La Morra

Hunt for truffles in the truffle capital of Alba

Indulge in gourmet food in the village or mountain restaurants

Marvel at the 15th-century frescoes in the villages above the Valle Maira and Valle Varaita

Hike in the beautiful Parco delle Alpi Marittime near Terme di Valdieri

Treat the body with healing waters at Terme di Valdieri

Above Abandoned brick bridge on the route to Bra, *see p43* **Below** Lofty mountain peaks of the Valle Maira near Elva, Stroppo and Acceglio, *see pp 45–6*

PLAN YOUR DRIVE

Start/finish: Barbaresco to Cuneo.

Number of days: 3–4, allowing for a day in the Langhe region and a day each for Valle Varaita and Valle Maira.

Distance: Approx 145 km (90 miles).

Road conditions: Roads are well-surfaced, but not always numbered. Rural routes are slow, winding and popular with motor bikers and cyclists at weekends. Mountain passes can be steep and mostly single track with few passing places. Roads from Saluzzo onwards may be impassable from Oct–May/Jun; only attempt these roads with snow chains, if experienced in driving in snow. Late autumn sees fog throughout.

When to go: Spring and autumn are best for travelling and wine festivals. The woods are most colourful in autumn; October is white truffle time in Alba.

Opening times: Shops tend to open 9am–1pm and 4–7pm Mon–Sat, with some closing on Monday morning. Churches are generally open 9am–noon and 4–7pm. Museums vary; those in smaller places close in the week's early part. Check ahead out of season.

Main market days: Alba: truffle market Sat (Oct–Dec); Bra: Wed; Savigliano: Piazza Santa Rosa, Tue; Cuneo: Piazza Galimberti, Tue.

Shopping: Alba is full of shops selling truffles and truffle-infused products – oil, pasta, purée – as well as hazelnut cakes and sweets. Cuneo is famous for chestnuts and Bra for its cheese.

Major festivals: Alba: Vinum (wine fair), late-Apr/May; Fiera del Tartufo Bianco (white truffle fair), Oct–Nov; Palio degli Asini (donkey derby), first Sun in Oct; La Morra: Mangialonga (food tour of vineyards), last Sun in Aug; Bra: Cheese fair, alternate years from 2013; Cuneo: Fiera del Marrone (chestnut fair), Oct.

DAY TRIP OPTIONS

Wine buffs will enjoy exploring the Langhe **vineyards** and **museums**, not to mention tasting the superior produce. **Outdoor enthusiasts** can head for the **pretty villages**, **valley greenery** and **mountain scenery** of the Valle Varaita. For full details, *see p47*.

Above Alba's main shopping street, Via Vittorio Emanuele II

WHERE TO STAY

AROUND ALBA

Villa La Meridiana
Cascina Reinè *inexpensive*
A liberty-style villa with great views, set among vineyards and orchards a short drive east of Alba on Viale Cherasca. Truffle hunts can be arranged.
Località Altavilla 9, 12051; 0173 440 112; www.villalameridianaalba.it

AROUND BAROLO

Cà San Ponzio *inexpensive*
This farmhouse offers charming rooms and large breakfasts with delicious cakes. A short drive southwest of La Morra, it's a good base for wine-country tours.
Via Rittane 7, Frazione Vergne, 12060; 0173 560 510; www.casanponzio.com

LA MORRA

Hotel Corte Gondina *moderate*
Stylish and elegant, this hotel has fine antiques and furnishings, a lush garden and pool. Good breakfast too.
Via Roma 100, 12064; 0173 509 781; www.cortegondina.it

① Barbaresco
Cuneo, Piemonte; 12050
Barbaresco, overlooking the Tanaro river, makes a good introduction to the hilltop villages of the Langhe area, whose vineyards spill down the slopes in geometric patterns towards the rolling hills beyond. A stroll down Via Torino reveals characteristics typical of a wine-country village – a square 12th-century stone tower, one of a string of medieval watch-towers that once studded the region; a sundial (1999) illustrating the wine-making process painted over a whole wall of a house, and of course the ubiquitous regional *enoteca*, housed in the former church of San Donato.

🚗 *Follow SP3 south to Tre Stelle and continue along Via Rio Sordo to Alba. Cross the railway line into Viale Cherasca and take fourth exit into Corso M Coppino to a large parking place at Piazza San Paolo.*

② Alba
Cuneo, Piemonte; 12051
Alba rose to prominence in medieval times, when 100 brick towers reportedly dominated its skyline. Nowadays, there are only a few left around the Piazza Duomo, but the town stakes its claim to fame on the white truffle. During October and November, swarms of chefs and food enthusiasts descend on the town to sample its musky delights. It seems appropriate that the pink-brick **cattedrale** *(open daily)* is dedicated to San Lorenzo, the patron saint of chefs. On its façade, he is portrayed

holding in his right hand the griddle on which he was martyred. Step inside the cathedral to see the lovely wooden choir stalls depicting still lifes and townscapes, inlaid in 1512 by Bernardino Fossati. The main street, Via Vittorio Emanuele II, is lined with shops selling truffles, oils, pastas, wines, cheeses and chocolates.

🚗 *Exit by Viale Torino to SP3bis, signed Barolo. Turn left at Gallo for Grinzane Cavour (signposted). Park by the castle.*

Slow Food
The region is known for its many food festivals. The pleasures of the table were held in high regard even before the Slow Food movement, which originated in Bra in 1986 in protest at the opening of a McDonald's near the Spanish Steps in Rome. The movement promotes traditional, local, seasonal and sustainable food. Piedmont restaurants serve their local delicacies with pride. Look for *bagna cauda* (hot dip) – an olive oil dip with anchovies and garlic, *fritto misto* (fried meats), *bollito misto* (boiled meats), *tajarin* (egg tagliatelle) and *agnolotti* (egg ravioli), the mountain cheese *castelmagno*, and the "testicles of the earth" – white truffles.

③ Grinzane Cavour
Cuneo, Piemonte; 12060
The magnificent 16th-century **Castello** *(closed Tue)* dominates Grinzane Cavour. It was once the home of Count Camillo Cavour, the town mayor for many years and a leading figure in the Italian Unification Movement of the 19th century. His bed, mayoral sash

*Below left Green rolling hills and vineyards around Barbaresco **Below right** The famous truffle castello at Grinzane Cavour, looming high over the village*

and some of his belongings are on show, as well as a barrel-maker's workshop and an 18th-century distillery. In November, the castle gains worldwide attention with its prestigious white truffle auction, when astronomical amounts of money – sometimes in excess of £100,000 for a single lot – change hands. More affordable for visitors are the fine wines and grappas for sale in the attached regional *enoteca*.

🚗 *Follow SP3 southwest to Barolo and park in Piazza Colbert.*

Above left The exquisite dome of the Chiesa Santa Chiara, Bra **Above** Atmospheric mist cloaking vineyards around La Morra

Above Road winding through the fertile vineyards around La Morra

④ Barolo
Cuneo, Piemonte; 12060

The highlight of this diminutive town is the **Castello dei Marchesi Falletti di Barolo** – the birthplace of Barolo, the "King of Wines". The vineyard has increased its reputation as a centre of wine production with its innovative interactive wine museum, **WiMu** *(open daily; closed 10–26 Dec, Jan–mid-Feb)*. Through three floors of the castle, visitors are enveloped in the history, art, food, music, films, literature and local traditions relating to the ambrosial liquid. The tour ends in the *tempio dell'entourista* (Wine Tourist's Temple), where visitors can taste quality Barolo for themselves. There's an *enoteca* on hand for those who want to buy.

🚗 *Take the SP3 and at the roundabout, take the first exit, SP58, to La Morra. Park in Piazza Martiri.*

⑤ La Morra
Cuneo, Piemonte; 12064

La Morra is another town that focuses on wine, with plenty of atmospheric bars for tasting. A climb up through the narrow streets to the Piazza Castello is rewarded with superb views across wine country. Pick up a map for vineyard hikes at the **Cantina Comunale di La Morra** here, or from the tourist office. It's an easy 15-minute walk to the **Cappella del Barolo** *(open daily)* at Brunate, a deconsecrated little church that was painted in strikingly bold colours by American artists Sol Lewitt and David Tremlett in exchange for a supply of Barolo wine. Or, drive to nearby Annunziata, where the **Ratti Abbey and Wine Museum** offers weekday guided tours and tastings.

🚗 *On leaving La Morra take the left fork, follow SP58 and then SP661 following signs to Bra. Park in Piazza XX Settembre.*

⑥ Bra
Cuneo, Piemonte; 12042

This lively town (its name coming from *braida* – planting vines in rows wide enough for grain to grow in between) is known as the headquarters of the Slow Food movement. As a result, food is an important part of any visit. Look for *salsiccia di Bra* (Bra sausage – a mixture of veal, pork, herbs and spices) on the menus of the excellent restaurants here. The tall church of **Santa Chiara** *(open daily)*, built in 1742, has a lovely Rococo interior and, in the words of its creator Bernardo Antonio Vittone, "a diaphanous dome" with an inner and outer shell, which creates wonderful plays of light. **Chiesa di Sant'Andrea** *(open daily)* is giddily Baroque, from its statue-topped façade to its altar packed with candles. Antique toys feature in the **Museo del Giocattolo** *(open Sun and by appointment)*.

🚗 *Take SS231 and SP662 westwards to Savigliano. Park in Viale del Sole or Viale Gozzano around the Parco Graneris.*

EAT AND DRINK

BARBARESCO

Antinè *expensive*
Michelin-starred restaurant serving veal with fried quail's eggs and black truffle. There's also a well-priced tasting menu. *Via Torino 16, 12050; 0173 635 294; www.antine.it; closed Wed, Jan & mid-Aug; booking advised*

ALBA

Piazza Duomo and La Piola *moderate–expensive*
Upstairs, the elegant Piazza Duomo comes under the Michelin-starred chef Enrico Crippa. On the ground floor, La Piola offers less expensive, rustic fare. *Pza Risorgimento 4, 12051. Duomo: 0173 366 167; www.piazzaduomoalba. it; closed Sun & Mon. Piola: 0173 44 28 00; www.lapiola-alba.it; closed Sun eve & Sun lunch Dec–Sep*

Other options
Check out **Tartufi Morra** *(Piazza Pertinace 3)* for truffles and the *pasticceria* **Tartufi Ponzio** *(Via Vittorio Emanuele II 7A)* for hazelnut chocolate truffles.

AROUND BAROLO

Del Buon Padre *moderate*
In a quiet village, this place serves *fonduta Piemontese* (Piedmont cheese fondue) and beef braised in Barolo. *Via delle Viole 30, Vergne 12060; 0173 56192; www.buon-padre.com; closed Wed & Mon–Fri lunch*

BRA

Osteria del Boccondivino *moderate*
A founding member of the Slow Food movement, this serves rabbit *tajarin* (thin tagliatelle) with butter and sage. *Via Mendicità 14, 12042; 0172 425 674; www.boccondivinoslow.it; closed Mon, Sun lunch Jun–Mar & Sun eve Jan–Sep*

Other options
Stock up on a Bra speciality, *ciuk* ("drunken" cheese aged in grape skins), from **Giolito** *(Via Montegrappa 6)*.

Eat and Drink: inexpensive, under €25; moderate, €25–€45; expensive, over €45

Above Riverbed on the way to Sampeyre in the Valle Varaita **Above right** The historic centre of Saluzzo, with views across the valley

⑦ Savigliano
Cuneo, Piemonte; 12038

Despite losing out to Turin in the bid to be the capital of the Savoy kingdom, the citizens of Savigliano still built their triumphal arch (1585), which leads onto the broad, arcaded Piazza Santarosa – a good place for refreshments. Close by is the Baroque **Palazzo Taffini d'Acceglio** (open Fri–Sun), which celebrates the exploits of Vittorio Amedeo I, Duke of Savoy, in a series of bold military frescoes, and has more decorative feminine rooms too. The **Museo Civico e Gipsoteca** (open Sat & Sun) contains sculptures by the 19th-century artist Davide Calandra, paintings and a reconstruction of an 18th-century pharmacy.

🚗 Follow the signs for Saluzzo directly westwards on the SP662.

⑧ Saluzzo
Cuneo, Piemonte; 12037

Renaissance houses, churches, palazzos and a castle all spill down from Saluzzo's historic hilltop. Almost in France, the city was constantly changing hands between the French and the House of Savoy. On a walk through the narrow lanes and steep cobbled alleyways and steps up to the old town, it feels as though time has stopped here.

A 90-minute walking tour

From the car, walk up Via Ludovico II to Corso Italia, which follows the medieval walls. To the left stands the late-Gothic **Cattedrale di Santa Maria Vergine** ① (open daily), whose façade has three round windows. The interior contains a beautiful polyptych by the 15th-century Flemish painter Hans Clemer (also known as the Master of Elva). The tourist office is further on the left. Cross Corso Italia and turn left through the **Porta Santa Maria** ② and follow Via Alessandro

VISITING SALUZZO

Parking
Park in Piazza Garibaldi.

Tourist Information
Piazza Risorgimento 1, 12037; 0175 46710; www.saluzzoturistica.it; closed Mon

WHERE TO STAY

SALUZZO AND AROUND

Persico inexpensive
Friendly, modern hotel in the centre of town with plainly furnished rooms. It has a good restaurant on the premises. Vicolo Mercati 10, 12037; 0175 41213; www.albergopersico.net

Castello Rosso moderate
Set on a hill amid parkland, this 16th-century castle offers a taste of luxury and spacious and colourful rooms. A good restaurant, pool and beauty treatments are also available. Via Ammiraglio Reynaudi 5, Costigliole Saluzzo, 12024 (next to Piasco on SP1); 0175 230 030; www.castellorosso.com

Where to Stay: inexpensive, under €100; moderate, €100–€200; expensive, over €200

Volta, lined with porticoes, to **Piazzetta dei Mondagli** ③, where, at number 5, the 19th-century writer and leading figure of the Risorgimento, Silvio Pellico, was born. Go up a steep flight of cobbled steps to Salita al Castello, past Renaissance houses with frescoes, loggias and terracotta decoration, and on to the **Torre Civica** ④ *(closed Fri–Sun)*, built in 1462. Climb up for marvellous views over the medieval rooftops to the mountains. At the top of the Salita are the **Piazza Castello** ⑤, the Fontana della Drancia (a favourite spot for newly married couples to be photographed), and the bulky **Castiglia** ⑥ with its formidable keep – once home to the marquises and later (until 1922) a prison.

Retrace your steps from the castle to see the brick church and the Romanesque bell tower of **San Giovanni** ⑦, begun in 1330. If the church is open, look in at the frescoes by Pietro da Saluzzo and, in the apse, the Cappella dei Marchesi, burial place of Ludovico II, who is ornately displayed as a medieval knight.

Continue along Via San Giovanni to the 15th-century palazzo, **Casa Cavassa** ⑧, which now houses the Museo Civico *(10am–1pm & 2–5pm Tue–Sun; tours at 11am & 4pm Sat–Sun & hol. Closed Mon & Wed)*. Originally the home of the Vicar General of the Marquis, Galeazzo Cavassa, it was restored by a devotee of the arts in the 1880s and filled with Renaissance art and antiques. There are also fine frescoes, friezes and coffered ceilings. Hans Clemer painted the *grisaille* (monochrome) frescoes of the *Labours of Hercules* on the courtyard arcades,

Above Painted *trompe l'oeil* doorway in the heart of Saluzzo's old town

and the exquisite *Madonna della Misericordia* altarpiece in Room 5. Don't miss the glorious panoramic view.

Go down steps to Via Deodata and Via Gualtieri and exit the walls at Piazza Vineis into Corso Italia (and the cathedral again). Head back along Viale della Liberazione and Via Savigliano to the car.
🚗 *Take SP589 to Verzuolo, then SP8 to Sampeyre. The road is slow, with some sharp bends. Park in Piazza della Vittoria.*

⑨ Sampeyre
Cuneo, Piemonte; 12020

The road follows and crosses the Varaita river as it winds its way through the Valle Varaita to the largest town in the area, Sampeyre, which is a popular base for summer hikes. Visit the tourist office in Piazza della Vittoria for information. Along the way, leafy woods and lofty mountains frame the views. Of interest are the terracotta church of **Santi Pietro e Paolo** *(open daily)*, which has frescoes by the Biazaci brothers, and a small, but packed **Museo Etnografico** *(Jul & Aug: open daily; Sep open Sun and last Sat)*. The more adventurous can drive up to the **Colle di Sampeyre**, the less adventurous can take the chairlift to the Sant'Anna valley. Either way, the view is dramatic and awe-inspiring. On the way to Sampeyre, stop at Piasco (look for the brown sign) to visit the **Victor Salvi Harp Museum** *(Jun–Sep: open Mon–Fri; Oct–May: open Sun–Fri)*.
🚗 *Follow the signs for Elva, turning right onto the SP335 at Goria Ugo. The road is extremely steep and mostly single track with hairpin bends.*

⑩ Elva
Cuneo, Piemonte; 12020

There's plenty of space to stop and admire the awesomely rugged view from the southern side of the Colle di Sampeyre. Wood and rubble houses line the isolated valley at Elva, a village once famous for collecting and selling women's hair for wigmaking. The 15th-century **Chiesa di Santa Maria Assunta**, decorated with animal and human heads on its exterior capitals, is adorned inside with a colourful series of frescoes by Hans Clemer.
🚗 *The SP335 is signposted to Stroppo. Park in the square by the church.*

Above The rugged Valle Maira seen from the road to Elva **Below** Stream cascading through the lush Valle Varaita

EAT AND DRINK

SALUZZO
Casa Pellico *moderate*
Located in the historic centre, this restaurant offers traditional Piedmontese dishes with an innovative twist. Dishes feature superb local ingredients including Cuneo ham and a range of excellent cheeses. Good wine list, friendly service and a modern atmosphere.
Piazzetta dei Mondagli, 12037; 0175 468 33; www.casapellico.it; closed Mon

Eat and Drink: inexpensive, under €25; moderate, €25–€45; expensive, over €45

Above left and right The pleasant townscape of Cuneo in Piedmont

VISITING DRONERO

Visitor Information
Piazza XX Settembre, 12025; 0171 91 70 80

WHERE TO STAY

STROPPO

Locanda alla Napoleonica *inexpensive*
Four prettily furnished rooms in a typical rustic 19th-century village house, accessed down steep cobbled stone steps. There's also a restaurant offering refined *occitan* specialities.
Bassura di Stroppo, 12020; 0171 999 277; www.locandanapoleonica.it

CUNEO AND AROUND

Tetto Garrone *inexpensive*
Surrounded by nut groves, this lovely farmhouse has large modern rooms, a courtyard garden of white flowers and a kitchen for the use of guests.
Via Campagna 45, Roata Rossi, 12100 (Roata Rossi is signposted off SR589); 0171 682 841; www.tettogarrone.it; closed in winter

Lovera Palace *moderate*
Elegant hotel with 40 rooms, central location and garage parking – a king and a pope have been past guests. It can organize truffle hunts in autumn.
Via Roma 37, Cuneo, 12100; 0171 690 420; www.palazzolovera.com

Other options
For those who fancy a traditional spa hotel, the **Hotel Royal** at Terme di Valdieri opens from June to September.
0171 97106; www.termerealidivaldieri.it

⑪ Stroppo
Cuneo, Piemonte; 12020
The Valle Maira is lined with leafy orchards, thick woods and lush pastures that tinkle with the sound of cow bells. Stroppo, the valley's capital in medieval times, has one church in its square and another jutting out dramatically on the spur above. This is the 12th-century **Chiesa di San Peyre**, which has a rocket-like bell tower and contains beautiful frescoes by the Master of Stroppo. To see inside, ask around for the key, then drive further up to park on a small patch of grass opposite the church.
🚗 *Take the slow SP422 west to Acceglio.*

⑫ Acceglio
Cuneo, Piemonte; 12021
At an altitude of 1,220 m (4,000 ft), Acceglio is the last town of the Valle Maira. During the 16th century, it was a stronghold of Calvinism, allowing the Huguenots to flee here over the nearby French border. Trees line the broad river, peaks loom above and the

stone houses with their wooden roofs recall much earlier times. There are lovely walks leading to waterfalls and lakes from here (and from Chiappera, a little further on), but arm yourself with a good map before setting off.
🚗 *Take SP422 back through Stroppo and east to Dronero. Park in Piazza XX Settembre on the west side of town. For the Riserva Ciciu, take the SP24 towards Busca for 2 km (1 mile), then turn left at the crossroads for Villar San Costanzo and follow the signs.*

⑬ Dronero
Cuneo, Piemonte; 12025
Dronero, where the old men play *petanque* and you'll hear the Occitan language spoken, is home to the crenellated **Ponte del Diavolo** (Devil's Bridge), built in 1492 across the Maira river. It's a peaceful viewpoint over the vegetable gardens and trout ponds to the mountains beyond. Also of interest are the octagonal grain market and the **Museo Civico Luigi Mallé** *(open Sat & Sun)*, with displays on art, the town and art historian Luigi Mallé's life. Drive to the nearby **Riserva Naturale Ciciu del Villar** at Villar San Costanzo. Clustered in the woods, the *ciciu* ("puppets") are huge, eroded rocks with stone caps, up to 10 m (30 ft) high. They were left behind after the glaciers retreated. There are some great views and it is an excellent spot for a picnic.
🚗 *Follow SP422 to Caraglio, then the SP23 to Borgo San Dalmazzo and the SS20 towards Valdieri. Look for signs*

Right Lago della Rovina, in the pristine environment of the Parco delle Alpi Marittime

Where to Stay: inexpensive, under €100; moderate, €100–€200; expensive, over €200

for Valdieri and Terme di Valdieri on
SP22 which turns into the SP239.
There is parking beyond the baths.

⑭ Terme di Valdieri
Cuneo, Piemonte; 12011
This pleasant spot in the Valle Gesso
was a popular summer retreat for
Italian aristocracy in the 19th century.
Set in the **Parco delle Alpi Marittime**
(www.parcoalpimarittime.it), it's a good
base for trips into the mountains –
get a map from the visitor centre *(Jun–
Sep: open daily)* or simply relax and
take some of the algae or sulphur
treatments. Don't miss a wander
through the **Giardino Botanico
Alpino Valderia** *(mid-Jun–mid-Sep:
open daily)*, where the confluence of
mountain and marine climates has
produced over 400 species of plants.
🚗 *Retrace the journey here, turning
right for Entracque before Valdieri.
Bypass Entracque village by taking first
right, signposted San Giacomo. Bear
right at Ponte di Rovine for the Lago
della Rovina. Park (paid) by the lake.*

⑮ Lago della Rovina
Cuneo, Piemonte; 12019
The drive climbs gently through the
mountains to the Parco del'Argentura
and ends at Lago della Rovina, popular
with fishermen. It's impossible to miss
the looming **ENEL hydroelectric
pumping station** *(tours available)*, the
largest in Italy at San Giacomo. Take
a gentle hike through the woods
around the lake, or make a full day
of it and head over the ridge to Lago
del Chiotas and Lago Brocan. Look
out for marmots, chamois and eagles.

🚗 *Return to Valdieri on SP22 and
continue to Borgo San Dalmazzo to
take SS20 to Cuneo. Follow signs for
Torino to the roundabout just after
the hospital. Take the third exit, go
straight over the next roundabout
into Lungostura Kennedy and park at
the Piazza Foro Boario on the right.*

⑯ Cuneo
Cuneo, Piemonte; 12100
The university town of Cuneo,
wedged between the Gesso
and Stura rivers, has a purposeful,
bustling air and is a good base for
exploring many parts of Piedmont.
The historic area of town lies to
the west of the wide 19th-century
streets. The **Museo Civico** *(closed Mon)*
traces local customs and costumes
and displays prehistoric, Roman
and medieval artifacts. Strolling
through the town, look out for
tempting displays of chestnut
sweetmeats and Castelmagno
cheese from the mountains.

Above View of Dronero and its 15th-century
Ponte del Diavolo

EAT AND DRINK

STROPPO
Locanda Codirosso
inexpensive–moderate
Offering views of the Maira Valley, this
restaurant serves traditional dishes
featuring locally sourced ingredients.
Homemade dessert and craft beers..
*Frazione Ruata Valle 8, 12020; 380 533
3955; www.codirosso.it; closed Nov–
Apr; booking advised*

CUNEO
Osteria della Chiocciola *moderate*
The first-floor restaurant serves great
specialities such as *ravioli ripieni di
castagne* (ravioli stuffed with chestnuts)
and *vitello tonnato* (veal in tuna sauce).
*Via Fossano 1, 12100; 0171 66277; www.
osteriadellachiocciola.it; closed Sun*

Arione *moderate*
The local delicacy is *Cuneesi al rhum* –
a kind of bittersweet chocolate truffle
made with rum. Ernest Hemingway
stopped by to try it in 1954.
*Piazza Galimberti 14, 12100; 0171 692
539; www.arionecuneo.it*

DAY TRIP OPTIONS
It is possible to make a circular tour
from Alba to appreciate the excellent
food and wine of the Langhe
vineyards and the hilltop villages.
The stunning mountain scenery and
wilderness is easily reached from
Saluzzo or Cuneo.

Vineyard tour
Based in Alba ❷, head for the
wonderful wine museum WiMu at
Barolo ❹, which will set visitors up
for La Morra ❺, a town with great
views over the rolling hills and
vineyards. Take a walk through the

glorious countryside from here.
Then aim for the village of Barbaresco
❶, another good vantage point,
especially in the golden evening
light, before returning to Alba.

🚗 *From Alba take SP3 to Barolo, then
SP3 and SP58 to La Morra. Head
eastwards to Grinzane Cavour and
pick up SP3 through Alba, aiming for
Località Altavilla and Barbaresco,
returning to Alba by SS231.*

Mountain and valley greenery
Drive at a leisurely pace through the
lovely Valle Varaita from Saluzzo ❽,

before reaching Sampeyre ❾, where
the Museo Etnografico is worth a
visit. Drive on through spectacular
mountain scenery to the villages
of Elva ❿ and Stroppo ⑪. Here,
admire the frescoes in the churches
before returning through the
verdant Valle Maira through Dronero
⑬ and back to Saluzzo.

🚗 *From Saluzzo take SP589 to
Verzuolo, then SP8 through Piasco to
Sampeyre. From here, head up to the
Colle di Sampeyre and down on SP335
to Stroppo. Follow SP422 to Dronero,
then SP589 to Saluzzo.*

Sacred Mountains & Island Palaces

San Carlone to Varese

Highlights

- **Lakeside gem**
  Relax at the enchanting lakeside village of Orta San Giulio and explore its pretty island and Sacro Monte

- **Sacri Monti**
  Wander through small, tree-shaded chapels on the Sacri Monti (Sacred Mountains) and savour the quiet

- **Borromean Islands**
  From Stresa, island-hop by ferry, to tour the extravagant island palaces with their lakeside gardens and waterside restaurants

- **Lago Maggiore Express**
  Enjoy a day trip via boat across Lake Maggiore and on the private Centovalli railway to stunning alpine valleys and mountain towns

A view of the island of Isola Bella in Lake Maggiore

Sacred Mountains and Island Palaces

Popular in the 19th century as a stop on the Grand Tour, Lago Maggiore is a beautiful stretch of water reaching north into Switzerland. Nearby, little Lago d'Orta holds the bewitching village of Orta San Giulio with its magical island and laid-back atmosphere. The resort of Stresa, with its grand hotels, is the departure point for boats to the lavish palaces and gardens of the Borromean Islands. The area's temperate climate sets the gardens ablaze with camellias, azaleas and rhododendrons. Above this perfect setting, the steep hillsides are dotted with extraordinary 17th-century chapels forming the Sacri Monti (Sacred Mountains). Away from the lake, to the east, the little known town of Varese is a fine discovery, with its pretty centre, country walks and top-class art gallery.

Above Sailing in front of the terraced gardens of Isola Bella, see p53 **Opposite** People enjoying lunch at a lakeside restaurant next to Lake Orta see p52

ACTIVITIES

Explore the sleepy town of Orto San Giulio and catch a boat to its island

Stride up steep hillsides to marvel at the chapels and the views from the region's three Sacri Monti

Sail across the waters to the splendid palaces and gardens on the Borromean Islands

Walk or cycle up the Val Cannobina to picnic by the Sant'Anna gorge.

Enjoy a stroll past the colourful blooms in the gardens at Villa Taranto

KEY

Drive route

Val Cannobina

Cavaglio
34
Monte Cadringa
1300m
Traffiume
4 CANNÓBIO
Maccagno
Trarego
Cânnero
394
Dumenza
Oggebbio
Luino
34
Germignaga
SACRO
MONTE DELLA
S TRINITÀ DI GHIFFA
69
Ghiffa
Porto Valtravaglia
Maggiore
394
Castelveccana
Mesenzana
Val
Marchirolo
43
Monte Colonna
1198m
Cunardo
Monte Nudo
1237m
aveno
Sasso del Ferro
1062m
8 ARCUMEGGIA
Rancio
Valcúvia
Monte Piambello
1123m
CASALZUIGNO **7**
Cittiglio
Cuveglio
Bedero
Valcuvia
233
Fracce
Brinzio
Gemonio
62
Monte Martica
1025m
Leggiuno
LOMBARDIA
Campo dei Fiori
1227m
629
Rasa di
Varese
Arcisate
Monvalle
394
Santa Maria
del Monte
344
Besozzo
Gavirate
Induno Olona
Comério
Sant'
Amrogio
rebbia
Casciago
18
Calcinate
del Pesce
394
9 VARESE
629
Biandronno
Lago di
Varese
Bobbiate
342
adrezzate
Travedona
Monate
Brabbia
Lago di
Monate
33
Ternate
36
Buguggiate
Comabbio
18
Galliate
Lombardo
17
A8
57
Lago di
Comabbio
Mercallo
Corgeno
629
Sesto Calende
17
33

0 kilometres   5

0 miles   5

PLAN YOUR DRIVE

Start/finish: San Carlone to Varese.

Number of days: 4–5 days, including a day on Lago Maggiore and a day's activity exploring the Val Cannobina.

Distance: Approx 160 km (99 miles).

Road conditions: The higher roads can be steep and winding, and often have poor surfaces after icy winters. The lakeside roads are good, although winding, and they get very busy in summer, especially at weekends. Use snow chains in winter.

When to go: Easter–Jul and Sep are the best months to avoid the summer crowds. The villa gardens are at their best in late spring and early summer. Many hotels and restaurants close down for winter at the end of October.

Opening times: Shops tend to open Mon–Sat 9am–1pm and 3–7pm. Hours for villas vary – some are closed on Mon and most close early in winter.

Main market days: Arona: Tue am; Orta San Giulio: Wed am; **Stresa:** Fri am; **Cannobio:** Sun am; **Laveno:** Tue am; **Varese:** Mon.

Shopping: Small boutiques sell turned wood, original paintings and hand-made jewellery in Stresa, Orta San Giulio and Cannobio. All villages have good *alimentari* (grocers) selling local salamis, cheeses, dried mushrooms and good Piedmont red wines.

Major festivals: Orta San Giulio: Firework festival, July; **Stresa:** Classical music festival, Aug–Sep; Camelia Festival, 3rd week of March.

DAY TRIP OPTIONS

Leave the car behind for the day and head for the famous **Borromean Islands by boat** from Stresa and explore them on foot; or opt for the **Lago Maggiore Express** – a trio of **ferry and mountain train trips** into neighbouring Switzerland. Alternatively, an attractive, circular route south and west from Stresa takes in the views, from the giant **statue of San Carlone**, the **pretty town** of Orta San Giulio and the **Alpine pastures** between. For full details, *see p55*.

Above View across the rooftops of Stresa and over Lago Maggiore

VISITING ORTA SAN GIULIO

Parking
Use the car park by the tourist office (Via Panoramica). From here, a tourist train heads to the centre and Sacro Monte.

Tourist Information
Via Panoramica, 28016; 0322 905163; www.distrettolaghi.it; closed Mon, Tue

WHERE TO STAY

ORTA SAN GIULIO

Leon d'Oro *moderate–expensive*
This family-run three-star hotel has en-suite rooms and a lakeside location. *Piazza Motta 42, 28016; 0322 911 991; closed Jan; www.albergoleondoro.it*

STRESA

Hotel Verbano *moderate–expensive*
On the northernmost of the Borromean Islands, this romantic, 12-bedroom hotel is handsomely furnished. Once the last boat has gone, the island is all yours. *Via Ugo Ara 2, 28838, Isola dei Pescatori; 0323 304 08; closed Nov–mid-Mar; www.hotelverbano.it*

① San Carlone
Arona, Piedmont; 28041
Completed in 1698, one of Europe's highest statues rises 35 m (115 ft) above the town of Arona. It is a monument to the archbishop of Milan, Carlo Borromeo, an important figure in the Counter-Reformation. Climb up inside for superb views from inside the statue's head *(Mar: open Sun & hol; Apr–Sep: open daily); Oct–Nov: Sat, Sun & hol; Dec: Sun).*

🚗 **Turn west off S33 onto SP35 for Montrigiasco. Follow SP110 and SP34 through Invório and Monticelli to SP43. Follow signs to Gozzano till SS229. Turn right, heading north along the lake to Orta San Giulio.**

② Orta San Giulio
Novara, Piedmont; 28016
Perched on a promontory, this medieval town, the jewel of Lago d'Orta, is a confection of frescoed pastel-coloured houses lining a maze of romantic cobbled alleys and piazzas. The traffic-free centre makes exploring the island's intriguing nooks and crannies a delight.

A two-hour walking tour
From the car park and tourist office, walk south along Via Fava to the Moorish fantasy hotel **Villa Crespi** ① *(www.villacrespi.it).* Follow the lakeside road to the main square, **Piazza Motta** ②, with cafés, shops and hotels and a weekly market held since 1228. The 16th-century town hall, **Palazzo della Comunità** ③, holds art shows and nearby **Rovera** *(Largo de Gregori 15; 0322 90123)* is a trove of local delicacies and wines. From the piazza, take a boat to **Isola di San Giulio** ④. Legend has it that, in AD 390, Giulio, a Christian preacher, rid the island of its dragons and serpents and built the Romanesque Basilica di San Giulio *(open daily)* – his

Statue of St Francis of Assisi, Orta San Giulio

remains are in the crypt. The only street, Via del Silenzio, becoming the Via della Meditazione, leads past the Benedictine convent Palazzo dei Vescovi. The abbess has put up signs encouraging meditation on "the island within".

Back at Piazza Motta, take the Salita della Motta, a stepped lane past the late-Renaissance **Palazzo Gemelli** ⑤ and other elegant palazzi such as the **Casa dei Nani** ⑥ (House of Dwarves) ⑥. Orta's oldest house, dating from the 14th century, this building takes its name from its four tiny windows. Passing by houses in a profusion of architectural styles, head up to the 15th-century Baroque church **Santa Maria Assunta** ⑦.

LAGO MAGGIORE EXPRESS

For a scenic day trip, start from Stresa with a leisurely ferry ride (tickets at ferry stations and tourist offices) to the end of the lake and into Switzerland (passports are a must). Stroll through lakeside Locarno and hop on board the Centovalli express, a Swiss train that passes through stunning Alpine scenery to Domodossola, Italy. There is time for a wander and a meal before catching the train back to Stresa (www.lagomaggioreexpress.it).

VISITING STRESA

Parking
There is a large pay-and-display at Piazza Marconi by the ferry terminal.

Tourist Information
Piazza Marconi 16, 28838; 0323 30150; www.distrettolaghi.it

EAT AND DRINK

ORTA SAN GIULIO

Al Boeuc *inexpensive*
Away from the crowds, this cosy wine bar serves delicious Piedmontese cheese and *affettati misti* (cold cuts). *Via Bersani 28, 28016; 339 5840039; www.alboeuc.beepworld.it; closed Tue mid Mar–Oct; open by reservation only Nov–mid Mar*

Villa Crespi *expensive*
This two-Michelin-starred restaurant, set in a Moorish-style luxury hotel, serves innovative Mediterranean cuisine. *Via G Fava 18, 28016; 0322 911 902; www.villacrespi.it*

STRESA

Il Clandestino *moderate*
Creative dishes using seasonal produce are beautifully presented here. The fish and seafood are particularly good. *Via Rosmini 5, 28838; 0323 30399; www.ristoranteilclandestino.com*

From here, take Via Gemelli and turn left to the **Sacro Monte di Francesco** ⑧ *(open daily)*. Set on a hillside above the lake, with views to Isola di San Giulio, this is a devotional path with 21 chapels illustrating the life of St Francis of Assisi. Built between 1591 and 1750, the chapels contain 376 sculptures and 900 frescoes and alternate between Baroque and Renaissance styles. The restaurant here has a pretty, ivy-clad terrace. Return to the car park on the train.

🚗 *Leaving Orta San Giulio, cross the roundabout to follow narrow SP114 past the station. Turn left on SP114, becoming SP39 later through Armeno. Drive over the hill, past small villages, and down the narrow lanes to Stresa.*

Sacri Monti

These devotional complexes are made up of a series of chapels, lining a path to the top of a mountain. The chapels illustrate the lives of Christ, the Saints or the Virgin Mary and were built in beautiful locations over the 16th and 17th centuries during the Counter-Reformation. There are nine such complexes across northern Italy, all UNESCO World Heritage Sites.

reach the islands. **Isola Bella** *(open end-Mar–end-Oct)* has a grand Baroque palace with terraced gardens. Visit quieter **Isola Madre** *(open end-Mar–end-Oct)* for its 16th-century villa and extensive gardens, with splendid magnolias and camellias in spring. **Isola dei Pescatori**, also called Isola Superiore, is an erstwhile fisherman's village of narrow lanes and higgedly-piggedly houses, now given over mainly to restaurants.

A 5-minute stroll north of the centre of Stresa leads to the Lido, where a cable car ascends Monte Mottarone, stopping halfway at the lovely **Giardino Botanico Alpinia** *(closed Oct–Mar)*. There are attractive walks at the summit and the 3-hour descent can be done on foot – or, if you prefer, by mountain bike.

🚗 *Take the lakeside SS33 northeast out of Stresa to Fondotoce. Continue along the waterside SS34 to Cannobio.*

Top Pretty Isola di San Giulio, a short boat ride from Orta San Giulio **Below** Statue of Carlo Borromeo, Arona **Below right** View from the cable car up Monte Mottarone, Stresa

③ Stresa
Verbano-Cusio-Ossola, Piedmont; 28838
When the Simplon Tunnel opened in 1906, linking northern and southern Europe by rail, sleepy lakeside Stresa became a favourite of the European nobility. The town is is now a sedate place with grand hotels, manicured gardens and a pedestrianized centre. It is beautifully located with stunning views up the lake to the Alps, and across to the famous treasures of the Borromean Islands. Take a ferry or boat taxi from the Stresa landing stage to

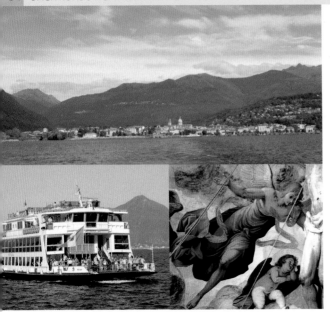

Top Lago Maggiore and Verbania, ringed by forest-clad hills **Above** Ferry taking visitors across Lago Maggiore **Above right** Fresco at Varese's Sacro Monte

VISITING CANNOBIO

Parking
There are several well signposted pay-and-display car parks; Piazza Martiri della Libertà at the northern end is the largest.

Tourist Information
Via A Giovanola 25; 0323 71212; www.procannobio.it

VISITING VARESE

Tourist Information
Via Romagnosi 9, Piazza del Podestà, 21100; 0332 28191; www.varesecittagiardino.it

Funicular
www.varesefunicolari.org

WHERE TO STAY

CANNOBIO
Pironi *moderate*
A friendly hotel in a 15th-century former monastery with comfortable rooms.
Via Marconi 35, 28822; 0323 70170; www.pironihotel.it; closed Oct–Feb

Residenza Patrizia *moderate*
This modern hotel is near the beach.
Via Vittorio Veneto 9, 28822; 0041 41 410 7830; www.residenzapatrizia.com

AROUND VARESE
Borducan *moderate*
This is a historic antique-filled hotel set in a Liberty villa on the hillside.
Via Beata C Moriggi 43, 21100; 0332 22 05 67; www.borducan.com

Where to Stay: inexpensive, under €100; moderate, €100–200; expensive, over €200

④ Cannobio
Piedmont 28822
An attractive village close to the Swiss border, Cannobio is a relaxed holiday resort, popular with families. It has a good beach, a wide choice of watersports and plenty of cycle trails and hikes inland. Accommodation and restaurant options are dotted among the pretty, stepped lanes. The town is also famous for its statue of the Virgin Mary said to have started bleeding in 1522. The **Santuario della Santissima Pietà** was built at the site in 1578.
🚗 *Take SS34 south to Ghiffa. Then turn right, following signs to Sacro Monte up steep lanes to the car park.*

Below Alfresco seating on one of the café-lined streets in Verbania

⑤ Sacro Monte della SS Trinità di Ghiffa
Verbano-Cusio-Ossola, Piedmont; 28055
Set in a stunning position with views across the lake to the foothills of the Alps, the 17th-century complex on this sacred mountain is incomplete, with three main chapels and two smaller ones flanking the central sanctuary. They were built between 1605 and 1617 and contain depictions of biblical scenes, including the baptism of Jesus by John the Baptist, with God looking down from above.
🚗 *Return to SS34 and turn right towards Verbania. After 6 km (4 miles), once in Intra, follow signs to Villa Taranto, where there is a car park.*

Val Cannobina
Explore the secluded Val Cannobina up to Traffiume and Orrido di Sant'Anna, a small gorge spanned by a Roman bridge. This pretty riverside path is an 8-km (5-mile) round trip and navigable on foot or by bike. Bikes can be hired from **Cicli Prezan** *(Viale V Veneto, 9, Cannobio 28822; 0323 712 30)*. There are many picnic spots and a restaurant *(see right)*.

⑥ Verbania
Verbano-Cusio-Ossola, Piedmont; 28922
Mussolini merged the villages of Suna, Intra and Pallanza under the Roman name for the lake, Verbania. This is an attractive town with narrow shop-lined lanes in the centre. The key draw is the **Villa Taranto** *(open mid–Mar–end Oct)*. In 1931, capitalizing on the region's microclimate, Neil McEacharn, a retired Scottish captain, began landscaping a botanical garden with species from around the

world. The resulting 7 km (4 miles) of pathways meander through beds of dahlias, camellias and rhododendrons, past ponds with spectacular fountains and giant lily pads and lotus flowers. It all makes a wonderful retreat.

🚗 *Follow the road for 500 m (547 yards) to the Intra ferry station and catch the car ferry to Laveno. Take SS394 (signposted Gavirate) out of Laveno to the roundabout in Fracce. Continue on Via Valcuvia, turning left up Via Sciareda into Casalzuigno.*

Above Manicured garden at Villa Taranto, Verbania
Top right A cobbled street in Arcumeggia

🕖 Casalzuigno
Varese, Lombardia; 21030
Set in the chestnut-tree valley of Cúvia is the village of Casalzuigno, whose main attraction is the 15th-century **Villa della Porta Bozzolo** (closed mid-Sep–Feb; Mar: Mon & Tue; Apr–mid-Sep: Mon) and its 18th-century terraced gardens. The villa has frescoes, period kitchens and farm buildings.

🚗 *Return to the main road and then left on SP7, up the steep switchback to Arcumeggia.*

🕗 Arcumeggia
Casalzuigno, Varese; Lombardia 21030
The stone houses and crumbling courtyards of this mountain village are decorated with 20th-century frescoes. Figurative works by artists such as Aligi Sassu and Remo Brindisi adorn the façades of some houses as part of an ongoing regeneration project that began in the 1950s.

🚗 *Backtrack to the main road and head east on SS394 to Rancio Valcúvia. Take SP62 southeast and climb up the wooded Campo dei Fiori to Varese.*

🕘 Varese
Varese, Lombardia; 21100
Nicknamed "The Garden City", Varese is a pleasing mix of early 20th-century villas and 17th-century Baroque buildings set in verdant parks. At the heart of the town's pedestrianized centre is the Church of San Vittore and its 12th-century frescoed baptistry. To the north of town (well signposted and with its own car park), the 18th-century **Villa Panza** (closed Mon) houses an impressive collection of contemporary art with site-specific installations in the old stables and works by Dan Flavin. There are also landscaped gardens and a good café. Follow signs north out of town along Via Virgilio and Via Prima Cappella to the **Campo dei Fiori** national park, once a hunting ground for the medieval dukes of Milan. From the park's ridge, the Via Sacra, a 2-km (1-mile) cobbled path, leads up the mountain past a series of 16th-century chapels, containing life-size scenes illustrating the Mystery of the Rosary. They form a **Sacro Monte** that culminates in the Baroque Santuario di Santa Maria del Monte and the village of Santa Maria del Monte. A 3-minute funicular (open weekends and end Jul–end Aug) whisks less energetic visitors up the mountain.

EAT AND DRINK

CANNOBIO
La Streccia *moderate*
Informal restaurant in a narrow alleyway, serving Piedmontese dishes featuring mushrooms and game.
Via Merzagora 5, 28822; 0323 70575; www.ristorantelastreccia.it; closed Thu

VERBANIA
Il Milano *expensive*
The dishes at this waterside restaurant combine creativity and local traditions.
Corso Zanitello 2, 28922; 0323 556 816; www.ristorantemilanolagomaggiore.it; closed Tue Jan–mid-Mar

VARESE
Bologna *inexpensive–moderate*
This classic trattoria serves traditional fare: the *antipasto della casa* (mixed hors d'oeuvres) is a delicious meal in itself.
Via Broggi 7, 21100; 0332 234 362; www.albergobologna.it; closed Aug

AROUND VARESE
Taverna delle Ruote *inexpensive*
This country trattoria serves seasonal produce and decent house wine.
Via Marconi 29, Bedero Valcuvia (just off the SP62, north of Varese), 21039; 0332 724 572; www.tavernadelle ruote.net; closed Tue eve & Wed

DAY TRIP OPTIONS
Stresa is a good base for exploring the area. Chugging across the lakes on a ferry really should not be missed.

Lake Maggiore Express
A very reasonably priced round trip from Stresa ❸, on a scenic rail and ferry route exploring the valleys and towns on the Swiss–Italian border.

Borromean Islands
Catch a boat from Stresa ❸ to explore **Isola Bella** before moving on to **Isola Madre** for a picnic lunch, or **Isola dei Pescatori** for a meal of lake fish at one of the waterside restaurants. Aim to return to Stresa in the late afternoon, when the light on the water is particularly special.

Saints and swimmers
Enjoy sweeping views of the lake from the statue of San Carlone ❶, then head to Orta San Giulio ❷ for lunch. Catch a speedboat to its island and have a dip in the lake before driving to Stresa for dinner.

Take the SP114 on the return trip, followed by the SP39.

Eat and Drink: inexpensive, under €25; moderate, €25–€45; expensive, over €45

Turin

ITALY • Venice

Genoa • • Bologna

Florence •

• Perugia

• Rome

Como's Villas and Villages

Como to Brunate

Highlights

- **Lakeside splendour**
  Enjoy the serene gardens and magnificent villas that have made Lake Como so famous

- **A change of view**
  Let someone else do the steering and see things from a different perspective on Lake Como's *traghetto* (ferry) service

- **Bella Bellagio**
  Visit the prettiest of the lakeside villages, set on the tip of a promontory with a scenic wooded hill behind it

- **Romance and panoramas**
  Explore romantic Varenna's exquisite villa gardens and climb up to Castello di Vezio for panoramic lake views

A view of houses on the hillside by Lake Como on a sunny day

Como's Villas and Villages

Famed for the sparkling beauty of its water, romantic villas and serene lakeside gardens, Lake Como does not disappoint. The natural setting of thickly wooded mountainsides rising up from beside the lake has been drawing visitors since Roman times – the 19th-century Romantics were particularly attached to the area. This route includes ferry crossings, shore-hugging roads and country lanes with several leg-stretching jaunts up to panoramic viewpoints. Como, Bellagio, Varenna and other villages are perfect spots to pause and enjoy the water for an afternoon – or longer.

KEY

Drive route

Above Appreciating the lakeside scenery from Bellagio, *see p61*
Opposite The winding road up to Santuario della Madonna del Ghisallo, *see p63*

ACTIVITIES

Go shopping for silk in stylish Como town

Walk up to the enchanting Sacro Monte di Ossuccio, high above the lake

Explore the fabulous lakeside gardens of villas Balbianello, Serbelloni and Melzi

Cycle or hike in the countryside around Menaggio where there are trails to suit all levels

Play a round of golf in the hills above Menaggio

Zig-zag acoss the waters on a *traghetto* (ferry) for pure lake romance

Watch a falconry display at the Castello di Vezio, Varenna

0 kilometres 3

0 miles 3

Bellano

340d

Plésio

Nobiallo

Cardano

Croce

5 MENAGGIO

VARENNA **7**

Griante

Cadenabbia

340

mezzo

Loppia

S. Giovanni

Pescallo

6 BELLAGIO

Ortanella

Como

di

Visgnola

583

Limonta

Lierna

Guello

Grumo

Perlo

41

Ólcio

Civenna

Lago di Lecco

SANTUARIO DELLA
MADONNA DEL
GHISALLO **8**

*M. S. Primo
1683m* △ *M. Ponci
1450m*

Magréglio

72

Mandello
del Lário

Barni

Onno

44

d' Tivano

44

9 VALASSINA AND
PIAN DEL TIVIANO

Colma

41

Sormano

Lasnigo

Cáglio

Rezzago

Valassina

Lambro

PLAN YOUR DRIVE

Start/finish: Como to Brunate.

Number of days: 2–3 days, allowing
half a day in Varenna.

Distance: Approx 100 km (62 miles).

Road conditions: Roads are generally
good, but with some tight bends on
the narrow lakeside roads between
Como and Menaggio and some steep,
winding lanes after Bellagio. In summer,
the lake roads can get very busy.

When to go: Visit Easter to July and
during September to beat the worst
of the summer crowds. Many of the
gardens are in full bloom in May–June.
Most lake hotels and restaurants close
from the end of October until Easter.

Opening times: Shops tend to open
9am–1pm and 3–7pm Mon–Sat. Villa
opening hours differ; some are closed
on Monday and the gardens usually
close early in winter.

Main market days: Como: Tue
and Thu morning and all day Sat;
Menaggio: 2nd and 4th Fri morning
of month; **Varenna:** Wed.

Shopping: Como is famous for its high-
quality silk, supplying Milan and the
world's fashion houses. There are some
outlets and factory shops around the
town. Workshops in Bellagio produce
ceramics, jewellery and leather goods.
Stock up too on Valtellina red wines
from the northern end of the lake.

Major festivals: Across the lake: Sagra
di San Giovanni (fireworks and boat
races), nearest Sat to 24 Jun; **Bellagio:**
Festa Patronale San Giacomo (town's
patron saint), 25 Jul. **Varenna:** Festa
del Lago (recalls the attack by Como),
1st weekend of Jul.

DAY TRIP OPTIONS

Tire energetic **youngsters** with a tour
of Como, a lakeside drive past **stately
villas**, then **climb up** the Sacro
Monte di Ossuccio before finishing
at Menaggio lido. For a more restful
time, take a **drive** on the quiet **back-
roads** away from the lake's bustle. Or
make use of the **ferries** by crossing
to Villa Balbianello, then back to
explore Varenna with its **villas** and
castle. For full details, see p63.

Above View from behind Bellagio out over Lake Como to Varenna **Below left** Church of the Madonna del Soccorso overlooking Menaggio **Below right** Inside the Church of the Madonna del Soccorso at the Sacro Monte di Ossuccio

VISITING COMO

Parking
Follow signs to a central multi-storey car park rather than look for an expensive roadside space with jacketed attendant.

Tourist Information
Via Pretorio, 22100; 031 304137; www.visitcomo.eu; closed Mon

WHERE TO STAY

COMO

Del Duca *moderate*
This comfortable three-star hotel has en suite air-conditioned rooms and a good-value restaurant, Le Colonne.
Piazza Mazzini 12, 22100; 031 264 859; www.albergodelduca.it; closed Jan

AROUND MENAGGIO

La Marianna *inexpensive-moderate*
This inviting family-run hotel has eight traditional rooms, most with lake views.
Via Regina 57, Cadenabbia di Griante, 22011 (on SS340, 3 km/2 miles south of Menaggio); 0344 43 095; www.la-marianna.com

Regina Teodolinda *expensive*
Set in lovely grounds, this carefully restored villa is serene, luxurious and has its own small swimming pool.
Via Vecchia Regina 58, Laglio, 22010 (on SS340, 21 km/13 miles south of Menaggio); 031 400 031; www.villareginateodolinda.com

BELLAGIO

Belvedere *expensive*
This hotel offers lake views, gardens, a pool, spacious rooms and parking too.
Via Valassina 31, 22021; 031 950 410; www.belvederebellagio.com; closed Nov–Easter

① Como
Como, Lombardia; 22100

The comfortable provincial town of Como sits on the southern tip of the western arm of Lake Como. It is best enjoyed by wandering the cobbled, criss-crossing grid of narrow lanes, a reminder of its Roman origins, and by taking in the lake vistas from the promenade or on the hill above town in Brunate *(see p63)*. An ancient silk-producing town, Como is a good place to shop for silk products.

In the main piazza, close to the harbour, the **Duomo** is a pleasing mix of Gothic and Renaissance styles with a Baroque dome. Next door is the medieval *broletto* (market hall) built in striped marble. Around the corner, the strong lines and functional style of the **Casa del Fascio**, completed in 1936 by architect Giuseppe Terragni, is one of the finest examples of Rationalist architecture in the country.

🚗 From Como, head north on SS340, the lakeside road signposted for Cernobbio. Through the village and past the luxury hotel Villa d'Este, branch off onto the SP71 or Via Vecchia Regina.

② Vecchia Regina: the SP71
Como, Lombardia

This narrow, winding road shows Lake Como in all its splendour. Running along the water's edge, the route weaves past private jetties, glorious retreats and splendid gardens built by European aristocrats and wealthy industrialists over the last few hundred years. Villa owners have included opera composer Vincenzo Bellini, fashionista Gianni Versace and, recently, Hollywood film star George Clooney. Most of the traffic takes the faster SS340, away from the lake, so drivers on this road are free to enjoy the views, stop to explore the little hamlets or peek into the celebrity-owned gardens.

🚗 Rejoin SS340, just before Brienno, and continue north to Ossuccio. Turn left to the Santuario just after a bend in the centre of the village. Park at the end of the road in the little square at the bottom of the grassy footpath.

③ Sacro Monte di Ossuccio
Como, Lombardia; 22016

Set in the folds of the hills above the lake, the Sacro Monte di Ossuccio is one of a series of UNESCO-recognized Sacred Mountains built across Northern Italy in the 17th century. Climb up through olive groves, past 14 chapels – each containing painted life-size plaster figures in scenes from the Bible – to the Church of the Madonna del Soccorso. It is a wonderful retreat from the lakeside hustle and bustle, with superb views of the water at the top of the steep 1-km (half-a-mile) long path.

🚢 *Follow the road back to the SS340 and continue north for 1 km (half a mile), then follow signs to the parking on the right.*

④ Villa Balbianello
Lenno, Como, Lombardia; 22016
One of many sumptuous lakeside villas, 18th-century Villa Balbianello *(mid-Mar–mid-Nov: open Tue & Thu–Sun)* stands on a verdant promontory with lovely views across the lake to the Grigne mountains. Paths lead down from the delightful loggia through beautiful terraced gardens to the water. Film buffs might recognize the location from *Star Wars: Episode II* (2000) and *Casino Royale* (2006), parts of which were filmed here. The house contains a small museum to its last owner, the explorer and mountaineer Guido Monzino and his Chinese, African and pre-Columbian art.

🚢 *Continue north on the SS340 to Menaggio and its roadside, town-centre parking. The road gets very crowded on this section.*

⑤ Menaggio
Como, Lombardia; 22017
Lakeside Menaggio is more a working village than a resort. It is a great base for enjoying strolls, hikes and cycle rides in the surrounding area and there is even a good golf course – set up by four British visitors in 1907; the tourist office *(Via Lusardi 26, 22017; 0344 364 11; www.menaggio. com)* has maps and information and

you can hire bikes from most hotels. In the village centre, **Piazza Garibaldi** offers some of the best restaurants and an attractive promenade leads down to the lido.

🚢 *There is a ferry station in Menaggio for the* **traghetto** *to Bellagio (or return 3 km/2 miles on SS340 to Cadenabbia).*

Above Palm-lined lakeside promenade, or *lungolago,* in the heart of Menaggio

⑥ Bellagio
Como, Lombardia; 22021
On the tip between the two arms of Lake Como, pretty Bellagio has been attracting visitors for centuries. The village centre is a criss-cross of steep, stepped lanes lined with boutiques, hotels, eateries and several handsome villas and gardens. The 17th-century **Villa Serbelloni**, a Rockerfeller institute, is closed to the public, but its formal terraced gardens can be visited on a guided tour *(mid-Mar–Oct: open Tue–Sun)*. The Neo-Classical **Villa Melzi** *(end Mar–Oct: open daily)* has an orangery and a Japanese garden. From town, it's a half-hour stroll to the fishing hamlets, Loppia (west) or Pescallo (east).

🚢 *Leave the car in Bellagio and catch one of the regular ferries to Varenna. Tickets available at the ferry terminal.*

Above left Elegant Villa Balbianello, built in 1787 on Lake Como **Above centre** Life-size statue in Chapel V of the Sacro Monte di Ossuccio **Above** Como's Piazza San Fedele, the site of law courts in Roman times

VISITING BELLAGIO

Parking
The centre of Bellagio is car-free so use the spaces on the edge of the village. Limited free spots (green paint) are available around the communal gardens up the hill from the ferry station. Otherwise, the blue pay-and-display bays are the only option. Some hotels have special deals for parking.

EAT AND DRINK

COMO

Castiglioni Gastronomia *inexpensive*
This family-run delicatessen offers mouthwatering home-made pasta, salamis and cheeses, and serves a good-value lunch in a pretty courtyard. *Via Cesare Cantù 9, 22100; 031 263 388; www.castiglionistore.com*

La Colombetta *expensive*
Simple, elegant dining rooms provide the backdrop for Sardinian-inspired fish specialities, often including home-made pasta, accompanied by good Italian wines. *Via Diaz 40, 22100; 031 262 703; www.colombetta.it; closed Sun*

MENAGGIO

Il Ristorante di Paolo *moderate*
Excellent food served in a relaxed and elegant atmosphere. The staff are helpful about the good wine list. *Largo Cavour 5, 22017; 0344 32 133; www.ilristorantedipaolo.it; closed Tue*

BELLAGIO

Silvio *moderate*
The simple, refined meals based around the freshest fish – often caught by Silvio or his son – and magical lake views make this place a treat. *Via Carcano 12, 22021; 031 950 322; www.bellagiosilvio.com*

Eat and Drink: inexpensive, under €25; moderate, €25–€45; expensive over €45

Right The grandiose lakeside frontage of Villa Cipressi, Varenna **Far right** Varenna's village centre backed by a steep mountainside **Below** Spectacular view of Lake Como from Castello di Vezio

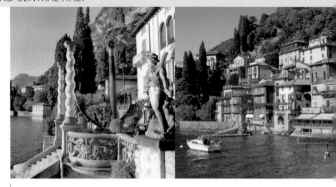

➐ Varenna

Lecco, Lombardia; 23829

Set on the eastern shore of Lake Como and backed by steep mountains, Varenna is a sleepy fishing village that sparkles in the afternoon sun. The castle on the hillside above is said to be haunted by a 7th-century queen, Theodolinda, and in the 12th century, the village itself was involved in bloody wars with its bigger neighbour, Como.

VISITING VARENNA

Tourist Information
Via IV Novembre 7, 23829; 341 830 367; www.varennaturismo.com

WHERE TO STAY

VARENNA

Hotel Milano *moderate*
This stylish hotel is centrally located, with a good restaurant, great lake views and charming owners.
Via 20 Settembre 35, 23829; 0341 830 298; www.varenna.net

Hotel Du Lac *expensive*
Tucked in a quiet corner of the village, this comfortable hotel offers spacious bedrooms. There is a shaded waterfront bar and breakfast is served outside.
Via del Prestino 11, 23829; 0341 830 238; www.albergodulac.com

A two-hour walking tour

The short ferry crossing from Bellagio is possibly the most romantic way to arrive in Varenna. Head uphill from the **ferry station** ① to the main road. Turn right and cross over to where the signposted path to the castle begins, next to the Hotel Ristorante Monte Codeno. A 15-minute walk up this very stepped mountain path leads to Vezio, an ancient hamlet of stone houses whose conquest by the Romans in 196 BC is described by the Roman author Pliny the Younger. Follow the signs through tiny lanes, past the Piazza della Chiesetta di Sant'Antonio Abate, named for its tiny 16th-century church, and through an olive grove to the 13th-century **Castello di Vezio** ② *(Mar–Oct: open daily)*, which offers stunning views, lawns and ruined towers. There are falconry displays at the weekend and an outdoor trattoria serving good, local specialities.

Return to the little piazza in front of the church, from where a panoramic path, called the Scabium, runs back down to Varenna. From the church,

Where to Stay: inexpensive, under €100; moderate, €100–€200; expensive, over €200

turn right, if facing the church, and then right again after a 90-degree turn. Continue along, under a stone bridge, and take the signposted right fork downhill. A few minutes' steep walk or drive, accompanied by glorious views, leads to the main road into Varenna. Turn right and cross over to the luxuriant terraced gardens and museum at the 17th-century **Villa Monastero** ③ *(open mid-Mar–end Oct, Jan–Feb: Sun)*, built on the site of a 13th-century Cistercian monastery. The rooms are grandly decorated and the garden's avenues and terraces are shaded by cypress, oleander and citrus trees.

Turn left out of the villa and pop into the splendid garden with its relaxing viewpoint at the hotel next door, **Villa Cipressi** ④.

Left out of Villa Cipressi leads into Varenna's main square, **Piazza San Giorgio** ⑤, with its 13th-century parish church and the 10th-century chapel of **San Giovanni Battista** ⑥, which has excellent frescoes. From here, head down into the grid of cool lanes to Varenna's waterfront cafés. Walk past the tiny harbour on the left and continue along the **walkway** ⑦ back to the ferry station and Bellagio.

Falconry display at Castello di Vezio

🚗 *Leave Bellagio on SP41 (see below), which winds for 5 km (3 miles) up to Magreglio. Park near the sanctuary.*

⑧ Santuario della Madonna del Ghisallo
Bellagio, Lombardia; 22030

The Madonna del Ghisallo has been the patron saint of cyclists since 1949 and this sanctuary is a very popular destination for two wheelers; it is often on the route of the annual Italy-wide cycle race, Giro d'Italia. Next door there is a specialist museum with bicycles and Giro-winners' pink jerseys, donated by Italy's cycling greats. From the Romeo Belvedere nearby there are unbeatable views of the eastern arm of the lake and the Grigne mountains. 🚗 *Continue south along the SP41.*

⑨ Valassina and Pian del Tiviano
Como, Lombardia; 22030

Crossing this rural corner of the lake takes drivers along winding lanes through chestnut woods and medieval hamlets. At **Colma**, there is an astronomical observatory and great views in three directions. Head towards the lake across the bowl of the Pian del Tiviano, which is carpeted with narcissi, lilies of the valley and bluebells in springtime. Here, the road switchbacks down to **Nesso**, a pretty lakeside village. 🚗 *Drive along SP41, turn right onto SP44 signed Sormano, carry on for 19 km (12 miles) till Nesso. At SS583 turn left to Como 16km (10 miles). Follow signs to the funicular and nearby car park.*

⑩ Brunate
Como, Lombardia; 22034

Catch the funicular up to Brunate *(every 15 min from 6am till 10:30pm; Jun–Aug: till midnight)* to finish the drive with some more spectacular views of the lake. The steep 6-minute ascent passes attractive 19th-century villas and their gardens to the summit where a small Art Nouveau resort offers a few restaurants and cafés as well as strategically sited places to drink in the lake views one last time.

Above Monument to cyclists at Santuario della Madonna del Ghisallo **Below** Steep alleyway between the houses of Varenna

EAT AND DRINK

VARENNA

Il Castello di Vezio *inexpensive*
This informal al fresco restaurant serves lake fish, grilled meats and their own organic vegetables and olive oil. Wash it all down with local Valtellina wine. *Vezio, 23828 Perledo, Lecco; 3334 485 975; www.castellodivezio.it; open Mar–Nov daily 10am–7pm; reservation needed for evenings*

Il Cavatappi *moderate*
Reservations are needed at this tiny, intimate place. The dishes are excellent and include local lake-fish specialities. There is also a good list of local wines. *Via XX Settembre 8, 23829; 0341 815 349; www.cavatappivarenna.it; closed Mar–May & Oct–Dec; Wed Jan – Feb*

DAY TRIP OPTIONS
Several parts of this drive would make comfortable, varied day trips – with or without the car.

Villas and views
After exploring the lanes of Como ①, follow the lake road past splendid villas. Take a detour to walk up to Sacro Monte di Ossuccio ③ for panoramic views, before ending up in Menaggio ⑤ for a swim at the lido.

Back roads from Bellagio
Head away from the bustle of Bellagio ⑥ on this back route to Como, which heads up to the Santuario della Madonna del Ghisallo ⑧, dedicated to the patron saint of cyclists, before winding through

Drive north from Como on SS340, branching off on to SP71 and up to the Sacro Monte di Ossuccio, then return via SS340 to Menaggio.

wooded valleys to the lake road and back to Bellagio or Como ①.

Leave Bellagio on SP41, take winding SP44 and then SS583 to reach Como.

Ferry-hopping tour
Leave the car in Bellagio ⑥ and take the ferry *(www.my-lake-como-holiday.com)* to Lenno/Villa Balbianello ④. Return to Bellagio for lunch, then hop onto the ferry to Varenna ⑦ to see the town and Castello di Vezio.

Lombardy's Glacial Valleys

Bergamo to Erbusco

Highlights

- **Split-level Bergamo**
  Explore ancient lanes of the charming Upper Town, and the grand buildings and avenues of the Lower Town

- **Untouched valleys**
  Well away from the tourist trail, the Bergamasco and Brescian valleys are an insight into life in Lombardy through the ages

- **Low-key lakeside**
  Slow down to the gentle pace at quiet Lago d'Iseo – a world away from the international holiday resorts of the other northern lakes

- **Sparkling vintages**
  Sip the country's best fizzy wines among the vineyard-clad, gently rolling hills of Franciacorta

Steep wooded hillside and mountains ringing Lago d'Iseo

Lombardy's Glacial Valleys

Many years ago, when Northern Italy's glaciers retreated to the Alps, they left behind a series of fertile valleys and pretty lakes backed by rugged hills. Strategically located cities such as Bergamo and Brescia have a long history as Roman, medieval and even Venetian strongholds. But there's evidence of much older human occupation up in the hills of the Val Camonica, where the rocks and caves are peppered with extraordinary prehistoric petroglyphs. Further down the valley, Lago d'Iseo is the perfect place to unwind, while the sparkling wines and hills of the Franciacorta provide relief from summer heat. Throughout the region, hearty pastas, polenta, salamis and cheeses are washed down with good table wines.

Above Bergamo's Upper Town, dominated by the Torre Gombito, *see p68* **Below** Houses lining the banks of Lago d'Iseo, *see p70*

KEY

Drive route

ACTIVITIES

Ride the funicular to Bergamo's Upper Town to uncover its history

Take a relaxing boat trip on the sparkling waters of Lago d'Iseo

Explore the Roman mosaics and other historic treasures in ancient Brescia

Tour the vineyards of the Franciacorta and sample its sparkling wines

Hike through the pre-Alpine valleys and discover the prehistoric rock art

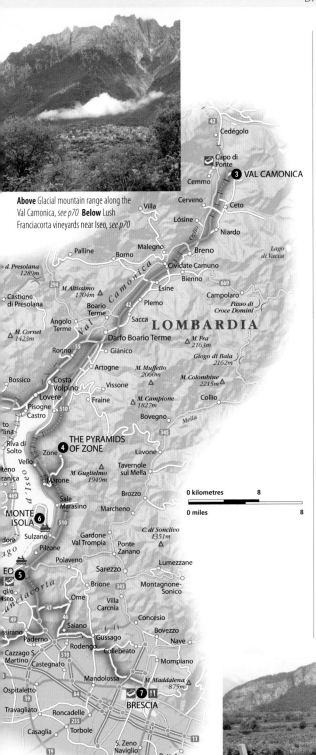

Above Glacial mountain range along the Val Camonica, *see p70* **Below** Lush Franciacorta vineyards near Iseo, *see p70*

PLAN YOUR DRIVE

Start/finish: Bergamo to Erbusco.

Number of days: 3 days.

Distance: Approx 230 km (143 miles).

Road conditions: Light industry and heavy traffic mar the roads near to the cities, but the number of cars decreases further up the valleys. Roads will be busy on summer weekends. Tunnels should be taken with care.

Opening times: Shops tend to open 9am–1pm and 3–7pm Mon–Sat, although some shops in small villages are closed on Mon morning.

When to go: Spring and early summer see the Alpine flowers at their best, while autumn is marked by wild mushrooms and wine festivals.

Main market days: Clusone: Tue morning; **Iseo:** Fri morning; **Lovere:** Sat morning.

Shopping: Look out for local produce such as mountain cheese *(formagella)*, salami and pasta *(casoncei, scarpinocc)*, as well as Franciacorta sparkling wines.

Major festivals: Bergamo: Sant' Alessandro, 26 Aug; Santa Lucia, 13 Dec; **Brescia:** Mille Miglia vintage car race, 2nd week of May; **Erbusco:** Franciacorta festival, 3rd weekend of Sep.

DAY TRIP OPTIONS

See the **medieval** and **Renaissance buildings** of Bergamo and then drive along **Val Seriana** to Clusone. Or, from Lago d'Iseo, spend time on Monte Isola for some **lakeside relaxation**, finishing with a trip to Zone to see the **stunning rock formations**. Explore the **wineries**, **vineyards** – and **wines** – of beautiful Franciacorta. For full details, *see p71*.

Above The spectacular dome in the Basilica di Santa Maria Maggiore, Bergamo

VISITING BERGAMO

Parking
On-street parking is hard to find in Bergamo's centre. Head for the underground car parks at Piazza della Libertà or Piazzale della Repubblica, off Viale Vittorio Emanuele II. If you've got one, show a funicular ticket when paying, to get a discount on Sundays.

Tourist Information
There are guided walking tours *(Apr–Oct: 3pm)* and bicycles can be hired. *Città Bassa: Viale Papa Giovanni XXIII 57, 24122; 035 210 204. Città Alta: Torre Gombito 13, 24129; 035 242 226; www.comune.bergamo.it*

VISITING CLUSONE

Tourist Information
Piazza Orologio 21, 24023; 0346 21 113; www.turismoproclusone.it

Market day
On Mondays, the lanes are taken over by a market selling local salamis, cheese and fresh pasta. Smallholders from the hills nearby sell home-grown produce.

WHERE TO STAY

BERGAMO

La Valletta Relais *inexpensive*
This spick and span, family-run hotel on the hillside has pretty rooms.
Via Castagneta 19, Città Alta 24129; 035 242 746; www.lavallettabergamo.it

Torre Gombito *expensive*
Set in a medieval tower in the heart of the Upper Town, this contemporary boutique hotel offers small, tidy rooms.
Via Mario Lupo 6, Città Alta, 24129; 035 247 009; www.gombithotel.it

CLUSONE

Albergo Commercio e Ristorante Masci *inexpensive*
Simple, attractive rooms and a good restaurant in the village centre.
Piazza Paradiso 1, 24023; 0346 21 267; www.mas-ci.it

❶ Bergamo
Bergamo, Lombardia; 24100

In the foothills of the Alps, prosperous Bergamo has an attractive Città Alta (Upper Town) whose Renaissance buildings and medieval lanes are encircled by impressive 17th-century Venetian walls. The medieval neighbourhoods and elegant avenues of the Città Bassa (Lower Town) are good for shopping and transport.

A three-hour walking tour
From the car park, turn right up the sweeping main road, Viale Vittorio Emanuele II, taking in the mix of attractive gated villas and 1930s Fascist architecture. Just around the bend is the **funicular** ① that takes visitors up to the Città Alta. Trundling up through the city walls and splendid palazzo gardens, this 7-minute ride ends near the medieval **Piazza Mercato delle Scarpe** ②, once home to a shoe market. Follow Via Gombito, almost opposite, past the 12th-century **Torre Gombito** ③, the only extant medieval tower of which there were about 20; this one marks the main crossroads of the Roman city. Continue up to **Piazza Vecchia** ④, the city's Renaissance showpiece and site of the medieval Palazzo della Ragione *(temporary exhibitions: 10am–6pm Tue–Sun)*. The piazza is lined with cafés and at its heart is the 18th-century Contarini fountain with white marble lions. Next to the palazzo, the Torre Civica belltower rises 52 m (170 ft), offering splendid views of Bergamo and the

Contarini fountain statue, Piazza Vecchia

countryside. The bells strike 100 times at 10pm, recalling an era when the gates would be closed for the night.

Pass under the arcade of the *palazzo* into Piazza del Duomo. The highlights here are the Romanesque church of Santa Maria Maggiore, with its opulent Baroque interior, and the funerary chapel Cappella Colleoni (1472), a Renaissance extravagance of twisted columns and pastel marble decorated with Giambattista Tiepolo's frescoes (1733).

Return to Piazza Vecchia, then turn left up Via Colleoni past boutiques. Head through the arch at Piazza Mascheroni into Piazza della Cittadella, once the heart of this military stronghold. Cross the courtyard to the gateway diagonally opposite, then turn left into **Colle Aperto** ⑤ for views of the gardens and vineyards around the city walls. Head through Porta Sant'Alessandro to the upper funicular station.

Take the funicular up to the **San Vigilio** ⑥ neighbourhood, ideal for a

Below left Façade of the Cappella Colleoni, Bergamo **Below right** View along Bergamo's funicular

Above View of the Duomo and its Neo-Classical west façade from Torre Civica, Bergamo

drink with sweeping views across the city to the plains. Exit the funicular station and follow the road round to the left and on to the belvedere area, which has splendid views over 19th-century villas and gardens – the summer homes of wealthy Milanese. Rest here, then head down steep Via San Vigilio, keeping the funicular lines on the left. Turn left through Porta Sant'Alessandro to return to Colle Aperto. Here, catch the bus (line 1) to the car park or walk back along the lovely Venetian walls. To do the latter, head down Viale delle Mura, on the right, all the way to **Porta San Giacomo** ⑦, then take winding Via Sant'Alessandro down through a medieval neighbourhood to Via Don Carlo Botta, which leads left, back to Viale Vittorio Emanuele II and the car park at Piazzale della Repubblica.

🚗 *South of Bergamo, pick up the SS671 (signed Val Seriana) and follow signs to Clusone for 32 km (20 miles). On the roundabout after the small Fonti Pineta mineral water plant, follow signs to the centre and use one of the marked car parks.*

② Clusone
Bergamo, Lombardia; 24023
High in the mill-lined Val Seriana, Clusone is an appealing medieval town of pastel-coloured houses and

cobbled lanes rising up to the Piazza Orologio, where the frescoed and porticoed Palazzo Comunale sports a working astronomical clock from 1585. Still higher stands the Baroque **Basilica di Santa Maria Assunta**, with a wonderful 15th-century fresco of the *Triumph of Death* and a *Dance Macabre* next door; note the rich kings and bishops trying to bribe their way out of death.

🚗 *Back at the roundabout, take the SS671 left towards Rovetta, then right on SP53 to Lovere. Through Lovere, follow signs to Darfo Boario Terme on the SR55, then take the SS42 north up the Val Camonica to Capo di Ponte. At the roundabout at the village entrance, follow the brown signs to Naquane and Parco Nazionale delle Incisioni Rupestri over the railway line. Park by the 15th-century church. The park entrance is a 10-minute walk uphill.*

Bergamo's polenta
The yellow cornmeal staple, polenta, features heavily on many of Bergamo's restaurant menus and has been enjoyed in the region for centuries. It can be served with salami, wild mushrooms, melted Taleggio cheese or roast veal. Or you might find it sliced and chargrilled along with a selection of fresh vegetables.

EAT AND DRINK

BERGAMO
Cooperativa Città Alta *inexpensive*
Great-value, hearty portions of local pasta, polenta and grilled meats are served under the vines.
Vicolo Sant'Agata 19 (off Via Colleoni), 24129; 035 218 568; www.ilcircolino cittaalta.it

Baretto di San Vigilio *moderate*
The views from this elegant restaurant create a romantic atmosphere.
Via al Castello di San Vigilio 1, Colle San Vigilio, 24129; 035 253 191; www.barettosanvigilio.it

Vineria Cozzi *moderate*
This is a classy *enoteca* with a stylish, good-quality restaurant attached.
Via Colleoni 22/A, 24129; 035 238 836; www.vineriacozzi.it

Below Panificio Tresoldi, a bakery-patisserie in Bergamo's medieval Città Alta (Upper Town)

Eat and Drink: inexpensive, under €25; moderate, €25–€45; expensive, over €45

Above View of Sale Marasino, one of Lago d'Iseo's pretty villages **Top right** Sale Marasino's church, seen from the lake ferry
Above right Iron Age rock carvings at Parco Nazionale delle Incisioni Rupestri

VISITING VAL CAMONICA

Tourist Information
Via S Briscioli 42, Capo di Ponte, Brescia 25044; 0364 42 080; www. invallecamonica.it

WHERE TO STAY

VAL CAMONICA

Casa Visnenza *inexpensive*
This comfy B&B in Cemmo, right next to Capo di Ponte, is run by owners who are knowledgeable about local sights.
Via San Faustino 7, 25044 Cemmo di Capo di Ponte; 320 906 4557; closed Mon –Fri Mar–Nov; www.casavisnenza.com

ISEO

La Tesa *inexpensive*
An organic farm in the hills above Iseo offering simple apartments and rooms.
Via Silvio Bonomelli, Colline d'Iseo 25049; 030 982 2984; closed Jan–Feb; www.latesa.it

BRESCIA

Albergo Orologio *inexpensive*
Something of a boutique hotel, this is a cosy place in the centre of town.
Via Cesare Beccaria 17, 25121; 030 375 5411; www.albergoorologio.it

ERBUSCO

L'Albereta *expensive*
Every comfort is catered for at this luxurious Relais & Chateaux hotel.
Via Vittorio Emanuele 23, 25030; 030 776 0550; www.albereta.it

Where to Stay: inexpensive, under €100; moderate, €100–200; expensive, over €200

③ Val Camonica
Brescia, Lombardia; 25044
Scattered over the hillsides of the Val Camonica are thousands of stones inscribed with fascinating prehistoric rock carvings. Dating from Neolithic times through to the Iron Age, together they are recognized as a UNESCO World Heritage Site. One of the largest concentrations is found just outside Capo di Ponte. The **Parco Nazionale delle Incisioni Rupestri** *(open 8:30am–dusk Tue–Sun; www. parcoincisioni.capodiponte.beniculturali. it)* is an attractive, open-air site littered with more than 100 carved boulders that can be explored over a couple of hours. Wonderfully evocative and dynamic, scenes portray hunts and funerals, boats, and people dancing, farming, fighting and worshipping.

🚗 *Return back down the SS42, forking right on SP510 towards Brescia. After a series of tunnels, turn right onto the lakeside SP510bis, signed Lago d'Iseo. In Marone, just after the parish church on the right, take the poorly signed left turn to Zone SP32 (down the side of the Municipio building), then drive up the winding road to the car park at Zone.*

④ The Pyramids of Zone
Brescia, Lombardia; 25050
Strange rock formations, resembling giant anthills, pepper the natural reserve around the village of Zone, high above Lago d'Iseo. Rain erosion

on the area's moranic sand has created these extraordinary columns which are often topped by a granite boulder. At the entrance to the park stands the 12th-century **Chiesa di San Giorgio**, with frescoes of Saint George slaying dragons and the the profile of Florentine writer Dante, who visited the area in the 14th century.

🚗 *Return to Marone via SP32, take SP510bis south to Iseo, which has several pay-and-display car parks.*

⑤ Iseo
Brescia, Lombardia; 25049
The largest village on the eastern side of Lago d'Iseo, ancient Iseo was an important trading post before it was sacked by Federico I Barabarossa in the 12th century. Now a low-key resort, the semi-pedestrianized medieval village centre boasts an arcaded main square, stone lanes, a handful of decent restaurants and a lakeside promenade with views across the water to the wooded cliffs of the opposite shore. Ferries leave here for destinations around the lake, most notably to Monte Isola.

🚗 *Leave the car behind and catch a ferry across to Monte Isola.*

⑥ Monte Isola
Brescia, Lombardia; 25050
The largest lake island in Europe, Monte Isola is 9 km (6 miles) around and more than 600 m (2,000 ft) high, topped by the Santuario della Madonna della Ceriola, with fabulous 360-degree views. Arriving is part of the fun, with lovely views of lakeside villages along the way. Stroll along

Below Passenger ferry cruising across Lago d'Iseo past stunning mountain scenery the waterfront, or hire a bicycle and explore its tiny villages, stopping for a meal en route – strong legs are needed to get up to the Santuario.

🚗 *From Iseo, take a right on SP47bis to Ome, then SP46 to Rodengo-Saiano, through Gussago past the church on the left and after the town centre take right. From here take the main road out of town and follow signs to Brescia, which has plenty of on-street pay-parking.*

June 9.30am–4.30pm; www.bresciamusei. com) has fine Roman mosaics and medieval treasures, including a 4th-century bronze *Winged Victory.*

🚗 *Retrace route back towards Iseo (follow signs to "Milan, Bergamo and Lago d'Iseo"), but turn left on SP49, follow signs to the autostrada that leads to the Strada del Franciacorta.*

🞸 Erbusco
Brescia, Lombardia; 25030
This village lies at the heart of a small wine-producing area – known as Franciacorta – dotted with ancient religious buildings. The monasteries that cultivated this land in the Middle Ages were tax exempt, leading to the name Franciacorta. See *www.franciacorta.it* for information on drives and cycle rides through the idyllic countryside.

Franciacorta wines
The pleasant hills south of Lago d'Iseo have been a wine-making area for centuries. Attention turned to sparkling wines in the 1960s, and in 1995 the area was awarded the DOCG, in recognition of the quality of the sparkling wines made using the champagne method, involving a second fermentation in the bottle.

🞷 Brescia
Brescia, Lombardia; 25121
Known for its arms industry and engineering factories, Brescia also has an attractive medieval centre and well-preserved Roman ruins. At the heart of the city is the broad, arcaded **Piazza della Loggia** with an imposing *palazzo* at one end and the Torre dell'Orologio opposite. Via dei Musei follows an ancient Roman road to the site of the forum, now Piazza del Foro, which is topped by the columns of the **Tempio Capitolino** from AD 73. The nearby **Museo di Santa Giulia** (open Tue–Sun: mid-Jun–Sep 10.30am–6pm, Oct–mid-

Above Small vineyard in Franciacorta, near Erbusco **Left** Ruined columns of the Roman Tempio Capitolino in Brescia

EAT AND DRINK

ISEO
Da Piccioli *inexpensive*
Fried seafood, frogs legs & chips are on offer at this lakeside establishment.
Via Cristini, Marone, 25054; 333 724 6847

Osteria Il Volto *moderate–expensive*
Blends mountain and lake flavors.
Via Mirolte 3, 25049; 030 981 462; www. osteriailvolto.it; closed Wed & Mon lunch

BRESCIA
Osteria la Grotta *moderate*
Expect Brescian food – *casoncei* (salami-stuffed pasta) – in an elegant setting.
Vicolo del Prezzemolo 10, 25121; 030 44 068; www.osterialagrotta.it

WINERIES IN FRANCIACORTA

CA' DEL BOSCO
Via Albano Zanella 13, 25030, Erbusco; 030 776 6111; www.cadelbosco.com

CAVALLERI
Via Provinciale 96, 25030, Erbusco; 030 776 0217; www.cavalleri.it

BELLAVISTA
Via Bellavista 5, 25030, Erbusco; 030 776 2000; www.terramoretti.it

FERGHETTINA
Via Saline 11, 25030, Adro; 030 745 1212; www.ferghettina.it

DAY TRIP OPTIONS
There are options for a city walk followed by a country drive, some lakeside relaxation or a wine tour.

Urban and rural exploration
Spend the morning on a walking tour of Bergamo ❶, enjoying funicular rides and architecture from the 12th to the 18th century. After lunch, enjoy the countryside of the Val Seriana on the way to medieval Clusone ❷.

Follow the drive's instructions, and back.

Monte Isola and the Pyramids
In Iseo ❺, stock up with picnic provisions before taking the ferry to Monte Isola ❻ to explore the island for most of the day. Cycle round the island, stopping to eat al fresco on the way. Return to Iseo in the late afternoon, then drive to Zone to see the extraordinary rock formations.

Take the ferry to Monte Isola; afterwards follow the SP510bis to Zone.

Romans and wine tasting
Explore Roman Brescia ❼, then enjoy a tour of the Franciacorta wine region. Head for Erbusco ❽ and visit a few of its wineries – perhaps on a bike.

Follow the drive's instructions to Erbusco. You may be able to hire a bicycle from a hotel or agriturismo.

Eat and Drink: inexpensive, under €25; moderate, €25–€45; expensive, over €45

Switchbacks and Limonaie

Arco to Gargnano

Highlights

- **Lake Garda**
  Indulge in watersports at Riva del Garda, or visit the lemon-growing glasshouses along the lakeshore, where olive groves and citrus trees carpet the hillsides

- **Austrian heritage**
  Explore the Germanic heritage and cuisine of Lake Garda's northernmost towns, which were once part of the Austro-Hungarian Empire

- **Adrenalin-fuelled drives**
  Corkscrew through the Brasa gorge away from the lake into the wooded, Alpine interior of the Tremosine

- **Enchanting Gargnano**
  Be charmed by this laid-back lakeside village and its peeling Art Nouveau villas and ancient churches

The broad Gardesana Occidentale, winding along the steep banks of Lake Garda

Switchbacks and Limonaie

Running along the northwestern shore of Lago di Garda, this route is for those who enjoy challenging drives. From the medieval village of Arco and the lakeside resort of Riva del Garda, the road skirts the lake before branching on to an exhilarating switchback – the eighth wonder of the world, according to Winston Churchill – up to the comune of Tremosine. The climb through thick woodland brings breathtaking views and, at the end, a walk up to the Santuario della Madonna di Montecastello. The drive ends in dreamy Gargnano, set among olive groves and the *limonaie* (sheltered lemon groves) that give this shoreline its name.

KEY

Drive route

Above The Torre Apponale on the Riva del Garda waterfront **Below** View from Arco's castle
Opposite Narrow streets and brightly painted townhouses, Arco

PLAN YOUR DRIVE

Start/finish: Arco to Gargnano.

Number of days: 1 day.

Distance: Approx 60 km (37 miles).

Road conditions: Roads are narrow and winding, and busy in summer. In winter, the switchbacks are impassable due to snow. The lakeside road plunges through galleried tunnels into dazzling sunlight.

When to go: Apr–Jun is ideal. Autumn, too, is pretty, but most places shut up shop from the end of Oct until Easter.

Opening times: Shops tend to open 9am–1pm and 3–7pm Mon–Sat. In villages, some are closed on Mon mornings.

Main market days: Arco: Wed; antiques market every 3rd Sat; Riva and Gargnano: Wed am; Tignale: Tue.

Major festivals: Gargnano: Centomiglia Regatta, 2nd week in Sep; Pieve: Easter Sunday.

① Arco
Trento, Trentino-Alto Adige

The **Castello** (*Jan: open Sat & Sun, Feb–Dec: open daily*) atop the rocky outcrop looming over Arco was built in the 12th century, and the 30-minute wander up to it from the central Piazza 11 Novembre affords panoramic views. Arco became a popular winter retreat in the 19th century, when, as part of the Austrian Empire, its mild climate attracted Central European aristocracy. Explore the wonderful public gardens on Viale delle Palme and an impressive arboretum in the **Parco Arciducale Arboreto** (*open daily*), which formed the grounds of the Habsburg Archduke Albert's winter palace.

🚗 *Follow the well-signposted SS45b for 6 km (4 miles) to reach the centre of Riva del Garda, from where the car parks are clearly signposted.*

② Riva del Garda
Trento, Trentino-Alto Adige; 38066

Always a strategic trading post, and part of the Venetian, then the Austro-Hungarian Empire until 1918, this fine lakeside resort of cobbled piazzas, stone buildings and atmospheric lanes is now a focus for watersports, with windsurfing and sailing opportunities galore. Offering beautiful views of Lago di Garda, the town's broad Piazza 3 Novembre is lined with porticoed buildings and watched over by the 13th-century **Torre Apponale**. To the west, above the waterfront, is the 12th-century **Bastione**, built by the Venetians in 1508, on Monte Rocchetta. The pleasant walk up to this ruined fortress is rewarded with sensational views over the lake.

🚗 *Leave Riva on SS45bis, heading south past Limone sul Garda, for about*

17 km (11 miles). Take the second right turn for Tremosine up SP38.

③ Porto to Pieve: SP38
Brescia, Lombardia

When the SP38 opened in 1913, the German newspaper *Frankfurter Zeitung* dubbed it "the most beautiful road in the world". Linking isolated mountain communities with the lake, this exhilarating road switchbacks through narrow tunnels and wooded valleys, squeezing impossibly through the spectacular Brasa gorge, and up to the green hills of Tremosine. The SP38 has been the setting for numerous car commercials, as well as breathtaking car chases in the Bond film *Quantum of Solace*.

🚗 *Follow SP38 for about 6 km (4 miles) from the lake to Pieve at the top of the mountain, where many village centre car parks are signposted.*

④ Pieve
Tremosine, Brescia, Lombardia; 25010

One of the many hillside villages in the comune of Tremosine, Pieve has an attractive centre of stone-built houses. At 350 m (1,148 ft) above the lake, there are wonderful views across the sparkling waters to Monte Baldo opposite. The town's church has an 11th-century Romanesque bell tower but its main building, built later, is lit by Murano glass chandeliers, adding to its elegant Baroque interior.

🚗 *From the centre, head southwest out of town, following the signposted route to the next village, Arias, and then on towards Tignale.*

Above left Living on the edge in Pieve
Above The Castello di Arco, high above the town

VISITING ARCO

Tourist Information
Viale del Palme 1, 38062; 0464 532 255; www.gardatrentino.it

VISITING RIVA DEL GARDA

Tourist Information
Largo Medaglie d'Oro 5, 38066; 0464 554 444; www.gardatrentino.it

VISITING PIEVE

Tourist Information
Piazza Marconi 1, 25010; Tremosine; 0365 953 185; www.infotremosine.it, www.gardalombardia.com

WHERE TO STAY IN RIVA DEL GARDA

Restel de Fer *inexpensive*
Owned by the friendly Menghelli family for more than 600 years, this farmhouse offers a handful of atmospherically furnished rooms. The locally sourced food in the restaurant is also excellent. *Via Restel de Fer 10, 38066; 0464 553 481; www.resteldefer.com*

EAT AND DRINK IN RIVA DEL GARDA

Osteria il Gallo *moderate*
This friendly, informal eatery in Riva centre serves hearty dishes of polenta, dumplings and home-made pasta, accompanied by good local wines. *Piazza San Rocco 12, 38066; 0464 556 200; www.osteriailgallo.com*

Eat and Drink: inexpensive, under €25; moderate, €25–€45; expensive, over €45

(half a mile) beyond the woodmill outside Prabione. To reach the sanctuary by car, follow signs on the road that descends to SS45bis.

⑥ Santuario di Madonna di Montecastello
Tignale, Brescia, Lombardia; 25080
This 17th-century sanctuary is built over an ancient castle has an older chapel decorated with Renaissance frescoes. It is a peaceful spot, reached by a steep 20-minute walk that is rewarded with magnificent views and a small café _(Mar–Oct: open daily)_. Extend the walk for another 20 minutes by following the path past the _eremo_ (hermitage) up to the cross at the top of nearby Monte Cas.

🚗 _Continue down the mountain to the lakeside road, the SS45bis. Turn right and head south to Gargnano, to the signposted, covered car park opposite the tourist office on the main road._

Above left View over the Santuario di Madonna di Montecastello **Above right** Fresco in the Santuario di Madonna di Montecastello **Below** Boats at Gargnano's harbourside

VISITING GARGNANO

Tourist Information
Piazzale Boldini 2, 25084; 0365 791 243; www.gargnanosulgarda.it

⑤ Pieve to Tignale Road
Brescia, Lombardia
Driving through valleys of beech, ash and chestnut, past cool streams, Alpine meadows and sheer mountain bluffs, it is easy to forget the bustle of the lake below. There are several viewpoints and picnic spots along the way.
🚗 _Follow signs to Tignale. The roadside car park for the sanctuary is 1 km_

WHERE TO STAY IN AND AROUND GARGNANO

Hotel Du Lac _moderate_
Superbly located on the lakeside, in a quiet corner of the village, this is the smaller of two neighbouring hotels run by the same family for three generations. Rooms have fine period furniture and there is a pretty terrace and pergola with panoramic views.
Via Colletta 21, 25084, Villa di Gargnano; 0365 71107; www.hotel-dulac.it; closed Nov–Mar

Hotel Villa Sostaga _expensive_
On the hillside above Gargnano, this welcoming, family-run villa offers informal luxury in 11 handsomely furnished rooms. There are splendid views from the lovely grounds and pool. A well-priced restaurant (open to non-residents) serves memorable seasonal specialities.
Via Sostaga 19, 25084, Navazzo; 0365 791 218; www.villasostaga.com

⑦ Gargnano
Brescia, Lombardia; 25084
Perhaps the prettiest village on Lake Garda, Gargnano is a series of _frazione_ (neighbourhoods) strung out along the waterfront between olive woods and secluded _limonaie_. The village is relatively untroubled by tourism and is perfect for a gentle wander or a lazy afternoon in the shade of an orange tree with dreamy lake views.

A two-hour walking tour
From the car park, walk down Via Roma away from the main road. The cloister of a 13th-century Franciscan monastery stands next to the Baroque **Church of San Francesco** ① just down on the right. The columns in the cloister are decorated with citrus fruits – a reference to the Franciscan introduction of lemon cultivation to the area. Legal wrangles keep the cloister closed to the public, but it is possible to peek inside by climbing the steps leading to the locked door just before the church. Continue down the lane to reach the pretty main square of Gargnano and its little marina. A building near the 16th-century **Palazzo Comunale** ②, displays cannonballs that were wedged into its walls during the 1866 War of Independence against Austria.

Head round the waterfront and east out of the square to Via Rimembranza to take in the 19th-century **Palazzo Feltrinelli** ③ on the right. Now part of the University of Milan, the palace was built by the paper and publishing magnates whose patronage can be seen throughout the village – in the hospital, the infant school and numerous family houses. The public **beach** ④ is a few minutes further along on the right in a grassy olive grove. The lane continues past several splendid Liberty (Italian Art Nouveau) villas,

Where to Stay: inexpensive, under €100; moderate, €100–€200; expensive, over €200

notably the luxurious **Villa Feltrinelli** ⑤, now a top-class hotel, but formerly home to the Fascist leader Benito Mussolini and his family during the Republic of Salò *(see p83)*. Continue along the peaceful lane, past olive groves and occasional glimpses of the lake, to reach a large *limonaie* and the tiny Romanesque chapel of **San Giacomo di Calino** ⑥. This 11th-century church is one of the oldest on the lake. It is a peaceful place, with a 14th-century fresco of St Christopher on the lakeside wall, opposite the tiny shingle beach. This lovely spot is ideal for a picnic.

Return to the harbour in the village centre and take the lakeside lane round Hotel Gargnano, where the English novelist DH Lawrence spent a night in 1912. Continue along the walkways, past the waterfront villas and their boathouses, keeping the

abandoned olive oil factory on the right. This scrubby path leads back to the car park, from where Via Donatore di Sangue branches off to the Escola Materna Feltrinelli, an infant school, on the left and the working *limonaie* on the right, on the other side of the main road (the SS45bis). The shady cobbled lane continues into the charming neighbourhood of **Villa** ⑦, which has a couple of hotels and a tiny picture-postcard port with a popular bar. Down at **Via Colletta 44** ⑧, a plaque declares that DH Lawrence lived here with his lover Frieda over the winter of 1912–13 while writing *Twilight in Italy*, an evocative piece on village life and the beauty of this area. Retrace your steps to the car.

Lemon Cultivation

In the 13th century, Franciscan monks founded a monastery in Gargnano and introduced citrus cultivation to the Lake Garda area. *Limonaie*, or purpose-built terraces for growing lemon trees, were introduced in the 17th century to protect the plants during the winter months. Dotted on the hillsides, these skeletal structures have brick walls and terraced lines of narrow pillars. Citrus farming on a commercial scale had ended by the 20th century, because of blight and cheaper alternatives, but some *limonaie* are still open to the public.

Above Stone buildings of pretty Gargnano
Below right View of the Riviera di Limonaie
Bottom left *Limonaie* along the shoreline of Lake Garda **Below left** Lemon souvenirs from the Riviera di Limonaie

EAT AND DRINK IN GARGNANO

Miralago *moderate*
This lakefront restaurant serves well-judged fish and seafood dishes. The service is relaxed and professional.
Via Zanardelli 5, 25084; 0365 71209; closed Tue, Jan & Feb

La Tortuga *expensive*
This Michelin-starred restaurant has a stylish dining room and knowledgeable staff. The wines are well priced.
Via XXIV Maggio 5, 25084; 0365 71251; www.ristorantelatortuga.it; closed Tue & Nov–1st wk Mar

⑥ San Giacomo di Calino

VIA MUSLONE
VIA DEGLI OLEANDRI
VIA SAN GIACOMO
VIA REPUBBLICA
VIA RIMEMBRANZA

⑤ Villa Feltrinelli

Lago di Garda

VIA REPUBBLICA
VIA RIMEMBRANZA

④ Beach

VIA REPUBBLICA

③ Palazzo Feltrinelli
② Palazzo Comunale
PIAZZA FELTRINELLI
VIA ROMA
① Church of San Francesco
ℹ️ P

0 metres   500
0 yards   500

VIA DELLA LIBERTÀ

⑦ Villa
⑧ Via Colletta 44

Eat and Drink: inexpensive, under €25; moderate, €25–€45; expensive, over €45

From the Lake to the Plains

Salò to Mantua

Highlights

- **Laidback lakeside resorts**
  Relax in the low-key towns that line the lake with their pretty harbours, *belle époque* villas and fine shingle beaches – perfect for a quick dip

- **Wonderful wines**
  Sip the delicious light wines produced by the temperate climate and rolling hills of Cavaion Veronese, to the east and south of Lake Garda

- **Renaissance showpiece**
  Explore medieval and Renaissance Mantua whose elegant piazzas are dominated by the palazzos of power

- **Ruins with a view**
  Clamber the picturesque ruins of a 1st-century AD Roman villa in a charming olive grove at the very tip of Sirmione's promontory

Grotte di Catullo, ruins of a Roman villa at Sirmione, Lake Garda

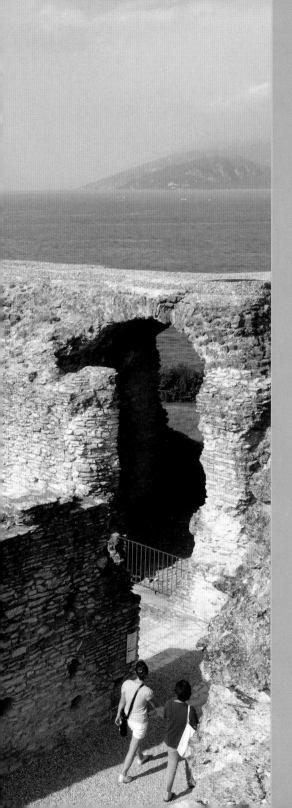

From the Lake to the Plains

Exploring Lake Garda reveals the fascinating multilayered history of the region: the Romans enjoyed the natural spas on the lake's southern shore; the mighty Venetian Republic dominated the area during the 15th and 17th centuries; and the modern era of the 20th century dotted the lakeside with elegant *belle époque* resorts. Inland, it was the bloody battle for Italian independence that marked the wine-growing hills around San Martino, while Mantua was a centre of Renaissance power, as revealed by its rich art and architecture. This itinerary also showcases the different facets of this water-dependent region, from rice-covered plains to olive-grove and vineyard-clad hills. The drive can also be linked with Drive 6 to Gargnano (*see pp76–7*) for a longer trip.

Above Salò overlooked by the bell tower of its cathedral, *see p82* **Below** Pretty harbour front with fishing boats at the resort of Bardolino, *see p83*

ACTIVITIES

Enjoy an open-air concert at Il Vittoriale in summer

Swim in Lake Garda from the shingle beach just south of Torri del Benaco

Immerse yourself in the thermal spa waters in Simione for some welcome relaxation

Climb the poignant memorial tower at San Martino della Battaglia

Sample fabulous local produce: oil and wine from Bardolino, and tortellini pasta from Valeggio sul Mincio

Cycle among the picturesque rice fields – thankfully quite flat – around Mantua

Take a daytrip to Venice by boat from Mantua

0 kilometres   6

0 miles   6

KEY

Drive route

PLAN YOUR DRIVE

Start/finish: Salò to Mantua.

Number of days: 3 days.

Distance: Approx 115 km (71 miles).

Road conditions: Lakeside roads get busy at weekends and in summer. The outskirts of the towns are lined by light industry but the roads are flat and well maintained.

When to go: Avoid the stifling summer heat on the plains by visiting in autumn, when the menus are full of pumpkin and chestnut dishes; spring is an attractive time, too. August sees the lake chock-a-bloc and the hotels close between Nov and Easter.

Opening times: Shops tend to open 9am–1pm and 3–7pm Mon–Sat, although in the small villages some will be closed on Monday morning.

Main market days: Sirmione & Torri del Benaco: Mon am; **Lazise:** Wed; Bardolino & Mantua: Thu am; San Martino della Battaglia: Sat am; **Valeggio sul Mincio:** 4th Sun of the month (antiques and bric-à-brac).

Shopping: Mantua has some small attractive boutiques and wonderful delicatessens. Be sure to stock up on locally made olive oils and wines in Bardolino and around the Moreniche hills to the south of Lake Garda.

Major festivals: Bardolino: Festa dell' Uva (grape festival), Oct; **Valeggio sul Mincio:** Festa del Nodo dell'Amore (love knot or tortellini festival), 3rd Tue in Jun; Fiera di Valeggio (music and dance), 1st week in Jul.

DAY TRIP OPTIONS

Lake Garda has plenty for families, history buffs and activity addicts. Kids will love the varied and **macabre exhibits** at Il Vittoriale, followed by a **ferry ride**, **castle** visit and a **swim**. History buffs can start at Sirmione with **Roman** and **medieval remains**, before climbing the **memorial tower** at San Martino and finishing in the **gardens** of pasta-loving Valeggio sul Mincio. Mantua itself deserves a day: walk the **Renaissance city**, buy a **picnic**, then explore the countryside **on two wheels**. For full details, see p85.

VISITING SALÒ

Parking
There are pay-and-display parking sites around town, although the multi-storey car park on Via Brunati is the best bet.

Tourist Information
Piazza Sant'Antonio 4, 25087; 030 374 87 45; www.rivieradeilimoni.it

VISITING TORRI DEL BENACO

Parking
The main car park is immediately opposite the ferry point on the south side of town. It is free out of season and pay and display at other times.

Tourist Information
Via Gardesana, 37010; 045 62 96 482; www.tourism.verona.it

WHERE TO STAY

AROUND IL VITTORIALE

Hotel Villa Florida *moderate*
This hotel has small suites and apartments, plus gardens and a pool.
Corso Zanardelli 113, 25083; 0365 21836; www.hotelvillaflorida.com; closed mid-Oct–Mar

Hotel Bolsone *expensive*
This secluded 15th-century manor house is set high above Lake Garda and has six rooms. No children under 12.
Via Panoramica 23, 25083; 0365 21 022; www.dimorabolsone.it; closed Nov–Feb

TORRI DEL BENACO

Garnì Onda *inexpensive*
All rooms here have balconies or terraces. A good breakfast is included.
Via per Albisano 28, 37010; 045 722 5895; www.garnionda.com; closed mid-Nov–Mar

Hotel del Porto *moderate*
Located lakeside, this hotel offers stylish rooms and even swisher bathrooms. Self-catering suites are also available.
Lungolago Barbarani 6, 37010; 045 722 5051; www.hoteldelportolagodigarda. it; closed Nov–Mar

SIRMIONE

Grifone *moderate*
Five-star lake views compensate for the no-frills rooms at this friendly hotel.
Via Bocchio 4, 25019; 030 916 014; www.sirmionehotelgrifone.it; closed mid-Jan–mid-Mar

AROUND SAN MARTINO DELLA BATTAGLIA

Selva Capuzza *inexpensive*
Selva Capuzza has a winery, self-catering apartments and a good restaurant.
Agriturismo Borgo San Donino, 25015 Desenzano del Garda (just outside San Martino della Battaglia); 030 991 0279; www.selvacapuzza.it; closed mid Jan–mid Feb

① Salò
Brescia, Lombardia; 25087
An attractive and historic town, Salò basks in its own sunny bay on the western shore of Lake Garda. For more than 400 years it was the capital of the communities known as the Magnifica Patria, which were under Venetian domination until the Republic's fall in 1797. The town briefly came to the fore again during World War II when Hitler and Mussolini made it the capital of the Republic of Salò *(see right)*. Fronting the handsome lakeside promenade, **Lungolago Zanardelli**, is the porticoed 16th-century town hall, **Palazzo della Magnifica Patria**, not far from the unfinished Renaissance **Duomo**.
🚗 *Follow Via Trento (SS45bis) NE out of town through Gardone to a signed left turn to Il Vittoriale and car park.*

② Il Vittoriale degli Italiani
Brescia, Lombardia; 25083
The extravagant home and gardens of the poet and nationalist hero Gabriele d'Annunzio sprawl across the hillside above the *belle époque*

resort of Gardone. A controversial figure, he was known for his affair with the actress Eleanor Dusé and, more famously, his fiery relationship with Mussolini, for whom he wrote the (meaningless) Fascist war cry "Eia, eia, eia! Alalà!" It is an egocentric place cluttered with the poet's possessions, which range from a gilded tortoise to the prow of the boat *Puglia*, which d'Annunzio commanded during World War I – and his own macabre mausoleum. Concerts are performed in the amphitheatre in summer.
🚗 *Return to the main road and turn left onto Via Roma (SS45bis). Continue into Toscolano-Maderno and catch the car ferry (traghetto), signed to the right.*

③ Torri del Benaco
Verona, Veneto; 37010
The swallow-tail battlements of the **Castello Scaligero** guard the pretty little harbour at Torri del Benaco. The castle offers wonderful views from its towers and an engaging museum on olive cultivation and local fishing methods, as well as information about

Below left Café-lined harbour front at Lazise **Below right** San Severo church frescoes, Bardolino **Bottom** Grotte di Catullo, ruins of a 1st-century AD Roman settlement with lake views at Sirmione prehistoric rock carvings in the woods inland. It is also home to one of the oldest *limonaie*, or lemon tree glasshouses, on the lake. South of the village's network of quiet cobbled lanes lies a pleasant shingle beach.

🚗 *Take the main SS249 south to Bardolino. Parking in the centre is easy.*

❹ Bardolino
Verona, Veneto; 37011

This pleasant resort has a medieval warren of lanes and the frescoed 9th-century Romanesque **Chiesa di San Severo**. Away from town, the soft rolling hills of Cavaion Veronese are carpeted with vineyards and olive groves. The tourist office lists routes to oil and wine producers, and the **Museo del Vino** *(closed Nov–mid-Mar)* gives an insight into the history of these key local industries. Plus, the end products can always be sampled at the resort's many *enoteche* and restaurants.

🚗 *Take SP31 (Via Croce) out through the vineyards, turn right on Strada Villa. Carry straight onto Strada Tre Contrè, turn right on SP31, through Calmasino, follow signs left to Lazise. Turn left for pay-and-display car parks.*

❺ Lazise
Verona, Veneto; 37017

A popular tourist town, Lazise's ancient centre is enclosed within beautiful **medieval walls**. Next to the small port stands the **Dogana Veneta**, the customs house used to tax goods on the lake during Venice's 400 years of rule. Next door, the small Romanesque church of **San Nicolò** holds 13th-century frescoes.

🚗 *Take SR249 south to Peschiera del Garda. Drive through the town centre, following signs to SR11 and Sirmione. Park outside the walled town.*

Mussolini's Republic of Salò

In November 1943, Mussolini and Hitler made a last-ditch attempt to rally Fascist Italy against advancing Allied troops by establishing the Italian Social Republic of Salò. Villas and palaces on Lake Garda became ministries, while Mussolini and his family lived in Gargnano. The Republic limped on ineffectually until Italian liberation on 25 April 1945; three days later Mussolini was executed by partisans on Lake Como.

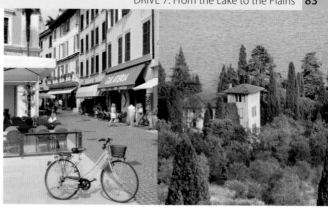

❻ Sirmione
Brescia, Lombardia; 25019

This historic town on a promontory jutting into the waters of Lake Garda is guarded by a mighty 13th-century castle, the **Rocca Scaligera** *(closed Mon)*. The café-lined lanes lead north to the ruins of a 1st-century Roman villa, the **Grotte di Catullo** *(closed Mon)*, set among olive trees on the lake's edge. Visitors since Roman times have been drawn by the spa waters (tourist office has details).

🚗 *Follow signs south for Brescia, then follow signs to SP13 to Milan. The tower is just beyond the village.*

❼ San Martino della Battaglia
Brescia, Lombardia; 25010

A long spiral ramp leads up to the panoramic terrace at the top of this frescoed tower *(closed Mon)*, built in memory of those who died fighting during the Risorgimento, the movement for Italian unification. In 1859, during the wars of independence from Austria, these hills saw some of the bloodiest battles in history. On 24 June, during the Battle of Solferino, 40,000 men were killed or injured in one day. A Swiss businessman, Henry Dunant witnessed the carnage and saw the local people helping the wounded, regardless of nationality. His suggestion of creating a neutral hospital corps to help during wartime led to the founding of the Red Cross in 1863. There is also an ossuary and a museum here, displaying love letters, bloodied uniforms and tattered flags.

🚗 *Follow SP13 to Pozzolengo, then SP18 towards Monzambano. Turn left onto SP74 (Strada Moscatello), then right onto SP19 (towards Volta Mantovana). Turn left onto SP3 to Vallegio sul Mincio.*

Above left Cafés and shops close to Piazza Vittoria, Salo's main square **Above** Lake view from Il Vittoriale

EAT AND DRINK

SALÒ

Ristorante 100km *expensive*
The contemporary restaurant in Hotel Bellerive serves locally sourced creations. *Via Pietro da Salò 11, 25087; 0365 520 410; www.hotelbellerive.it; closed Nov–mid-Mar*

TORRI DEL BENACO

Trattoria Bell'Arrivo *moderate*
By the little harbour, this trattoria is a cosy spot for tasty, good-value food. *Piazza Calderini 10, 37010; 045 629 9028; closed Mon (Mar–May & Oct) & Nov–Feb*

SIRMIONE

La Rucola *expensive*
Enjoy the fish in this smart restaurant near the castle. Ideal for a treat. *Passaggio Strentelle 7, 25019; 345 619 5728; www.ristorantelarucola.it; closed Jan & Feb, Thu & Fri*

SAN MARTINO DELLA BATTAGLIA

Osteria alla Torre *moderate*
This friendly place offers old-fashioned cooking – try the home-made pasta. *Via Torre 1, 25015; 030 910 8261; www.osteriaallatorre.it; closed Thu*

Below Colourful boats moored at Torri del Benaco on Lake Garda

Eat and Drink: inexpensive, under €25; moderate, €25–€45; expensive, over €45

VISITING MANTUA

Tourist Information
Piazza Andrea Mantegna 6, 46100;
0376 432 432; www.turismo.mantova.it

Bike and Boat Hire
To hire a bike for a day, register with a
passport and leave a deposit at **Casa del
Rigoletto** *(Piazza Sordello 23)*. Longer-
term bike hire is available at **Mantua
Bike** *(Viale Piave 22b; 0376 220 909;
www.mantuabike.it)*. Many hotels also
have cycles for guests.

Lake and river cruises range from an
hour's round trip to a day cruise to
Venice. Contact the tourist office.

WHERE TO STAY

VALEGGIO SUL MINCIO

La Finestra Sul Fiume B&B *moderate*
This converted mill in an idyllic riverside
location offers attractive suites and a
spacious garden. Cycles can be hired
nearby. *Corte Sega 2, 37067; 045 795
0556; www.lafinestrasulfiume.it*

MANTOVA AND AROUND

Consorzio Agrituristico Mantovano
This co-operative coordinates many
farmstay and B&B options across the
fertile surrounding countryside.
www.agriturismomantova.it

Ostello del Mincio *inexpensive*
In Rivalta sul Mincio, 10 km (6 miles)
west of town, this well-run YHA hostel
offers doubles, family rooms and dorm,
plus bike and canoe hire.
*Via Porto 23-25, 46040; 340 9300509;
www.ostellodelmincio.it*

Casa Poli *moderate*
This minimalist boutique hotel with
small but comfortable contemporary
rooms is located a 10-minute walk
from the city's central squares.
*Corso Garibaldi 32, 46100; 0376 288
170; www.hotelcasapoli.it*

Residenza Ca' delle Erbe *moderate*
Stay in airy rooms in a palace
overlooking the square. A great mix
of classic and contemporary styles.
*Via Broletto 24, 46100; 0376 226 161;
www.cadelleerbe.it*

Below Fresco showing the Titans attacking
Olympus, in the Palazzo Te, Mantua

8 Valeggio sul Mincio
Verona, Veneto; 37067
On the western border of the Venetian
empire, this sleepy town played a
strategic role supported by its imposing 14th-century **Castello Scaligero**.
In pretty riverside **Borghetto** the
Ponte Visconteo, built by the Dukes
of Milan in 1393, protected the edge
of their territory. These days, Valeggio is
more famous for tortellini, served in
family-run restaurants all over town.

Close to the centre, the woodland,
lawns and ornamental gardens of

Parco Giardino Sigurtà are perfect
for stretching your legs. Highlights
include the tulips and irises in spring
and the water lilies in summer.

🚗 *Follow SS249 to Roverbella. From
the centre follow signs to Santa Lucia.
Pass the left turn to Santa Lucia and
turn right onto road to Mantua. Overlook signs to the centre, follow signs to
Padova, taking the "tangenziale nord"
round to the SS10. Cross the bridge,
head towards the Castello, turn right at
the mini roundabout to the free parking along the town wall on Via Mincio.*

9 Mantua (Mantova)
Mantua, Lombardia; 46100
Rising out of the rice fields around the River Mincio, Mantua (Mantova)
is ringed on three sides by lakes awash with lily flowers in season. It's
impossibly romantic, with cobbled lanes linking the piazzas, a clutch
of Renaissance masterpieces of art and architecture and a comfortable,
relaxed pace of life. In autumn, all the city's restaurants feature *ravioli
alla zucca* (pumpkin stuffed ravioli) with sage butter.

A two-hour walking tour
Follow the city wall east from the car
parks to Via San Giorgio, next to the
castle, which leads into **Piazza Sordello**
①. The thin square is dominated on
its eastern side by the sprawling
Palazzo Ducale ② *(closed Mon)*. The
largest palace in medieval Europe, it
incorporates the 14th-century Castello

di San Giorgio, churches, courtyards,
gardens and the Palazzo del
Capitano and Magna Domus. Once
home to the ruling Gonzaga dynasty
(1328–1707), the palace is a labyrinth
of frescoed and mirrored rooms, the
highlight being the *Camera degli Sposi*
(the Married Couple's room) with
frescoes by Andrea Mantegna (1474).

Across the square, the **Duomo** ③ has an 18th-century façade and its interior was reconstructed from the Gothic original by Giulio Romano in 1545. Leave the piazza through the southern arch with the red-brick Torre Della Gabbia on the right, where people were punished by being hung in a cage and left to die. In Piazza Broletto, the façade of the 13th-century **Palazzo del Podestà** ④ has a statue of local Roman poet Virgil.

Duck left down Via Accademia to look into the 18th-century **Teatro Scientifico Bibiena** ⑤ (mid-Nov–mid-Mar: closed Mon; visit tourist office for concert details). Opened with a recital by Mozart in 1770, the theatre still performs work by Monteverdi, the Mantovan father of opera, and puts on productions of Verdi's opera *Rigoletto*, which is set in the city.

Return to the covered arcade on Piazza Broletto and head left past elegant shops into **Piazza delle Erbe** ⑥ and the 13th-century Palazzo della Ragione. The square is dominated by the Torre dell'Orologio with its astronomical clock dating from 1472. Visit Mantua's oldest church, the pretty 11th-century Rotonda di San Lorenzo, discovered in 1908 during the dismantling of the Jewish ghetto that had grown around it.

Round the corner, Piazza Mantegna holds more cafés and Mantua's most important church, **Sant'Andrea** ⑦, begun in 1472 by Leon Battista Alberti. Home to Andrea Mantegna's tomb, the barrel-vaulted interior houses two vases said to hold the blood of Christ.

Head south along Via Roma and across Piazza Marconi to the canal where, on the left, a small covered bridge is part of the **Fish Market** ⑧ built in 1536 by Giulio Romano. Fork left down Via Principe Amadeo, into Via Acerbi, where the temple-like **Casa del Mantegna** ⑨ was lived in briefly by the artist and now holds exhibitions. Across the road, the deconsecrated **Tempio di San Sebastiano** ⑩, built by Alberti in 1458, is now a monument to Mantovans fallen in war.

Cross busy Viale Risorgimento to perhaps the city's greatest treasure, the **Palazzo Te** ⑪ (closed Mon am), an island retreat for Federico Gonzaga and his mistress Isabella, designed by Giulio Romano and completed in 1535. The palace is a world of frescoes with a peaceful lawned garden. The *Sala di Amore e Psiche* is awash with erotic frescoes while the Sala dei Giganti, with its paintings of falling columns, appears to be collapsing around you.

Head back in a straight line northeast on either Via Giovannic Acerbi or Via Nazario Sauro to the car park.

Above left Parco Giardino Sigurtà, Valeggio sul Mincio **Above** Shady cafés and arcades in Mantua's Piazza delle Erbe

EAT AND DRINK

MANTUA AND AROUND

La Loggetta *inexpensive*
The fantastic ice-cream served here comes in a variety of flavours to reflect the seasons. It also serves vegan ice-cream, milkshakes and *granite*.
Piazza Broletto 12, 46100; 0376 181 2866

Due Cavallini *moderate*
Good-value traditional cooking served by welcoming staff in a rustic dining room or walled summer garden. The *ravioli alla zucca* is highly recommended.
Via Salnitro 5, 46100; 0376 322 084; www.trattoriaduecavallini.mantova.it; closed mid-Jul–mid-Aug & Tue

Dal Pescatore *expensive*
Set in a country house, a 40-minute drive from Mantua, this family-run restaurant – with three Michelin stars – serves unforgettable, innovative meals in an elegantly relaxed atmosphere.
Località Runate 15, Canneto sull'Oglio, 46013; 0376 723 001; www.dal pescatore.com; closed Mon & Tue

Il Cigno dei Martini *expensive*
In an elegant dining room overlooking a beautiful garden, well-judged cooking is matched by impeccable service.
Piazza d'Arco 1, 46100; 0376 327 101; www.ristoranteilcignodeimartini.com; closed Aug, Mon & Tue

DAY TRIP OPTIONS

Visitors are spoilt for choice when it comes to days out near Lake Garda.

Family day
Based in Salò ❶, tour Il Vittoriale ❷, then cruise across the lake on the car ferry to Torri del Benaco ❸, where you can eat well, explore the village, play "King of the Castle" and have a dip from the village beach.

Follow driving instructions to Il Vittoriale and Torri del Benaco, and then back.

War and peace
Visit the Roman remains at Sirmione ❻, then drive to San Martino della Battaglia ❼ to climb the tower, a memorial to the war dead. Head to Valeggio sul Mincio ❽, home of tortellini pasta and also the peaceful green spaces of Parco Giardino Sigurtà.

Follow driving instructions from Sirmione to San Martino and Valeggio, then return.

Town and country
Spend the morning exploring the majestic architecture of Mantua ❾ – the Castello, palazzos and piazzas. Buy a picnic, then take the cycle path or a boat (visit the tourist office for routes). There are canals, rivers and pretty countryside to admire.

Eat and Drink: inexpensive, under €25; moderate, €25–€45; expensive, over €45

The Hidden Valleys of the Alto Adige

Merano to Brunico

Highlights

- **Alpine hospitality, designer spas**
  Enjoy cosy alpine bars, hearty food and top-quality Alto Adige wines at traditional mountain inns; then, sweat it out in luxury at chic spa retreats

- **Churches, abbeys and castles**
  Enjoy wine tasting at Novacella Abbey; stroll among the frescoed Gothic cloisters of Bressanone cathedral; and admire the well-preserved bastion of Castel Tirolo

- **High-altitude challenge**
  Drive over the Passo di Monte Giovo (Jaufenpass) – the most northerly road pass in Italy – with stunning vistas of jagged mountains covered with a dusting of snow

The road "over the roof of Italy", the SS44, with outstanding Alpine views

The Hidden Valleys of the Alto Adige

A cheerful "Grüss Gott" rather than "ciao" is the greeting visitors will hear on this tour through Italy's South Tyrol. This fascinating borderland, passed back and forth between ruling powers down the years, is proud of its Germanic roots. The drive begins in the spa town of Merano – or Meran – and wends its way through secluded valleys where the traditional Alpine way of life continues much as it has for centuries: cattle and sheep are led up to high pasture in summer, cheese is made in huts on the mountainside, and sweet hay is still cut by hand. After crossing the Monte Giovo/Jaufen pass, the route drops down to the Isarco (Eisacktal) valley for the Baroque splendours of the Abbazia di Novacella (Neustift) and the cathedral town of Bressanone.

ACTIVITIES

Soak in outdoor thermal pools and sunbathe below mountain peaks in Merano's state-of-the-art spa

Take a cable car to the 12th-century church of San Vigilio in a quiet mountain-top location above Merano

Go for a hike in the Parco Nazionale dello Stelvio near the Val d'Ultimo, or walk the high-altitude Adolf Munkel footpath in the Val di Funes

Learn how to smelt copper at a re-created Neolithic village near the Val Senales glacier

Shop for art and speciality foods in Bressanone's medieval arcades

Breathe in the smell of freshly cut hay on walks through velvety Alpine pastures

Above Vine terraces near the Abbazia di Novacella, *see p92* **Below left** The Art Nouveau Kurhaus, Merano, *see p90* **Below right** Pretty houses in the spa resort of Merano, *see p90*

KEY

🚋 Drive route

[Map of the region showing the drive route with locations including Ritzeil, Valles (Vals), Mezzaselva (Mittewald), Maranza (Meransen), Rio di Pusteria (Mühlbach), Aica (Aicha), Rodengo (Rodeneck), Sciaves (Schabs), Luson (Lüsen), Scaleres (Schalders), ⑧ ABBAZIA DI NOVACELLA (NEUSTIFT), Varna (Vahrn), ⑨ BRESSANONE (BRIXEN), S. Andrea (St. Andrä), Velturno (Feldthurns), Lazfons (Latzfons), Chiusa (Klausen), Albes (Albeins), Funes (Villnöss), ⑩ VAL DI FUNES (VILLNÖSS), Santa Maddalena, Furchetta 3028m, Peitlerkofel 2874m, Plancios (Palmschoß), ⑪ PASSO DELL'ERBE (WÜRZJOCH), Padraces, Antermoia, Mantana (Monthal), S. Lorenzo di S. (St. Lorenzen), Plan de Corones (Kronplatz) 2273m, Longega (Zwischenwasser), Rina, Riscone (Reischach), S. Martino i. B. (St. Martin i. T.), S. Vigilio di M. (St. Vigil), MMM RIPA AT BRUNICO (BRUNECK) ⑫, Lüsner Alpe]

see p94

PLAN YOUR DRIVE

Start/finish: Merano to MMM Ripa at Brunico.

Number of days: 3, allowing half a day to explore Bressanone, and a visit to the thermal baths in Merano.

Distance: 290 km (180 miles).

Road conditions: The roads are well paved and well signposted. Mountain routes can be slow. The road to Monte Giovo is steep, with many switchback bends. Late snow may keep the Passo dell'Erbe/Wurzjoch closed into July.

When to go: Late Jun–late Sep is best, when the mountain passes and refuges are open, the summer hiking season is in full swing and cable cars are running. For tourist information, visit *www.suedtirol.info.*

Main market days: Merano: Tue & Fri; Bressanone: Mon & Sat morning; Brunico: Wed.

Shopping: Look for mountain cheeses and chutneys, *speck* (smoked ham), jams and preserves made from mirtillo berries, and quality Alto Adige wines. Interesting mountain products include *loden* (traditional jackets and hats made from wool felt) and crib figures from Bressanone.

Major festivals: Throughout the region: Törggelen *(see p94)* mid-Sep–Nov; **Merano:** Easter horse races; Wine and food festival, Nov; **Bressanone:** "Treffpunkt" wine festival, end Jul; "Musik und Kirche" (classical music in churches), mid-Jul–mid-Sep; bread and strüdel market, Oct; International Mountain Summit, late Oct–early Nov; **Bressanone & Brunico:** Christmas markets, late Nov–early Jan; **Val di Funes:** Speck festival in Oct.

DAY TRIP OPTIONS

The drive can be broken up into day trips. Families can see the **castle** at Tirolo, then try **living like a Copper Age man** at the Archeoparc in Val Senales. Adults might prefer a Tyrolean **history museum**, a drive over a **mountain pass,** then a **soak** in a **spa.** Alternatively, stock up on an **Alpine picnic, hike** on a **high-altitude trail,** then explore a **museum** about **mountain survival.** For full details, *see p95.*

Right Fresco of St Christopher on the exterior of Merano's Duomo **Right centre** The Church of San Vigilio, in a beautiful mountain setting **Far Right** The quaint village of Unser Frau in the Val Senales **Below** View of Merano, beside the Passer river

WHERE TO STAY

MERANO (MERAN)

Terme Merano *expensive*
Stunning town-centre hotel designed by Matteo Thun with restful interiors. Rooms are spacious, with balconies.
Piazza Terme 1, 39012; 0473 259 259; www.hoteltermemerano.com

Vigilius Mountain Resort *expensive*
This luxury eco-spa, reachable only by cable car (15 mins from Lana), is a wonderfully relaxing place to stay. There's a fabulous quartzite-lined pool.
Monte San Vigilio (Vigiljoch), 39011 Lana; 0473 556 600; www.vigilius.it

VAL D'ULTIMO (ULTENTAL)

Arosea Life Balance *expensive*
This modern hotel offers understated luxury and sunny terraces. Some suites have outdoor saunas and showers.
Kuppelwies am See 355, 39016 St Walburg; 0473 785 051; www.arosea.it

Other options *inexpensive*
For farmhouse B&Bs offering spotless rooms, breakfasts from locally grown products, and often a pool and free Wi-Fi, visit *www.redrooster.it*

VAL SENALES (SCHNALSTAL)

Zur Goldenen Rose *moderate*
Wood-panelled *stuben* and snug rooms with wooden floors make this a good bolt-hole halfway up the Val Senales.
Karthaus 29, Senales (Schnals); 0473 679 130; www.goldenerose.it

① Merano (Meran)
Alto Adige; 39012

Tourists started flocking to Merano at the end of the 19th century, after Empress Elizabeth of Austria – known as Sissi – chose the town for her winter cure, and a resort of pastel-coloured Art Nouveau palaces and riverside promenades evolved. Sissi stayed at **Trauttmansdorff castle**, now home to interesting botanical gardens *(open daily)*. Take time to enjoy the town's landmark **thermal baths** *(open daily)*, designed by architect Matteo Thun, which opened in 2005. They offer thermal pools, and treatments using mud, chestnuts and apples.

🚗 *From the centre, follow signs for Bolzano (Bozen), then signs for Lana. Follow the brown signs for Val d'Ultimo (Ultental) and the "Seilbahn" (cable car). Turn right and park at the cable car station in Lana.*

② San Vigilio (Vigiljoch)
Alto Adige; 39011

Step into the cable car at Lana and travel back in time to 1912, when it was built. It's the second oldest in Europe and climbs *(May–Oct: daily)* in stately fashion to Vigilius Mountain Resort – an eco-resort built from larch that wraps around the mountain. From there, hop on a chairlift and soar above the larch woods of Monte San Vigilio (Vigiljoch), which has been a sacred place since prehistoric times. There's a café with panoramic views at the top, from where an uphill hike (15 minutes on Path 4) leads to the beautiful, simple Romanesque **Church of San Vigilio**, with 14th-century frescoes. Return on foot (1 hour; Path 3, then 34) or by chairlift to Vigilius – its restaurant (Ida) is a popular stop for hikers.

🚗 *Return to Lana. Follow the brown road signs for Val d'Ultimo (Ultental). Pass through San Pancrazio (Sankt Pankraz) to San Nicolò (Sankt Nikolaus) and the Lahnersäge Visitor Centre.*

③ Val d'Ultimo (Ultental)
Alto Adige; 39016

The first part of the valley is the most dramatic, climbing steeply through orchards and vineyards, past signs for *waalwegs* (the ancient irrigation channels that make farming possible on the sunny, south-facing hillsides). The valley opens out into lush pastures dotted with traditional chalets topped by wooden roof shingles weighted with stones against stormy weather. Stop for refreshments at the village of San Pancrazio before heading on to San Nicolò and the **Lahnersäge Visitor Centre** *(mid-May to Oct: open Tue–Sun)* with its water-driven sawmill, just before the climb into the village of St Gertraud (1,519 m/ 4,984 ft), the starting point for hikes in the **Parco Nazionale dello Stelvio** *(www.stelviopark.bz.it)*.

🚗 *Return to Merano on SS38, skirting to west of town centre and turning west into Venosta (Vinschgau) valley. Soon after Naturno (Naturns) turn right and take the long, winding road into the Senales (Schnalstal) valley.*

Matteo Thun
Born in Bolzano, architect Matteo Thun has designed some ground-breaking buildings in Alto Adige, from the Vigilius resort, which won *Wallpaper* magazine's design award in 2004, to the spa complex in Merano. In the 1980s, with Ettore Sottsass and others, he co-founded the Memphis Group, which injected colour, humour and pizzazz into everyday design.

🚗 *Continue north up the Val Passiria (Passeiertal) for 15 km (10 miles). Look out for the Sandwirt inn on the right, just before San Leonardo. The museum is next to it. Park outside the restaurant or in the car park left off the main road.*

Andreas Hofer

An innkeeper and cattle dealer, Andreas Hofer (1767–1810) fought for the Tyrol's autonomy after it was ceded to Bavaria in 1805. He became a reluctant hero of the people after successful uprisings against Bavarian and Napoleonic troops. However, larger political forces overtook him and he was betrayed to the invaders. Napoleon supposedly gave the order to "give him a fair trial and then shoot him". He was executed in Mantua in 1810.

④ Val Senales (Schnalstal)
Alto Adige; 39020

Perched on a rocky outcrop, the little church of Monte Santa Caterina (Katharinaberg) is one of the few landmarks on the drive up the steep, wooded Senales valley. Many twists and turns lead to **Certosa (Karthaus)**, a village with a famous church and cloister, home to a silent order of monks from 1326–1725. Continue higher still to the **Archeoparc** *(Jun–Nov: open daily)* – a fascinating re-creation of a late Neolithic village in an Alpine landscape (1,500 m/4,921 ft) that was home to Ötzi the Iceman. The fascinating remains of this Copper Age man were found mummified in the glacier above the valley in 1991, and now rest in Bolzano *(see p100)*. At the Archeoparc, visitors can try their hand at archery, making fire, smelting copper ore, working a flint tool or baking bread in the typical domed ovens of 5,000 years ago.
🚗 *Drive back down the valley and turn left to Merano. In the town centre, pick up the brown signs for Val Passiria (Passeiertal), then Tirolo (Tirol). Parking is on the left, before the castle.*

⑤ Castel Tirolo (Schloss Tirol)
Alto Adige; 39019

Such was the power of the counts of Tirol, who built their mountain eyrie in a strategic position on a hillside above Merano, that the whole region was named after them. Surrounded by lush forest, this huge 12th-century castle is well preserved and its keep, temple, knight's hall (an occasional concert venue) and refectory are all open to visitors. Within the complex is a **museum** *(mid-Mar–early Dec: open Tue–Sun)* of daily life in the Middle Ages, with interactive displays.

⑥ MuseumPasseier
Alto Adige; 39015

The Sandwirt inn was the birthplace of Andreas Hofer – the former stables next door are now a museum *(closed Mon except Aug & Sep)* in his memory. A short film (in Italian, German and English) tells Hofer's story, giving an insight into the Tyrolean fight for independence – always with a strong identity, Alto Adige is, to this day, an autonomous province. The museum reveals traditional Alpine life via indoor displays and an open-air exhibition of wooden chalets, with barns and grain storage, a skittle alley, beehives, a communal oven, a mill for making *loden* (local felt fabric) and a schnapps still.
🚗 *Continue into San Leonardo in Passiria (St Leonhard). Take a right, following the brown signs for the Passo di Monte Giovo (Jaufenpass).*

EAT AND DRINK

MERANO

Trattoria Mainardo *moderate*
This simple eatery is popular for its hearty, delicious dishes made with fresh ingredients. Lovely, cozy atmosphere and attentive service.
Via Mainardo 19; 0345 157 5412; closed Sun

Sissi *expensive*
A top restaurant where renowned chef Andrea Fenoglio produces modern Italian cuisine with a regional bent.
Galileistrasse 44, 39012; 0473 231 062; www.sissi.andreafenoglio.com; closed Mon

AROUND SAN VIGILIO

Pfefferlechner *moderate*
A down-to-earth place dating back to 1297, where they brew their own beer, distill their own schnapps and produce their own smoked bacon and trout. Order the "Gupffleisch" in advance – neck of pork in schnapps, with bacon dumplings and white cabbage. Kid-friendly, there's also a beer garden and playground outside and the medieval dining rooms overlook the stables.
St Martinsweg 4, 39011 Lana; 0473 562 521; www.pfefferlechner.it

AROUND MUSEUMPASSEIER

Trattoria Lamm *moderate*
In the main square of the village, the 17th-century Lamm inn prides itself on its simple Tyrolean dishes, such as home-made pasta, and a lovely strudel made with local honey.
Via Villaggio 36, 39010 San Martino in Passiria (just before MuseumPasseier); 0473 641 240; www.gasthaus-lamm.it; closed Sun eve & Mon

Below 12th-century Tirol Castle looks down on 13th-century Brunnenburg Castle

Eat and Drink: inexpensive, under €25; moderate, €25–€45; expensive, over €45

Above The road over the top of Italy at Passo di Monte Giovo (Jaufenpass)

VISTING BRESSANONE

Parking
Park off Via Brennero (Brennerstrasse) on the road from Novacella. Free parking (max 2 hrs) just outside the pedestrian zone by the riverside at Stufles.

Tourist Information
Viale Ratisbona 9 (Regensburger Allee 9); 0472 836 401; www.brixen.org

WHERE TO STAY

ABBAZIA DI NOVACELLA

Pacherhof inexpensive
Near the abbey, this hotel makes its own wine from vineyards dating from the 11th century. Rooms have wooden floors and spacious bathrooms; some have balconies, and there's a huge pool. Vicolo Pacher 1, 39040 Novacella; 0472 835 717; www.pacherhof.com; closed mid-Jan–mid-Mar

BRESSANONE AND AROUND

Elephant inexpensive
This hotel has an elegant touch of faded grandeur, and is centrally located. It also has a formal restaurant and more casual enoteca (wine bar). Via Rio Bianco 4, Bressanone; 047 283 2750; www.hotelelephant.com

Ansitz zum Steinbock moderate
Beamed ceilings and white-washed walls characterize the uncluttered bed-rooms in this imposing building, 18 km (11 miles) southwest of Bressanone, just beyond Chiusa (Klausen). Vicolo F. v. Defregger 1439040 Villandro (Villanders); 0472 843 111; www.zumsteinbock.com; closed Jan

Right Pedestrians wander the narrow streets of Bressanone's old town

➐ Passo di Monte Giovo (Jaufenpass)
Alto Adige; 39010

Leaving the Passeier valley behind, there will be plenty of bikers and perhaps a few hardy cyclists for company on the ear-popping ascent to the Passo di Monte Giovo (2,094 m/6,870 ft). This is the most northerly road pass in Italy, giving access to stunning views of ridge after ridge along the Austro-Italian border. The big skies and saw-toothed peaks, with a dusting of snow even in summer, make it feel like driving over the top of the world. As the landscape opens out to high moorland, there are opportunities to stop for a coffee and admire the glorious views at makeshift roadside bars before making the long, winding descent to Vipiteno (Sterzing) in the Isarco (Eisack) valley.

🚗 Join A22 south towards Bolzano (Bozen)/Verona. Take Bressanone Nord (Varna) exit and turn right towards Bressanone. Exit from SS12, pass through Varna following brown signs for Quartiere Leone (Löwenhof), then take the road for Abbazia di Novacella on the left.

➑ Abbazia di Novacella (Neustift)
Alto Adige; 39040

In the 17th century, the Augustinian monks of Novacella commissioned a Weltwunder-Brunnen, a depiction of the Seven Wonders of the World, for their abbey, which had long been an important centre of learning in the Tyrol. In a moment of immodesty, they added their church to the picture as world wonder number eight. The abbey (closed Sun; Jan–Mar also closed Mon) offers a lot for the visitor to see, with its impressive bell tower and basilica, medieval cloister with 14th-century frescoes, its maze of painting-lined galleries, gardens and a library in which the monks still work. The complex, built in southern German Baroque style, is a great place to wander and enjoy: surrounded by vineyards, the abbey makes its own wine which can be sampled in the small restaurant (closed weekends), or bought from the shop.

🚗 Exit the abbey and take SS12 (not the motorway) into Bressanone. Park just outside the pedestrianized historic centre.

➒ Bressanone (Brixen)
Alto Adige; 39042

With its cobbled streets, medieval arcades and classic beer gardens, Bressanone (Brixen) seems like a busy metropolis after the quiet valleys earlier in the drive. Rich and powerful, Bressanone became an independent principate in the 11th century and its ruling bishops were constantly jockeying for power with the counts of Tyrol. Today, this attractive town is the artistic and cultural capital of the region.

A two-hour walking tour
This walk is best done Tue–Sat, when the shops and museums are open and the town is bustling. It begins in Piazza Duomo (Domplatz), still the focus of the town.

Bressanone's cathedral, **The Dom** ① (open daily), was built in the 10th century, rebuilt in the 13th century and rebuilt again, in lavish Baroque style, between 1745 and 1758, when its twin onion domes were added. The broad, vaulted nave is richly decorated in marble and stucco with a ceiling fresco of the Adoration of the Lamb by Paul Troger (1698–1762), an Austrian known for his illusionist paintings. Through the cathedral's right door is

the Gothic **Kreuzgang** ② (cloister), with a series of richly frescoed vaulted archways painted between 1370 and 1510 by artists from Bressanone and Brunico (Bruneck).

Return to Domplatz and turn into Piazza Parrocchia (Pfarrplatz), passing the **Pfaundlerhaus** ③ – a Gothic palazzo with a lavish Renaissance façade. At the crossroads, turn right into Via San Albuino (Albuingasse) and walk to Piazza Seminario (Seminarplatz) and the interesting 18th-century **seminary** ④ (now a theology college) with views of Plose mountain (2,500 m/8,200 ft) behind it. Backtrack to the riverside Vicolo della Ghiare (Griesgasse) to the Aquila (Adler) bridge, crossing the River Eisack into the **Stufels (Stufles)** ⑤ district, the oldest part of Bressanone, doing a loop past the Schutzangelkirche (church) and the theatre back to the bridge. Recross the river to the **Museo della Farmacia (Pharmaziemuseum)** ⑥ *(Tue–Wed 2–6pm, Sat 11am–4pm; Jul & Aug open Mon–Fri & Sat, same hours).* This contains a fascinating collection of antique vials for lotions and potions, as well as ornate medical manuals covering 400 years of medical history. Re-enter the historic centre by the **Torre Bianca (Weissenturm)** gate ⑦ – the white tower is actually

part of St Michael's parish church. At the cathedral, bear right into the **Portici Maggiori (Grosse Lauben)** ⑧, a shopping arcade that dates back to medieval times, but is now home to fashion and speciality food shops. Take a left turn into the small galleries of the **Portici Minori (Kleine Lauben)** ⑨, built in the 1400s, then continue along Vicolo Vescovado (Hofgasse) to the **Palazzo Vescovile (Hofburg)** ⑩ (Bishop's Palace), surrounded by a moat. The inner courtyard has Renaissance archways that lead to the Museo Diocesano (Diozesanmuseum) *(closed Mon, Nov & Feb–mid-March).* The exhibits reveal just how powerful Bressanone's bishop-princes were: among the fine displays is a Byzantine silk cloak decorated with a stylized eagle, the personal emblem of Bishop Albuino – a gift from Emperor Henry II. Next to the palace is the **Giardino dei Signori (Herrengarten)** ⑪, a peaceful monastery-style garden growing vegetables, herbs and flowers.
🚗 *Follow the road for the highway, but before Chiusi's exit, turn left and follow the brown signs for Val di Funes (Villnöss).*

Above left The Abbazia di Novacella, set among vineyards **Above right** The Colossus, one of the Wonders of the World, Abbazia di Novacella

TYROLEAN FOOD SHOPPING

Located just the other side of the river to the Abbazia di Novacella, **DeGust** *(Zona Bsackerau 1 Löwecenter, Varna; 0472 84 9873; www.degust.com; closed Sun)* sells well over 100 Italian artisan cheeses, including Alpine styles such as the bittersweet blue cheese Golden Gel, matured in sweet grapes and wrapped in hay. There are also preserves, chutneys, salamis and South Tyrolean speck (smoked ham) for sale.

EAT AND DRINK

ABBAZIA DI NOVACELLA

Other options *moderate*
Pacherhof *(see p92)* has four panelled *stube*, one of which is said to be the oldest in South Tyrol. The menu gives a modern spin on Tyrolean cuisine, using vegetables from their own garden.

BRESSANONE

Oste Scuro (Finsterwirt) *expensive*
Excellent local delicacies and a great atmosphere in this much-loved restaurant; good wine list, too.
Vicolo del Duomo 3, Bressanone; 0472 835 343; www.finsterwirt.com; closed Sun eve & Mon, Jun

Eat and Drink: inexpensive, under €25; moderate, €25–€45; expensive, over €45

Above The church of Santa Maddalena, in an idyllic setting in the Val di Funes (Villnöss)

HIKING IN THE VAL DI FUNES

Kompass walking maps (1 cm : 500 m) are essential as they show footpaths, level of difficulty and the steepness of the terrain. Trails are simple to follow – red and white blazes painted on rocks and trees to keep walkers on the right path. Mountain refuges offer good food and drink en route.

WHERE TO STAY

AROUND VAL DI FUNES

Ansitz Ranuihof *inexpensive*
Once a hunting lodge, this farmhouse offers six comfortable doubles; breakfast includes milk and eggs from the farm. *San Maddalena (St Magdalena) 39, 39040 Val di Funes (Villnöss) (after Funes, veer south to San Maddalena then take the road to St Johann and Ranui); 0472 840 506; www.ranuihof.com*

Below Alpe di Zannes and Le Odle ranges with Geisler Spitzen

⑩ Val di Funes (Villnöss)
Alto Adige; 39040
A real gem of a valley, the spectacular Val di Funes is characterized by walls of grey saw-toothed peaks – the Puez Odle (Puez Geisler) mountains – rising above the lush, green rolling meadows that open out after Funes. It's a beautiful part of the drive for a gentle walk, or to spend a half-day on a more ambitious hike such as the Adolf Munkel path – a five-hour circular trail that starts and ends in Zannes (Zanser Alm) at the head of the valley (see *www.suedtirol.info; Kompass map 55)*. The path climbs to 2,000 m (6,560 ft), at one point, giving panoramic views, and there are huts or *rifugi* en route for revitalizing refreshments.

🚗 *From Funes, take SP163 uphill to the signposted Kopfel Joch pass. There, turn right on SP29 to the Passo dell'Erbe (Würzjoch). Park at Ütia de Börz inn.*

⑪ Passo dell'Erbe (Würzjoch)
Alto Adige; 39030
This road pass reaches more or less the same giddy heights as some of the more famous Dolomite passes, but is one much less commercialized and the view of the mountains on the approach is sensational. Alta Via 2, one of the high-level trans-Dolomite footpaths, crosses the road between Kopfel Joch and Würzjoch, so parking and having a half-hour or so walk in either direction will give a flavour of hiking these high trails. A visit to the Ütia de Börz inn at the pass is recommended – the food is good and it is also a fabulous base for a few days hiking (half-board and minimum three-day stay preferred).

🚗 *From the pass, descend to San Martino (St Martin) in Badia, passing Ciastel de Tor. Turn left on the SS244 towards Brunico. Follow the signs for Brunico centre and the MMM Ripa. Park at the castle.*

Törggelen
An old South Tyrolean tradition, the Törggelen season roughly coincides with the arrival of the new season's wine (Oct–mid-Nov). It's a time when people go for hikes and gather to feast on local specialities before the onset of winter. The name comes from the Latin word *torquere*, to turn or squeeze – referring to pressing grapes to make wine. Some say the tradition came from wine merchants visiting the wine growers to try the new wine – after the tasting, they would be given a feast. A typical Törggelen spread involves *speck* or sausage, roast chestnuts and breads.

Reinhold Messner

Mountaineer Reinhold Messner grew up in Val di Funes (Villnöss) and learnt to climb with his father. Messner thought the usual "siege" techniques used on mountaineering expeditions were disrespectful to the environment and pioneered the Alpine style of climbing – using minimal equipment – in the Himalayas. He is famous for making the first solo Everest ascent without oxygen and went on to become the first man to climb all 14 of the world's peaks over 8,000 m (26,250 ft). He founded a mountain museum at five locations in the South Tyrol: the newest opened in 2011 in Brunico (Bruneck).

⑫ MMM Ripa at Brunico (Bruneck)
Alto Adige; 39031

The main market town of the Val Pusteria (Pustertal), Brunico (Bruneck) grew up around the castle built in 1250 by the Prince-Bishop of Brixen, Bruno of Wullenstätten, and flourished

thanks to its position on the trade route between Venice and Germany. In 2011, Reinhold Messner opened the doors to this fifth part of the Messner Mountain Museum Ripa – inside the Castello di Brunico *(Jun–Sep & 8 Dec–Easter Mon: open Wed–Mon)*. The display is a tribute to the mountain peoples of the world who have made their homes at the very margins of where it is possible to live – Sherpas, Indios, Tibetans, Walser, Mongols and Hunzas.

Above left Houses from the 16th and 17th centuries, Brunico **Above** Castello di Brunico, home to the Messner Mountain Museum Ripa **Below left** Cycling on the Alta Pusteria bikepath near Brunico (Bruneck)

EAT AND DRINK

AROUND PASSO DELL'ERBE

Hotel Lech da Sompunt *expensive*
Try spit-roasted *porchetta* (suckling pig), fondue, and fresh trout from their pond. Other specialities include *canederli* (dumplings) and *Kaiserschmarren* (sweet cranberry pancake). They also offer simple, Tyrolean rooms to stay in. *Str Sompunt 36, 39036 Pedraces (about 12 km/8 miles south of San Martino on SP244); 0471 847 015; www.lechdasompunt.it; closed 7 Apr–10 Jun, Oct & Nov*

Maso Runch *expensive*
Just east of Badia, this restaurant is popular for its hearty six-course menu. After rustic appetisers, expect homemade ricotta and spinach ravioli, pork shin with sauerkraut, local wine to drink and apple strudel for dessert. *Runch 11, 39036 Pedraces (about 12 km/8 miles south of San Martino on SP244); 0471 839 796; www.masorunch.it*

DAY TRIP OPTIONS
To break up the tour into day trips for adults and children, use either Merano or Bressanone as a base.

Ice Man adventure
Children will enjoy travelling from Merano ❶ and visiting the castle and interactive museum at Castel Tirolo ❺. Next, it's off to the Archeoparc in Val Senales ❹ to discover how the Ötzi the Ice Man lived. Enjoy dinner at Pfefferlechner in Lana *(see p91)*, with its adventure playground and animals as well as great food and beer brewed on the premises.

Take SS44 north from Merano, turn left to Tirolo. Return to Merano, access Val Senales via SS38, picked up just outside Merano. Lana is also close to Merano – follow SS238 for Bolzano/Bozen/Lana.

Tyrolean treats
Plunge into the Tyrolean past at the MuseumPasseier ❻, then head up to "drive over the roof of Italy" and enjoy a high-altitude coffee or drink at the Passo di Monte Giovo ❼. Return to Merano ❶ to explore the botanical gardens of Trauttmansdorff Castle. Finish off the day with a relaxing splash in the thermal pools at Merano's beautiful new spa complex.

Access all from the Passiria/Passeier valley road (the SS44).

Taste of the mountains
Stock up on an Alpine picnic at the bustling Saturday farmer's market in Bressanone ❾ or DeGust in Varna *(see p93)* and hit the high-level trails in the Val di Funes ❿ or do a bit of the Alta Via 2 footpath from Passo dell'Erbe ⑪. Head on to the mountain museum at Brunico ⑫ to learn about real mountain living.

Follow the driving instructions from Bressanone to Val di Funes, Passo dell'Erbe and Brunico. Return via SS49.

Eat and Drink: inexpensive, under €25; moderate, €25–€45; expensive, over €45

Classic Dolomites Tour

Bolzano to Alpe di Siusi

Highlights

- **Famous road passes**
  Negotiate exhilarating hairpin bends and switchback roads that wind like ribbons around the Dolomites

- **Michelin-starred hot-spots**
  Dine at top-class restaurants on dishes made from the finest local produce

- **Time-travel experience**
  Visit Ötzi – the remains of a 5,000-year-old Ice Man in Bolzano's archaeological museum – and follow the trail of dinosaurs in the Bletterbach gorge

- **Award-winning wine producers**
  Stop for tastings along the Strada del Vino, in the oldest wine region of the German-speaking world

Corvara nestles beneath the impressive Col Alt mountain on the floor of the Badia valley

Classic Dolomites Tour

This itinerary is for those who like heights: it offers switchback roads, chairlift and cable car rides – and dizzying haute cuisine. A popular skiing and hiking area, there are exceptional hotels and restaurants in this province, which has more Michelin stars than any other in Italy. The route crosses the most famous passes of the Dolomites, a range of limestone mountains raised skywards 250 million years ago when Africa collided with Southern Europe. Bring hiking boots; it's worth getting out of the car and walking, not least for a glimpse of history. Some trails lead along the World War I front line, where Italian and Austrian troops dug themselves into the mountains to survive. In 1919, after war ended, this German-speaking region – known as South Tyrol – became a part of Italy.

[Map of the Trentino Alto Adige region showing the Classic Dolomites Tour route, with labelled towns including Bolzano (Bozen), Castel Roncolo (Schloss Runkelstein), Strada del Vino (Weinstrasse), Geoparc Bletterbach, Val di Fiemme, Alpe di Siusi (Seiser Alm), Ortisei (St. Ulrich), and Val di Fassa. Scale: 0 kilometres 8, 0 miles 8.]

ACTIVITIES

Taste the superb wines of the Alto Adige on the Strada del Vino

Walk back in time to the last Ice Age in the gorge at the Geoparc Bletterbach

Ride up in a chairlift and hike in the Catinaccio mountains, and enjoy delicious hearty food in a mountain refuge

Drive over the roof of Italy across the stunning Pordoi, Falzàrego, Valparola and Gardena passes of the Dolomites

Climb through World War I galleries blasted into the rock at Lagazuoi and view wartime memorabilia at the Tre Sassi fort

Catch the *enrosadira*, when the Dolomites glow in the rays of the setting sun

PLAN YOUR DRIVE

Start/finish: Bolzano to Alpe di Siusi.

Number of days: Approx 4–5.

Distance: 219 km (136 miles).

Road conditions: The roads are pretty good. Routes over mountain passes are narrow with steep turns and can be busy. The A22 motorway can get heavily congested with long queues of traffic near tolls – leave plenty of time to get to and from airports. Beware speed limit of 110 kmh, lower than on other Italian motorways.

When to go: May to Oct (some cable cars only operate mid-Jun–mid-Sep). Early or late snow may close the passes – look for signs on the approach roads or call 0471 200 198.

Main market days: Bolzano: fruit and vegetable market at Piazza Erbe (Obstplatz), Mon–Sat; La Villa: last Thu of month; Corvara: 2nd & last Sat of month; Ortisei (St Ulrich): Fri.

Shopping: Look for local wine, liqueurs and grappas, wild honey, cheeses and salami; *loden* (traditional felt jackets and hats); fruit compôtes and preserves; and *kräutersalz* (salt and herb mix).

Major festivals: Across region: Törggelen *(see p94)*, mid-Sep–Nov; Bolzano: Transart (festival of contemporary culture), Oct; Christmas market, late Nov–23 Dec; Appiano (Eppan): medieval horsemanship, Whitsun Castelrotto (Kastelruther): Spatzen folk festival, Oct; Christmas market in Dec; Val Gardena (Gröden) & Alta Badia: Ski World Cup events, Dec.

KEY

🚍 Drive route

Above The limestone peaks of the Dolomites as seen from Marmolada, *see p102* **Below** Typical valley scenery on the Strada del Vino, *see p101* **Below left** Wall painting on the side of a Bolzano "Torgglhaus", or restaurant, *see p100*

DAY TRIP OPTIONS

Using Bolzano as a base offers family day trips exploring an **archaeological museum**, enjoying a **picnic** then going on a **hike** to look for **dinosaurs** in a **gorge**, before admiring the **frescoes of dwarves and giants** in a **castle**. Adults may prefer a **wine tour** (including a visit to a **wine museum**) through famous **wineries** of the Alto Adige, enjoying a **gourmet lunch** along the way. For full details, *see p103*.

Above Statue of Walther von der Vogelweide in Piazza Walther (Waltherplatz), Bolzano

VISITING BOLZANO (BOZEN)

Parking
Park in Piazza Walther (Waltherplatz), on Via Laurin or outside the train station (in the Central Parking facility).

Tourist information
Via Alto Adige 60, 39100; 0471 307 000; www.bolzano-bozen.it

WHERE TO STAY

BOLZANO

Greif *expensive*
This central, 500-year-old inn is now a chic 33-bedroom haven filled with original art and Biedermeier furniture.
Piazza Walther, Bolzano; 0471 318 000; www.greif.it

AROUND GEOPARC BLETTERBACH

Krone *inexpensive*
This 16th century friendly family-run village inn has an excellent restaurant.
Dorfplatz 3, Piazza Principale, 39040 Aldino (Aldein); 0471 886 825; www.gasthof-krone.it

❶ Bolzano (Bozen)
Alto Adige; 39100

In a valley at the junction of the Talvera and Isarco rivers, Alto Adige's main town has changed hands several times over the centuries. In the Middle Ages it was controlled by the Counts of Tirol, then by the Bishops of Trento; next it passed to the Habsburgs, then to Bavaria and Austria. Although it was given to Italy at the end of World War I, there's still a real Germanic feel to the town centre.

A two-hour walking tour

Via Laurin connects the train station to the start of the walk at **Piazza Walther** ①. Passing the statue of Walther von der Vogelweide (1170–1230), a great German poet of the Middle Ages, head to the Gothic **Duomo** ② *(open daily)* with its elaborate steeple and lozenge-pattern roof. A short walk leads to the **Chiesa dei Domenicani** ③ *(open daily)*, with Gothic frescoes from the Giotto school and fine 15th-century frescoes by Friedrich Pacher in the cloister (separate entrance). Head up Via Goethe-Strasse to the food market on **Piazza Erbe (Obstplatz)** ④. On one corner stands the fountain of Neptune (1745), known as Gabelwirt (Innkeeper with a Fork) – walk past this and head up Via dei Francescani (Franziskanergasse) to the **Convento dei Francescani** ⑤ *(open Mon–Sat)*, dating to the first half of the 14th century. Inside is one of Bolzano's finest treasures: a superb Gothic wooden altar carved by Hans Klocher.

Detail of a fresco from Bolzano's Gothic Duomo

Backtrack a little to the top end of the market and take a left into the road named after **Dr Joseph Streiter** ⑥ – a mayor of the town in the mid-19th century – here are shops selling chocolate, vintage clothes and accessories here. Continue to Via dei Bottai (Bindergasse) and turn right to **Piazza Municipio (Rathausplatz)** ⑦, lined with beautiful Rococo stucco façades. Another right turn leads down **Portici (Lauben)** ⑧, a porticoed shopping street with oriel windows and elegant Baroque floral plasterwork.

Continue along Via Museo to the **Museo Archeologico** ⑨ *(10am– 6pm Tue–Sun; also Mon in Jul, Aug & Dec)*. The prize exhibit here is Ötzi – the remains of a man in his 40s from the Copper Age, preserved in the ice of the Alps on the Italian-Austrian border. There's a video reconstruction of how Ötzi may have met his end in 3500 BC. Cross the River Talvera (Talfer) to the arch on **Piazza Vittoria (Siegesplatz)** ⑩, commissioned by Mussolini in 1928. Return back over the bridge, carrying straight on to Piazza del Grano, then turn right back to Piazza Walther.

🚗 *From central Bolzano, follow signs for Funivia (cable car) di S Genesio and for Castel Roncolo. Turn right, crossing the river to the car park. Walk up the steps (slippery when wet) to the castle.*

② Castel Roncolo (Schloss Runkelstein)
Alto Adige; 39100

Pier Paolo Pasolini filmed his version of Boccaccio's (1313–75) bawdy tales *The Decameron* (1971) in this 13th-century castle *(closed Mon)*. The secular frescoes are some of the best in the world. Images of giants and dwarves, the legendary lovers Tristan and Isolde and the world of chivalry were painted to impress in the 14th century – the castle was part of the Vintler family's bid to be accepted into noble society.

🚗 *Return to Bolzano centre, cross the Ponte Druso and go straight. Take SS42 for Appiano (Eppan) and Strada del Vino (Weinstrasse). Turn right to Caldaro. Park in the wine centre car park or in the blue boxes outside the town centre.*

③ Strada del Vino (Weinstrasse)
Alto Adige; 39052

Although it's one of the smallest wine regions in Italy, Alto Adige produces more DOC wines than any other. This section of the drive follows part of the South Tyrolean Wine Road. Start at Caldaro's **Winecenter della Cantina** *(open daily)*, with wines for any budget. More tasting opportunities are on offer at the wine bar/visitor centre, **Punkt** *(closed Mon)*, on the main square. Enjoy, too, Caldaro's 16th-century Uberetsch architecture, which mixes Gothic and Renaissance styles.

🚗 *Follow Strada del Vino (Weinstrasse) through Termeno (Tramin) and Magre*

(Magreid), then take the minor road to the station and cross over A22 and River Adige. Turn left onto SS12 to Egna (Neumarkt) and turn right through the village. Turn right onto SS48 towards Val di Fiemme. After two sharp bends follow signs left for Aldein (Aldino). Turn right after village and park at the Geoparc.

④ Geoparc Bletterbach
Alto Adige; 39040

Rock fans can see how the Dolomites were formed, epoch by epoch, as well as spot the tracks of prehistoric reptiles by walking the length of this 8-km (5-mile) fossil-packed gorge *(admission charge)*, which has carved its way down the mountain since the last Ice Age. The **Geopath** is for experienced walkers (with hiking boots); an easier 30-minute forest path (wheelchair accessible) from the visitor centre gives views into the canyon.

🚗 *Descend via Aldein (Aldino) to SS48. Turn left to Cavalese in the Val di Fiemme. Park in the main square.*

⑤ Val di Fiemme
Trentino; 38033

The focus of Cavalese's town centre is the **Magnifica Comunità**, a medieval palazzo *(not open to public)* frescoed with images of San Vigilio. This was once the summer palace of the Bishops of Trento, who used to stay here to escape the summer heat. Stay for a coffee or lunch before carrying on along SS48 to Tésero. This is known for its **Chiesa di San Rocco**, frescoed with activities not allowed on a Sunday, such as drinking and playing dice.

🚗 *From Tésero, take the minor road (not SS48) to Predazzo, then before Moena make a deviation to the right. Head past Lago di Soraga and return to SS48. Drive through Pera di Fassa and park at the Vajolet chairlift station.*

Above left Magnifica Comunità, Cavalese's historic parliament building **Above right** Vines on the slopes above Lago di Caldaro, on the Strada del Vino **Below** Bustling market on the Piazza Erbe, Bolzano

EAT AND DRINK

BOLZANO

Ca' de Bezzi (Batzenhäusl) *inexpensive*
This 600-year-old inn offers mixed plates served in cast-iron pans. Good wine.
Via A Hofer (Andreas-Hofer-Strasse) 30; 0471 050 950; www.batzen.it

Franziskanerstuben *moderate*
This homely restaurant offers a mix of Italian and Tiroaean dishes.
Via Dei Francescani 7, 39100; 0471 976 183; www.franziskanerstuben.com; closed Sun

STRADA DEL VINO

Ansitz Pillhof *inexpensive*
The best wines from South Tyrol are on display in the *enoteca* (wine shop) here; try by the glass at the bar or in the bistro.
Via Bolzano 48, 39010 Frangart, Appiano (Eppan) (on SS42 south of Bolzano); 0471 633 100; www.pillhof.com

Zur Rose *expensive*
The elegant food is Michelin-starred and includes seafood and flavours from across Italy. The cellar is well-stocked.
Via Josef Innerhofer 2, 39057 San Michele, Appiano (Eppan); 0471 662 249; www.zur-rose.com; closed Sat eve & Sun

Restaurant Ritterhof *expensive*
This restaurant serves locally sourced dishes with an imaginative twist and has a good wine list.
Weinstrasse 1/A, Kaltern; 0471 963 330; www.restaurant-ritterhof.it; closed Jan–mid-Feb: Mon–Thu, mid-Feb–Dec: Mon & Tue lunch

VAL DI FIEMME

El Molin *expensive*
Great *stuzzichini* (snacks), a superior pizzeria and even Michelin-starred food.
P.za Cesare Battisti 11, 38033 Cavalese; 0462 340 074 (book for lunch); www.elmolin.info; closed lunch Mon–Fri & Tue

Eat and Drink: inexpensive, under €25; moderate, €25–€45; expensive, over €45

Above left Mountain scenery behind Corvara
Above centre Lago di Fedaia, near Canazei **Far right** Hiking in the Dolomites at Marmolada
Below The glacier on top of Marmolada

WHERE TO STAY

VAL SAN CASSIANO

Garni Ai Pini *inexpensive*
A family-run guesthouse with sauna.
*Strada Glira 4, 39030 San Cassiano;
0471 849 541; www.ai-pini.it; closed
Easter–early Jun, Oct & Nov*

Chalet Susi *expensive*
A simple and well-presented apartment.
*Via Sotsas 4, 39030 La Villa; 0471 847
015 ; www.chaletsusi.it; closed Easter–
mid-Jun, Oct & Nov*

Rosa Alpina *expensive*
Understated luxury at this spa hotel.
*Strada Micura de Rü 20, 39030 San
Cassiano in Badia; 0471 849 500;
www.rosalpina.it*

CORVARA

La Perla *expensive*
Luxury hotel with exceptional food.
*Strada Col Alt 105, 39033; 0471 831
000; www.hotel-laperla.it; closed Apr–
mid-May & mid-Sep–Nov*

ALPE DI SIUSI (SEISER ALM)

Cavallino d'Oro *inexpensive*
A 700-year-old inn with 40 rooms.
*Piazza Kraus, 39040 Castelrotto; 0471
706 337; www.cavallino.it*

Romantik Hotel Turm *expensive*
A superb spa hotel with great food.
*Piazza Chiesa 9, 939050 Fie allo Sciliar;
0471 725 014; www.hotelturm.it; closed
first 2 wks Apr & early Nov–21 Dec*

⑥ Val di Fassa
Trentino; 38039

Popular with skiers, Val di Fassa's classic sight is the **Rosengarten mountain range** (Catinaccio in Italian). A chairlift *(end Jun–early Sep)* climbs from Pera to Ciampedie at 2,000 m (6,562 ft), where it's possible to walk among the peaks. An easy one-hour forest trail (Path 540) leads from Ciampedie to the Gardeccia refuge – perfect for a lunch stop.

🚗 *Continue on SS48 to Canazei, and begin the signposted ascent to the Passo Pordoi. Bear right on SS48 up a series of steep switchbacks to Passo Pordoi, which has ample free parking.*

Rosengarten (Rose garden)
Ladin legends are part of an epic oral tradition. One has it that the dwarf King Laurin, angry when his beloved Princess Similde was taken away from him, put a spell on his rose garden so that no one would see it again by day or night – but he forgot to include dawn and dusk – when the sun gives the mountains their rosy glow.

⑦ Passo Pordoi
Alto Adige; 38032

For the best views of glacier-topped Marmolada (3,246 m/10,650 ft), take the cable car *(late May–late Oct)* from Passo Pordoi (2,239 m/7,346 ft) up to **Sass Pordoi**. Alternatively, stretch the legs for half an hour or so along the Viel del Pan ("trail of bread") – an old grain-smuggling route which begins at the pass behind the Albergo Savoia (hiking boots essential). Once back in the car, descend through a series of steep switchbacks to pretty **Arabba**. Carry on along the Livinallongo valley, passing the 11th-century Andraz castle, which once defended the iron ore mines and foundries producing swords for export across Europe.

🚗 *Descend on SS48 through Arabba and Livinallongo; climb to the Passo di Falzàrego. Park at the cable car station.*

⑧ Lagazuoi (Lagació)
Veneto; 32043

A cable car whisks passengers up from Passo di Falzàrego to Lagazuoi at 2,778 m (9,114 ft) in just three minutes *(Jun–Nov & Dec–Easter)*. A short walk uphill leads to the Lagazuoi refuge, a large café/restaurant with stunning, far-reaching views of most of the Dolomites. In World War I, Austrian troops gained a bird's-eye view of the Passo Valparola from the exposed Kaiserjäger path to the northwest. Visitors with walking boots and a head for heights can turn right from the cable car station and head down the rock-cut steps that lead to the wartime galleries, blasted into the heart of the mountain (rent helmets/torches at the entrance). This exciting descent lasts about 90 minutes and is a hit with older children. Alternatively, return to the pass by the cable car.

🚗 *Turn left towards Passo di Valparola and drive for a few minutes to the Museum of the Tre Sassi Fort.*

⑨ Tre Sassi Fort
Veneto, 32043

Built in 1897 by the Austro-Hungarian army to defend the Passo Valparola (2,168 m/7,113 ft), this fort was opened as a museum *(15 Jun–30 Sep: open daily)* in 2003 to commemorate the 1914–18 war, with the entrance now guarded by "soldiers" in full uniform. Once home to a garrison, the fort now exhibits poignant memorabilia, letters, photographs and films showing the harsh icy conditions that the soldiers on both sides fought under during a conflict that saw tens of thousands die.

🚗 *Descend to Val San Cassiano.*

⑩ Val San Cassiano

Alto Adige; 39030

This is a lovely part of the Alta Badia, where footpaths lead through lush pastures from Capanna Alpina into the mountains of the **Fanes-Sennes-Braies Natural Park** – site of many Ladin legends. In this quiet valley, look for chamois, capercailies and eidelweiss. There are also traditional *vila* settlements – wooden homes with a galleried hayloft, built around a central square with a fountain, drinking trough and communal bread oven – a merging of sociable Roman customs with those of the more isolated Rhaetian and Bajuvares peoples centuries ago.

🚗 *Continue to La Villa (Stern). Turn left for Corvara.*

Ladin country

The third language in this region, after Italian and German, is Ladin – a combination of Latin, Celtic and Rhaetian. During the Roman Empire, Ladin territory ran from Switzerland to the Adriatic sea, but a Germanic culture from Bavaria took precedence around AD 400. There are about 30,000 Ladin speakers in the Dolomites today and the language is taught in schools and used in public administration. There are TV and radio programmes in Ladin, as well as the newspaper *Usc di Ladins.*

⑪ Corvara

Alto Adige; 39033

In 1930, mountain guide Franz Kostner saw the potential of Corvara as a ski resort and built Italy's large lift to Col Alt (1,980 m/6,496 ft). He then set up the first ski school and made the valley accessible to cars. The town is still unspoilt and is the centre of the Ladin-speaking area. A trip up Col Alt is worth it for the restaurant and views at the top.

🚗 *From Corvara, follow signs for the Passo Gardena (Grödner Joch). Park at the bar/restaurant at the top.*

⑫ Passo Gardena (Grödner Joch)

Alto Adige; 39033

A quieter pass than Pordoi, this route has outstanding views of moorland and mountain, with a café at the top at 2,121 m (6,959 ft). The descent leads into the **Val Gardena (Grödnertal)** and the villages of Selva (Wolkenstein), Santa Cristina (Sankt Christina) and Ortisei (Sankt Ulrich), which throng with skiers in winter but are relatively peaceful in summer.

🚗 *Descend on SS243 and turn right onto SS242. At Ortisei (St. Ulrich), turn left for Castelrotto (Kastelruth). Go straight on to Siusi (Seis). Park at the cable car for a walk or drive past Fié allo Sciliar (Völs am Schlern), then turn left to Prösels.*

⑬ Alpe di Siusi (Seiser Alm)

Alto Adige; 39040

The route runs below the Alpe di Siusi plateau at 2,000 m (6,560 ft) *(closed to traffic 9am–5pm, unless staying in a hotel on the mountain)*. The road is flanked by hay meadows, while above looms Sciliar (Schlern) mountain, symbol of the Dolomites, topped by two peaks. In early summer, the wild flowers are stunning – take the cable car from Siusi (Seis) to the pastures around Compaccio (Compatsch) to see them. From Siusi, continue past the onion-domed St Konstantin church to Fiè allo Sciliar. Carry on to forbidding **Castel (Schloss) Prösels** *(Apr–Oct: guided tours hourly 11am–4pm Mon–Sat; Jul & Aug: 10am–5pm)*, built around 1500 by the Lords of Völs – witch hunters, friends of Emperor Maximilian and owners of salt mines near Innsbruck.

Above The pretty ski resort of Corvara, a good base for a trip up Col Alt

EAT AND DRINK

VAL SAN CASSIANO

Rifugio Scotoni *expensive*
Walk to this popular mountain hut for its wood-fire cooked mixed grills.
Alpe Lagazuoi 2, 39030 La Villa in Badia (1-hour's hike on Path 20 from Capanna Alpina, off the San Cassiano valley road); 0471 847 330; www.scotoni.it; closed early Apr–mid-Jun & Oct–mid-Dec

St. Hubertus *expensive*
Outstanding restaurant in Rosa Alpina offering Michelin-starred refined cuisine.
Strada Micurà de Rü 20, 39030 San Cassiano; 0471 849 500; closed Tue

CORVARA

Rifugio Col Alt *expensive*
Enjoy dishes such as pasta with venison ragù or oysters and Champagne.
0471 836 324; www.rifugiocolalt.it; closed Apr–mid-Jun & mid-Sep–mid-Dec

AROUND PASSO GARDENA

Stüa Catores *moderate*
Try the deer ravioli with bilberry butter.
Via Sacunstr. 49, 39046 Ortisei; 0471 796 682; www.stuacatores.com; closed Tue

DAY TRIP OPTIONS

To break up the tour into day trips, use Bolzano as a base. Families will enjoy a look into the area's past. Adults will enjoy the wine tour – but may want to do it in a tour group minibus – contact *www.suedtiroler-weinstrasse.it.*

Family time-travel
Visit the Museo Archeologico at Bolzano ① to learn about Ötzi and life in the area in the Copper Age. Pick up a picnic in Bolzano, then drive to Geoparc Bletterbach ④ to search for dinosaur fossils. Enjoy lunch, then set off to Castel Roncolo ② for a classic castle with lively frescoes.

From Bolzano, take SS12 south to Ora, pick up SS48 east, turning off left to Aldino then Bletterbach. Return the same way, passing through Bolzano, then taking SS508 north.

Wine tour
From Bolzano ①, drive the Strada del Vino ③ to Caldaro to visit its wine centres and plan which wineries to visit. Head to Tramin, then Cortaccia, Magre, Egna and Ora. Enjoy tastings and lunching at a winery restaurant.

Follow the drive's directions for the Strada del Vino, but stay on the SS12 at Ora, returning back to Bolzano.

Eat and Drink: inexpensive, under €25; moderate, €25–€45; expensive, over €45

Mountains and Lakes
Laghi di Fusine to Trieste

Highlights

- **Stunning scenery**
  Visit the national parks and pretty mountain villages in the Alpi Giulie

- **Cultural capital**
  Wander past the palazzos and loggias of Udine, the historic capital of Friuli

- **Borderland vineyards**
  Explore the low-lying hills, dotted with vineyards, farms and country inns, close to Slovenia

- **Roman remains**
  Admire the remains of the Roman town of Friuli, now the most important archaeological site in northern Italy

- **Imperial grandeur**
  See the ruins left in Trieste by the Romans, and the grand palazzos and coffee houses left by the Habsburgs

The magnificient 14th-century Castello Duino, on the road to Trieste

Mountains and Lakes

Bordering Austria and Slovenia, Friuli-Venezia Giulia has a rich and complex history, reflected in its patchwork of languages and ethnic groups. The northern area around Tarviso – part of the Austro-Hungarian Empire till World War I – boasts stunning Alpine scenery, complete with braided rivers, pristine lakes and the high peaks of the Alpi Giulie. Towards the south, these mountains give way to the fertile hills and plains of Friuli. Dotted with castles, this land, home to wine making and ham-curing, has the charming city of Udine as its capital. To the east, near the Slovenian border, are two of Italy's most important fine-wine regions: Colli Orientali and the Collio. Closer to Gorizia, the stark, dramatic uplands of the karst plateau drop down to the Adriatic and the Neo-Classical city of Trieste.

Above Remains of the colonnaded Roman forum in front of the medieval Castello di San Giusto, Trieste, *see p113*

ACTIVITIES

Walk the loop of the Laghi di Fusine

Hear the call of the wild with some dog-sledding in Tarvisio

Cross-country ski or snow shoe in winter – or walk in summer – in the pristine countryside around Valbruna

Ascend to the spiritual heights of Monte Lussari by cable car

Scare yourself with the mummies in the Duomo, Venzone

Wander through the charming small town of Cividale del Friuli, with its 8th-century Tempietto Longobardo

Take a walk in the footsteps of Austrian poet Rainer Maria Rilke, along the cliffs at Duino

Spend a day exploring in Trieste's "museum quarter"

KEY

Drive route

Above Early autumn colours of the lakeside woodlands around the Laghi di Fusine, *see p108*

PLAN YOUR DRIVE

Start/finish: Laghi di Fusine to Trieste.

Number of days: 5 days, including half a day for Udine; 1 day for touring the wine regions and a day in Trieste.

Distance: 270 km (168 miles).

Road conditions: The road to the Laghi di Fusine is easy to drive as most of the Alpine routes are wide. Signage is good but scarce around Gorizia and on small vineyard roads. Snow chains are obligatory in winter.

When to go: The Alpi Giulie's autumn hues are glorious, while winter offers endless opportunities for skiing. Udine and the wine regions are best visited Apr–Nov. Maritime Trieste can be mild – but also windy – at any time of the year.

Opening times: Shops tend to open 9am–1pm and 4–7:30pm Mon–Sat (food shops are shut Mon and Wed afternoon, all other shops are shut Mon morning). Church and museum times vary, but are usually 9am–noon and 4–7 or 8pm. Many museums are closed on Monday.

Main market days: Tarvisio: daily; Udine: Via Zanon, daily; Via Redipuglia, Sat; **Cividale del Friuli:** Sat; **Cormòns:** Fri; **Trieste:** Wed.

Shopping: Look out for salt-cured, air-dried hams and salami throughout the region, and grappa and wines from the Collio and Colli Orientali.

Major festivals: Tarvisio: Krampus (St Nicholas Eve), Dec; **Udine:** Friuli DOC food and wine, Sep–Oct; **Cividale:** Palio di San Donato (medieval festival), late Aug; **Trieste:** Barcolana regatta, Oct; **Palio di Trieste:** Carnevale, late Jan–mid-Feb across Friuli.

DAY TRIP OPTIONS

From Tarvisio, take **cable cars** to hilltop **churches** and **walk** in the mountains. Explore ancient **castles** and **towns** rebuilt after earthquakes. See the **Roman ruins** in Aquiléia. Drive around the **vineyards** of the Collio, before visiting **lively** and **cultured** Trieste. For full details, *see p113*.

Above The picturesque hamlet of Valbruna, in the shadow of the Alpi Giulie

GETTING TO LAGHI DI FUSINE

From Tarvisio, take the SS54 east through Fusine in Valromana and then the small Via dei Laghi on the right about 3.5 km (2 miles) to the two lakes.

WHERE TO STAY

TARVISIO

Edelhof *moderate*
At the edge of a forest, this grand residence has 17 rooms and a restaurant. *Via Diaz 13, 33018; 0428 400 81; www.hoteledelhof.it*

VALBRUNA

Valbruna Inn *moderate*
This cosy village inn has rooms that look from flower-decked balconies on to the Alpi Giulie. *Via Alpi Giulie 2, 33010; 0428 660 554; www.valbrunainn.com*

MALBORGHETTO

Casa Oberrichter *inexpensive–moderate*
A hotel housed in a wood-beamed 15th-century palace with a restaurant. *Via Superiore 4, 33010; 0428 41888; www.casaoberrichter.com*

AROUND UDINE

La Faula *inexpensive–moderate*
This working farm, set in idyllic countryside, offers nine characterful rooms. *Via Faula 5, Ravosa di Povoletto, 33040 Udine (A23 exit Udine Nord in direction of Tarvisio). From SS13 Pontebbana drive towards Povoletto-Cividale. At roundabout, turn right to Povoletto); 333 171 9514; www.faula.com; closed Oct–Feb*

① Laghi di Fusine
Udine, Friuli-Venezia Giulia; 33018
The two lakes of Fusine, the Lago Inferiore and the Lago Superiore, occupy a glacial basin set amid dense forests of red fir trees, framed by curving hills and a crown of Alpine summits. The colours of the mirror-like surfaces of the lakes vary, as the seasons and light change. And in autumn, the forests are ablaze with intense hues. Walk a circuit of the lakes on the Sentiero del Rio del Lago.

🚗 *Head on to the SS54, and follow the sign to Tarvisio. Parking in Tarvisio can be tricky as it gets extremely busy – use on-street parking, which is best at the northern end of town.*

② Tarvisio
Udine, Friuli-Venezia Giulia; 33018
In the far northeast of Friuli-Venezia Giulia, where Italy, Slovenia and Austria meet, Tarvisio flies the flags of the three border communities. Nestled in an amphitheatre of valleys and peaks, the town is charming and very Alpine-oriented – the local hero is Julius Kugy, who climbed the Alpi Giulie (Julian Alps) in the early 1900s. Ski outlets, hotels and smart food shops line the main street.

Alpine sports such as skiing, snow-boarding, dog-sledding and walking are the main attractions, so visit the Tourist Office *(Via Roma 14, 33018; 0428 2135; www.tarvisiano.org)* for information on these and other outdoor activities, including a programme of guided walks. Enjoy the village ambience and the daily market in Piazza Mercato.

🚗 *Take the SS13 in the direction of Udine, and turn left onto Via Saisera and follow signs for Valbruna.*

③ Valbruna
Udine, Friuli-Venezia Giulia; 33010
This delightful Alpine hamlet in the Val Canale opens on to a beautiful world of mountain meadows and forests – habitats for roe deer and a myriad of birds. Throughout the year, Valbruna is the place for nature lovers. A network of walking trails leads into the valley, to mountain peaks and to the **Santuario Monte Lussari**, located at an altitude of 1,790 m (5,872 ft) *(open daily Jun–early Oct)*. The walk to the sanctuary takes about 3 hours; or you can take the cable car from neighbouring Camporosso. In winter, the plains of Valbruna transform into a fabulous cross-country ski domain right alongside the village, with a huge network of trails extending through the upper Val Saisera.

🚗 *Return to the SS13, following directions to Udine, then turn right to reach Malborghetto.*

④ Malborghetto
Udine, Friuli-Venezia Giulia; 33010
The main street of Malborghetto is tucked along the edge of a valley that is skirted on both sides by a ridge of mountain peaks. A sign points out the village's two main historic sights – the 13th-century **Santa Maria della Visitazione** *(open daily)* on the town hall square near the Municipio or town hall and, down the street, the dashing

Below Hotels with geranium-festooned balconies near the centre of Alpine Tarvisio

Above Fresco from the Duomo di Sant'Andrea Apostolo, Venzone

17th-century **Palazzo Veneziano**, which houses the **Museo Etnografico** *(closed Mon)*, an ethnographic museum with displays on geology, prehistory, ethnology and forestry.

🚗 *Return to the SS13, following directions to Udine. Turn off to Venzone. Park outside the walls or near Piazza Municipio.*

⑤ Venzone

Udine, Friuli-Venezia Giulia; 33010
The medieval town of Venzone prospered due to its position on an old trading route linking the Veneto to Carinthia (Austria), Kranjska Gora (Slovenia) and Bavaria. In 1976, an earthquake killed 3,000 people and destroyed most of the town's buildings. However, the citizens rallied and rebuilt them with meticulous care, skilfully renovating many medieval treasues – the town is now a historic monument.

Admire the walls, tower and old gate, the **Porta San Genesio**, as well as the loggia on **Piazza Municipio**, whose excellent museum has pictures and displays of Venzone before and after the earthquake. The 14th-century **Duomo di Sant'Andrea Apostolo** *(open daily)* is a noteworthy Romanesque-Gothic edifice whose interior is adorned with frescoes. Also of interest is the Duomo's chapel, **Cappella di San Michele**, which contains mummified corpses. On the other side of the SS13, visit Bordano and its delightful **butterfly house** *(Mar–Oct: open daily)*, home to more than 400 species of butterfly.

🚗 *Continue south on SS13 to Udine.*

⑥ Udine

Friuli-Venezia Giulia; 33100
Midway between the mountains and sea, Udine is a small powerhouse of art, architecture and gastronomy. Start out from **Piazza della Libertà**, referred to the most beautiful Venetian square on dry land – the city was conquered by Venice in 1420 – ringed by fine 15th–17th-century buildings whose façades are an elaborate lacework of arches and porticoes. Among these are the Venetian-Gothic **Loggia del Lionello** and the Renaissance **Loggia di San Giovanni**. The **Torre dell'Orologio** (clock tower), where the main castle gate once stood, is part of another portico. From here, take the path to the old castle, whose **Civici Musei di Udine** *(closed Mon)* houses valuable frescoes in the Galleria d'Arte Antica.

Piazza Matteotti, with its 1543 fountain, is the heart of the city's elegant café and shopping zone – reached by the old market street, Via Mercatovecchio. Lastly, pass in front of the Palazzo del Comune and head to the Piazza del Duomo to see the Latin cross-shaped **cathedral** *(open daily)*, whose foundations date to 1335. Masterful 18th-century frescoes by Tiepolo can be seen in the **Museo Diocesano** *(closed Tue)*, housed in the Palazzo Arcivescovile (Archbishop's Palace).

🚗 *Take the SS54 northeast following signs for Cividale del Friuli.*

Below Statue of Heracles in the beautiful Piazza della Libertà, Udine **Below right** The decorated window of a lavender shop in Venzone

EAT AND DRINK

TARVISIO

Tschurwald *moderate*
An interesting mix of Austrian and Italian food is on the menu here: home-made pasta, polenta with local cheese sauce and game dishes in season.
Via Roma 8, 33018; 0428 405 34; closed Thu

MALBORGHETTO

Antica Trattoria Da Giusi *moderate*
Savour cooking that reveals the strong culinary link between Alpine Italy and Austria – soups, air-dried meats, smoked pork with sauerkraut and desserts.
Via Bamberga 19, 33010; 0428 60014; www.dagiusi.it; closed Tue

VENZONE

Locanda al Municipio
moderate–expensive
This restaurant in the heart of Venzone if famous for its fish-based dishes and seasonal homemade pasta.
Via Glizoio di Mels, 33010; 0432 985801; www.locandaalmunicipio. com; closed Mon

AROUND VENZONE

Hotel Ristorante Carnia *expensive*
This highly feted restaurant is bright and contemporary, with a menu based on seafood and classic Friulian dishes.
Via Canal del Ferro 28, Loc. Carnia, 33010 (6 km/4 miles north of Venzone on SS13); 0432 978 013; www.hotelcarnia.it

UDINE

La Ciacarade *moderate*
This wood-beamed restaurant has a handful of tables plus a long bar. Enjoy smoked trout, cheese fritters with onion and *prosciutto cotto d'oca all'arancio* – orange-flavoured goose prosciutto.
Via S Francesco 6/A, 33100; 0432 510 250; closed Sun & Tue dinner

Eat and Drink: inexpensive, under €25; moderate, €25–€45; expensive, over €45

Above left River Natisone, Cividale del Friuli
Top right Statues in the Tempietto Longobardo,
Cividale del Friuli Right Piazza Paolo Diacono,
site of the daily market in Cividale del Friuli

WHERE TO STAY

CIVIDALE DEL FRIULI

B&B Dai Toscans *inexpensive*
This central B&B has a stylish interior
and serves up a delicious breakfast.
*Corso Giuseppe Mazzini 15/1, 33043;
0349 076 5288; www.daitoscans.it*

Locanda al Pomo d'Oro *inexpensive*
Located in the centre of town, this
modest hotel still serves its original
purpose of providing travellers with
shelter, tasty food and good wine.
*Piazzetta San Giovanni 20, 33043;
0432 731 489; www.alpomodoro.com*

Locanda al Castello *moderate*
A 20-minute walk from the centre, this
family-run inn offers old-fashioned
charm with the amenities and
services of a luxury hotel.
*Via del Castello 12, 33043;
0432 733 242; www.alcastello.net*

CORMÒNS

Agriturismo Domus Rustica
inexpensive
Set in bucolic vineyards just 2 km
(1 mile) outside Cormòns.
*Via Sottomonte 75, Brazzano 34071;
0481 60288; www.domus-rustica.it*

Albergo Ristorante Felcaro
moderate
A fine, antique-filled villa with a
sauna, pool and tennis courts.
*Via S Giovanni 45, 34071;
0481 60214; www.hotelfelcaro.it*

Where to Stay: inexpensive, under €100; moderate, €100–200; expensive, over €200

7 Cividale del Friuli
Udine, Friuli-Venezia Giulia; 33043
Set on the banks of the River
Natisone, Friuli traces its name
and origin to a Roman fortification
that was built here in 53 BC and
christened Forum Julii by Julius
Caesar. In AD 568, it became the
capital of the feudal Duchy of
Lombard and later, like much of this
region, fell under the dominion of
the mighty Venetian Republic. The
town contains treasures from all of
these epochs concentrated around
its historic centre and the eclectic
15th–17th-century cathedral, **Santa
Maria Assunta**, in the Piazza del
Duomo. Take the cobbled lane
through the oldest section of town,
past 14th-century houses, to the
8th-century frescoes and reliefs at
the **Tempietto Longobardo**. From the
chapel, there are wonderful views of
the Ponte del Diavolo and the
aquamarine River Natisone. Nearby,
the 16th-century Palazzo dei
Provveditori Veneti attributed to the
master architect Andrea Palladio
houses the **Museo Archeologico
Nazionale** *(open daily)*. From the
museum, take the main street, Corso
Mazzini, up to the Piazza Paolo
Diacono with its pretty fountain and a
myriad architectural styles.
🚗 *Take the SR356 south, follow the
signposts for Prepotto, travelling on
SP352 and SR48.*

8 Colli Orientali
Friuli-Venezia Giulia
It is worth taking some time to explore
this lovely, hilly vineyard area between
Cividale del Friuli and Cormòns. Several
indigenous grape varieties – rarely
found elsewhere – are grown here.
Look out for the perfumed red
Schioppettino and delicately sweet
Picolit, which can yield a dessert wine
of great finesse. At Prepotto, there
are two vineyards that offer a taste
of these exceptional wines – **Vigna
Petrussa** *(Via Albana 47, 33040,
Prepotto; 043 271 3021; www.
vignapetrussa.it)* and **Le Due Terre** *(Via
Roma 68/B, 33040, Prepotto; 043 271
3189; www.schioppettinodiprepotto.it)*.
🚗 *Continue on the small wine road
via Dolegna del Collio, Venco and
Brazzano to reach Cormòns.*

9 Cormòns
Gorizia, Friuli-Venezia Giulia; 34071
Cormòns was part of the Habsburg
Empire from 1497 to 1918, and its
architecture and statue of Maximilian
I in Piazza della Libertà are testimony
to its historical inheritance. The town
still toasts the Austrian Emperor
Franz Joseph (1830–1916) on his
birthday (Aug 18). The ruins of the
Castello di Cormòns can be seen on
the slopes of nearby Monte Quarin.
  Today this small town, surrounded
by vineyards, is the capital of the Collio
wine business. The **Franco Toros** *(Loc.
Novali 12, 34072; 048 1613 27; www.
vinitoros.com)* is a must-visit for wine
lovers. Cormòn's long main street, lined
with palaces and noble residences,
loops around from the Piazza XXIV
Maggio, home to the **Palazzo Locatelli**.
This Palladian-style edifice houses an
enoteca (wine shop), which showcases
and serves local produce and wines.
Maps of wine routes are available here.
🚗 *Take Via Roma/SR409, turn right
towards San Floriano in Localitá Zegla.*

10 Collio: Strada del Vino
Gorizia, Friuli-Venezia Giulia; 34170
Collio is the colloquial name given to
the sloping Isonzo hills to the north
of Gorizia. Wedged between Cormòns
and the Slovenian border, this narrow
strip of land is a pleasant patchwork of
vineyards, orchards and, more recently,
olive groves. Follow the network of
tiny roads forming the signposted

Strada del Vino e delle Ciliegie (Wine and Cherry Route). Between the mountains and sea, the microclimate and "ponka" soils (marl, clay-limestone) help create many celebrated DOC white wines – Pinot Grigio, Friulano, Ribolla Gialla and Malvasia Istriana. Maps, available by the roadside on the way out of town and in tourist brochures, mark out the wineries with tasting rooms. Pay close attention to the maps and signposts, as a wrong turn could lead to Slovenia.

Follow signs to Russiz – where the vineyards are spread across the hillsides. The splendid estate of **Villa Russiz** *(Via Russiz 4–6, 34070, Capriva del Friuli; 0481 800 47; open Mon–Fri)*, founded in 1869 by French Count Theodore de la Tour, was one of the first wineries in Friuli to use French vine varieties. The villa has tasting rooms, a park, a chapel and a small mausoleum whose tiled cupola perches above rows of vines. The count's wife had the mausoleum built for him in 1894.

From Russiz, continue towards Capriva del Friuli, stopping at **Castello di Spessa** *(open daily)*. This medieval castle was altered in the 1880s and is now the centrepiece of

a huge complex containing a winery, a golf course and a hotel.

🚗 *From Zegla, turn right towards Capriva del Friuli, cross Capriva's centre turn right and after the railway station turn left onto SR56 to Gorizia.*

⓫ Gorizia
Friuli-Venezia Giulia; 34170
The 11th-century **Castello di Gorizia** *(closed Mon)* hilltop district is an enclave of medieval architecture: the castle has glorious views. The nearby quarter of Santo Spirito is home to the Gothic **Chiesa di Santo Spirito** and the **Musei Provinciali** *(closed Mon)*, which houses displays on World War I and regional history. In the mesh of medieval, Baroque and 19th-century architecture in the town below, there are walkways along the River Isonzo and fine villas such as the **Palazzo Coronini-Cronberg** *(closed Mon & Tue; Nov–Mar)*, which is set in magnificent parklands.

🚗 *Take the SS351 to Gradisca d'Isonzo and continue to Cervignano del Friuli. From here, take the SS352 to Aquileia.*

Top Hillside vineyards along the wooded Strada del Vino **Below left** Townhouses on the curving main street of Cormòns **Below right** The 11th-century Castello di Gorizia

EAT AND DRINK

CIVIDALE DEL FRIULI
Al Monastero *moderate*
Set in an old monastery, this eatery offers classic Friulian dishes, including top quality hams and salamis and a good choice of home-made pasta and meat dishes. Desserts include *strucchi* (fruit- and nut-filled pastries).
Via Ristori 9, 33043; 043 270 0808; www.almonastero.com; closed Sun eve & Mon

Antica Osteria La Speranza *expensive*
This historic bar and *osteria* serves traditional fish dishes with a modern twist. The blackboard menu is complemented by a good wine list.
Foro Giulio Cesare 15, 33043; 043 273 1131; closed Mon

AROUND COLLI ORIENTALLE
Al Cjant dal Rusignul *expensive*
This attractive country restaurant is renowned for its home-made pasta, mushroom and game. Good wine list.
Via Mernico, 8 34070 Mernico-Dolegna del Collio (just east of Prepotto); 048 160 452; www.ferrucciosgubin.it; closed Mon–Wed

CORMÒNS
Trattoria Al Cacciatore *expensive*
A local landmark, this upmarket restaurant prepares traditional dishes with great finesse using the best local ingredients. *Località Monte 22, 34701; 048 160 531; www.lasubida.it; closed Tue & Wed*

AROUND CORMÒNS
Terra e Vini *moderate*
This beautifully renovated *osteria* has an interesting menu with cold meats, pasta and *frico* (fried cheese delicacy). *Via XXIV Maggio 34, 34071 Brazzano di Cormòns; 048 160 028; www.terraevini. it; closed Sun eve & Mon, 3 wks Jan*

Eat and Drink: inexpensive, under €25; moderate, €25–€45; expensive, over €45

VISITING TRIESTE

Parking
Narrow streets and a one-way system make driving in Trieste difficult. There are few car parks, although many hotels have undercover parking (at extra cost). Park in the car park on Riva Nazario Sauro or on-street in the residential area between the historic centre and the cathedral/castello. Check that it is not a tow-away zone. There is a big paid parking area in Molo IV and one near the station.

Tourist information
Via dell'Orologio 1, angolo Piazza dell'Unità; 040 347 8312; www. turismofvg.it

WHERE TO STAY

TRIESTE

Hotel Albero Nascosto *moderate*
This small, charming hotel is part of a project for the restoration of the historic centre of Trieste. It has been beautifully renovated using the best quality materials and craftsmen.
Via Felice Venezian 18, 34124; 040 300 188; www.alberonascosto.it

Hotel Miramare *moderate*
Near the Castello di Miramare, this grey slate, metal and glass hotel is modernist and minimalist. Rooms have sea-facing terraces and high-tech facilities. There is also a beach bar and restaurant.
Viale Miramare 325/1, 34136; 040 224 7085; www.hotelmiramaretrieste.it; closed mid-Nov–mid-Mar

⑫ Aquileia
Friuli-Venezia Giulia; 33051
Founded as a Roman colony in 181 BC, Aquileia was the Roman capital of Friuli and is now northern Italy's most important archaeological site. The attractive ruins include Roman houses, a forum and an impressive ruined harbour. What was once a great town with a population of 200,000 is now home to a mere 3,500 people who live by tending their vineyards or catering to the tourists who come to marvel at the mosaics. The best of these are in the **basilica**, whose extraordinary floor mosaic of 700 sq m (837 sq yards) is the largest early Christian mosaic in the West. Take a circular walk on the Via Sacra to visit the excavations and the **Museo Archeologico Nazionale** *(www. museoarcheologicoaquileia.beni culturali.it)*, a treasure trove of Roman artifacts, bas-reliefs and sculpture.

🚗 *Take the SS352 south to Grado, then the SP19 towards Monfalcone. In Monfalcone, take the SS14 to Duino.*

⑬ Duino
Trieste, Friuli-Venezia Giulia; 34100
The star attraction here is the **Castello di Duino** *(www.castellodiduino.it; closed Tue)*, which has played host to many illustrious guests in its time, notably the Austrian poet Rainer Maria Rilke (1875–1926). Do not miss the glorious gardens and the bunker constructed in 1943. To complete the visit, take the panoramic 2-km (1-mile) long Rilke walk along the clifftops.

🚗 *Take the coastal SS14 to Trieste.*

⑭ Trieste
Trieste, Friuli-Venezia Giulia; 34100

Once the third city of the Austrian Habsburg Empire, after Vienna and Prague, Trieste is now a cluster of Roman, eclectic-style, Art Nouveau and Neo-Gothic architecture. From the bay and waterfront promenades to the top of San Giusto hill, Trieste retains an international atmosphere among the salty breezes washing in from the Adriatic.

A two-hour walking tour
From the car park, head up Riva 3 Novembre towards **Piazza dell'Unità dell'Italia** ①. The grand sweep of façades includes the 1870 Palazzo Comunale, Palazzo del Governo, Palazzo del Lloyd Triestino – the shipping company's headquarters – and Casa Stratti, home to Caffè degli Specchi, an 1839 coffee house.

Visit the Tourist Information Office for maps, before heading northeast, through the small Piazza Verdi to the bottom of Corso Italia, the main road referred to locally as "Corso". Cross over and take the small Via Cassa di Risparmio to Via G Mazzini. Turn left and rejoin the waterfront avenue Riva 3 Novembre: on the corner is the Neo-Classical **Chiesa Greco-Ortodossa di San Nicolò** ②. Continue along to the picturesque warehouse-lined strip of the **Canal Grande** ③: dug in 1756 to allow ships to unload inside the city. The canalside **Via Rossini** ④ is lined with restaurants, bars and markets, leading to Piazza Ponterosso. James Joyce's statue adorns the bridge. The Irish writer lived in Trieste for over a decade. Cross the bridge to the Piazza Ponterosso and head for the church, the **Chiesa di San Spiridione** ⑤, a Neo-Byzantine Serbian Orthodox church. Take Via Dante Alighieri back to the Corso Italia, and cross over to the gaping pit of the **Teatro Romano** ⑥, a Roman amphitheatre built by Emperor Augustus around 30 BC.

The steps alongside the Teatro lead to the **Tor Cucherna** ⑦, the ruins of a medieval tower, with fantastic views from the street above. From here, take the Treppe Giuseppe Rota stairway for the final climb up to the hilltop of San Giusto. Named after one of the city's patron saints, this area has Roman relics, medieval churches, public gardens and viewpoints. The piazza around the **Monumento ai Caduti** ⑧, a World War I memorial, is a popular romantic spot with terrific views. Carry on through the colonnaded **Foro Romano** ⑨ and on to the 14th–16th-century **Castello di San**

Giusto ⑩ *(open daily)*. Across Piazza delle Cattedrale stands the Gothic stone lacework and trilobite arches of the **Cattedrale di San Giusto** ⑪, a fusion of two 15th-century churches – hence its asymmetrical façade. Look to the right of the rose window for two huge cannon balls wedged into the wall. Head downhill on Via della Cattedrale into suitably windy Via della Bora (Northeast Wind Street) and on to the **Arco di Riccardo** ⑫, a crumbling Roman gateway from the 1st century BC. Turn right and trace the walls of the Chiesa Santa Maria Maggiore perched on a ledge over the old town – alongside the small **Chiesa di San Silvestro** ⑬. A wide stairway leads down to the Via del Teatro Romano. Cross the street and head back to Piazza dell'Unità past the pretty square of Piazza Piccola. Museum lovers may wish to see the unofficial museum quarter – near Piazza Hortis – with three museums: the Civico Museo di Storia ed Arte e Orto Lapidario (archaeology), the Civico Museo di Storia Naturale (natural history) and the Civico Museo Sartorio (art and culture) *(all closed Mon)*. Return to the car park via Via F Venezian.

Far left The clifftop Castello di Duino **Centre** The 18th-century Canal Grande in Trieste **Right** Caffè degli Specchi, founded in 1839, in Trieste's Piazza dell'Unità dell'Italia

EAT AND DRINK

AQUILEIA

La Capannina *moderate*
Overlooking the ancient harbor of Aquileia, serving a variety of fish dishes
Via Gemina 10, Aquileia, 33051; 0431 91019; www.ristorantelacapannina. net; closed Wed in winter

DUINO

Sardoc *moderate*
Robust cuisine such as *jota* (a thick cabbage, beans and potato soup), followed by veal shanks and strudel.
Loc. Slivia 5, 34013 Duino-Aurisina; 040 200 146; www.sardoc.eu; closed Mon–Wed

TRIESTE

Osteria da Marino *moderate*
This tavern serves Mediterranean staples such as mozzarella with tomatoes and Ligurian olives in a jovial ambience.
Via del Ponte 5/A, 34100; 040 366 596; www.osteriadamarino.com; closed Sat & Sun lunch

Pepenero Pepebianco Ristorante *expensive*
This restaurant is modernist in food and atmosphere, serving innovative dishes.
Via Rittmeyer 14/a, 34134; 040 760 0716; www.pepeneropepebianco.it; closed Sun

---

<table>
<tr><td>

DAY TRIP OPTIONS
The incredibly varied landscape gives a choice of three enjoyable day trip.

Alpine village tour
From Tarvisio ②, walk a loop of the Laghi di Fusine ①, then on to Valbruna ③, stopping to take the cable car from Camporosso to Monte Lussari, and finish in Malborghetto ④.

Take SS54 east to reach the lakes, then SS13 west to the other alpine villages.

</td><td>

Archaeological sites
See the beautiful piazza and frescoes of Udine ⑥, then drive to Aquileia ⑫ to see its fantastic Roman remains and enjoy lunch. Finish the day at the architectural jewel of Trieste ⑭.

Take SS352 from Udine to Aquiléia. Continue on SS352, left on to SS14 all the way along the coast to Trieste.

</td><td>

Vineyards to the coast
From Gorizia ⑪, visit Russiz and Collio ⑩ winding through vineyards and stopping for a tasting on the way to Cormòns ⑨. Then its off to Trieste ⑭ and the coast for an afternoon walk around the city and perhaps an evening's entertainment.

Roads in the wine area are narrow and winding: use the SS55, then the A4 (E70) to Trieste to save a little time.

</td></tr>
</table>

Eat and Drink: inexpensive, under €25; moderate, €25–€45; expensive, over €45

The Veneto Plain

Verona to Venice

Highlights

- **Romantic Renaissance city**
  Soak up the atmosphere in beautiful Verona, the setting for Shakespeare's tale of hapless love, *Romeo and Juliet*

- **A Baroque garden masterpiece**
  Wander around Valsanzibio's strictly ordered hedges, lawns and paths, virtually unchanged since the 1670s and set in idyllic countryside

- **An ancient city, full of young life**
  Visit Padua's Basilica di Sant'Antonio, the university where Galileo taught and a medieval marketplace – all infused with the buzz of student life

- **Timeless city of bridges**
  Explore magical, waterborne Venice, where the grand palaces, churches, museums and squares are joined by a labyrinth of alleyways and canals

Basilica di Santa Giustina, Padua, seen across
Prato della Valle

The Veneto Plain

The great Veneto plain is dotted with some of Italy's most magnificent cities and impressive fortified medieval towns, filled with priceless artworks and architecture. These cultural treasures are further enhanced by their exquisite natural setting among the rolling Euganean Hills, the lush Riviera del Brenta and the Venetian Lagoon. Meandering roads lead to rustic-style restaurants, and spa resorts that have been popular since Roman times. Padua's world-class art and serene churches and gardens bustle with youthful excitement, thanks to its student population. The winding Riviera del Brenta is a natural and architectural delight, famous for its Palladian villas – country homes for the Venetian nobility. The drive's conclusion is magical Venice, its Grand Canal lined with palaces. Although it's busy with visitors year round, it is simply unmissable.

KEY

═══ Drive route

ACTIVITIES

Experience the thrill of live opera in Verona in the wonderful Roman arena (*www.arena.it*)

Ramble or ride on the pathways and cycle tracks in the lovely Euganean Hills

Find peace and spiritual calm on an overnight stay at the Abbazia di Praglia

Take a leisurely boat trip on the Riviera del Brenta and admire its architectural wonders (*www.ilburchiello.it*)

Go island hopping in Venice's lagoon

Left Cyclists negotiating the winding streets of Arquà Petrarca, *see p119*

Above Driving through the Euganean Hills, *see p118*

0 kilometres 10

0 miles 10

Below View across Prato della Valle in Padua, *see p119*

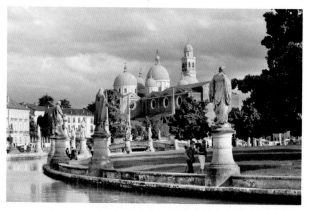

PLAN YOUR DRIVE

Start/finish: Verona to Venice.

Number of days: 4, allowing a full day for the Euganean Hills, half days for the smaller towns and a full day for Venice.

Distance: Approx 153 km (95 miles).

Road conditions: A mix of hilly and flat roads makes for easy-to-medium drives.

When to go: Visits are feasible year round, though spring (Mar–May) and autumn (Sep–Oct) are best for more pleasant temperatures. The foothills and plain can get hot during Jul–Aug, while fog is not uncommon in winter.

Opening times: Shops tend to open 9am–1pm and 3–7pm Mon–Sat. Villa opening hours differ; some are closed on Mondays and the gardens usually close early in winter.

Main market days: Montagnana: Thu; **Este:** Sat; **Padua:** Mon–Sat; **Venice:** Mon–Sat.

Shopping: Look out for ceramics in Este, local delicacies (wine, honey, jujube or *giuggiole*) in the Euganean Hills and handicrafts (glass, paper, jewellery) in Venice.

Major festivals: Verona: opera season Jun–Aug (*www.arena.it*); **Montagnana:** antiques market, every 3rd Sun Oct–May; Palio dei 10 Comuni (medieval horse race and pageantry festival), Aug–Sep (*www.palio10comuni.it*); **Venice:** Carnival, Feb–Mar; Film Festival, Aug–Sep; Regata Storica, 1st Sun in Sep; Biennale Art, Jun–Nov in odd-numbered years (*www.labiennale.org*).

DAY TRIP OPTIONS

Those with an interest in the performing arts will love a day in **Verona** with Juliet's **famous balcony** and an amphitheatre, home to **open-air opera**. Magical **Venice** rewards lovers of art – modern as well as classical – with a wealth of **museums**, **galleries** and **churches** full of priceless works. A foray into the Euganean Hills will delight lovers of **rural landscapes**, **elegant gardens** and **pretty abbeys**. For full details, *see p121*.

Above left The Castello di San Pietro, on a hill above Verona Above centre Giardini Dell' Arena, in the heart of Padua Above right Padua's 13th-century Basilica di Sant'Antonio

VISITING VERONA

Visitor Information
Via degli Alpini 9, 37100; 045 806 8680; www.tourism.verona.it

WHERE TO STAY

VERONA

Hotel Aurora *moderate*
This hotel has a lovely roof terrace overlooking the central square.
Piazzetta XIV Novembre 2, 37121; 045 594 717; www.hotelaurora.biz

Hotel Torcolo *moderate*
This charming, family-run place is in a quiet street, but close to the arena.
Vicolo Listone 3, 37121; 045 800 7512; www.hoteltorcolo.it; closed end Jan–Feb

MONTAGNANA

Hotel Aldo Moro *moderate*
This provides top service and spacious rooms, as well as a delicious breakfast.
Via G Marconi 27, 35044; 0429 81351; www.hotelaldomoro.com; closed 2 wks Jan & 1–20 Aug

ESTE

Agriturismo Barchessa *moderate*
Four self-catering apartments make up this 18th-century villa.
Via Cappuccini 9, 35042; 333 391 4733; www.agriturismobarchessa.com

ARQUÀ PETRARCA

Alloggio Franciscus Agriturismo *inexpensive*
These are country-style rooms in restructured farm buildings.
Via Valleselle 20, 35032; 0429 718 245; www.enotecadaloris.it

PADUA

Albergo Verdi *moderate*
A central hotel with bright rooms.
Via Dondi dell'Orologio 7, 35139; 049 836 4163; www.albergoverdipadova.it

❶ Verona
Veneto; 37100

Top of most visitors' list is the romantic shrine **Juliet's House** (*Casa di Giulietta; 27 Via Cappello*), the so-called home of the tragic heroine of Shakespeare's drama. Close by is the impressive **Roman arena**, where crowds once gathered to watch gladiator action and, today, watch open-air opera. Over the river are the Renaissance **Giardino Giusti** (1580), with its hedges and paths, as well as the **Museo Storia Naturale** (*closed Fri*), with displays of fossilized crocodiles and palm trees. Climb up to **Castello di San Pietro** for glorious views of the city. West of the centre, **San Zeno Maggiore** (1138) is a superb example of Romanesque architecture.

🚗 *Leave on SS11 east (signed Venezia) across river Adige. At San Bonifacio, turn right to SP7 through Arcole, Cologna Veneta and on to Montagnana. Follow signs to "stazione" and car park.*

❷ Montagnana
Veneto; 35044

Before entering the town, wander along the grassy moat to admire the sturdy, red-brick castellated walls and 24 defensive towers erected by the town's rulers between the 14th and 18th centuries. All four massive gateways lead to the main square and 15th-century **Duomo**, which holds works by Renaissance masters Paolo Veronese and Giorgione. Be sure to try the local prosciutto and, perhaps, the *stracotto d'asino* (donkey stew).

🚗 *From the car park, turn right along the walls. Around the corner, turn right at the traffic lights on the SR10 (towards*

Statue at the Casa di Giulietta, Verona

Padua). At a medieval tower on the right, turn left into Via Augustea. At the crossroads, turn right into Via Schiavin to car park No.3 (Castello), in Via Vigo di Torre, just past the Tourist Office.

❸ Este
Veneto; 35042

Once the capital of the pre-Roman Veneti, Este was absorbed into the Roman Empire before being razed to the ground by Attila the Hun. The town rose again under local nobility, the Signori d'Este, who constructed its imposing **castle** (*open daily*). In 1405 it came under the protection of the Venetians. The **Museo Nazionale Atestino** (*closed Mon*) has evidence of this turbulent history. Este also has a tradition of fine porcelain, especially good-quality hand-decorated pieces.

🚗 *Carry on along the walls to a roundabout and take 2nd right onto SP6. Follow signs for Baone, then SP21 into the Euganean Hills.*

❹ Euganean Hills
Veneto

The Colli Euganei is an area of beautiful rolling hills cloaked in woods full of wild boar and deer. The volcanic origins of these hills means fertile soil for crops and vines, and quarries that yielded the trachyte used for paving the streets of Venice. Wildflowers abound and there are special pockets, such as Monte Ceva, where mini prickly pears grow. Rewarding walks abound (for maps of routes – in Italian – visit *www.parcocollieuganei. com*). At the foot of the hills are spa resorts such as Abano and Montegrotto Terme.

Where to Stay: inexpensive, under €100; moderate, €100–€200; expensive, over €200

🚗 *Once in the hills, follow one of many signs to Arquà Petrarca along winding roads. Follow sign for "Arquà Alta: centro storico" up the hill to the car park.*

5 Arquà Petrarca
Veneto; 35032

This utterly charming town – with steepish, paved streets leading past Venetian-Gothic stone palaces – is named after the great medieval Italian poet Petrarch, who spent his final years here. Visit his lovely house, **Casa di Petrarca** *(closed Mon)*, which has his mummified pet cat on display. Shops sell *giuggiole* (the jujube fruit) steeped in liqueur as well as local wines.

🚗 *Head in the direction of Padua on the SP16 and, 2 km (1 mile) on, branch left onto the SP25 for Valsanzibio. Park outside the villa's entrance.*

6 Valsanzibio
Veneto; 35030

Spend an afternoon exploring these exquisite Baroque gardens *(open Mar–Nov; www.valsanzibiogiardino.it)* created in 1669 for the Venetian noble Zuane Francesco Barbarigo on shady terraces that appear to grow out of the hillside. Fountain after fountain is draped with Classical allegorical statues, and water games amuse young and old alike, as does a maze of box shrubs. The house, **Villa Barbarigo**, is of a simple design compared to the gardens.

🚗 *Continue north on SP25 to Galzignano Terme. Turn left to a T-junction and left again on SP99, then right for the winding ascent of Monte Venda, the highest Euganean Hill. Then carry on the descent into Torreglia, head left (towards Padua), turn left to Tealo, and follow signs for Praglia.*

7 Abbazia di Praglia
Teolo, Veneto; 35037

This pretty Benedictine **abbey** *(closed Mon; www.praglia.it)*, set in gorgeous countryside, was founded in the 11th century and renovated in the 15th and 16th centuries. A monk-led tour reveals how the brothers restore ancient books and grow herbal products for sale along with cosmetics and honey. It is possible to stay here overnight.

🚗 *Drive north to SP89, turn right to join SS250. Through Tencarola, head into Padua (around SR47), right on Via Castelfidardo, then right on Via Cernia, and left to park at Prato della Valle.*

8 Padua (Padova)
Veneto; 35100

There's plenty to see here, from the **Prato della Valle** – Italy's largest square – to the country's second-oldest university, the **Palazzo del Bo**, founded in 1222 and visited on a fascinating guided tour *(Mon–Sat)* that takes in Galileo's rostrum and a 16th-century anatomy theatre. A short stroll away is **Piazza delle Erbe**, where a market *(Mon–Sat)* is held. Nearby, too, is the **Duomo**, partly built to a plan by Michelangelo, and frescoed **baptistry**. Don't miss the gardens of the **Orto Botanico** *(closes 3pm in winter)*, close to the **Basilica di Sant'Antonio**, a major destination for pilgrims. Padua's major art attraction is the **Cappella degli Scrovegni** *(advance booking essential; 049 201 0020; www.cappelladegliscrovegni.it)*, with Giotto's lyrical 14th-century frescoes of Bible stories – a masterpiece of Western art.

🚗 *Backtrack a little and follow signs to the "tangenziale" northeast. After the IKEA exit, follow signs for Venezia and SS11, turn left and follow signs to Stra.*

Above Cappella degli Scrovegni, Padua, Giotto's masterpiece **Below left** Prato della Valle, Padua, Italy's largest square **Below right** The thickly wooded Euganean Hills

VISITING PADUA

Tourist Information
Galleria Pedrocchi, 35100; 049 820 1676; www.turismopadova.it

EAT AND DRINK

VERONA

Antica Bottega del Vino *expensive*
Try the *risotto all'Amarone*, a rice dish with the robust local Amarone wine.
Via Scudo di Francia 3, 37121; 045 800 4535; www.bottegavini.it; closed Sun Nov–Mar

MONTAGNANA

Il Ristorante Aldo Moro *inexpensive*
The mouthwatering dishes include *tortellini con zucca* (pumpkin-filled pasta) and *oca al forno* (baked goose).
Via G Marconi 27, 35044; 0429 81351; www.hotelaldomoro.com; closed Mon

EUGANEAN HILLS

Rifugio Re del Venda *inexpensive*
Enjoy grilled meats in a shady courtyard at this country-style restaurant.
Via San Pietro 35, loc. Sottovenda, Cinto Euganeo; 0429 94122; closed Mon

ARQUÀ PETRARCA

La Montanella *moderate*
Try the *risotto alla quaglia* (quail) and *papera alla frutta* (duck baked with fruits) followed by dessert.
Via dei Carraresi 9, 35032; 0429 718 200; www.montanella.it; closed Tue eve, Wed & 6–16 Jan

PADUA

Ristorante Antico Brolo *moderate*
The signature food here is *Fantasia di baccalà*, a special salt cod dish.
Corso Milano 22, 35139; 049 664 555; www.anticobrolo.it; closed Mon lunch & 1 wk Aug

Above Grand Canal and the Church of Santa Maria della Salute, Venice

VISITING VENICE

For information on getting to and around Venice, see *www.hellovenezia.it*. It is possible to tour the other islands in the lagoon, such as Murano, Burano and Torcello, by waterbus.

Tourist Information
Giardini ex Reali, San Marco; 041 529 8711; www.turismovenezia.it

SHOPPING IN VENICE

For handmade paper, visit Rivoaltus *(Ponte di Rialto, 11 San Polo, 30125)* or pick up Venetian velvet slippers at Pied à Terre *(Sottoportego di Rialto, San Polo 60, 30125; www.piedaterre-venice.com)*. For a unique African slant on Murano beads, visit Niang Moulaye *(Salizada del Pignater, 3545 Castello 30122)*.

WHERE TO STAY

RIVIERA DEL BRENTA

Hotel Villa Ducale *moderate*
Enjoy the waterside elegance at this villa, set in gardens just beyond Dolo. *Riviera Martiri della Libertà 75, Dolo 30031; 041 560 8020; www.villaducale.it*

VENICE

Fujiyama B&B *moderate*
Find minimalist calm in this small but central hotel above an Asian tea house. *Calle Lunga San Barnaba 2727A, Dorsoduro 310123; 041 724 1042; www.fujiyama.life*

Palazzina Grassi *expensive*
Relax in the luxury of a Venetian palazzo set on the glorious Grand Canal. *Ramo Grassi 3247, San Marco 30124; 041 528 4644; www.palazzinag.com*

⑨ Riviera del Brenta
Veneto; 30039
The Brenta canal is lined with a number of splendid, elegant villas in Neo-Classical and Renaissance styles. Owned by Venetian nobility from the 1300s, they are a window into a long-vanished lifestyle. Just across the River Brenta, off the main road (SR11) and set in lush parkland, the grandest is the magnificently porticoed **Villa Pisani** *(Via Doge Pisani 7; 049 502 074; www.villapisani.beniculturali.it; closed Mon)*, which has a wonderful maze, and frescoes by Tiepolo. Just before the Marghera industrial build-up, fork right across the canal for Malcontenta (the villa's nickname), then follow signs to **Villa Foscari**, designed by Andrea Palladio in 1555 *(041 5470 012; www.lamalcontenta.com; open May–Oct Tue–Sat, morning only)*. For more villas, see *www.riviera-brenta.it*.

🚗 *From Villa Foscari, follow the river southeast to Fusina. Park and catch the ferry to Venice. Or, return to SR11 and pass through Marghera, then cross the causeway to Venice. Park at Tronchetto (to the right) or Piazzale Roma (straight on). Take a vaporetto into the city.*

⑩ Venice
Veneto; 30100
A whole city floating on a lagoon, Venice is a magical combination of grand palazzos, magnificent churches and ordinary houses amid a network of age-old alleyways and canals. Museums and art galleries attest to the city's glorious past, when it was a wealthy superpower. A stroll through some of the quieter *sestieri* (districts) is the best way to gauge the pulse of this unique city.

A four-hour walking tour
From Tronchetto or Piazzale Roma, catch a *vaporetto* (waterbus) down the Grand Canal and alight at **Rialto Mercato ①**, the commercial heart of the city since medieval times, with pioneer private banks such as the Banco Giro, dating back to 1157. It is now a wine bar with a great canalside terrace. Nowadays, Rialto is the site of a lively market *(8am–1pm Mon–Sat)*. Close by is the most famous of the city's 350 bridges, the 16th-century **Ponte di Rialto ②**. Spanning the Grand Canal at its narrowest point, the bridge is lined with craft shops and jewellers.

Take the canalside walkway **Riva del Vin ③**, where wine was once unloaded. This is a perfect place to enjoy the bustling activity on the Grand Canal – Venice's 3.5-km (2-mile) principal artery for goods, gondolas and all. Turn right into Rio Terà San

Where to Stay: inexpensive, under €100; moderate, €100–€200; expensive, over €200

Above left The Danieli Palace, one of Europe's most famous hotels **Above centre** Gondolas on Venice's Grand Canal **Above right** One of the arcades around Piazza San Marco, Venice

Silvestro. This is San Polo, Venice's smallest district, crammed with craft ateliers and shops, jewellers and glassmakers. Following signs for Ferrovia, turn left through Campo San Aponal and on to **Campo San Polo** ④. This spacious square once hosted bullfights, but now is a favourite with local kids, who zoom about on their bikes. During Venice's prestigious Film Festival, it is transformed into a huge open-air cinema.

Pass the church and cross Ponte San Polo to wind through the maze of alleys from Campo San Tomà to **Campo dei Frari** ⑤. This square is mostly taken up by the towering brick Basilica di Santa Maria Gloriosa dei Frari, the final resting place of the Renaissance composer Claudio Monteverdi. Keep left to Sotoportego San Rocco and over **Rio de la Frescada** ⑥ into Dorsoduro. Turn left along Crosera San Pantalon, then right, to cross the bridge to **Palazzo Foscari** ⑦, possibly the birthplace of the great Doge Francesco Foscari (r.1423–57). Continue through the peaceful square **Campiello dei Squelini** ⑧ to Ca' Rezzonico, a Gothic palace with the **Museo del Settecento**

Mooring post, Grand Canal

Veneziano ⑨ *(closed Tue)*. Cross Ponte San Barnaba and the eponymous square, and take Calle della Toletta to the **Gallerie dell' Accademia** ⑩ *(closed Mon pm)* in Campo della Carità. This former Palladian convent holds a priceless collection of 15th–18th century paintings by Titian, Carpaccio, Giorgione and Bellini. Italy's leading gallery of early 20th- century art is nearby, after San Vio – the **Peggy Guggenheim Collection** ⑪ *(closed Tue)*. Peggy's former home, the Palazzo Venier dei Leoni, houses key works by Giacometti, Picasso and Pollock, as well as a sculpture garden and terrace on the Grand Canal. From here, it is a short walk via Campo della Salute to the old customs warehouse, renovated by Japanese architect Tadao Ando into the gleaming **Punta della Dogana** ⑫ *(closed Tue)*. It now features contemporary works from the collection of François Pinault. Take the *vaporetto* from La Salute across to Venice's famed **Piazza San Marco** ⑬ and Doges' Palace. If time allows, head out to the lagoon's islands of Murano, Burano or Torcello by *vaporetto*, otherwise return to Piazzale Roma or Tronchetto.

EAT AND DRINK

RIVIERA DEL BRENTA

Osteria da Caronte *moderate*
Enjoy traditional cuisine with a refined touch at this riverside restaurant.
Via Dolo 29, Paluello di Stra, Dolo 30030; 041 412 091; www.osteriadacaronte.it; closed Tue eve, Wed, 2 wks Jan & Aug

Villa Nani Mocenigo *expensive*
A sophisticated restaurant in a grand villa on SR11 between Dolo and Mira.
Riviera Martiri della Libertà 113, 30031; 041 560 8139; www.villananimocenigo. it; closed Mon & Tue–Sat lunch

VENICE

Bar a Toletta *inexpensive*
A humble snack bar frequented by locals.Try the traditional venetian *tramezzino* (sandwiches).
Calle della toletta, 1191 Dorsoduro; 0415 200 196

Osteria L'Orto dei Mori *expensive*
An inventive Sicilian chef provides an innovative take on local dishes.
Campo dei Mori, 3386 Cannaregio 30121; 041 524 3677; www. osteriaortodeimori.com; closed Tue, 2 wks Dec, 1 wk Jul & Nov

DAY TRIP OPTIONS

Verona and Venice deserve at least a day's exploration, and the pretty Euganean Hills merit a day trip, too.

Performing arts in Verona
In Verona ①, start at Piazza dei Signori and Dante's statue. Head to nearby Juliet's House and then cross the River Adige to the Teatro Romano – where the Bard's plays are still performed. Walk along the river to the Ponte Scaligero footbridge. Cross

back over and carry on to the Roman arena, now a venue for open-air opera.

Venice's canalside treasures
Take a *vaporetto* down Venice's ⑩ Grand Canal to the Punta dell Dogana, then walk to the Peggy Guggenheim Collection for modern art, before admiring the medieval works in the Gallerie dell'Accademia. Lunch in a back-street *osteria*, then wander slowly to the Ponte di Rialto. Cross over and walk to Piazza San Marco to see the

Basilica and Doges' Palace. Hop on a *vaporetto* to get back to the car park.

Green delights
From Este ③, drive into the Euganean Hills ④, through the vineyards, up to pretty Arquà Petrarca ⑤. Move on to Valsanzibio ⑥ and its Baroque garden. Lunch around Monte Venda, then on to Abbazia di Praglia ⑦.

Follow the drive's instructions to the Abbey, then return via SP89 and SP247.

Eat and Drink: inexpensive, under €25; moderate, €25–€45; expensive, over €45

Dolomites to Veneto Hills

Cortina d'Ampezzo to Treviso

Highlights

- **Alpine wonders**
  Explore the magnificent Dolomites, which crown the fashionable resort of Cortina d'Ampezzo

- **Renaissance towns of the foothills**
  Visit superb Renaissance Feltre, utterly charming Asolo and laid-back Bassano del Grappa, set among rolling hills

- **Scenic war memorial**
  Ascend to the sombre memorial at Monte Grappa – a key battleground of World War I in a spectacular setting

- **Gourmet food**
  From Treviso's radicchio and tiramisù to Monte Grappa's fiery spirit and asparagus, enjoy treats galore

Charming Belluno, between the River Piave and the Dolomites

Dolomites to Veneto Hills

Rising to breathtaking heights in the far north of the Veneto region are the inspiring Dolomites mountains – elegant pale towers soaring above emerald meadows ablaze with brilliant wildflowers. Resort towns such as Cortina d'Ampezzo serve visitors in glorious summer as well as in winter, when the ski slopes are buzzing. This leisurely drive touches on traditional villages in picturesque spots that have inspired centuries of artists, including Titian. A thrilling bonus is majestic Monte Grappa (1,775 m/5,823 ft), all but unknown to overseas visitors. At the lower altitudes, walled towns nestle into the rolling foothills, cloaked with vines and woodland. The drive concludes in delightful Treviso, proud home of tiramisù and red chicory.

Above Detail of the façade of the historic cathedral at Asolo, *see p129*

Above Dramatic landscape of the tree-covered Dolomites mountains, *see pp126–7*
Below right View of the bridge designed by Palladio, Bassano del Grappa, *see p128*

ACTIVITIES

Go mountain walking or rock climbing on clearly signed routes in the Dolomites at Cortina d'Ampezzo

Clamber through World War I trenches at the Cinque Torri

Hike through the Parco Nazionale Dolomiti Bellunesi near Belluno and Feltre

Explore the solemn memorial to the fallen of World War I at Monte Grappa

Eat a bowl of creamy tiramisù in quiet Treviso, the place where it was invented

KEY

Drive route

PLAN YOUR DRIVE

Start/finish: Cortina d'Ampezzo to Treviso.

Number of days: 4 days.

Distance: 270 km (168 miles).

Road conditions: Fairly hilly and, on occasion, mountainous and winding.

When to go: Jun–Oct for outdoor activities, though the plains can get hot Jul–Aug. Winter brings snow and skiing to the mountains, so carry snow chains. Main roads are kept clear but mountain roads may be closed.

Opening times: Shops tend to open 9am–1pm & 4–7:30pm Mon–Sat (food shops are shut Mon & Wed afternoon). Church and museum times vary, but are usually 9am–noon & 4–7 or 8pm. Many museums are closed on Mon.

Main market days: Cortina d'Ampezzo: Tue & Fri; **Belluno:** Mon–Sat; **Feltre:** Tue & Fri; **Bassano del Grappa:** Mon–Sat; **Asolo:** Sat; **Treviso:** Mon–Sat.

Shopping: Look for ceramics at Bassano del Grappa and cheese around Feltre and Monte Grappa.

Major festivals: Feltre: Palio (medieval pageantry), 1st week in Aug; **Bassano del Grappa:** Mestieri in Strada (street market), Sep; **Asolo:** Incontri Asolani (chamber music), Aug–Sep.

DAY TRIP OPTIONS

Nature lovers can concentrate on the scenic Ampezzo valley with a **walk**, spectacular **mountain views** and a visit to the home of a **grand master**. From Treviso, enjoy a Renaissance tour starting at the **pretty town** of Asolo, then on to the **walls** of Feltre, the **palazzos** of Belluno and the **garden** at Nevegal. For full details, see p129.

Above Cortina d'Ampezzo, nestling below the dramatic Dolomites **Below** View of mountains, forests and a lake from Pieve di Cadore

VISITING CORTINA D'AMPEZZO

Tourist information
Piazza Roma 1, 32043; 0436 869 086; www.infodolomiti.it

WHERE TO STAY

CORTINA D'AMPEZZO

Meublé Montana *inexpensive*
A friendly, well-kept hotel in the centre of town, Meublé Montana is close to shops, restaurants and transport.
Corso Italia 94, 32043; 0436 860 498; www.cortina-hotel.com; closed May, Nov

❶ Cortina d'Ampezzo

Veneto; 32043
Chic Cortina, a leading winter ski resort, was part of the Habsburg Empire from the 16th century until after World War I and is today a charming mix of Tyrolean and Italian. The pretty town is set in a natural amphitheatre formed by the breathtaking crags and spires of the Dolomites, whose lower slopes are cloaked in thick forest and lush flower-filled meadows. The central pedestrian street, the Corso, is lined with smart boutiques. Winter brings crowds of jet-set skiers, but during the summer months, Cortina is an excellent base for walkers and climbers with its many chair lifts and cable cars. Information on walks is available from the tourist office.

🚗 *From town, drive up SP48 for Passo di Falzarego. Park at Bai de Dones café.*

❷ The Cinque Torri

Belluno, Veneto; 32043
The leisurely chair lift ride to the Cinque Torri rock towers ends with spectacular views of Cortina d'Ampezzo nestled within its crown of Dolomites peaks, a stunning backdrop to an open-air World War I museum. Close to the Austrian-Italian border, this area was a key strategic location, heavily fortified by both sides. After exploring the trenches and gun emplacements, take the lovely woodland track – sturdy walking shoes are recommended – back to the road. Two mountain huts (rifugi) provide café facilities in summer.

A three-hour walking tour

From **Bai de Dones** ❶, take the Cinque Torri *seggiovia*, or chair lift (*10am–5pm daily*) up to **Rifugio Scoiattoli** ❷ (2,225 m/7,300 ft), which boasts a magnificent terrace facing the Tofane-Lagazuoi range, northwest of the valley. Close at hand are the jagged rock teeth of the Cinque Torri (Five Towers), rising from earthy gums. Once off the chair lift, turn immediately left and take the path downhill into the trench on the slope, brightly flowered in summer. Signs point out rest areas, observation points and artillery positions. At the end of the first line of **trenches** ③, turn right to go down the reconstructed timber steps, which conclude at a covered area. Fork right and immediately left again. A little way up the hill, veer right to the **signs for return** ④ indicating the route back up to Rifugio Scoiattoli. Approaching the *rifugio*, take the left fork along the grassy ridge towards the foot of the dramatic rock towers, whose sheer cliff faces attract many climbers. own this path to the welcoming **Rifugio Cinque Torri** ⑤. A quiet road leads downhill to the northeast, offering views of the majestic Sorapiss mountain. The way forks left and enters shady conifer woods where squirrels and roe deer are not uncommon. About 20 minutes further on, when the path veers right, follow the northwest road signed Bai de Dones. This pretty route meanders amid alpenrose shrubs and pine trees, before reaching a small **lake** ⑥. Close by are the café, chair lift and car park.

🚗 **Leave Cortina d'Ampezzo on SS51, go past Zuel and onto Dogana Vecchia, the old customs point between the Habsburg Empire and Italy. San Vito is the next main town.**

Outdoors in the Dolomites

A UNESCO World Heritage Site, these spectacular mountains in the far northeast of Italy are a superb destination for skiing in winter and climbing and trekking in summer. Aided climbs known as *vie ferrate* criss-cross the sheer rock faces and a network of paths link *rifugi*, or mountain huts, which provide refreshments in the summer season.

---

③ San Vito di Cadore
Veneto; 32046
Dramatic Monte Antelao, at 3,264 m (10,709 ft) the highest mountain in the eastern Dolomites, rises over the village of San Vito di Cadore, while breaks in the trees afford inspiring views of the Pelmo massif. Further along the SS51, at Valle di Cadore, the **Chiesa di San Martino** occupies a high promontory, the site of an ancient castle. Near the valley floor is the covered wooden **Ponte di Rualan**.

🚗 *Continue through Tai di Cadore, taking SS51bis to Pieve di Cadore.*

④ Pieve di Cadore
Veneto; 32044
Pieve di Cadore stands at the foot of the Marmarole mountain range. A **statue** in the main square recalls its native son Titian, the foremost painter of the 16th-century Venetian school. His pretty home, **Casa di Tiziano** *(open May–Sep)*, has been maintained as a small museum.

🚗 *Head back towards Tai di Cadore and branch left on SS51 past Longarone. Exit for Ponte nelle Alpi and follow signs for Belluno "centro". Follow signs for Nevegal and from Piazzale Nevegal, take the way indicated for Faverghera. The car park is located at the top.*

⑤ Nevegal
Belluno, Veneto; 32100
On an elongated ridge marking the end of the mountains and the start of the Veneto plain, this tiny village is surrounded with dairy farms and ski slopes. A 30-minute walk from the car park leads to the **Giardino Botanico delle Alpi Orientali** *(open mid-Jun–mid-Sep; closed Mon except Aug)*.

🚗 *Return to Piazzale Nevegal and return to SP1. Across the river, fork right for Belluno "centro". Follow signs to the Lambioi car park and take the escalator (scala mobile) to town centre.*

Top Dramatic cloud-topped Dolomites above the Pieve Valley   **Above left** Statue of the artist Titian, favourite son of Pieve di Cadore   **Above right** View of a mountain village in the Dolomites   **Below** Casa di Tiziano, Titian's home in Pieve di Cadore

---

EAT AND DRINK

CORTINA D'AMPEZZO

El Zoco *moderate*
Top Italian cuisine and excellent wines. *Via Cademai 18, 32043; 0436 860 041; closed Mon, Apr–May & last 2 wks Nov*

Ristorante Tivoli *expensive*
Refined Italian cuisine with one Michelin star and a superb panoramic terrace. *Via Lacedel 34; 0436 866 400; www.ristorantetivoli.it; closed Mon & Tue lunch, Easter–Jun & Oct–Nov*

NEVEGAL

Ristorante La Casera *inexpensive*
Offers delicious rustic food, such as polenta with sausage and mountain cheese, and pasta with wild mushrooms. *Via Faverghera 751, 32100; 0437 908 180; closed Mon; booking advised*

WHERE TO STAY

BELLUNO

Albergo delle Alpi *moderate*
Furnished with all mod cons, this hotel,
built on the site of a historic inn in the
town centre, also has a good restaurant.
*Via Jacopo Tasso 13, 32100;
0437 940 545; www.dellealpi.it*

FELTRE

Via Paradiso 32 *moderate*
This comfortable modern renovation
in the town centre has three suites
and serves local delicacies at breakfast.
*Via Paradiso 32, 32032; 348 870 9622;
www.viaparadiso32.it*

MONTE GRAPPA

Albergo Forcelletto *inexpensive*
This simple mountain inn is managed
by a friendly local family and set in a
superbly panoramic location.
*Località Forcelletto, 32030; 349 954
4757; www.forcellato.it; closed Tue &
Mon–Fri in winter*

BASSANO DEL GRAPPA

Hotel Al Castello *inexpensive*
This traditional inn has cosy rooms
and is well placed for sightseeing.
*Via Bonamigo 19, 36061; 0424 22 8665;
www.hotelalcastello.it*

ASOLO

Albergo Al Sole *moderate*
This is a captivating 16th-century villa
with mod cons, near the main piazza.
*Via Collegio 33, 31011; 0423 951 332;
www.albergoalsole.com; closed Jan*

TREVISO

Albergo Il Focolare *moderate*
This popular hotel is charming,
comfortable and handily located.
*Piazza Ancilotto 4, 31100; 0422 56601;
www.ilfocolarehotel.com*

SHOPPING IN THE VENETO

In Monte Bassano, look for fine cheese
such as Morlacco and Bastardo del
Grappa in **La Speloncia** *(Via Bocchette
di Mezzo; 0439 438 260; Jun–Sep).*
   For hand-decorated ceramics in
Bassano del Grappa, try **L'Arte della
Ceramica** *(Via Angarano 21; 0424 503
901);* or taste the wide range of grappa
and liqueurs at **Osteria Grapperia
Nardini** *(Ponte Vecchio 2;
0424 227 741; www.nardini.it).*
   Gourmet goodies such as potted
red chicory *(radicchio rosso)* abound
in Treviso, especially at **Bottega del
Baccalà** *(Via S Parisio 15–17; 0422 540
818; www.fermi-treviso.com).*

Right View of Bassano del Grappa from its
famous wooden bridge **Top** Boating on one
of Treviso's many tree-shaded canals

---

⑥ Belluno
Veneto; 32100

Backed by the soaring Schiara massif,
pretty Belluno, the provincial capital,
is worth a visit for its grand squares,
such as **Piazza del Mercato** (also
known as Piazza delle Erbe), lined
with splendid Renaissance palaces
and home to an elegant 15th-century
fountain. Nearby, the 16th-century
Duomo has a Baroque campanile
that affords excellent views in all
directions. The town's **Museo Civico**
is worth visiting for its paintings by
local 16th–18th century masters.

🚗 *Head back to SP1 and turn right to
Feltre, past Trichiana and Mel. After
Lentiai, fork right on the SS50 to cross
the River Piave towards Feltre. Follow
signs for "centro", then "centro storico",
circling the town to the car park. Yellow
signs direct pedestrians into Feltre.*

⑦ Feltre
Veneto; 32032

This charming walled Renaissance
town comes alive in mid-Aug for
its colourful Palio horse race and
medieval pageantry festival. Only
3 km (2 miles) away is **Pedavena**,
known for its brewery. It is also the
gateway to the wild Vette Feltrine
mountain range, part of the Dolomiti
Bellunesi National Park, where there
are spectacular walks to be enjoyed
(www.dolomitipark.it).

🚗 *Leave Feltre on the SS50, towards
Bassano, then turn left at Cáupo
following signs for "Monte Grappa"
on the scenic SS148 as it winds its
way up the northernmost flank of
the mountain. Drive on past Osteria
Forcelletto and take the fork to SP149
to Cima Grappa.*

⑧ Monte Grappa
Veneto; 36061

Towering over the edge of the vast
Veneto plain is 1,775-m (5,823-ft)
high Monte Grappa. The peak is
home to **Cima Grappa**, a monumental
terraced *ossario*, a poignant memorial
to the Italian and Austrian troops
whose bones rest there. Lush
meadows now cover the World War I
battlefields. On a clear day, the views
extend all the way to the Adriatic
coast and Venice.

🚗 *Return to SS148 and turn left for
the zig-zag descent to Romano
d'Ezzelino. Turn right on SP74 and
follow signs for "centro". Park on
Viale Fosse by the town walls.*

⑨ Bassano del Grappa
Veneto; 36061

With a charming, traffic-free centre,
Bassano is well-known for ceramics,
fiery grappa spirit and the prized
white asparagus (in spring). For some
wonderful rooftop views, climb the
43-m (141-ft) high **Torre Civica**.
Straddling the River Brenta is the
landmark bridge **Ponte degli Alpini**,
designed by Andrea Palladio in 1571
(rebuilt 1948), from which there are

Far left Road leading to Belluno **Left** Delightful Belluno with its Duomo and Baroque campanile **Below** Flowers adorning houses in the pretty hillside town of Asolo

EAT AND DRINK

FELTRE

Osteria Crash *moderate*
A fun and friendly eatery with an excellent selection of wines and beers.
Via Paradiso 46, 32032; 0439 81169; closed Mon & Sun eve

MONTE GRAPPA

Osteria Forcelletto *inexpensive*
Hearty country fare and views over the Valsugana to the Asiago plateau.
Località Forcelletto, 32030; 349 954 4757; closed Tue & Mon–Fri in winter

BASSANO DEL GRAPPA

Belvedere Ristorante del Buon Ricordo *moderate*
Refined restaurant whose specialities include pheasant.
Viale delle Fosse 1, 36061; 0424 524 988; www.bonotto.it

Antico Ristorante Cardellino *moderate*
Try the *baccalà alla Vicentina*, a local cod speciality.
Via Bellavitis 17, 36061; 0424 220 144; closed Sun

ASOLO

Antica Osteria Al Bacaro *moderate*
Enjoy *spezzatino* (stew) and *baccalà* (salt cod) at wooden trestle tables.
Via R Browning 165, 31011; 0423 55150; closed Thu

TREVISO

Locanda Ponte Dante *moderate*
Close to the river, this eatery serves stews, polenta, octopus and sardines.
Piazza Garibaldi 6, 31100; 0422 178 5946; closed Sun eve & Mon

Toni da Spin *moderate*
Historic trattoria in the town centre – try the *pasta e fagioli* for lunch.
Via Inferiore 7, 31100; 0422 543 829; www.ristorante tonidelspin.com; closed Mon lunch

---

impressive views of the town. The **Museo Civico** *(closed Mon)* contains works by 19th-century sculptor Canova. In Piazza Garibaldi stands the 11th-century Romanesque-Gothic **Chiesa di San Francesco**.
🚗 *Leave on Viale Venezia (SP248) for Asolo, turning left for "centro" after 16 km (10 miles). Park at Piazza Garibaldi.*

⑩ Asolo
Veneto; 31011
The peaceful setting of this beautiful hillside town has long attracted poets (Robert Browning), aristocrats (Caterina Cornaro, 15th-century queen of Cyprus) and travellers (Freya Stark). A visit should start at **Piazza Garibaldi**, its fountain fed by underground aqueducts that once filled the Roman baths. Just across the main street stands the venerable **Cattedrale**. Pass through a city door on Via Collegio and walk uphill to the 14th-century fort, **La Rocca** *(open Sat & Sun)*, for views over the town and lush countryside.
🚗 *Return to SS248 and drive through Montebelluna towards Conegliano. Turn right at the roundabout before Venegazzu onto SR348 and follow signs straight to Treviso. Take the first turn-off for "centro" and park at Viale Battisti.*

⑪ Treviso
Veneto; 31100
This charming walled market town-cum-city on the River Sile is scored with waterways from the long-gone days of canal navigation. Stroll east along the banks to a poignant "barge cemetery", where the old timber craft were sunk when road transport took over. The lively fish market has its own island, modelled by Venetian architect Carlo Scarpa (1906–78). One of Treviso's claims to gastronomic fame is that it invented the classic Italian dessert tiramisù; it also purports to be the home of *radicchio* (red chicory) and *pasta e fagioli* (pasta/bean soup).

DAY TRIP OPTIONS
Choose between the wonders of nature and the man-made splendour of the Renaissance.

Painterly landscapes
Using Cortina d'Ampezzo ❶ as a base, do a little shopping before heading up to the Cinque Torri ❷. Work up an appetite climbing to see the views – if painting isn't an option, take a photo.

Lunch at a mountain hut, then drive to San Vito di Cadore ❸, with more photo opportunities at the Ponte di Rualan. Drive on to Pieve di Cadore ❹ to see the place of Titian's birth.

Follow the drive's instructions.

Renaissance tour
From Treviso ⑪, head to pretty Asolo ⑩, the "pearl of the province", then

on to walled Feltre ❼ with its historic Renaissance centre. After lunch, drive to Belluno ❻ to explore its grand palazzo-lined squares, 16th-century Duomo and Renaissance paintings.

Take the SP55 then the SS248 to Asolo. Retrace route back on SS248, then take SS348 to Feltre. Take the SS50, then SP1 to Belluno. To return quickly, take SS50 north to A27. Take this south to Treviso.

Eat and Drink: inexpensive, under €25; moderate, €25–€45; expensive, over €45

IEREMIA

The Po Delta

Ferrara to Ravenna

Highlights

- **Courtly capital**
  Explore Ferrara's Renaissance palazzos, medieval churches and magnificent castles, built by its powerful d'Este rulers

- **The mighty Po**
  Follow Italy's longest river as it heads to the sea over rich alluvial plains, reclaimed since Roman times

- **The lagoons of Comacchio**
  Discover these superb wetlands, an important sanctuary and breeding ground for migrating water birds

- **Byzantine majesty**
  Feast your eyes on splendid Ravenna – the last great capital of the Roman empire – rich in glittering mosaics

Mosaics inside the Presbytery of the Basilica di San Vitale, Ravenna

The Po Delta

The massive River Po winds across its expansive delta in large, lazy arcs. Somewhat tamed by reclamation, the largest flood plain in Italy is an easy place to explore. This drive starts at Ferrara and then wanders through rich agricultural lands, along the massive, protective river banks to wild wetlands of superb natural beauty with excellent cycling paths and well-marked walking trails. After the ancient forest of Mesola, the beauty of the Pomposa monastery, the busy fishing village of Porto Garibaldi and the fascinating town of Comacchio, the journey ends with the world's greatest Byzantine treasures in the charming city of Ravenna.

ACTIVITIES

Catch a fish with local fishermen in Porto Garibaldi; and stay overnight on board a traditional fishing boat

Photograph the birdlife of the Valli di Comacchio at sunset including the migrating flamingos

Take a class in mosaic-making and learn the ancient Byzantine art of designing with glass in Ravenna

Ride a bicycle across the Valli di Comacchio – the delta is very flat here and perfect for cycling

Hike in Il Bosco della Mesola, the last forest in the delta, and look out for fallow and red deer

Take a dip at a sandy-beached lido along the delta coast from Porto Garibaldi

0 kilometres 8

0 miles 8

KEY

Drive route

Left Ferrara's Loggia of the Merchants, Piazza Trento Trieste, *see p134* **Above right** Mudflats and reed beds in the wildlife haven Valli di Comacchio, *see p138*

PLAN YOUR DRIVE

Start/finish: Ferrara to Ravenna.

Number of days: 2–3 days.

Distance: Approx 240 km (150 miles).

Road conditions: Generally excellent.

When to go: Summer is best, with clear skies and good beach weather. The Po valley around Ferrara and the coast is prone to fog in winter.

Opening times: Most museums open 10am–6pm, with small museums often only open on weekends outside the summer months. Churches are usually open 7:30am–noon and 3–7:30pm.

Main market days: Ferrara: Mon & Fri; Ro & Comacchio: Wed; **Argenta:** Thu; **Ravenna:** Wed & Sat in Via Sighinolfi; **Mesola:** Sat.

Specialized markets: Ferrara: Antique Market, 1st weekend of month (except Aug); **Ravenna:** Antique and Handicrafts Market, 3rd weekend of month.

Shopping: Modern mosaic gifts and all tools and requirements for making mosaics are available in Ravenna.

Major festivals: Ferrara: Buskers Festival, last week in Aug; Ferrara Palio di San Giorgio (medieval horse race and pageantry), last Sun in May; Ferrara Hota: Air Balloon Festival, 3rd week in Sep; **Porto Garibaldi:** Festa della Madonna del Mare (boat festival and celebration), 4 Jun; **Comacchio:** Sagra dell'Anguilla (eel festival), first 2 weekends in Oct; **Ravenna:** Ravenna Festival (music, drama and dance; www.ravennafestival.org) Jun–Jul.

DAY TRIP OPTIONS

Architecture enthusiasts will enjoy the **frescoes**, **duomo** and **castle** in Ferrara, one of the **delta's oldest buildings** in the Po Delta at Argenta and more **mosaics** and **great architecture** in Ravenna. Nature-loving families can head to the Valli of Comacchio to enjoy the **waterbirds** and pristine **delta** environment and visit the **eel factory** at Comacchio. Next, they can visit the coast for a **swim** at a lido or carry on to Il Bosco della Mesola to see the **deer**. For full details, *see p139*.

Above A narrow alley through the historic centre of Ferrara

VISITING FERRARA

Getting to Ferrara
From the A13 toll road, take exit Ferrara Nord onto Via Eridano/SP19. The nearest airports are Bologna and Venice.

Parking
Centro Storico, Via Darsena

Bicycle hire
Rent-a-bike Ceragioli (*Piazza Travaglio, 44121; 339 405 6853*)

Tourist Information
Castello Estense, 44121; 0532 299 303; www.ferraraterraeacqua.it

WHERE TO STAY

FERRARA AND AROUND

Hotel Touring *inexpensive*
Set in the town centre and offering excellent value for money, this 1950s hotel has quiet rooms, excellent staff and parking permits for a small fee.
Viale Cavour 11, 44100; 0532 206 200; www.hoteltouringfe.it

Alla Cedrara a Ferrara *inexpensive*
This *agriturismo* (farm stay) in parkland 7 km (4 miles) from the historic centre, serves generous breakfasts (on the terrace in fine weather). Exit Ferrara on Via Modena, left after bridge, then right into Via Arginone, first left Via Pelosa. At Via Aranova turn left for the *agriturismo*.
Aranova, 102–104 Lat. Via Pelosa, 44044; 345 013 54 24, 340 934 30 96; www.allacedrara.it; offers bicycle hire

Hotel Ferrara *moderate*
This central hotel combines a sleek modern style with a characterful old building – some rooms have views onto neighbouring Castello Estense.
Largo Castello 36, 44121; 053 220 5048; www.hotelferrara.com; free bicycle hire

❶ Ferrara

Ferrara, Emilia-Romagna; 44121–44124

The d'Este dynasty ruled over Ferrara from the 13th to the 16th century, enriching it with a splendid castle, medieval architecture and fine Renaissance palaces. This stroll leads through the oldest part of the city to the sombre, moated castle at its centre, Castello Estense.

A two-hour walking tour

From the car park on Via Darsena, enter the city to the right of the 17th-century Porta Paola. Cross Piazza Travaglio diagonally right to the busy shopping street Via San Romano. Cross Via Ripagrande/Carlo Mayr and turn right on **Via Volte** ①, one of the oldest parts of the city. The archways once joined the river warehouses on the right to the merchants' houses on the left. At the end, turn left, then right into Vicolo Granchio. Go straight on, in a series of dog-legs, into Via Carmellino and Via Borgo di Sotto.

This leads to the **Oratorio dell'Annunziata** ②, with superb frescoes, including a 15th-century fresco by the school of Pisanello. Continue into Via Scandiana – on the right is the **Chiesa di Santa Maria in Vado** ③. In 1171 a priest celebrating mass broke the host, which sprayed blood over the vault above the altar, confirming the miracle of the Eucharist.

On the left is **Palazzo Schifanoia** ④ *(closed Mon)*, which belonged to the d'Este family and is now home to a museum containing artifacts from the d'Este court as well as some of

Detail from the façade of Ferrara's Duomo

the most significant 15th-century fresco cycles in Italy showing court life, zodiac signs and Roman gods.

Return past the oratory, turn right at Via Pergolato, then left at Via Savanarola past **Casa Romei** ⑤ *(closed Mon)*, a fine example of a Ferrerese nobleman's house combining medieval and Renaissance elements. Turn left at Via Terranuova, then right into Via Mazzini past the **Synagogue and Jewish Museum** ⑥ *(open Sun–Thu, guided visits only: 10am, 11am, 12 am)*. On the left of Via Mazzini is the Ghetto. In 1492, Ercole I gave shelter to Jews fleeing persecution in Spain. When d'Este power waned, the community was gated in 1627 and closed in 1859. Now a charming area, it was the setting for Giorgio Bassani's 1962 novel, *The Garden of the Finzi-Continis*.

Via Mazzini opens into a series of squares in the city's heart. On the right of Piazza Trento Trieste is a Renaissance bell tower, attributed to Leon Battista Alberti (1404–72), and the medieval Loggia of the Merchants. Facing west is the Duomo, the magnificent 12th-century **Basilica di San Giorgio** ⑦

Below Statue of Niccolò III d'Este 1383–1441), the Marquess of Ferrara, outside the Palazzo Municipale
Below right The glassy waters of a peaceful wooded pond near Il Mulino del Po

EAT AND DRINK

FERRARA

Leon d'Oro *inexpensive*
Almost a Ferrara institution, this central café and *pasticceria* opposite the Duomo is famous for its *pampapato*, a nutty, nougat-style sweet dipped in chocolate.
*Piazza della Cattedrale 8, 44121;
0532 20 9318; closed Tue*

Caffetteria Ristorante Schifanoia *inexpensive*
This small pavilion has been turned into a delightful garden café by artist Simone Bavia.
*Palazzo Schifanoia, Via Scandiana 21,
44100; 340 617 8870; lunch only;
closed Mon*

Cà d' Frara *moderate*
As you would expect in a restaurant in Via del Gambero (Prawn Street), this pleasant restaurant serves seafood, but also home-made pasta specialities such as *cappellacci di zucca* (pumpkin pasta).
*Via del Gambero 4, 44121; 0532 205
057; www. ristorantecadfrara.it; closed
Tue & Wed lunch*

L'Oca Giuliva *moderate*
A small restaurant with an excellent wine cellar: try their splendid *salama da sugo*, a spicy sausage in ragù sauce.
*Via Boccacanale di Santo Stefano 38,
40100; 0532 207 628; closed Tue;
booking advised*

Osteria Del Ghetto *moderate*
In the heart of the Jewish ghetto, this small *osteria* has a typically local menu: try the *cosciotto di maialino in porchetta* – ham-wrapped roast pork with fennel.
*Via della Vittoria, 26, 44121; 0532 764
936; www.osteriadelghetto.it*

IL MULINO DEL PO

VenTo di Supa *moderate*
Simple outdoor restaurant-bar on the shores of the Po river. Offers excellent meat and fish dishes. Try the roasted eel, a local specialty..
*Via Dazio, 52 44030; 345 610 80 08;
www.ventodisupa.com; closed Mon*

(open daily). The lower part of the façade is Romanesque while the intricately carved upper part was built later in Gothic style.

Directly opposite is the **Palazzo Municpale** ⑧, a 12th-century d'Este residence remodelled in the 16th century to house the City Hall. To the right, above an arch designed by Leon Battista Alberti, is a statue of Niccolò III d'Este on horseback; to the left, seated on a column, is his son Borso.

Turning right up Corso Martiri della Libertà, the last column on the left has marks from when the River Po burst its banks, flooding the city. Nearby is the statue of the Ferrarese Dominican monk Girolamo Savonarola, a leader of Florence whose passionate sermons started the Bonfire of the Vanities in 1497, when all "sinful goods" were taken from the city's houses and burnt.

Surrounded by a moat is the symbol of Ferrara, the **Castello Estense** ⑨ *(closed Mon)*, built in the 15th century to protect Niccolò II d'Este against his own people. As d'Este rule became established, the castle grew into a fine home with terraces and frescoed apartments. Return to the car park.

🚗 *Leave Ferrara on Via Pomposa, towards Copparo – turn left into Via Pontegradella, then left into Via Caretti, and right into SP2. Just before Corlo, take 1st left onto SP14 (towards Ro). At Ro follow signs to "Centro Storico", left at Via Dazio, follow signs for Area Golenale del Po - Mulino sul Po. Park in the designated area. Walk over the embankment to the park.*

Cycling in the Po Delta
Geographically the whole area of the Po Delta is very flat, making it ideal for exploring on a bike. Ravenna has free bicycles for hire – yellow/red for tourists/residents. Register at the tourist office *(Via Salara 8, Ravenna 48100; www.turismo.ra.it)*. Many hotels supply bikes free to guests.

Route maps and information are available at www.ferrarabike.com and www.cycle-r.it, including the Destra Po Route, part of the Eurovelo cycle routes from Athens to Cadiz. Most locals are keen cyclists, and hotels and guides can offer biking tours not easily found elsewhere.

❷ Il Mulino del Po
Ro, Ferrara, Emilia-Romagna; 44030
This small parkland with picnic areas and bicycle hire, on the banks of the river near the Polesella bridge, featured in a 1940 novel by Riccardo Bacchelli, *Il Mulino del Po* (The Mill on the Po), evoking the harsh realities of life on the river. There is a small museum in the barge/houseboat that was used in a 1949 film of the book. The tethered barge was manoeuvred into mid-stream, where the force of the water turned the waterwheel it carried, grinding the corn. The tall mooring poles are an indication of how high the river flows when in flood.

🚗 *Returning to Ro, take 1st left onto Via Vallalbana/SP24, following signs to Berra. At Canova, turn left into Via Brusantina Pampano/SP12 to Ariano. At Piazza Garibaldi turn left to SP11 to Mesola. Use car park on Viale Roma.*

Above The Castello Estense, or castello di San Michele, in Ferrara

Eat and Drink: inexpensive, under €25; moderate, €25–€45; expensive, over €45

Right top The impressive red-brick Treponti Bridge, Comacchio **Right below left** Boats in the harbour at Porto Garibaldi **Right below right** Detail of the façade at the Abbazia di Pomposa

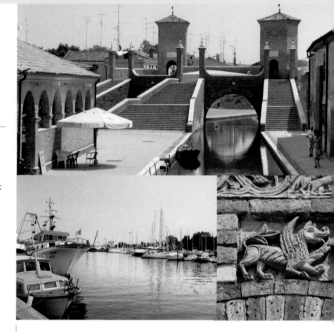

VISITING COMACCHIO

Consorzio del Parco Regionale del Delta del Po
This office provides information on bike hire, boat tours and walking trails throughout the Po Delta.
Via Cavour 11, 44022; 0533 314 003; www.parcodeltapo.it

WHERE TO STAY AROUND IL BOSCO DELLA MESOLA

L'Oasi di Valle Cannevié-Porticino
inexpensive
Combining tourism and wildlife preservation, this mini ecopark near the Lido di Volano is run in conjunction with the Province of Ferrara and offers accommodation and a restaurant and bar as well as guided tours of the surrounding wetlands (in Italian).
Via per Volano 45, 44020 Volano di Codigoro; 0533 719 014; tours: Apr–Sep daily, closed Mon Oct–Mar; also offers bicycle hire

Below The square-turreted 16th-century Castello di Mesola

3 Castello di Mesola
Ferrara, Emilia-Romagna; 44026
One of the last *Delizie* (pleasure lodges) built by the Ferrara dukes, the Castello di Mesola was part of a huge hunting estate. Building started in 1578, creating a central block with four towers surrounded by a semi-circular porticoed courtyard. The former stables and granary now contain bars, a restaurant and a local produce shop. The filmic nature of the setting was used by director Mario Soldati for his 1954 film *La Donna del Fiume*, with Sophia Loren.
🚗 *Head east on Via 25 Aprile, then right at Strada Statale Romea/SS309. Fork left to Bosco Mesola and Gigliola, turning left and following the signs to Bosco della Mesola and car park.*

4 Il Bosco della Mesola
Ferrara, Emilia-Romagna; 44026
Once an extensive forest, only 1,000 hectares (4 sq miles) of Il Bosco della Mesola (*www.parcodeltapo.it*) remain and are now under the protection of the Corpo Forestale. Explore the forest on foot or by bicycle (hire available near front gate) along the 1.5 km (1 mile) of paths. These lead through an attractive setting of English oak, holm oak and pine, inhabited by the shy red deer of Mesola, the only native population of red deer in Italy.

🚗 *Return to Gigliola, then turn left at Via Vecchia Corriera and right at Strada Giralda Centrale, continuing to Abbazia di Pomposa and car park.*

5 Abbazia di Pomposa
Via Pomposa Centro, 12, Codigoro Ferrara; 44020
This superb Romanesque abbey was first established in the 7th century, and by 1001 it had been made a royal abbey by Emperor Otto III. However, after several centuries of decline, the last monks left Pomposa in 1671. The abbey was built in the style of a basilica, with a central nave and an aisle on each side, using material salvaged from other sites. The two carved roundels came

Below Fishermen unloading the day's catch at Porto Garibaldi from Ravenna. The complex is an architectural delight – the 48-m (157-ft) bell tower, or campanile, is typical Lombard Romanesque. The interior is covered with frescoes of biblical scenes by Bolognese masters and the floor was created in the 11th and 12th centuries by Venetian craftsmen.

In the 11th century, the monk Guido d'Arezzo is said to have invented modern musical notation while teaching music here.

🚗 *Head south on Loc. Lovara/SS309, turn left at SP54 to Lido di Volano, then right at Strada Panoramica Acciaioli. At Porto Garibaldi, fork left on Via Cacciatori, then left into Via Florido Braga, right at Via Volturno to the port.*

⑥ Porto Garibaldi
Ferrara, Emilia-Romagna; 44029
Named in honour of the Risorgimento hero Giuseppe Garibaldi (1807–82), who landed here during his flight from the Austrians in 1849, this busy fishing port has several sandy beaches, perfect for a dip in the Adriatic. The **Lido delle Nazioni**, **Lido di Pomposa**, **Lido degli Scacchi** and the **Lido degli Estensi** are all accessible from here by ferry for foot or bicycle passengers.

The town also was one of the largest fishing fleets in the Adriatic, with boats leaving the Magnavacca Canal early in the morning and returning later to unload their catch. It's easy to charter a boat for a fishing trip from the harbour.

🚗 *Head west on Via Giacomo Matteotti, which becomes Strada Provinciale di Comacchio/SP1. At Comacchio, turn left at Via Trepponti/ SP1 and follow the road around the town. Turn right at roundabout to Corso Giuseppe Mazzini and ample parking.*

⑦ Comacchio
Ferrara, Emilia-Romagna; 44022
This picturesque town has derived its prosperity from many centuries of fishing, salt harvesting and catching eels from the nearby lagoon. Founded by the Etruscans and annexed by the Romans, who built a canal to deepen the lagoon, Comacchio went on to prosper under the Goths, Lombards, Venetians and finally the Papal States. The historic centre is divided by canals with ten brick bridges. The **Treponti Bridge**, built in 1634, has five staircases, five semi-circular arches and crosses five different canals. It's also possible to visit the eel pickling factory, **La Manifattura dei Marinati** *(Corso Mazzini 200; open daily).*

🚗 *Continue along Corso Mazzini, past La Manifattura dei Marinati, turn left, then right into Via Spina/SP1, left at Strada Poderale Belfiore, crossing the canal, straight onto Via Arsa and Via Anita in Loc. Fosse passing Via Agosta along the edge of the lagoon, then turn left on Via Martinella Rotta and park in a layby for the view.*

Above left Comacchio, a town of canals, boats and bridges **Above right** The elegant 14th-century bell tower at the Abbazia di Pomposa **Below** One of the well-tended sandy beaches at Porto Garibaldi

EAT AND DRINK

CASTELLO DI MESOLA
Ristorante Al Castello *moderate*
Set within the walled courtyard of the castle, this trattoria puts on a good show for locals and visitors alike. Try steamed asparagus with cheese and truffles, pasta with venison ragù, and chicken pieces covered with sesame seeds and fried.
Piazza Umberto I 9, 44026; 0533 993 088; closed Mon & Tue

IL BOSCO DELLA MESOLA
Il Bischero *moderate*
This restaurant has a warm and intimate atmosphere and serves robust Tuscan cuisine such as choice salamis, tagliatelle with wild boar sauce and chargrilled steak Florentine.
Via Sacche, 344026; 3474 209 506; www.ristorantelafalce.it; closed Mon & Tue; also has gluten-free menu

ABBAZIA DI POMPOSA
Corte Madonnina *moderate*
This *Azienda Agricola* (farm business), just south of the abbey, sells its own wines direct to the public. The adjoining farmhouse serves typical cuisine: *salama da sugo* (medieval sausage), pumpkin ravioli and eels.
SS Romea (Località per Volano 1), Pomposa, 44020; 0533 719 002; www.cortemadonnina.it; closed Mon

Eat and Drink: inexpensive, under €25; moderate, €25–€45; expensive, over €45

Above Flamingos feeding on the wetlands, Valli di Comacchio **Above right** Sumptuous mosaic inside Ravenna's Basilica di San Vitale **Below** Frescoed nave in the Basilica di Sant'Apollinare Nuovo, Ravenna

VISITING RAVENNA

Tourist Information
Ravenna's tourist offices sell a **combined ticket** that includes entry to: the Basilica di Sant'Apollinare Nuovo, the Neonian Baptistry, the Basilica di San Vitale and the Mausoleum of Galla Placidia. A clear map is provided with the ticket.
Via Fiandrini Benedetto, Via Di Roma or Piazza Duomo; 0544 541 688; www.turismo.ravenna.it

WHERE TO STAY

AROUND ARGENTA

Val Campotto *inexpensive*
This farm stay, just south of the lagoon, has nine rooms and a pleasantly rustic ambience. There is local produce for sale and an onsite restaurant.
Strada M Margotti 2, 44011 Campotto di Argenta; 0532 800 516; www.valcampotto.it; offers bicycle hire

RAVENNA

Hotel Centrale Byron *inexpensive*
This budget hotel is in the historic centre and offers basic, but clean and comfortable facilities. There is parking in a nearby private garage.
Via IV Novembre 14, 48121; 0544 212 225; www.hotelsravenna.it

Villa Santa Maria in Foris *moderate*
Set in a comfortable, restored villa in the historic centre, this hotel offers pleasant, modern rooms.
Via Giuseppe Pasolini 61, 48100; 0544 212 163; www.villaforis.it

Albergo Cappello *moderate–expensive*
A superb Renaissance palazzo only a few steps from Piazza del Popolo – some rooms and suites have period furnishings with elegant frescoes.
Via IV Novembre 41, 48121; 0544 219 813; www.albergocappello.it

⑧ Valli di Comacchio
Ferrara, Emilia-Romagna; 44022

The lagoons of Comacchio are wetlands of international importance and the centrepiece of the Parco Delta del Po *(www.parcodeltapo.it/er)*, which covers an area of 3,500 hectares (14 sq miles) and stretches from Chioggia to Comacchio. It was designated a World Heritage Site in 1999. Large raised banks divide the lagoons, providing flat paths perfect for cycling along, and here and there stand the remains of fishing lodges and small salt pans. The shallow, brackish waters are an ideal habitat for more than 300 species of water birds. Species that can often be sighted include flamingoes, avocets, spoonbills, shelducks, black-winged stilts, slender-billed gulls and Mediterranean gulls. Visitors can also view the lagoon by boat or from walking trails.

🚗 *Return along Via Martinella Rotta. Turn left at Via Valle Umana, at Anita turn right on Via Fossa dei Socialisti and left on Via Pagana that leads to Longastrino. Turn right at Via Molinetto/SP10, which curves left. Turn right at Via Giovanni Amendola/SS16, which continues to Argenta.*

⑨ Argenta
Ferrara, Emilia-Romagna; 44011

As the mouth of the Po Primario, the old River Po, silted up, channels were cut to the sea. One of these became known as the River Reno. On its northern bank lies quiet Argenta, an ideal spot for bird-watching forays to the **Campotto Oasis**, three small lagoons south of the town. Just by the oasis stands the **Parish Church of San Giorgio** *(Via Cardinala)*, built in 569, it is one of the oldest buildings in the delta. Although the church is rarely open, its portal of Roman marble is worth a look. Further south, on the same road, is the excellent **Museo delle Valli** *(closed Mon; www.vallidiargenta.org)*. Traditional life in the delta, land reclamation and local wildlife are well covered by its displays and bicycles are available to hire for an excursion around the lagoon.

🚗 *From Argenta, turn right into Via Nazionale Ponente/SS16 for 36 km (22 miles). Take the exit for Ravenna Centro, follow Via Faentina/SS253, then go left at Circonvallazione San Gaetanino. Turn sharp right at Via Don Giovanni Minzoni, fork right, then turn left into car park at Largo Giustiniano.*

⑩ Ravenna

Ravenna, Emilia-Romagna; 48100
From AD 402 until 476, Ravenna was the capital of the Western Roman Empire and remained the capital of Byzantine Italy until the 8th century. The city's importance in the early Christian era endowed it with astonishing monuments and lavishly decorated churches – eight buildings have been listed by UNESCO. But Ravenna is a living city and not just an architectural museum – its piazzas and historic monuments are linked by pleasant streets bustling with local life. The octagonal **Basilica di San Vitale** *(open daily)*, built 527–48, is the only major church from the period of Emperor Justinian I to survive virtually intact. Its colourful mosaics are the height of Byzantine splendour – look for the emperor portrayed with court officials, and on the opposite wall, the Empress Theodora. Within the complex is the small building of the **Mausoleum of Galla Placidia** *(included in group ticket)*, regarded as the best preserved of the mosaic monuments, and the **Museo Nazionale di Ravenna** *(separate ticket)*, in the cloisters, with 14th-century frescoes of Santa Chiara and a

Below The exterior of the Byzantine Basilica di San Vitale, Ravenna

collection of fabrics, ivories, coins and icons. To the left, in Via San Vitale/Via Salara, the **information office** offers free bicycles for exploring the city. Nearby Via Cavour is a fine shopping street, which leads to Piazza Andrea Costa and the **covered market** *(morning only)* selling flowers, fish, meat and cheese and all manner of fresh local produce. Via IV Novembre leads straight to elegant **Piazza del Popolo** with its two Venetian-style columns with saints Apollinare and Vitale perched on top. Behind is Palazzo Communale and to the left, Palazzo Veneziano, built when Ravenna was part of the Venetian Republic in the 15th century. The archway in Palazzo Veneziano leads to **Via Cairoli**, a narrow shopping street with Liberty-style shop façades.

The **Basilica di Sant'Apollinare Nuovo** *(combined ticket)*, in Via di Roma, has a cylindrical bell tower and some of the largest Byzantine mosaics (6th century). Directly opposite, Via Negri leads into Largo Firenze and the side door to the **Basilica di San Francesco**, its 10th-century crypt full of water with fish swimming over the 5th-century mosaic floor. Leave by the front door into Piazza San Francesco. Through the garden to the right is the Neo-Classical **Tomb of Dante** *(open daily; free entry)* – the Italian poet died here in 1321. In Piazza Duomo stands the last of the combined ticket sites: the late 4th- or early 5th-century **Neonian Baptistry**. The octagonal building contains delightful Greco-Roman influenced frescoes. From here, Via Cavour runs towards the imposing 16th-century **Porta Adriana**. Left at Via Barbiani is the **Domus dei Tappeti di Pietra** *(open daily, entry through San Eufemia)*, the site of a Roman villa and beautiful Byzantine mosaics.

Above Free yellow bicycles available for tourists in Ravenna

EAT AND DRINK

ARGENTA AND AROUND

Oasi *inexpensive*
This is the closest bar/trattoria to the Museo di Valli and it is possible to pick up a picnic lunch to enjoy in the park.
Via Vallesanta 6, 44011; 0532 808 017; open Tue–Sun lunch, Fri–Sun eve

Ristorante Patuelli *moderate*
Situated opposite the parkland south of the museum, this place serves superb chargrilled eel and other local delicacies.
Via Cardinala 11/a, Campotto 44011; 0532 808 314; closed Mon & Tue

RAVENNA

Gustavo Bizantino *inexpensive*
Eat with the locals at this busy self-service buffet within the covered market. Great fresh food and you can pile your plate high with delicious bread, grilled vegetables and fresh salads.
Mercato Coperto, Piazza Andrea Costa, 48100; 0544 32073; lunch only

Osteria dei Battibecchi *moderate*
This small place has a small but tasty menu – home-made lasagne, pork hot pot with cardoons, and caramelized figs.
Via Della Tesoreria Vecchia 16, 48100; 0544 219 536; closed Mon

Enoteca Ca' de Ven *moderate*
This bar/restaurant, in a historic palazzo near Dante's Tomb, is a Ravenna institution – try the *piadina* and *crescioni* (filled Italian flatbreads).
Via Corrado Ricci 24, 48100; 0544 30163; www.cadeven.it; closed Mon

---

DAY TRIP OPTIONS

Adults will enjoy Ferrara and Ravenna's historic buildings, while the watery wildlife-filled Po Delta and the beach will keep young families busy.

Art and architecture

At Ferrara ①, spend half a day seeing the city's frescoes and Renaissance architecture, then head off to Argenta ⑨ to visit one of the delta's oldest

buildings and lunch in the countryside. Next explore the great churches and Byzantine mosaics in Ravenna ⑩.

The SS16 joins all these stops.

The natural world

From Ravenna ⑩, pack a picnic and set off early to Valli di Comacchio ⑧, to spend a couple of hours watching the water birds on the lagoon. Carry on to Comacchio ⑦ to visit the eel

pickling factory, then head off to Porto Garibaldi ⑥ for lunch on the beach. Drive north to the woods of Bosco della Mesola to glimpse the shy deer, or just stay on the beach.

Head north from Ravenna on SP1, turning left at Cruser following signs to Comacchio. Retrace drive instructions to Porto Garibaldi, then head up along the coast to Bosco Mesola.

Eat and Drink: inexpensive, under €25; moderate, €25–€45; expensive, over €45

The Azure Coast to the Po Valley

Genoa to Portovenere

Highlights

- **Magnificent palazzos**
  Explore the grand historic palaces and the dark tangle of ancient alleyways in vibrant Genoa

- **Ham, violets and fine art**
  Discover the architectural and artistic gems amid the gourmet delights of historic and affluent Parma

- **Golfo dei Poeti**
  Take in the exquisitely framed views of the sea at beautiful Portovenere where Lord Byron once swam

- **Apennine scenery**
  Zig-zag around the mountains and through the untouched countryside of the tree-clad Apennines

The pretty seafront at Portovenere and the Chiesa di San Pietro

The Azure Coast to the Po Valley

At the western end of the Riviera di Levante, Genoa, the capital of Liguria, is a dynamic, multi-layered city, with the extra spice of being a working port. Built on the wealth of merchants, it's a city of glittering Baroque churches, of 16th- and 17th-century palazzos and of fish and oranges spilling out of dark alleyways. At the eastern end of the Riviera, literary La Spezia, the naval capital of Liguria, is big brother to pretty Portovenere, and gateway to the Cinque Terre. Inland, above the farms and unspoilt Apennine countryside, affluent Parma and Reggio Emilia take well-deserved pride in what they have produced – fabulous art and architecture and the famed prosciutto and Parmigiano.

Above Basilica San Prospero and Piazza San Prospero, Reggio Emilia, *see p146*
Below right Cattedrale di San Lorenzo, Genoa, *see p144*

KEY

🚗 Drive route

ACTIVITIES

Explore Genoa, Europe's largest medieval centre, and climb the hills above for a panoramic overview

Take a boat from Portovenere for the sparkling Golfo dei Poeti (Gulf of Poets) and the lovely islands of Palmária, Tino and Tinetto

Sample the delights of the Po Valley – from the freshest of fish on the coast to the renowned Parmigiano and prosciutto from Parma

Go hunting for mushrooms in the Apennines

Cycle around the historic sites of Parma at a leisurely pace

Below Picturesque scenery en route to Langhirano, *see p145*

PLAN YOUR DRIVE

Start/finish: Genoa to Portovenere.

Number of days: 4–5, allowing a day for Genoa, a trip to Parma and time to enjoy La Spezia and Portovenere.

Distance: Approx 325 km (200 miles).

Road conditions: Mountain roads are twisting and slow, and the coast road coast is winding and busy in summer.

When to go: Genoa can be good to visit in winter. It gets full during the Boat Show in Sep, and some places close for Aug. The interior is accessible all year, although snow chains may be needed in winter. The coast gets busy Jul & Aug.

Opening times: Major museums open 9am–7pm Tue–Fri and from 10am Sat & Sun. Some museums and smaller churches close early afternoon. Shops are closed all day Sun and Mon am, and open 9am–12:30pm and 3:30–7:30pm on other days (large shops stay open all day). Parma's shops close Thu pm.

Main market days: Genoa: Mon–Sat; Parma: Wed & Sat; Reggio Emilia: Tue & Fri; La Spezia: Fri.

Shopping: In Genoa, look for pesto, *trenette* (short linguini) and *trofie* (pasta twists); in Langhirano, prosciutto and *culatello* (hams) and, in the mountains, porcini mushrooms. Parma is justly famous for its ham, cheese and Parma violets. Reggio Emilia's shops also sell Parmigiano-Reggiano cheese.

Major festivals: Genoa: Holy Week processions, Easter; Festival Musicale del Mediterraneo (concerts at the port), Jul & Aug; International Boat Show, 2nd week in Sep; **La Spezia**: Palio del Golfo (rowing race), 1st Sun in Aug; **Parma**: Festival del Prosciutto, Sep; Palio (medieval sports), Sep; Verdi Festival, Oct; **Portovenere**: Festa della Madonna Bianca (religious procession), mid-Aug.

DAY TRIP OPTIONS

It takes a full day to see the sights and spend time in the **museums**, **churches** and **palazzos** in Genoa. From there, drive along the **coast** to visit the port of La Spezia and romantic Portovenere with its **castle**, **grotto** and **islands**. For full details, see p147.

Above The huge arch of medieval Porta Soprana, the main entrance to Genoa

VISITING GENOA

Parking
The main car park is under Piazza della Vittoria, where bus tickets for the city can be bought. The centre is closed to traffic.

Tourist Information
Via Garibaldi 12r; 010 557 2903; open daily; www.visitgenoa.it

WHERE TO STAY

GENOA

Cristoforo Colombo *moderate*
Colourful and elegant rooms in the historic part of the city. In summer, breakfast is served on the roof terrace.
Via Porta Soprana 27, 16123; 010 251 3643; www.hotelcolombo.it

Cairoli *moderate*
Contemporary art inspires the bright and fresh rooms in this palazzo hotel, with an outdoor terrace and small gym. Garage parking is available.
Via Cairoli 14/4, 16124; 010 246 1454; www.hotelcairoligenova.com

Locanda di Palazzo Cicala *expensive*
Chic hotel with large rooms and stucco ceilings in an 18th-century palazzo near the cathedral. Paid parking nearby.
Piazza San Lorenzo 16, 16123; 010 251 8824; www.palazzocicala.it

AROUND BERCETO

Villa Tre Angeli *inexpensive*
The owners of this pretty pink Liberty-style villa are very helpful and can arrange mushroom-picking expeditions and Parmigiano and prosciutto tours.
Via Roma 37, Bedonia 43041; 0525 824 841; www.villatreangeli.com

❶ Genoa (Genova)
Genoa; 16100

Surrounded by hills and looking out to sea, proud Genoa was transformed in the 16th and 17th centuries, when its wealthy merchants commissioned grand palazzos in what was then named "Strada Nuova" (New Street) – now called Via Garibaldi, it is a UNESCO World Heritage Site and three of the palazzos are world-class museums. For stunning views of the historic centre, take the lift to Castelletto.

A three-hour walking tour

Start from the De Ferrari metro station and follow Via Dante to the two towers of the **Porta Soprana** ①, a gate in the 12th-century walls that separate the historic from the modern city. The Vico Dritto di Ponticello leads past the **Chiostro di Sant' Andrea** ②, a ruined 12th-century cloister that was once part of a Benedictine monastery. **Casa di Christoforo Colombo** ③, the supposed boyhood home of Christopher Columbus, is next door. Return to Porta Soprana and turn left into Via Ravecca, past the bell tower and cloisters of the 13th-century Chiesa di Sant' Agostino, now the **Museo di Sant' Agostino** ④, with works by Giovanni Pisano (1250–1315) and Antonio Canova (1757–1822). The museum fronts **Piazza di Sarzano** ⑤, so long, that it was once used for jousting and rope-making.

Stradone di Sant'Agostino leads to the Romanesque **Chiesa di San Donato** ⑥ with an octagonal campanile, a rose window and, inside, striped columns and a painted ceiling. Follow Via San Donato round the church to Piazza delle Erbe, with a full range of bars, including lively **Bar Berto** ⑦ (1904), decorated with tiles from Albisola. Walk back past the church to Via San Bernardo and look for the **Antica Drogheria Torielli** ⑧, filled with all kinds of herbs and spices.

Via San Bernardo leads to arcaded Via Turati. Turn right and keep going until the sign for Vico dei Caprettari is on the right. Look in (or get a haircut) at the **Barbiere** ⑨, to admire the Art Deco ornamentation. The alleyways here have an enticing mix of shops.

Turn left into Via di Cannetto then right into Via San Lorenzo with its striped 12th-century **Cattedrale di San Lorenzo** ⑩, flanked by two lions. Look inside for the Renaissance Cappella di San Giovanni Battista, once home to St John the Baptist's ashes. Carry on to Piazza Matteotti and the 16th-century **Palazzo Ducale** ⑪. Look inside for exhibitions. For some Baroque pomp, continue to the right of Piazza Matteotti and the **Chiesa del Gesù** ⑫, full of coloured marble, gilt stucco and frescoes. Take Salita Arcivescovado, turn left onto Vico San Matteo, then right to Via Soziglia for a drink and a cake in coffee houses **Klainguti** or **Romanengo** ⑬, dating from 1800s. A left turn at the end of Via Soziglia onto Vico del

Ferro leads to Via Garibaldi and its great palazzos. Step inside **Palazzo Doria-Tursi** ⑭ for the beautiful courtyard and double marble staircase and view the stucco work. The **Palazzo Bianco** ⑮ has wonderful paintings by Filippino Lippi, Veronese and Caravaggio, as well as Dutch and Flemish masters Rubens, Van Dyck and Memling. The **Palazzo Rosso** ⑯ has paintings, furniture and 17th-century frescoes. Continue to Piazza Fontane Marose and Via XXV Aprile, passing the 19th-century **Teatro Carlo Felice** ⑰, home of Genoa's opera house.

If there's still time, take the Liberty-style lift from Piazza Portello, off Via Garibaldi, up to **Belvedere Montaldo** ⑱ for sweeping views. If staying longer in Genoa, take time to explore the port area.

🚗 *Follow signs to motorway A12 east to the Chiavari exit, signed Parma then SP225 to Carasco. Take SP586, then turn right on SP26bis. Continue up the Passo del Bocco and take the SP3 through Bedonia. Follow signs for A15 on SP523. After railway bridge, turn right for Berceto. Park in Piazza San Giovanni. For Corchia, follow signs to Corchia.*

② Berceto
Parma; 43042
The road to Berceto climbs through the Apennines and chestnut, beech and oak forests to the Valle del Taro, which is porcini mushroom country. Quiet Berceto, with its stone houses and cobbled streets, has changed little since it was an important stop on the Via Francigena. Its main attraction is the Romanesque **Duomo di San Moderanno**, which has a 12th-century lunette of the Crucifixion.

Time has also passed by the village of **Corchia**, tucked away in chestnut groves a little west of Berceto. Dating back to the 13th century, everything here is made of stone. For 400 years

the village depended on its nearby mines, which only closed in 1943.

🚗 *Take SP15 to Calestano, then follow signs for Langhirano.*

③ Langhirano
Parma; 43100
It is a lovely drive through Calestano, where the countryside opens out into green terraced meadows, vines and orchards. The next town, Langhirano, is dedicated to the curing of air-dried ham; its many factories open their windows to what is said to be a perfect combination of sea and mountain air. The **Museo del Prosciutto** *(open weekends)* in the Foro Boario, a former cattle market, tells the history and process from pig to plate.

🚗 *Take SP665 to the signposted Castello di Torrechiara and car park.*

④ Castello di Torrechiara
Parma; 43010
This impressive castle *(closed Mon)* was built in the 15th century for defence, as can be seen by the three rings of walls and four square towers, and also as a family residence. There are a series of vivid 16th-century frescoes: the *Salone degli Acrobati* (Acrobats' Room) shows gymnasts in a human pyramid on the backs of lions and the *Camera d'Oro* (Golden Room) tells the love story between Count Pier Maria Rossi, for whom the castle was built, and his lover, Bianca Pelligrini.

🚗 *Take SP665 to Parma. Use a free car park off the tangenziale (ring road). Buy a ticket from machine for bus to centre.*

Above top The port of Genoa, facing the Ligurian Sea **Above left** Mural of St George slaying the dragon on the town hall, Genoa **Above right** The spectacular Castello Torrechiara, near Langhirano **Below left** The picturesque village of Calestano

SHOPPING IN TORRECHIARA
Buy prosciutto, salami and Parmigiano at **Salumeria da Gardoni** *(Piazza Leoni 5, 43010; 0521 355119; www.www. facebook.com/gardonitorrechiara).*

EAT AND DRINK

GENOA
Il Cadraio *moderate*
Traditional genoese specialties served in a cozy, rustic trattoria. Great wine list. *Vico dietro il coro della Maddalena, 26r, Genoa 16124; 010 247 4095; www. facebook.com/ilcadraio/*

Da Rina *expensive*
This restaurant in an old warehouse overlooking the Porto Antico serves fish dishes and excellent antipasti. *Mura delle Grazie 3r, 16128; 010 246 6475; www.ristorantedarina.it*

Other options
For great focaccia, try **Forno Patrone** *(Via Ravecca 72r, 16128; 010 251 1093; closed Wed pm)* near the Porta Soprana.

AROUND BERCETO
Trattoria Corchia *inexpensive*
The small trattoria in tiny Corchia specializes in local game and mushroom dishes and is also known for its pizzas. *Corchia 43042; 0525 61814; closed Mon*

La Pergola *moderate–expensive*
This traditional restaurant puts mushrooms to the fore – expect porcini risotto and wild mushroom soufflé. *Via Garibaldi 19, Bedonia 43041; 0525 826 612; www.ristorante-lapergola.it; closed Thu*

Eat and Drink: inexpensive, under €25; moderate, €25–€45; expensive over €45

Above left Boats in La Spezia's harbour
Above right Piazza Prampolini, Reggio Emilia
Below Statue of the 16th-century artist Parmigianino in Piazza Santa Maria della Steccata, Parma

ACTIVITIES IN PARMA

Explore the car-free centre of town by hiring a bike from one of the **Punto Bici** (www.infomobility.pr.it) pick-up and drop-off points in the city. For tours of prosciutto and Parmigiano factories with tastings, try **Food Valley Gourmet Tours** (Viale Frati 38D; 0521 798 515; www.foodvalleytravel.com).

WHERE TO STAY

PARMA

Hotel Torino moderate–expensive
This comfortable hotel, furnished in modern style, is right in the historic centre and has garage parking.
Borgo Angelo Mazza 7, 43121; 0521 281 046; www.hotel-torino.it

REGGIO EMILIA

Albergo delle Notarie moderate
In the heart of the city, this hotel has views of the cathedral, a good restaurant and parking.
Via Palazzolo 5, 42121; 0522 453 500; www.albergonotarie.it

LA SPEZIA

Hotel Firenze e Continentale moderate
This large hotel with an attractive marble and wood interior offers stylish and comfortable accommodation.
Via Paleocapa 7, 19122; 0187 713 200; www.hotelfirenzecontinentale.it

PORTOVENERE

Belvedere moderate
This family-run hotel offers a terrace overlooking the sea, rooms with balconies and on-site parking.
Via Garibaldi 26, 19025; 0187 790 608; www.belvedereportovenere.it

⑤ Parma

Parma; 43100
Seductive Parma is a treasure house of art and architecture, and a store of gastronomic delights. The 11th-century **Duomo** reflects both aspects. It is home to works by two sons of Parma – Parmagianino (1503–40) and Correggio (1489–1534), who painted the *Assumption* (1534) in the central cupola, and at the main entrance is the earliest known bas-relief of the slaughter of a pig. Next door, the 13th-century octagonal baptistery, by architect and sculptor Benedetto Antelami (c.1150–1230), is a confection of pink and white Verona marble. Don't miss the decorative interior.

Stroll over the green lawn to the vast Palazzo della Pilotta, built by the Farnese family and housing several museums. A visit to the **Galleria Nazionale** (Tue–Sun) allows a closer look at works by Parmagianino, Correggio and others. Here, too, is the **Museo Archeologico Nazionale** (open daily) and the wooden **Teatro Farnese**, inaugurated in 1628, when the auditorium was flooded to present a *naumachia* (naval battle). The three-tier auditorium has a revolving stage, the first in Italy.

The **Museo Glauco Lombardi in Via Garibaldi** is testament to Maria Luigia, who became Duchess of Parma in 1815 after Napoleon's abdication, and was a famous fan of Parma violets. Her dresses, jewellery, family portraits and watercolours are all on show.

🚗 *From the tangenziale take SS9 to Reggio Emilia. Park in the centre at Caserma Zucchi on Viale Isonzo.*

⑥ Reggio Emilia

Emilia Romagna; 42100
As affluent as its neighbour Parma, if less glamourous, Reggio Emilia is a pleasant town to visit, with two large, lively central squares. Piazza Prampolini holds the **Duomo**, topped by a brick octagonal lantern tower, its Romanesque upper half in contrast to the 16th-century marble lower half, where Adam and Eve appear in the lunette over the doorway. In the same square, in 1797 the **Palazzo del Capitano del Popolo** flew the red, green and white tricolor that was later – in 1848 – to become Italy's national flag. It's a brief walk along the colonnaded street to Piazza San Prospero and the Baroque **Basilica San Prospero**, its façade busy with statues of saints, and guarded by six pink Verona marble lions. The profuse displays of sculpture, natural history and archaeology in the antique glass cases of the **Musei Civici** are a work of art in themselves. Don't miss the fine black and white medieval mosaics in the entrance hall.

🚗 *Take SS63 south towards La Spezia. At Aulla, join SS62 and follow signs for A15 to La Spezia and the road by the port. Turn right on Viale Amendola and park in Piazza d'Armi (2nd left).*

⑦ La Spezia
La Spezia, Liguria; 19100
With its mild climate and stunning position at the head of the Golfo della Spezia, backed by mountains, it's easy to see why Byron, Shelley, George Sands and DH Lawrence all loved the area. Nowadays, it is a thriving port and Italy's chief naval base, and it's still a treat to take a boat out into the bay. Standing back from the palm-fringed Giardini Pubblici along the sea front is Piazza Chiodi, site of the naval Arsenale from the 1860s. Next to it is the grand **Museo Tecnico Navale** *(open daily)* with model ships, figureheads and submarines. Wide boulevards lead to the centre and the modern market in Piazza Cavour with its wavy roof. Close by, the **Museo Amedeo Lia** *(closed Mon)* has first-class enamels and ivories, Roman bronzes and works by Tintoretto, Cranach and Canaletto. Next door, the **Museo del Sigillo** has the world's largest collection of seals, including Chinese jade and Art Nouveau objects by René Lalique.

🚗 *Take SP530 to Portovenere. Park on the main road before the village.*

⑧ Portovenere
La Spezia, Liguria; 19025
Dependent on fish in Roman times, when it was known as Portus Veneris (Port of Venus), Portovenere is still a typical Ligurian fishing town, with tall ochre and pink tower houses rising up from the small harbour. A walk along the harbour front and up the marble steps leads to the striped Genoese-Gothic **Chiesa di San Pietro**, stunningly sited on the tip of the rocky promontory that borders the western side of the Golfo dei Poeti. Alongside is the **Arpaia Grotto**, or Byron's Grotto, where a plaque on the wall commemorates the poet's swim to Lerici. Windows in the wall provide perfectly framed views of the Cinque Terre. Turning back towards the town, steep alleyways lead up to the chunky 16th-century **Castello Doria**, with more stunning views, and then back down to the main Via Capellini, a run of little bars, restaurants and boutiques. If time allows, take a boat from the port to explore one of the lovely islands nearby – Palmária, Tino or Tinetto.

BOAT TRIPS AND FERRIES
For information on passenger boats between La Spezia and Portovenere, Isola Palmária and the Cinque Terre, visit **Consorzio Marittimo Turistico** *(5 Terre, Via Don Minzoni 13, La Spezia 19121; 0187 732 987; www.navigazionegolfodeipoeti.it).*

WHERE TO EAT

PARMA
Enoteca Fontana *inexpensive*
This restaurant, popular with locals, serves wine by the glass from an extensive wine list (the Lambrusco is good). Snacks feature local specialities. *Strada Farini 24a, 43121; 0521 286 037; closed Mon & Tue*

Gallo D'Oro *moderate*
Rabbit and horsemeat feature on the menu here apart from classic Parma dishes, a variety of salads and stuffed pastas. It is located in the historic centre. *Borgo della Salina 3, 43121; 0521 208 846; closed Sun*

LA SPEZIA
Il Ristorantino di Bayon *expensive*
Stylish and intimate restaurant with the accent on fish. Enjoy Palmária mussels and *trofie* (tightly twisted pasta) with shrimps and almonds. *Via Felice Cavallotti 23, 19121; 0187 732 209; closed lunch & Sun; booking advised*

AROUND PORTOVENERE
Locanda Lorena *expensive*
It takes a boat trip to reach this excellent seafood restaurant on the Isola Palmária, but it's well worth it. They also have rooms. *Via Cavour 4, Isola Palmária 19025; 0187 792 370; closed Wed & Nov–Feb; www.locandalorena.com*

Above Portovenere's harbour, with its pastel-coloured tower-houses **Left** Fishing boat in the sea beneath Castello Doria, Portovenere

---

DAY TRIP OPTIONS
Genoa easily deserves a day to itself for exploration and from there you can head down the coast to La Spezia and a boat trip to Portovenere.

Medieval Genoa
Simply spend the whole day in Genoa ❶, investigating the maze of alleyways that make up the medieval centre, the Baroque jewel of San Gesù and the magnificent Cattedrale di San Lorenzo before discovering the artistic treasures of the palazzos. Stop for a coffee at Pasticceria Klainguti and be sure to end the day with a seafood supper.

Big port and little harbour
From Genoa ❶, enjoy the coastal road to La Spezia ❼, stroll the port's pleasant boulevards, take in some maritime history, then hop on a boat to lovely Portovenere ❽ and soak up the wonderful views of the Cinque Terre from the Chiesa di San Pietro.

For La Spezia from Genoa, choose between SP1 which gives good views of the coast until Sestri Levante, or the quicker A12/E60 motorway, which gives a journey time of 1½ hours.

Eat and Drink: inexpensive, under €25; moderate, €25–€45; expensive over €45

The Ligurian Coast and Apennines

Camogli to Riomaggiore

Highlights

- **Parco Nazionale delle Cinque Terre**
  Explore the five exquisite villages of
  this UNESCO World Heritage Site in a
  dramatic setting on the Ligurian coast

- **Fruits of the forest and sea**
  Sample the freshest seafood and
  enjoy produce from Apennine farms
  such as pestos, chestnuts and honey

- **Peaceful Parco dell'Antola**
  Hike among the wooded hills, dotted
  with lakes and ancient villages, in
  this overlooked part of Liguria

- **Jewel of the Riviera**
  Enjoy lovely Portofino, squeezed
  between turquoise waters and the
  lush greenery of its promontory

The picturesque harbour of Portofino – an
iconic fishing village on the Italian Riviera

The Ligurian Coast and Apennines

Sparkling waters lap the Ligurian coast. Beach resorts, tiny fishing harbours, hidden coves and exquisite Portofino all vie for attention with the famous five villages of the Cinque Terre, where colourful mosaics of houses tumble down steep cliffs to the sea. Inland lies a landscape of ancient hamlets and shady dry-stone terraces of vines, olives and aromatic basil. In contrast, the Ligurian Apennines are a world apart – one of medieval castles and agricultural villages set among lakes, meadows and chestnut forests, where sheep graze peacefully and horses are still used to log timber.

Above Typical tower houses of the Cinque Terre, Manarola, *see p158*

ACTIVITIES

Hike or cycle along the *sentieri* – trails – in the stunning Parco Nazionale delle Cinque Terre

Enjoy a panoramic picnic at the Santuario di Montenero above Riomaggiore

Taste the speciality of Vernazza – honey-coloured *sciacchetrà*, a sweet dessert wine

Surf the waves or laze on the beach at Levanto

Take a boat trip from Camogli for coastal views of San Fruttuoso, Portofino and the Cinque Terre coast

Play a round of seaside golf at Rapallo

Explore Lago di Brugneto amid beech and chestnut woods

0 kilometres   6

0 miles   6

KEY

Drive route

Above The popular Monterosso al Mare beach, Cinque Terre, *see p156*

PLAN YOUR DRIVE

Start/finish: Camogli to Riomaggiore.

Number of days: 4–5, allowing one day each for the coast and the interior and 2 days for the Cinque Terre.

Distance: Approx 182 km (113 miles).

Road conditions: Roads are slow, narrow, twisting, often very steep and sometimes single track with infrequent passing places. If you choose to visit the Cinque Terre by car rather than by public transport, arrive early in the day to be sure of a parking place. There are no fuel stops in the Cinque Terre.

When to go: Coastal resorts get very crowded Jul–Aug and roads may be impassable. Spring and autumn are cooler and less busy. Autumn makes for the best colour in the interior.

Opening times: Shops close 1–4pm; some in the main towns open on Sundays. Churches and museums vary, but are usually open in the mornings until 1pm and from 4–7pm. Museums are generally shut on Mondays.

Main market days: Bonassola: Thu; Levanto: Wed; Monterosso al Mare: Thu; Vernazza: Tue.

Shopping: Look for *sciacchetrà* (sweet wine) in the Cinque Terre, *castagnaccio* (chestnut cake), virgin olive oil, pesto, honey and Limoncino liqueur.

Major festivals: Camogli: Stella Maris (sea procession), 1st Sun in Aug; Sagra del Pesce (fish festival), 2nd Sun in May; Levanto: Festa del Mare (in honour of San Giacomo), late Jul; Monterosso al Mare: Sagra dei Limoni (lemon festival), late May; Torneo di Noci (walnut tournament), Sep; Manarola: Presepe di Manarola (Manarola Nativity), Dec; Pentema: Presepe di Pentema, Dec–Jan.

DAY TRIP OPTIONS

It's easiest to reach the Cinque Terre by train – once there, walk **La Via dell'Amore** (The Love Trail) from Riomaggiore to Manarola for views of **pretty villages** and **harbours**. Enjoy the **cable car** and **coastal delights** of Sestri Levante. Get away from it all in the **Apennines**, exploring Torriglia's **castle** and **walking** around Lago del Brugneto. For full details, *see p159*.

Right View of the Ligurian Appenines on the way to Torriglia **Below right** Rapallo castle, built in the 16th century to ward off pirates **Below left** Colourful façades on Camogli's beachfront promenade

WHERE TO STAY

CAMOGLI

La Camogliese *moderate*
Friendly, family-run 2-star hotel with balconies overlooking the sea, right in the centre of town.
Via Garibaldi 55, 16032; 0185 771 402; www.lacamogliese.it

Villa Rosmarino *moderate–expensive*
Chic villa high above Camogli, with six very contemporary, art-filled rooms, with terrace, pool, garden and views.
Via Figari 38, 16032; 0185 771 580; www.villarosmarino.com; no children under 8

PORTOFINO

Eden *moderate–expensive*
Set a little way back from the piazzetta, this is the most affordable hotel in town, with a charming garden and restaurant.
Via Dritto 18, 16034; 0185 269 091; www.hoteledenportofino.com

RAPALLO

Italia e Lido *moderate*
Enjoy the private beach and dining terrace at this historic promenade hotel next to the castle.
Lungomare Castello 1, 16035; 0185 50492; www.italiaelido.com

TORRIGLIA

Hotel della Posta *inexpensive*
Built in the early 1900s, this central hotel is simple, but well furnished.
Via Matteotti 39, 16029; 010 944 050

Below The picturesque harbour settlement of Portofino

① Camogli
Genoa; 16032
Steeped in seafaring tradition and once rivalling Genoa in naval power, the town acquired its name, Casa Mogli (house of wives), because the menfolk spent so much of their time at sea. The *case torri*, the colourful houses up to seven storeys high, threaded with steep alleyways that are the hallmark of the fishing villages of the Levante coast, are stacked up from the picturesque harbour. During the Sagra del Pesce (fish festival) in May, the harbour is the scene of a festive fry-up when thousands of fish are cooked in a giant 5-m (15-ft) pan and distributed free to the crowds. The 12th-century **Dragonara Castle**, set on a rocky promontory, separates the busy harbour from the beach,

and the **Museo Marinaro** *(closed Tue)*, full of models of ships, paintings and naval instruments, recalls the town's glorious maritime past.

For San Fruttuoso, take a boat from Camogli (along the coast, or walk about 3 hours in each direction).

② San Fruttuoso
Genoa; 16030
The boat from Camogli chugs round the Golfo del Tigullio to the ancient Benedictine **Abbazia di San Fruttuoso**, straddling a sandy cove; originally, boats would have moored under its arches. Sights include the 11th-century church, topped by a tiled cupola, the cloisters, and the 16th-century watchtower. The other attraction, visitable by glass-bottomed boat, is a bigger than life-size bronze statue of **Cristo degli Abissi** (Christ of the Deep), sunk out in the bay in 1954, hands raised in blessing for those who work on or under the sea. There are beachside cafés, bars and swimming, but no road access.

Head north out of Camogli to Via Aurelia/SP1, then turn right. Fork right onto the SP39, then right again on SP227 along the coast to Portofino. Park in the multi-storey car park.

③ Portofino
Genoa; 16034
Even those without a luxury yacht anchored in the enchanting harbour can appreciate how Portofino earned

Where to Stay: inexpensive, under €100; moderate, €100–€200; expensive, over €200

its reputation as one of Italy's most romantic spots. Window shopping at Missoni or Dior and people-watching from a waterside café may be a draw for many, but for the most gorgeous views, walk to **Castello Brown** (Nov–Mar: closed Mon–Fri), up in the pines on the peninsula. Montague Yeats Brown, the British consul, gave his name to this 16th-century castle when he lived here in the 1890s. From here, walk on to the **Faro**, the old lighthouse at the Punta del Capo. Art lovers should visit the **Museo del Parco** (winter: closed Tue), overlooking the harbour, which displays intriguing modern sculptures.

🚗 *Take the SP227 north to Rapallo. Park along the seafront or at the car park on Via Milite Ignoto.*

④ Rapallo
Genoa; 16035
The grand hotels and villas lining Rapallo's Lungomare still recall the 19th-century aristocrats and literati, among them Max Beerbohm and Ezra Pound, who were attracted by the town's inviting climate and location. Along the shore, past the ruined 16th-century castle jutting out into the sea, the ochre Villa Tigullio houses the **Museo del Merletto**, where drawers full of lace reflect the town's past history of lace-making. In the centre, the **Museo Gaffoglio** (closed Sun & Mon) holds an eclectic collection of Meissen porcelain, 19th- and 20th-century pastoral paintings and exquisite Fabergé pieces. For the best view of the area, take a ride up the *funivia* (cable car) from Piazza Solari to the striped and pinnacled **Santuario di Montallegro** (1559), which houses a Byzantine icon said to possess miraculous powers.

🚗 *Take the SP1 towards Genoa and, from Recco, turn right onto SP333. At Gattorna, take SP21 to Torriglia. Park in the main square.*

⑤ Torriglia
Genoa; 16029
A 30-minute drive on a steep and twisting road leads from the coast up to the chestnut forests, lakes and villages of the Ligurian Apennines. Verdant in spring and summer, and glorious in autumn, this is a much less-visited area than the coast. Torriglia's main sight is its castle, perched high above the town. The domain of the Fieschi from the mid-14th century, then the Doria family from the 16th to the 18th centuries, it is now in ruins. The area is known for its porcini mushrooms and *canestrelli* biscuits.

🚗 *Take the uphill road north to SP15-1 and turn left and left again, following brown signs to Pentema. Park at the road's end for the top of village or follow signs to Pezza for the lower part.*

Above The the small fishing village of Camogli **Below** The ruins of Torriglia castle, set among woods

WHERE TO EAT

CAMOGLI AND AROUND
La Cucina di Nonna Nina *moderate*
Whether dining in the blue and white rooms or outside in the garden, visitors will enjoy the best of Liguria's cuisine.
Via Molfino 126, Località San Rocco, 16032 (from Camogli take SP1 towards La Spezia, then turn right); 0185 773 835; www.nonnanina.it; closed Wed

La Bossa *moderate–expensive*
Wine bottles line the walls of this small *enoteca*, which has a daily-changing menu featuring dishes such as stuffed anchovies, rabbit or a fish ravioli.
Via della Reppublica 124, 16032; 0185 772 505; www.labossa.it; closed Wed & lunch Sep–Jun

PORTOFINO
O Magazin *moderate–expensive*
An ideal spot on the water for watching the world go by – be prepared to wait for a table. Try their ragù with pasta.
Calata Marconi 34, 16034; 0185 269 178

RAPALLO
Osteria O Bansin *moderate*
Long-established restaurant in the old town with an accent on fish and good-value fixed-price lunches.
Via Venezia 105, 16035; 0185 231 119; www.trattoriabansin.it; summer: closed Sun lunch; winter: closed Sun & Mon eve

TORRIGLIA
La Taverna dei Fieschi *moderate*
After admiring the Bakelite radios, sit down to dishes that celebrate local porcini mushrooms, chestnuts, wild boar and *canestrelli* (biscuits).
Via Magioncalda 30, 16029; 010 944 815; closed Mon

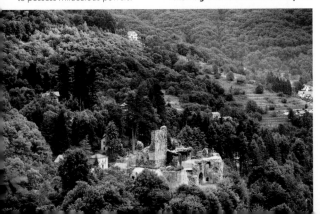

PARCO DELL'AVETO

This is an important protected area of mountain peaks, beech woods and glacial lakes, famous for its large number of insectivorous plants. The park office in Borzonasca can supply maps and information about walks and hikes in the area. *Via Mallè 75a, Borzonasca 16041; 0185 343 370; www.parks.it/parco.aveto*

WHERE TO STAY

PENTEMA

Locanda Al Pettirosso *inexpensive*
This rustic locanda/trattoria, set in the remote little mountain village in the Parco dell'Antola, offers three pretty rooms and a cosy place to eat. *Località Pentema 3, 16029; 010 944 802*

AROUND FONTANIGORDA

Due Ponti *inexpensive*
The peaceful location – surrounded by pines, with the River Trebbia lapping at the bottom of the garden – makes this a welcoming hotel. It has a good restaurant and bikes are available. *Via Nazionale 2, Loc. Due Ponti, (3 km/2 miles before Loco on SP45) 16023; 010 958 12; www.hoteldueponti.it*

BORZONASCA

Agriturismo Casa del Bosco *inexpensive*
This 19th-century villa has undergone a quality refurbishment and overlooks vine and fruit terraces, and a stream with waterfalls. It is eclectically furnished and can serve lunch and dinner, too. *Loc. Prato di Caregli 44, 16041; 340 728 4206; www.agriturismocasadelbosco.it*

SESTRI LEVANTE

Villa Agnese *moderate*
On the outskirts of town, this modern and eco-conscious hotel has light, airy rooms and a relaxing garden. Expect organic produce for breakfast. *Via alla Fattoria Pallavicini 1A, 16039 (close to Sestri Levante exit of A12); 0185 457 583; www.hotelvillaagnese.com*

Grand Hotel dei Castelli *expensive*
For a luxurious stay, head up to this 1920s cliff-top castle-hotel. The spacious rooms are filled with antiques and pictures, and outside there are gardens, a sea-water pool and roof-top terrace. *Via Penisola di Levante 26, 16039; 0185 487 020; www.hoteldeicastelli.it*

Other options

The **Hotel Helvetia** (*Via Cappuccini 43, 16039; 0185 41175; www.hotelhelvetia. it*) is close to the beach and has a shuttle parking service to the edge of town.

⑥ Pentema
Genoa; 16029

Still very much the isolated mountain village it has always been, Pentema clings to the hillside, stone houses and sheds fronting steep cobbled streets and steps. At Christmas, the village is much visited for its *presepe,* which consists of much more than the Christmas crib. Yellow numbers painted on the walls direct pilgrims on a journey through more than 40 life-size tableaux, reflecting all aspects of 19th-century village life and crafts, culminating in the Nativity scene. Many of these can actually be seen all the year round.

🚗 *Head back towards Torriglia until meeting SP15-1, then turn left towards Propata. Turn right just before a tunnel, following signed to Lago del Brugneto and park near the dam.*

⑦ Lago del Brugneto
Genoa; 16025

Lush terraced meadows, groves of hazelnut, beech and chestnut and horse-logged wood are hallmarks of the **Parco dell'Antola** (*www. parcoantola.it*), which encompasses the arms of Lago di Brugneto. An artificial lake constructed in 1959 to provide water for Genoa and Piacenza, the lake makes a good stopping point for a peaceful and

undemanding walk (see website for suggestions). A wooded path, following old mule tracks, skirts the arms of the lake close to the water, while other trails lead to waterfalls and an old mill.

🚗 *From the lake, follow signs for Montebruno, turning left at SS45. Carry on along SS45, signed Piacenza, turn right onto SP17 after Loco, then turn left onto SP18 to Fontanigorda. There is plenty of parking available.*

Below The Baia di Silenzio and the harbour at Sestri Levante **Bottom left** The peaceful, wooded countryside around Lago del Brugneto **Bottom right** One of Fontanigorda's 13 pineapple-topped fountains

Far left The Lago del Brugneto, an artificial lake that supplies Genoa with water **Centre left** The river that feeds Lago del Brugneto **Left** Hans Christian Andersen's favourite beach at Sestri Levante

⑧ Fontanigorda
Genoa; 16023
It is easy to while away half an hour or so here, walking the cobbled streets in search of all 13 of the pineapple-topped fountains for which this small, red-roofed mountain village is famous. The fountains are dedicated – aptly enough for a place with an abundance of water – to the Mater Dolorosa (Our Lady of Sorrows). The Baroque church of **Santi Antonio e Jacopo** has a decorative red-and-gold interior and impressive barley-sugar columns.

Follow the sign for Casoni on SP17, then SP48, drive over the Passo di Fregarolo and turn right at SP586 for Borzonasca, where the Abbazia di Sant/Andrea di Borzone (3 km/2 miles east of the village) is signposted along SP49. For Borzonasca, park in Piazza Garibaldi by the church.

⑨ Borzonasca
Genoa; 16041
After a spectacular journey over the 1,203-m (3,950-ft) Passo di Fregarolo, Borzonasca's main attraction is the **Abbazia di Sant'Andrea di Borzone** *(open daily)*, a short drive east of the town. Standing in peaceful isolation and guarded by a 600-year-old cypress tree, the Benedictine complex was founded in the 12th century on an earlier 9th-century Lombard building, and is characterized by its rows of blind brick and stone arcading. The bell tower was probably originally an ancient watchtower. In the town itself, shops sell local honey, San Stè cheese, and, in season, hazelnuts; and the Aveto Park office provides information about hikes in the area.

Take SP586 for Carasco and follow signs for Chiavari on SP225, then turn left on SP1 for Sestri Levante.

⑩ Sestri Levante
Genoa; 16039
Hans Christian Andersen enjoyed his visit here in 1833 so much that the town named the sandy beach **Baia delle Favole (Bay of Fairy Tales)**. On the other side of the peninsula along which this popular and cheerful resort clusters, lies the more intimate **Baia di Silenzio**, with its fleet of fishing boats and coloured houses. Close by, the **Galleria Rizzi** re-creates a palazzo interior of the 19th century, including engaging works of art such as still-lifes by the Baroque painter Felice Boselli. Lively Via XXV Aprile/Corso Colombo is packed with interesting shops and eateries, and the Hotel dei Castelli on the hill offers refreshments and panoramic views of both bays.

Take SP1 towards La Spezia until Passo del Braco, then turn right on SP332, then SP64 for Bonassola. Park along the seafront.

WHERE TO EAT

SESTRI LEVANTE

El Pescador *expensive*
This well-known restaurant, with a view over the Baia delle Favole, prides itself on serving the freshest fish of all types, shapes and sizes. *Via Pilade Queirolo 1, 16039; 0185 428 888; www.ristoranteelpescador.com; closed Tue*

Cantina del Polpo *moderate*
There's plenty of fish on the menu, but there are other options, too, such as *trofie* (or *trofiette*) *al pesto* (twisty pasta), *torte di verdura* (vegetable pie), plus excellent local wines and grappas. *Piazza Cavour 2, 16039; 0185 485 296; www.cantinadelpolpo.it*

Below Borzonasca, the closest village to the Benedictine Abbazia di Sant'Andrea di Borzone

Eat and Drink: inexpensive, under €25; moderate, €25–€45; expensive over €45

Right The curving bay of Levanto, flanked by two wooded headlands

WHERE TO STAY

LEVANTO

A Durmi *inexpensive*
Beautifully appointed bright and airy rooms around a quiet courtyard garden that has plenty of relaxing shady spots. Mini apartments are also available.
Via Viviani 12, 19015; 0187 800 823; www.adurmi.it

Stella Maris *moderate–expensive*
Colourful frescoes and antiques fill the rooms of this lovely 19th-century palazzo. Ample breakfasts are served under a pergola in the garden.
Via Marconi 4, 19015; 0187 808 258; www.hotelstellamarislevanto.com

MONTEROSSO AL MARE

Porto Roca *expensive*
Soak up the sea views from the beautiful verandas, terrace and garden of this luxurious hotel, set on the headland and with private beach below.
Via Corone 1, 19016; 0187 817 065; www.portoroca.it; closed Nov–Mar

Other options
La Spiaggia *(Via Lungomare 98, 19016; 0187 817 567; www.laspiaggiahotel. com)* offers beachfront rooms.

CORNIGLIA

Cristiana Ricci *inexpensive*
There are not many accommodation choices in Corniglia, but Cristiana has four small, quiet rooms.
Via Fieschi 123, 19018; 0338 937 6547; www.bebcorniglia.com

Below The village of Corniglia, set on 100-m (330-ft) high cliffs

⑪ Bonassola
La Spezia; 19011
A little quieter than Sestri Levante, the town of Bonassola shelters behind its sea wall, on top of which a boardwalk stretches the length of the dark, sandy beach. In the town centre, the **Chiesa di Santa Caterina** has a sumptuous Baroque interior with two stunning processional crosses of intricate silverwork. Paintings of ships hang on the walls – ex votos from thankful sailors. On a cliff west of the town, the **Cappella della Madonnina della Punta** beckons for a sunset walk.
🚗 *Follow signs for Levanto. There is a large car park next to the tourist office on the seafront.*

⑫ Levanto
La Spezia; 19015
With the best beach in the area – long and sandy – and good opportunities for kayaking and surfing, Levanto is a destination for lovers of the outdoors. It's also a good entry point for the

Cinque Terre. However, the historic centre provides plenty to see as well. The medieval walls, the **Castello di San Giorgio** *(not open to public)*, **Torre dell'Orologio** and the pretty **Loggia del Commune** all date back to the 13th century. But perhaps best of all is the lovely **Chiesa di Sant'Andrea**, a beautiful example of Ligurian Gothic with its striped, green serpentine and white Carrara marble façade and delicate lacy rose window.
🚗 *Take SP43 past the train station, then SP370, which finishes with a steep descent to Monterosso. Park at the seafront, or on Via Roma.*

> ### Walking in the Cinque Terre
> As well as the famous **Sentiero Azzuro (Blue Trail)**, which connects all five villages, there are numerous well-marked trails linking the shrines and hilltop hamlets of the **Parco Nazionale delle Cinque Terre**. Some of these trails can be covered by bike or on horseback. Pick up maps, bus and train timetables and information on the Cinque Terre card (required to access the trails) from information points or tourist offices at the train stations. The park's website, *www.parconazionale5terre.it*, is also a useful source of information.

⑬ Monterosso al Mare
La Spezia; 19016
Monterosso is the first of the five Cinque Terre villages encountered when approaching from the west, and the only one to be built on the flat. A tunnel hewn out of rock

connects the long sandy beach of the new town, **Fegina**, to the older part, where a huge modern statue of Neptune (14 m/45 ft), nicknamed "Il Gigante", stands in front of the harbour. Here, too, in Piazza Garibaldi, is the 13th-century serpentine and white marble striped **Chiesa di San Giovanni**, complete with rose window. Climb the hill to the **Convento dei Cappuccini** (1622) and its **Chiesa di San Francesco** for excellent artworks – *Crucifixion* by Van Dyck, *La Veronica* by Strozzi and two good pieces by Luca Cambioso.

🚗 *Take SP370, then a series of right turns on to Vernazza. There is a car park outside the village.*

Above Narrow alleyway in Corniglia, typical of all the Cinque Terre towns

⑭ Vernazza

La Spezia; 19018
Regarded by many as one of Italy's most perfect villages, Vernazza's pastel- and earth-coloured houses, strewn with washing, crowd the little piazzetta that fronts the natural harbour. Take time here to watch the locals fishing close to the stacks of striated rocks and the bobbing fishing boats. The harbourside **Chiesa Santa Margherita d'Antiochia** (1318), distinguished by its octagonal bell tower, is unusual in having its door on the eastern (altar) side. Perched on top of the rocky promontory, the watchtower of the **Castello Doria** was built in the 15th century, as were many others along this coast, to ward off marauding pirates.

🚗 *Head out of town on SP63 and follow SP61 and SP30 to Corniglia. Park before you get to the village.*

⑮ Corniglia

La Spezia; 19018
Compact Corniglia, the only Cinque Terre village not directly on the sea, sits high on a cliff amid terraced vineyards and olive groves. Less busy than its counterparts, it makes for a peaceful stroll through the boxy houses and eclectic mix of attractive gift, clothes and food shops lining the main Via Fieschi. Looking seaward from the dark and narrow alleyways, the Santa Maria Belvedere offers the chance to admire the dramatic, jagged edge of the coastline. To get to the beach or the train station, descend the famous **Lardarina**, the broad zig-zag path of nearly 400 steps, from where a coastal trail connects with Manarola.

🚗 *Head back on SP30, then turn right onto SP61 and right again onto SP51. At roundabout after Groppo, take SP59 to Manarola. Park outside the village.*

Below The harbour and the Chiesa Santa Margherita d'Antiochia at Vernazza

Left The popular sandy beach at Monterosso al Mare

EAT AND DRINK

LEVANTO

Taverna Garibaldi *inexpensive*
Popular with locals and located on a bustling street, this place specializes in pizzas of all varieties, including prawns and *bresaola* (air-dried beef).
Via Garibaldi 57, 19015; 0187 808 098; evenings only; Sep–Jun: closed Tue

Da Rino *moderate*
Sit outside and watch the local street life as you sample minestrone soup or simple seafood linguine presented on crisp white tablecloths.
Via Garibaldi 10, 19015; 0187 813 475; www.ristorantedarino-levanto.com; eves only, winter: closed Tue

VERNAZZA

Ristorante Pizzeria Vulnetia *inexpensive*
Popular place serving good fish dishes – try the marinated anchovies or linguine – as well as pizzas and pastas.
Piazza Marconi 29, 19018; 0187 821 193; closed Mon

Belforte *expensive*
This place serves creative cuisine, best eaten on the cliffside *terrazzo con vista* (terrace with view) at sunset.
Via Guidoni 22, 19020; 0187 812 222; www.ristorantebelforte.it; closed Tue

CORNIGLIA

Enoteca Il Pirun *inexpensive*
After sampling a glass or two of the local wine in this cosy wine bar, head upstairs for a bite to eat.
Via Fieschi 115, 19018; 0187 812 315

Other options
Stock up at **A Butiega** (*Via Fieschi 142, 19018*) for picnic supplies: sandwiches and seafood antipasti are on offer.

Above Manarola, a classic Cinque Terre village of pastel-coloured houses set by the sea

WHERE TO STAY

MANAROLA

La Torretta *moderate*
This chic and peaceful hotel has an elegant and eclectic style. The hot tub with a view, airy rooms and subtle lighting make for a pampering stay.
Vico Volto 20, 19017; 0187 920 327; www.torrettas.com

Ca' d'Andrean *moderate*
This hotel, in a typical Cinque Terre tower-house in the upper village, is family-run, has spacious modern rooms and a courtyard garden with fragrant lemon trees.
Via Discovolo 101, 19017; 0187 920 040; www.cadandrean.it

RIOMAGGIORE

Locanda del Sole *moderate*
This central establishment offers 10 modern rooms on different levels, all with a terrace. Breakfasts are generous and easy parking is a bonus.
Via Santuario 14, 19017; 0187 920 773; www.locandadelsole.net

⑯ Manarola
La Spezia; 19010

Manarola's pink- and ochre-washed houses and narrow streets cascade down to its tiny harbour, where an old-fashioned crane winches the boats in and out of the water. The little **Sciacchetrà Museum** *(open daily)* gives a good insight into the making of the eponymous local amber-coloured wine. From the Gothic **Chiesa di San Lorenzo** (1338), with its ornate rose window and separate square bell tower, previously an ancient lookout, there's a pleasant walk up through the vineyards and down to the classic viewing point at **Punto Bonfiglio**. At Christmas time, the hills above the village are decorated with prettily illuminated Nativity scenes – *presepe* – all made from recycled materials.

🚗 *Return up SP59, then take SP370 at the roundabout. Next, turn right onto SP32 to Riomaggiore. Park at the top of the village, paying at the booth.*

⑰ Riomaggiore
La Spezia; 19017

Named after the Rio Major (Main River) that now flows underground between houses clinging to the steep-sided ravine, Riomaggiore is a good place to start walking the Cinque Terre trail. There are great views on the climb to the 14th-century Santuario di Montenero.

A two-hour walking tour

This walk offers a quick tour of the village before the hard climb begins. From the car park at the top of the village, head down the steep Via Santuario and turn first right along Via Pecunia to the **Chiesa di San Giovanni Battisti** ①. Founded in 1340, its lovely rose window and Gothic doorways are a result of 19th-century remodeling and, inside, the graceful two-toned grey arches frame a life-size wooden crucifix by Baroque sculptor Anton Maragliano. Head down the broad steps to the bustling **Via Colombo** ②, where the river roars underfoot, and continue past the coloured houses, little shops and boats parked on the road near the harbour. On the right, there's a blue-lit tunnel towards the train station; walk through it to find one of the many **murals** ③ by Silvio Benedetto that decorate the village. This one depicts the building of the *muretti a secco* (dry-stone walls) that form the Cinque Terre terraces.

0 metres 200
0 yards 200

Where to Stay: inexpensive, under €100; moderate, €100–€200; expensive, over €200

Left Pretty Riomaggiore, built over the Rio Major **Below left** Dramatic rock formation, at Riomaggiore **Below right** Small shrine to the Madonna, by a doorway in Manarola

EAT AND DRINK

MANAROLA

Marina Piccola *moderate*
Sit outdoors and watch the walkers and swimmers as evening falls, while eating local treats – mainly seafood.
Via Lo Scalo 16, 19010; 0187 920 923; www.hotelmarinapiccola.com/ ristorante; closed Tue

RIOMAGGIORE

Ripa del Sole *moderate*
Dine al fresco with elegance here, at the top of the village, and tuck into the superb variety of seafood, vegetarian and organic dishes.
Via de Gasperi 282, 19017; 0187 920 143; www.ripadelsole.it; closed Mon

Other options
La Lanterna, in an old anchovy-salting warehouse *(Via San Giacomo 46, 19017; 0187 920 589; www.lalanterna. org; closed Tue)*, makes the most of the fish catches of the day.

Below Fishing boats in the clean waters of Riomaggiore's harbour

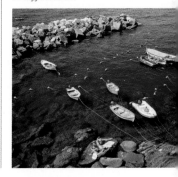

At the end of Via Colombo, a subterranean passage emerges at the **harbour** ④. Stop here to take in the views; admire the boys jumping off the rocks and look back at the houses tumbling higgledy-piggledy down the cliff. Then, follow the path to the left to see the little beach before returning through the tunnel to Via Colombo. Now the climb begins. Take the steps up Via Gramsci, and go round a children's playground to Via di Loca, past some handy seats. More steps, signed Santuario di Montenero, lead past terraces filled with rows of pepper and basil plants.

Go around the cemetery to the main Manarola to Riomaggiore road, where the views begin to open up – it's also the start of Sentiero 3a,

marked by red and white stripes. Cross the road, then turn right, taking the concrete steps on the left-hand side up through vineyards and scrub to the gleaming white **Santuario di Montenero** ⑤, set among the pines. At 341 m (1,120 ft), there are great views along the coast in both directions. Walk past the restaurant to spot the little cog railway – *trenino del vino* – used to take workers and grapes up and down the terraces at harvest time.

Energetic hikers can carry on to the Colle del Telegrafo (making a 9-km/6-mile round trip in total). To get back to the car, descend to the road, then follow it down to Riomaggiore. There is a bus service, but stop by the visitor information office for a timetable first.

DAY TRIP OPTIONS
The coastal towns of Levanto, Sestri Levante and Camogli all make good bases for day trips.

Cinque Terre experience
Starting from Levanto ⑫, get a flavour of the upper and lower Cinque Terre by exploring the pretty village and harbour of Manarola ⑯, then walk the easy Via dell'Amore trail to Riomaggiore ⑰. From here, hike up through the terraces of vines to the Santuario di Montenero.

From Levanto, the easiest option is to take the train, which stops at all five Cinque Terre villages.

Golfo del Tigullio
Enjoy the Golfo del Tigullio from Sestri Levante ⑩, exploring Rapallo ④, where you can spend time on the beach and take a cable-car ride. Then continue round to the little gem of Portofino ③, before returning.

From Sestri Levante take SP1 to Rapallo, then SP227 to Portofino, and back. Or,

relax and take one of the boats that ply the coast from town to town.

Explore the Ligurian Apennines
From Camogli ①, drive through the chestnut and beech woods to the castle at Torriglia ⑤, then head to the timeless village of Pentema ⑥. For exercise, the nearby Lago del Brugneto ⑦ is good for a walk.

From Camogli, take SP333 to Gattorna, then SP21 to Torriglia. The SP15-1 runs from Pentema to Lago del Brugneto.

Eat and Drink: inexpensive, under €25; moderate, €25–€45; expensive over €45

Sanctuaries and Forests

Fiesole to Anghiari

Highlights

- **Great Benedictine abbey**
  Wander around the Abbazia di Vallombrosa along heavily forested trails of beech and firs

- **Historic castles**
  Conquer the ruined Castello di Romena and climb the tower of the splendid Castello di Conto Guidi

- **Pristine forests**
  Visit the best preserved forests in all Italy, the Parco Nazionale delle Foreste Casentinesi, home to wild animals such as wolves, boars and mouflon

- **Holy sanctuary**
  Visited by St Francis and one of the holiest places of the Franciscan monks, the medieval Santuario della Verna is set in an untouched forest

Casentino Valley view with Poppi's Castello dei Conto Guidi in the distance

Sanctuaries and Forests

A thousand years ago, followers of the early Christian faith retreated from the everyday world of men and established monastic communities deep in Italy's forests. Their aim was to live a life of poverty, commune with nature and listen to the word of God resounding in the silence. While protecting the forests, the monasteries grew: some retained a sublime simplicity, others were decorated with great works of art. Forests such as Casentino and Vallombrosa are now national parks and part of Italy's natural heritage. This drive takes in sophisticated Fiesole, the Hermitage of Camáldoli, the castle town of Poppi and the La Verna Sanctuary, and visits Michelangelo's birthplace and the beautiful town of Anghiari overlooking the Upper Tiber Valley.

Above Benedictine monks at the Santuar della Verna, *see p168*

ACTIVITIES

Take a hike in the Casentino Forest among pine woods, beech and maple trees

Ride a bike along the River Arno as it approaches the town of Stia

Enjoy a picnic in the unspoiled Forest of Vallombrosa (Valley of Shadow)

Learn Italian at Poppi's cultural institute – or take a class in stone masonry

Feed the bears with chestnuts gathered in the forest at Poppi children's zoo

Listen to heavenly organ recitals and Gregorian chants at the La Verna Sanctuary

Below The ancient town of Anghiari, rising above the surrounding vines and fruit trees, *see p169*

Above Driving through the deep Casentino Forest at Vallombrosa, *see pp164–5*

PLAN YOUR DRIVE

Start/finish: Fiesole to Anghiari.

Number of days: 2–3 days.

Distance: Approx 140 km (87 miles).

Road conditions: Generally excellent.

When to go: Summer is best, with plenty of festivals and concerts. In spring, the weather can be changeable but often good. Autumn sees the forests change colour, but winter is not recommended. Many mountain passes close as do many restaurants and hotels, and travel can be difficult.

Opening times: Most museums open 10am–6pm (small museums only on weekends outside the summer). Monasteries and sanctuaries observe the religious calendar and churches usually open 9am–noon and 3–7pm. Sundays and major religious feast days are likely to be busy.

Main market days: Fiesole: Sat; Stia: Tue; Pratovecchio: Fri; Poppi: Sat; farmers' market, Tue; Anghiari: Wed.

Major festivals: Fiesole: Estate Fiesolana (music and arts), Jul & Aug; Vallombrosa: church music, Jul & Aug; Poppi: Il Gusto dei Guidi (food and wine), Aug; La Verna: Festival of Organ Music, Jul & Aug; Caprese Michelangelo: Festa della Castagna (chestnut festival), Oct. Anghiari: Festa dei Bringoli e di San Martino (pasta festival), Nov.

Shopping: The monks at Vallombrosa and La Verna sell products such as liquors, jams and CDs of monastic music. In Anghiari, buy oils, soap and creams from the medieval olive oil mill of Ravagni; nearby Bussatti make textiles on looms left by Napoleon's retreating troops.

DAY TRIP OPTIONS

There's lots for families to do here, from conquering **castles** with **towers** and **dungeons** to feeding the **animals** at Poppi's zoo. Or explore the **Roman ruins** of Fiesole – the **amphitheatre** and **museum**, then enjoy a **picnic** and **walk** in the forest of Vallombrosa. Adults may enjoy the spiritual peace of exploring the many ancient **churches**, **sanctuaries** and **monasteries** of the area. For further details, *see p169*.

KEY

Drive route

VISITING FIESOLE

Take the SS65 from Firenze. Turn right on Via Salviati and follow signs to Fiesole.

Tourist Information
The tourist office (*Via dei Partigiani 3; 055 596 1323; www.comune.fiesole. fi.it*) is next to the Area Archeologica. The three museums around the Roman theatre can be visited on one ticket and cover prehistory to the Renaissance.

WHERE TO STAY

FIESOLE

Villa San Michele *expensive*
Part of this Renaissance villa is attributed to Michelangelo. Expect total luxury.
Via Doccia 4, 50014; 055 567 8200; www.villasanmichele.com

ABBAZIA DI VALLOMBROSA

Grand hotel Vallombrosa *inexpensive*
This large hotel has simple rooms and is an excellent base for trekking.
Via G.Carducci 2, 50066; 055 862 012; www.vallombrosalberghi.com

Above The green serpentine and white marble façade of Badia Fiesolana **Below** Consuma Pass, a route through the Tuscan Hills west of Poppi **Below right** Statue of King Victor Emmanuel II in the Piazza Mino, Fiesole

1 Fiesole
Firenze, Toscana; 50014
This important Etruscan, then Roman, town was conquered by Florence in 1125. Its panoramic position and clear air induced the Medicis to build a villa here. At the town centre, Piazza Mino da Fiesole is overlooked by 14th-century **Palazzo Pretorio** with its handsome double loggia. The **Duomo di San Romulo di Fiesole** has an impressive polyptych by Bicci di Lorenzo (1373–1452) depicting stories of Saint Nicholas. Nearby, the **Area Archeologica** (*closed Tue in winter*) contains a superb Roman theatre and baths from the 1st century BC. Evidence of the Etruscans is still obvious from the city walls (Via della Mura Etrusche) and the tombs in Via del Bargellino. For sumptuous views of Florence, take Via San Francesco, by the side of the Duomo, up to the convent, which stands on the site of the original Roman acropolis.

From the centre of town, Via Vecchia Fiesolana leads to the hamlet of San Domenico, home to two important churches. **Badia Fiesolana** (*Via della Badia dei Roccettini 9; closed Sun and public holidays*) is a rare example of the Romanesque style in Tuscany. The abbey was consecrated in 1032 and dedicated to the martyred bishop, St Romulus. Its serpentine and marble façade was retained during 15th-century restorations attributed to architects Brunelleschi and Michelozzo. The interior, and the convent next door, show the rational style of the early Florentine Renaissance and use of the local grey stone, *pietra serena*. Nearby, the 15th-century **Chiesa di San Domenico** contains works by the locally born Renaissance painter and monk Fra Angelico (c1395–1455).

🚗 *Head back down the hill on SP53 towards Florence. Follow signs for SS67 autostrade to Pontassieve. Follow the brown signs for Vallombrosa, via Pelago on SR70, then right on SP83 then onto Via Vallombrosana (SP85). Turn right to the Abbey. Park on Via San Benedetto.*

2 Abbazia di Vallombrosa
Vallambrosa, Firenze, Toscana; 50066
Founded in 1036 by a Benedictine monk, the Vallombrosa Abbey has a large monastery, church, cloister, tower, sacristy and kitchens. Its first monks lived as hermits in primitive conditions and the woods around are dotted with their chapels and holy places. This walk is a good way to understand something of their way of life and history.

A one-hour walking tour
Pick up a free map and audio guide from the **Centro Visatori** ① (*Via San Benedetto 1; open Apr–Oct daily*). Walk back down Via San Benedetto and turn right into the road that runs in front of the monastery. There is a large gate to the abbey, **Church** ② and ancient pharmacy. The church

(*www.vallombrosa.it; open daily*) was remodelled in the 17th century and has a rich Baroque interior. The *trompe l'oeil* ceilings are a perfect example of the style. Exit the abbey complex to the right. The road turns round to the left and runs into an elegant avenue of trees. On the right is a small **Fish Pond** ③, still well

Above Grassy remains of the 1st-century BC Roman theatre, Fiesole **Below** Aerial view of Abbazia di Vallombrosa, set within the forest

EAT AND DRINK

FIESOLE

Ristorante Perseus *inexpensive*
Rustic tables and unfussy food are combined with great atmosphere, especially on summer evenings when booking is recommended.
Piazza Mino 9r, 50014; 055 591 43; closed Mon–Wed in winter

La Reggia degli Etruschi *moderate*
Excellent Tuscan cuisine is served in this large restaurant with panoramic views over Florence. Enjoy wine tasting in the *enoteca*.
Via San Francesco 18, 50014; 055 593 85; www.lareggiadeglietruschi.com

ABBAZIA DI VALLOMBROSA

Archimede *moderate*
This restaurant uses vegetables straight from the owner's farm. The Tuscan dishes include *ribollita* (bread and vegetable soup), mixed grills and meat and fowl roasted on a spit.
Loc. Ponte Casalino, 50066; 055 869 055; www.ristorantearchimede.it; closed Tue in winter

stocked with fish, which was a useful food source for the monks. Follow Via San Benedetto downhill; on the right are the well-ordered Giardino Botanico (Botanic Gardens) and, at the bottom of the hill, the chalet-like **HQ Corpo Forestale** ④. At this point, turn hard right. The path runs up the hill between some buildings of the Corpo Forestale. Pass the open area to the left, where an old saw mill once stood, to a pretty picnic spot where water flows into the old public washing basin from the pond above. With the pond to the right, take the track straight uphill, marked Scala Santa. At this point, the path becomes steeper and the irregular stonework makes sensible shoes preferable.

Once past the confines of the monastery, the path turns sharp left over a stone bridge to a small chapel, the **Cappella di San Torello** ⑤. This is the first of four chapels set in beautiful woodland, the others being **Cappella del Masso di San Gualberto** ⑥, **Cappella delle Colonne** ⑦ and, after a sharp right turn, **Cappella del Beato Migliore** ⑧. To the left of the last is a stone staircase leading up to the road and the **Paradisino** ⑨. This complex was originally a group of monk's cells clustered around the small church. As the monastery's fame grew and more visitors arrived, it became a type of hotel. It is believed that the

English poet John Milton stayed here, as he mentioned Vallombrosa in his poem, *Paradise Lost*. The terrace offers splendid views – on a clear day – all the way to Florence's Duomo.

Across the road from Paradisino is a gushing fountain of ice-cold water. The road now slopes down towards the abbey and soon reaches an open area and a rough stone path leading up to the woods. Beside it are steep, stone-lined cuttings forming artificial avenues called **Vie di Legni** (Wooden Roads) ⑩. These avenues once criss-crossed the mountains and were used to drag giant tree trunks to the Arno to be floated down to Florence.

Further on, to the left, is the chapel **Faggio Santo** (The Holy Beech Tree) ⑪, the holiest place here. The abbey's founder, St Gualberto, is said to have arrived in a snowstorm and rested beneath the tree. When he awoke, it had sprouted leaves to protect him from the elements. The tree is still there. A 10-minute walk leads back to the abbey complex and the car park. There is a good bar with toilet facilities above a large village green.

🚗 *Turn right along winding Via del Lago in Vallombrosa (to Consuma). Turn right signposted Passo della Consuma at Via Casentinese/SR70, then left at SP74. Follow the brown signs to Castello di Romena. Follow the road to the car park.*

Eat and Drink: inexpensive, under €25; moderate, €25–€45; expensive, over €45

WHERE TO STAY

STIA AND AROUND

Monastero Santa Maria della Neve *inexpensive*
Set in the historic centre and run by Dominican nuns, this guesthouse offers basic but comfortable rooms. Rules of the order apply (10pm curfew). *Piazza Landino 25, Pratovecchio 52015 (southeast of Stia on SP310); 0575 583 774; www.monasterystays.com*

Albergo Falterona *inexpensive*
This newly refurbished hotel in a Renaissance building in the historic centre of town has a comfortable and relaxed atmosphere. Rooms are beamed and some have frescoed ceilings. *Piazza Tanucci 85, 52017; 0575 583 545; www.albergofalterona.it*

Borgo Tramonte *inexpensive*
Simple, clean, rustic-style rooms in a large restored 18th-century farmhouse on the edge of the Casentino Forest. Enjoy the nearby walking trails, mountain bike and horse riding. *Loc. Papiano, 52017; 0575 581 404; www.borgotramonte.it*

CAMÁLDOLI AND AROUND

Monastery of Camáldoli *inexpensive*
Run by Benedictine monks, this offers basic but peaceful stays within the monastery – rules apply (11pm curfew). *Monastery of Camáldoli, 52010; 0575 556 012; www.monasterystays.com*

I Tre Baroni *moderate*
This resort in Moggiona, on the road to Camáldoli, is a combination of hotel rooms and apartments scattered through the village. The décor is period and the place is relatively relaxed. *Via di Camáldoli 52, 52010 Moggiona di Poppi; 0575 556 204; www. itrebaroni.it*

③ Castello di Romena

Pratovecchio, Arezzo, Toscana; 52015
Dating from the 10th century, this **Castello** *(Jul–Aug: open daily; Mar–Oct: open Thu–Sun; closed Nov–Feb)* once had three central towers and 11 smaller ones reinforcing the walls. Set on the highest defensive point of the Casentino valley, the castle is thought to have been visited by the poet Dante (c.1265–1321) – who mentions it in his *Divine Comedy* – after his exile from Florence. The castle still has its keep, central tower with drawbridge, prison tower and Piazza d'Armi, where the army was trained. Cypresses mark the position of the walls and there are fabulous views of the valley below.

The delightful **Pieve di San Pietro di Romena** is nearby – head back down the tree-lined avenue and take the track on the left. At the T-junction, turn right on SP73 and into the car park. The earliest reference to this church was in 1054 and the current building dates to 1152. There is evidence of an earlier building from an Etruscan or Roman cult. The simple Romanesque semicircular apse faces east towards Jerusalem

and the three naves, pillars with Lombard Christian capitals referring to fertility rites, and unadorned interior evoke a spiritual calm and tranquillity. There is also a picnic area looking out over the valley towards Poppi.

🚗 *Turn right on SP74 towards Stia, then right on Via Fiorentina/SP73 into Pratovecchio. After the piazza, turn left into Via Garibaldi, then Via Roma to "Centro Stia". Don't take SP556, keep straight, then right on Via Edmondo De Amicis. Take first left, under the arch and park in Piazza Bernardo Tanucci.*

④ Stia

Arezzo, Toscana; 52017
The pretty, historic town of Stia nestles between the River Staggia and the nascent River Arno, which runs down the Casentino valley and on to Florence. The town developed in the 11th century under the jurisdiction of the Guidi Counts from Poppi, who ruled over the area from the 11th–15th centuries. Stia prospered down the centuries due to its excellent woollen cloth production, an industry that continues to this day. The centre of town is set around Piazza Tanucci

Top The ruins of Castello di Romena, above the Casentino valley **Right** Piazza Tanucci's centrepiece, the Fontana dei Serpenti, Stia **Far right** The charming Romanesque Pieve di San Pietro di Romena, Castello di Romena

Where to Stay: inexpensive, under €100; moderate, €100–200; expensive, over €200

with the Fontana dei Serpenti and the **Pieve di Santa Maria Assunta**, a Romanesque church with a splendid *Annunciation* by Bicci di Lorenzo (1414). There's also a shop selling the famous local Casentino cloth.

🚗 *At lower end of Piazza Tanucci turn left before the bridge on SP310, back to Pratovecchio, turn left to Via Monte/SP72, then left onto Via Appennino/SP72. Turn left to stay on SP72 (signed Eremo di Camáldoli), then join SP69 to the hermitage.*

The Casentino Forest

This vast forest provided the wood used to build the great fleet of the Medicis and, today, the **Parco Nazionale delle Foreste Casentinesi, Monte Falterona e Campigna** *(www. parcoforestecasentinesi.it)* is still one of the most prized forests in Europe. The forest is an important sanctuary for the Apennine wolf, wild boar, deer, and mouflon (mountain sheep).

⑤ Camáldoli

Arezzo, Toscana; 52010

Italian monks sought to understand God better by withdrawing from the world to a life of contemplation in the forest. The **Eremo di Camáldoli** *(www. Camaldoli.it)* was one of the hermitages founded by the Benedictine monk San Romualdo (c. 953–1027), son of the duke of Ravenna. He established a community of five cells with a small oratory here in c.1024. Only 14 monks remain, cut off from visitors, but Romualdo's original austere cell is still visible. The Church of the Hermitage (c.1220) underwent an astonishing Baroque transformation in the late 16th century, giving it grand frescoes

and elaborate cornices. Look out for the fine altarpiece of the Madonna by Andrea della Robbia (1435–1525).

Neaby, along Località Camáldoli, lies another interesting monastic complex, run by the same order as the hermitage. The **Monastery of Camáldoli**, however, maintains closer community contact. At the centre of the hamlet is a large hostel, a monastery, and a church with major works by the late-Renaissance artist Giorgio Vasari (1511–74). Don't miss the Antica Farmacia (1543) – an old pharmacy – with walnut cabinets.

Camáldoli is also home to the **Foreste Casentinesi Visitor Centre** *(open spring & summer)*, which has good maps of the area, making it the perfect starting place for exploring the park's 600-km (373-mile) network of paths on foot, horseback or by bike.

🚗 *Head south along SP67 towards Poppi. At the junction with Via Roma/ SR70 turn right, then left on Piazza Garibaldi/SP65. Cross the bridge and turn left into Piazza 4 Novembre, follow round to Piazza Gramsci and park.*

Above left Eremo di Camáldoli, founded by San Romualdo **Above centre** The Casentino Forest, where the monks sought isolation **Above right** Façade of the Romanesque Pieve di Santa Maria Assunta, Stia

EAT AND DRINK

STIA

Il Ristorante Fattoria La Foresta
moderate
This simple and rustic restaurant serves typical local produce along with seafood, home-made pasta and Florentine steaks.
Via Roma 31, 52017; 0575 582 032; closed Tue

CAMALDOLI

Albergo Ristorante Camáldoli
inexpensive
This guesthouse has been looking after travellers for years. Rustic fare includes delicious *acquacotta* (literally "cooked water") – a hearty Tuscan soup, *ravioli all'ortica* made with ricotta and nettles, and roasted wild fennel.
Loc. Camáldoli, 52010; 0575 556 019

Below A glade at Camáldoli in the Casentino Forest

Eat and Drink: inexpensive, under €25; moderate, €25–€45; expensive, over €45

Above The medieval walled town of Anghiari, decked with flags **Above right** The birthplace of sculptor Michelangelo, Caprese Michelangelo

WHERE TO STAY

POPPI

Albergo Casentino *inexpensive*
The only hotel in the historic centre of Poppi fronts onto the piazza with comfy rooms, a garden and restaurant.
Piazza della Repubblica 6, 52014; 0575 529 090; www.albergocasentino.it

CAPRESE MICHELANGELO

Il Vigno *inexpensive*
A rustic collection of restored farm buildings with rooms and apartments at daily or weekly rates. Mountain bikes and trail maps available.
Loc. il Vigno 262, 52033; 0575 792 019; www.agriturismoilvigno.eu

Terra di Michelangelo *moderate*
This *agriturismo* (farm stay) is a complex of stone farmhouses, apartments and rooms offering daily and weekly rates.
Loc. San Polo 70, 52033; 0575 791 055; www.terradimichelangelo.com

Below The Santuario della Verna, where St Francis of Assisi once stayed

⑥ Poppi
Arezzo, Toscana; 52014

The historic heart of this castellated town rises majestically above the modern commercial centre. Poppi was the seat of power of the Guidi Counts until they picked the wrong side in the 1440 war between Florence and Milan. Fortunately, the splendid 12th-century **Castello dei Conti Guidi** *(open 10am–7pm daily)* remains, with its magnificent tower, mullion windows, battlements and stone staircases. Other highlights include the colonnaded **Piazza Amerighi**, and the 17th-century hexagonal **Chiesa di Madonna del Morbo** with a *Madonna and Child* by Filippino Lippi (1457–1504).

For something different, visit the **Poppi Zoo** *(open 9am–6pm daily; www. parcozoopoppi.it)*. This large parkland, dotted with pine, chestnut and oak trees, houses various European animals such as lynxes, wolves, deer, beavers and porcupines in generally spacious enclosures. The zoo was founded by

a local vet in 1972, and there is a small train to help visitors get about.
🚗 *Cross back over the Arno to Piazza Garibaldi, then turn right at SR70 towards Santuario della Verna/Via Bibbiena SR71. On SR71, keep left onto Viale Michelangelo, then a sharp left onto Viale Luigi Gori/SS208 all the way to La Verna. From the car park it's a 5–10-minute walk to the Sanctuary.*

Della Robbia
La Verna and the Casentino is home to terracotta masterpieces of the Della Robbia sculptors. Luca della Robbia (1400–82) perfected a white majolica with a blue background, and yellow and green glazes to protect the works from the elements. Andrea della Robbia (1435–1525) created the masterpieces *The Crucifixion* and *The Assumption* in the Basilica Maggiore at La Verna.

⑦ La Verna
Arezzo, Toscana; 52010

One of the holiest sites in Italy, **Santuario della Verna** *(www.laverna. it)* is a monastic community that developed around Saint Francis of Assisi (1182–1226) who spent 40 days in retreat here in 1224. While in La Verna, he developed stigmata – the wounds of Christ appeared on his body. Count Orlando of Chiusi gave La Verna to Francis as a retreat for contemplation and built him the chapel Santa Maria degli Angeli, the nucleus of the convent. The sanctuary appeals to believers and non-religious alike as its stunning views, pristine woods and fascinating collection of buildings and the stories associated with them are compelling.

🚗 *Head southeast on SP208, turn right onto Via Roma/SP60, then left on SP54 to Caprese Michelangelo. Turn left at Via Capoluogo, go up the hill and park.*

8 Caprese Michelangelo

Arezzo, Toscana; 52033a

This small mountain town is best known as the birthplace, in 1475, of Michelangelo Buonarroti, one of the greatest artists of all time. His father, a government function-ary, worked here briefly, but soon after the boy's birth, the family returned to Florence. It is said that the artist returned here frequently, but there's little evidence of his presence. In the remains of the castle is located a small **museum** *(www.capresemichelangelo.net; open 11am–6pm Tue–Sun)* for those who wish to pay homage.

🚗 *Head south on SP47 to Anghiari. Follow SP43 avoiding signs for Centro, then turn right up Corso Giacomo Matteotti to the car park. Walk via the tunnel to the elevator up to town centre.*

9 Anghiari

Arezzo, Toscana; 52031

The unquestionable antiquity of this medieval citadel gives it a special charm and its knot of ancient lanes and piazzas is pleasant to wander round. It was of strategic importance because of its position on the trading routes between the Adriatic and central Italy. Impressive sections of its 12th- and 13th-century walls remain intact, containing several gateways and even old churches. Apart from a reputed visit by Thomas Beckett in the 12th century, Anghiari is most famous for the decisive battle in 1440, when the Florentine Medicis defeated the superior forces of the Visconti Milanese. **Palazzo della Battaglia** *(open 9am–7pm daily)*, in the central Piazza Mameli, has scale models of the battle. The town's main square, Piazza Balduccio, has a statue of Garibaldi and has been a market area for 800 years.

COURSES IN POPPI

Centro di Cultura Italiana Casentino
This cultural centre runs courses on the Italian language and seminars on opera, cooking and even stone masonry. *Via Cesare Battisti 5, 52014; 0575 529 774; www.parlital.it*

EAT AND DRINK

LA VERNA

Refettorio del Pellegrino *inexpensive*
Visitors to the refectory can expect a wholesome, set-price three-course meal, including a glass of wine. *Santuario della Verna, 52010; 0575 5341; meals 12–1:30pm and 7:30pm*

CAPRESE MICHELANGELO

Il Rifugio *moderate*
Expect hearty mountain food such as home-made pasta with local truffles and mushrooms, and roast meats. *Loc. Lama di Caprese 47, 52033; 0575 793 752; www.ilrifugioristorante.eu; closed Wed*

Il Cerro *moderate*
This family-run restaurant pays great attention to local produce and wines. *Via Il CerRo 120, 52033; 0575 793 923; www.ristoranteilcerro.com; closed Mon & Tue*

ANGHIARI

Ristorante La Nena *moderate*
A cosy restaurant with attention to detail on classic Tuscan dishes. *Corso Matteotti 10, 52031; 0575 789 491; www.ristorantenena.it; closed Mon*

Da Alighiero *moderate–expensive*
Enjoy superb home-made pastas with porcini, Chianina veal with rosemary, and semifreddo with pistachios. *Via Garibaldi 8, 52031; 0575 788 040; www.daalighiero.it; closed Tue*

Top left Small shrine in the pristine woodland around La Verna **Left** The imposing tower of Castello dei Conti Guidi, Poppi

---

DAY TRIP OPTIONS

Younger kids will love the castles and the zoo, while older ones should enjoy Roman sights, a picnic and a forest walk. The more spiritual will enjoy the quiet forest holy places.

Castellos and animals

From pretty Stia ④, visit the impressive ruins of Castello di Romena ③, then drive on to the well-preserved Castello dei Conti Guidi in Poppi ⑥. For a final treat, hop on a train tour of Poppi zoo.

From Stia, take the SP della Scarpaccia to Castello di Romena. Take SP73 to SR70 to Poppi. Return on SR70, SP310.

Romans and a forest walk

Based at Fiesole ①, spend some time shopping for a picnic. Then tour the Roman sights and museums, climbing up to the acropolis. Drive to Abbazia di Vallombrosa ② and enjoy a picnic there, with the abbey's jam, then work off the food with a walk in the woods.

Follow the drive's directions, then return the same way.

Secluded retreats

Based at Poppi ⑥, see its *Madonna and Child*, then shop for picnic supplies. Drive to Camáldoli ⑤ to tour the monastery and then picnic at the hermitage. Next, stop at Stia ④ to see its Romanesque church and then visit the delightful church at Castello di Romena ③.

From Poppi, head north on SP67 and SP69 to Camáldoli. SP72, SP310 to Stia. SP della Scarpaccia, then left to Romena. Take SP73 to SR70 back to Poppi.

Val d'Arno and the Chianti Hills

Ponte Buriano to Volpaia

Highlights

- **Landscapes of Leonardo**
  See the ancient bridge and Le Balze scenery that so captivated Leonardo da Vinci that he put them in his paintings

- **Chianti Classico**
  Enjoy the rolling hills and neat vines that make Chianti one of Europe's most delightful wine-making areas

- **Soft stone villages of Chianti**
  Explore some of Italy's most beautiful small towns, producing excellent wine and the highest quality olive oil

- **The art of Nature**
  Explore the modern sculpture gallery at Pievasciata, where artists display their works in a natural park

Autumn vines, changing colour, near Castello di Brollio in Chianti

Val d'Arno and the Chianti Hills

Many of the mystical landscapes that glow in the paintings of Leonardo da Vinci can be seen in a little known part of Tuscany between the right bank of the River Arno and the Pratomagno mountain range. Crossing the Arno, the road soon leaves the industrial flatlands and rises into the delightful countryside of the Chianti. This area is most famous for the light red wine it produces that is the perfect match for a bowl of delicious pasta. Like the wine, the people of the area are generous and easygoing, and the light on the landscape has inspired painters and poets, while the local produce are specialities to be savoured.

ACTIVITIES

Photograph the brilliant autumn colours in Chianti as the vine leaves turn gold against the silver-green of the olive trees

Get married in Greve, where the Comune conducts the ceremony and there are villas and restaurants in abundance for guests and gourmets

Take a Tuscan cooking class in Chianti and learn about the local food that accompanies the wine

Jump on a bike and follow the path of the "Eroica" bike race along the back roads of Chianti

Above Looking towards the church of Santa Croce in Piazza Matteotti, Greve in Chianti, *see p174*

KEY

🚗 Drive route

Póggio Masserecci 1548m

Jane

Bagnena

Vezza

Bibbiano

Giustino Valdano

M. Capannino 747m △

Subbiano

ogialli

② BORRO

Castiglion Fibocchi

Arno

71

Laterina

Castelluccio

Ponte alla Chiassa

① PONTE BURIANO

Antria

Lago della Penna

Pratantico

69

Ponticino

Indicatore

AREZZO

Póggiola

Staggiano

Battifolle

73

San Zeno

Olmo

Civitella di Chiana

Pieve al Toppo

21

Below Glorious country villa and autumn vines in the Val d'Arno, *see p174* **Far left** A traditional majolica platter in Castellina in Chianti, *see p175*

PLAN YOUR DRIVE

Start/finish: Ponte Buriano to Volpaia.

Number of days: 2–3 days.

Distance: 100 km (62 miles).

Road conditions: Roads are generally good and well signposted. In winter the Chianti roads can be icy and snow chains may be needed on some roads.

When to go: Chianti has a definite season, May–Oct, and at other times of the year many restaurants and amenities close. Autumn is less crowded and the changing colour of the leaves is beautiful.

Opening: Major museums are open 8:30am–7:30pm and often close Mon. Small museums often only open on weekends outside the summer months. Churches vary but are generally open 7:30am–noon and 3–7:30pm. Shops open 10am–1pm and 4–8pm and close Sun and Mon mornings.

Main market days: Loro Ciuffenna: Mon; Pian di Scò, Greve in Chianti and Castellina in Chianti: Sat; Radda in Chianti: 4th Mon of month.

Major festivals: All over: Cantine Aperte (tasting day at wineries), last Sun in May; Calici delle Stelle, night of San Lorenzo (wine-tasting in the piazzas), Aug 10; San Martino, cantinas open for tasting of the new wine, 2nd week Nov. **Greve:** Chianti Classico Wine Festival, 2nd weekend in Sep.

Shopping: The area is famous for wines and olive oil. Wine shops and most vineyards have the capacity to ship locally and internationally.

DAY TRIP OPTIONS

Using Greve in Chianti as a base, families will enjoy the drive through **pretty hamlets** along the Via Sette Ponti, picking up a **picnic** on the way to Ponte Buriano **Natural Reserve**, ideal for a **walk**. Wine lovers can stay at Castellina in Chianti to enjoy a **wine tasting**, tour a **vineyard** and explore **cellars** in Chianti wine towns. History buffs will enjoy **medieval town halls** and **churches**, **castles** and **Etruscan finds**, then contrasting this all with a walk around an outdoor **modern sculpture park**. For full details, *see p177*.

Above Busy bric-à-brac market in Greve in Chianti

GETTING TO PONTE BURIANO

From A1 Florence-Rome, take Arezzo exit. Pass under Viale Don Minzoni, then left towards Bibbiena. At roundabout, take Via Sette Ponti/SP1 to Ponte Buriano. Cross bridge, through town, turn left and left again. Park near the river on the right.

WHERE TO STAY

PONTE BURIANO

Le Bilodole *inexpensive*
This central farmhouse has a pool and offers good breakfasts in quiet environs.
Loc. Cincelli 11, 52100; 0575 364 655; www.bilodole.it

AROUND PONTE BURIANO

Badia Di Campoleone *expensive*
This luxurious villa offers a wellness centre, pool and restaurants.
Loc. Castelluccio 38, Capolona 52010; 0575 451 561; www.badiacampoleone.it

BORRO

Il Borro *moderate–expensive*
Rent an 18th-century villa or a simple apartment. The staff is very helpful.
San Giustino Valdarno, Loc. Borro 1, 52020; 055 977 053; www.ilborro.com

VIA SETTE PONTI

Villa Belpoggio *moderate*
Only 2 km (1 mile) from Loro Ciuffenna this historic house in luxurious gardens has comfortable rooms and suites.
Via Sette Ponti Ponente 40, Loro Ciuffenna 52024; 055 969 4411; www.villabelpoggio.com

CASTELLINA IN CHIANTI

Palazzo Squarcialupi *expensive*
In the historic centre, this large hotel has comfy rooms, pool and terrace.
Via Ferruccio 22, 53011; 0577 741 186; www.palazzosquarcialupi.com

Right Typical Le Balze sandstone landscape near Piantravigne **Far right** The famous seven-arched bridge of Ponte Buriano

① Ponte Buriano
Arezzo, Toscana; 52100

With its seven beautiful arches crossing the River Arno, the 13th-century Romanesque Ponte Buriano is the start of an ancient pilgrim route, the Via Sette Ponti. The bridge also marks the start of a Regional Natural Reserve that runs along the river to the dam at Penna. These wetlands are key nesting grounds for migrating birds – find out about trails through the reserve from the **visitor centre** *(by the bridge; 393 53089; www.parks.it)* at Ponte Buriano. The bridge itself has not changed since Leonardo da Vinci visited it in the late 15th century, when he was so taken by its beauty he put it in the background of his *Mona Lisa*.

🚗 *Head northwest along Via Sette Ponti/SP1, through Castiglion Fibocchi. At San Giustino Valdarno, turn left for Borro. Follow signs to the car park.*

② Borro
Arezzo, Toscana; 52028

In the medieval era, this tiny clutch of houses could only be reached by a drawbridge spanning a deep gully. Today, this hamlet has been fully restored by the Ferragamo family (of the Florentine fashion house), and now houses artisans' workshops. The automated *presepe*, or **nativity scene** *(open daily)*, which rather surprisingly includes Pinocchio, was created by the local priest.

🚗 *Return to Via Sette Ponti/SP1 and turn left at Loro Ciuffenna, park in Piazza Vittorio Emanuele II. Return to SP1 and carry on before turning left on Strada Comunale di Piantravigne to town. Return to SP1 to Pian di Scò. In town, turn right into Viale Alessandro Volta/SP1 and use car park on right.*

③ Via Sette Ponti
Arezzo, Toscana; 52024, 52028, 52026

A series of pretty villages mark the defensive points on the Via Sette Ponti (Road of the Seven Bridges), with views over the lake basin of the Balze. In tiny **Loro Ciuffenna**, visit the Romanesque Pieve di San Pietro a Gropina, with a carved stone pulpit and capitals, and the ancient Tuscan mill.

Further along the SP1, **Piantravigne** perches perilously amid the towering sand and limestone pinnacles of Le Balze. The final stop, the parish church of Santa Maria in **Pian di Scò**, with its imposing bell tower, still has a simple Romanesque interior, largely unaltered since the 12th century.

🚗 *Leave on SP87 to Figline Valdarno. At roundabout, take 2nd exit onto Via Francesco Petrarca/SS69. Turn left at Via Nicolò Copernico/SP16 to Greve in Chianti. Follow signs to car park.*

④ Greve in Chianti
Florence, Toscana; 50022

At the heart of town, **Piazza Matteoti's** irregular architecture reveals Greve's prosperity in the Middle Ages, as the wealthy merchants were required to pay for their own *loggias* (porticoes) – now filled with shops, bars and restaurants. The statue in the piazza is of local explorer Giovanni da Verrazzano (1485–1528), the Italian who sailed to North America.

Chianti is a top cycling destination and the Eroica Trail is well signposted and suitable for all levels. Bikes can be hired from Officiana Ramuzzi *(Via Italo Stecchi 23, Greve in Chianti 50022; 055 853037; www.ramuzzi.com)*.

🚗 *Take SR222 south to Castellina in Chianti. Park to the south of the town centre on Via 4 Novembre.*

❺ Castellina in Chianti

Siena, Toscana; 53011

The rolling hills of the Chianti have always separated Florence and Siena, the two great Tuscan rivals for power. Barely touched over the centuries, the fields and vineyards remain as they were when they were first carved out by oxen. The towns, too, have changed little and reflect the intense respect of their residents for the traditional values.

Above The Neo-Romanesque Church of San Salvatore, Castellina in Chianti

A one-hour walking tour

Start from the car park with views east across the fields of Chianti. At the top of the steep entry ramp, join the main road that skirts the town. Follow this to the left, then on the right, on the corner of Via delle Mura, is **Enoteca Poggio Amorelli** ①, below a square castle-like bastion – taste its wines or arrange a vineyard visit. Continue along Via delle Mura up the hill to the Rocca della Comune. Walk past Remembrance Park on the left, with valley views, and turn right into **Piazza della Comune** ②, dominated by the huge Rocca built by the Medici to defend against Siena. The entire town was once fortified, but most of the walls and the gates are long gone. Left of the tower is the **Museo Archeologico del Chianti** ③ *(closed Wed)*, which contains mostly

The black cockerel insignia of Chianti

Etruscan exhibits from the area. Head out of the square to the right past the trattoria La Torre. Take Vicolo della Rocca downhill to the main street, Via Ferruccio, which can get busy in summer. Directly opposite is the Renaissance **Palazzo Squarcialupi** ④, now a fashionable hotel and the wine store Fattoria La Castellina *(0577 740454; www.lacastellina.it)*. Tastings and tours can be organized here. Over the road is a classic butcher's shop, **Macelleria Stiaccini** ⑤. Try a delicious *panino con la finochiana* (fennel salami sandwich). Slightly further up the hill is the **Tourist Office** ⑥ *(Apr–Nov: open daily)* for information on wineries and Etruscan tombs. If more refreshment is needed, the Chianti Bar, further uphill, provides simple snacks and wine by the glass. At the top of the street is the **Church of San Salvatore** ⑦, which was rebuilt after World War II. It contains a fresco, *Madonna Enthroned*, by the pre-Renaissance artist Lorenzo di Bicci (1373–1452). Return to Via Ferruccio and take the path to the left leading into **Via delle Volte** ⑧. This medieval enclosed walkway runs parallel to Via Ferruccio and was used for defensive and religious purposes. To the left, slit windows provide glimpses of the countryside, and to the right some of the old cellars have been turned into workshops and restaurants. The walkway finally returns to Via Ferruccio, close to the car park.

🚗 *Head south, turn left at Via del Mandorlo to SP102, then on to Vagliagli. Fork left to Monteliscai. At Via dei Ponti/SS408 turn left, then left again to Strada Comunale di Catignano. Turn left to Pievasciata, then left on Via del Campana to the sculpture park.*

PRODUCE IN THE VAL D'ARNO

Zolfino beans and Valdarno chicken – both local delicacies – as well as olive oil and Vin Santo can be bought from **Fattoria Casamora** *(Via di Casabiondo 5, Pian di Scò 52026; 055 960 046; www.casamora.it)*. For home-made yoghurt and cheeses, try **La Capanna del Sole** *(Loc. Casamona, Loro Ciuffenna 52024; 335 574 7699; www.capannadelsole.it)*. Call small farm suppliers before visiting.

EAT AND DRINK

AROUND PONTE BURIANO

Il Grano Arso *expensive*
Chef Andrea mixes local tradition with dishes from his native Apulia. .
Piazza Italia, 4R, 52029, Castiglion Fibocchi (Arezzo); 0575 1484731; www.ilgranoarso.it; closed Mon & Tue lunch

BORRO

Osteria del Borro *moderate*
A romantic setting, this place specializes in seafood and meat – superb gourmet treats from an open kitchen.
Via Pio Borri, 52024; 055 977 2333; www.osteriadelborro.it; closed Wed in winter

VIA SETTE PONTI

Ristorante La Torre *moderate*
Located inside a medieval tower. The fish dishes here are a highlight.
Via Alighieri, 20 Loro Ciuffenna 52024; 055 917 2032; www.ilristorantelatorre.it; closed Mon

GREVE IN CHIANTI

Da Verrazzano *moderate*
Enjoy Tuscan treats such as *ribollita* (hearty soup), *panzanella* (tomato and bread salad) and good wine on a splendid terrace overlooking the piazza.
Piazza Matteotti 28, 50022; 055 853 189; www.ristoranteverrazzano.it; closed Sun pm/Mon & Jan

CASTELLINA IN CHIANTI

La Torre *moderate*
Tuck into good traditional food in the central piazza.
Piazza Umberto 1, 53011; 0577 740 236

Eat and Drink: inexpensive, under €25; moderate, €25–€45; expensive, over €45

Above Radda in Chianti, once the capital city of Chianti **Above right** Volpaia, known for its blooming flowers in early summer

COOKERY COURSES IN CHIANTI

Preparing food can be as much fun as drinking the wine that goes with it, and at **Tenuta Casanova** (*Loc. Sant'Agnese 20, Castellina in Chianti 53011; www.tenutacasanova.it*) they show how to do both with gusto and finesse. Or learn to cook a four-course Tuscan meal in the grand **Villa Fattoria di Vistarenni** (*Loc. Vistarenni, Gaiole in Chianti 53013; 0577 738 476; www. villavistarenni.com*), located between Gaiole and Radda.

WHERE TO STAY

AROUND CHIANTI SCULPTURE PARK

Villa Astreo *moderate*
Each room in this exceptional and historic B&B has a truly individual style. *Via Del Colombaione 4, Vagliagli di Castelnuovo Berardenga 53010 (2km/1 mile northeast of sculpture park); 0577 322 624; www.astreo.it*

AROUND CASTELLO DI BROLIO

Villa di Sotto *inexpensive*
This simple B&B, about 2 km (1 mile) south of Brolio, offers genuine Italian warmth and hospitality on the edge of the sweet village of Villa a Sesta. *Via San Caterina 30, Villa a Sesta 53100; 347 932 7090; www.villadisotto.it*

AROUND RADDA IN CHIANTI

Villa Fattoria di Vistarenni *moderate*
This historic villa, between Gaiole and Radda, is a 16th-century residence with original period furniture. Enjoy B&B or even hire the entire estate. *Loc. Vistarenni, Gaiole in Chianti 53013; 0577 738 476; www.villavistarenni.com*

VOLPAIA

La Locanda *expensive*
This rustic converted farmhouse in the hills above Volpaia is a beautiful and peaceful Tuscan retreat. *Loc. Montanino di Volpaia 53017; 0577 738 833; www.lalocanda.it*

Wine tasting in Chianti

Vineyards are working enterprises, so try to book in advance for tours and tastings. Large operators usually have staff on hand, but smaller ones may need to call someone who can speak English. However, driving around, visitors will see "*cantina aperta*" signs, which indicate that the vineyard is open for tasting and buying wine. There is usually a small charge for a tour and tasting and this often includes snacks.

6 Chianti Sculpture Park
Pievasciata, Siena, Toscana; 53010

This contemporary sculpture park (*Apr–Oct: open daily; Nov–Mar: call 0577 357151; www.chiantisculpturepark.it*) is in a superb setting of macchia scrub, holm oak and pine trees. The one-hour trail visits 25 site-specific works by Italian and international artists, such as William Furlong's *Off the Beaten Track*: stainless-steel cubes that emit sounds of city life as you pass. Built in May 2004, the park was the inspiration of Rosalba and Piero Giadrossi, who are often at the nearby gallery La Fornace.

On leaving the park turn left (north). Drive 3 km (2 miles) on a dirt track. Turn right, then left onto SP408. Turn right towards Castelnuovo Berardenga; fork right, staying on SP484. Park on the left, opposite the Fattoria Castello Di Brolio.

7 Castello di Brolio
Siena, Toscana; 53013

This small village is surrounded by an enormous vineyard and castle with the same name that date back to the 10th century and have been owned by the Ricasoli family since then. Although it's now part of Siena, the castle (*Mar–Nov: closed Mon*) was a Florentine stronghold that was demolished by the Sienese army, then completely rebuilt in the 16th century. Baron Bettino Ricasoli (1809–80), who played a key role in the Unification of Italy and was twice Italy's prime minister, gave it its current mock-medieval style in the 19th century. There is still evidence of a mortar attack from World War II on the western wing. Taste the Baron's highly regarded wines at the wine shop (*open daily*).

Below The beautiful rolling hills of Chianti, dotted with vineyards

Where to Stay: inexpensive, under €100; moderate, €100–€200; expensive, over €200

🚗 *Return north on SP484, turn right at SP408 towards Gaiole. Fork left at SP2, then take SR429 into Radda in Chianti. Turn right at Piazza 4 Novembre to park.*

❽ Radda in Chianti
Siena, Toscana; 53017

The capital of Chianti in the 14th century, tiny Radda still retains its sense of import as one of the main towns in the Chianti League. Pride in its history is revealed by the family heraldic shields that adorn the front of the **Palazzo di Podestà** (now the town hall) in Piazza Ferrucci. This was where the *podestà* or magistrate was based. Across the square is the **Chiesa di San Niccolo**, its original Romanesque design still evident despite the fact that it was heavily remodelled in the last century.

🚗 *Drive back down the hill, turn right at the roundabout onto Via La Strada*

del Chianti/SP2bis (under SR429) towards Volpaia. Turn right on SR114C, then right on SP112.

The famous Gallo Nero
Archduke Cosimo III chose the black cockerel – Gallo Nero – as the symbol for the area's wine makers in the 18th century as he was sick of arguments about which was the "true" wine of Chianti. Since then, if the bottle has an image of the Gallo Nero in a red circle on the label on its neck, then it is Chianti Classico. However, it was Baron Ricasoli who first defined classic Chianti wine in 1874. It has to include 75 per cent Sangiovese and 25 per cent Malvasia and Trebbiano grapes.

❾ Volpaia
Siena, Toscana; 53017

First mentioned in the 12th century, Volpaia was repeatedly damaged, then rebuilt as a result of its strategic position between warring Sienese and Florentine forces. The walled village improved its economy during a period of stability in the 16th century. A central point for viniculture in the area, the village is essentially a large winery owned by the Stianti family. The village cellars, such as those in the crypt of 15th-century **Commenda di Sant'Eufrosino** (*guided tours by appointment; www.volpaia. com*), designed by Michelozzo, contain vast wooden barrels, a wine bar, bottling plant and olive mill. The *enoteca* also sells a booklet mapping out various countryside walks.

Above Bell tower or campanile in the little hamlet of Volpaia **Below left** The façade of the Palazzo di Podestà, Radda in Chianti

EAT AND DRINK

NEAR CHIANTI SCULPTURE PARK
La Taverna Di Vagliagli *moderate*
This restaurant, between Castellina and Pievasciata, offers an intimate, elegant atmosphere with excellent service, superb food and good wine. *Via del Sergente 4, Vagliagli 53019; 0577 322 532; closed Tue*

RADDA IN CHIANTI
Le Forchette del Chianti *moderate*
On the town wall overlooking the valley. Run by two sisters serving honest traditional Tuscan dishes alongside a good wine list. *Viale Matteotti 5, 53017 ; 0577 738 923; www.leforchettedelchianti.it; closed Thu*

VOLPAIA
La Bottega *moderate*
Come here for the hearty, unpretentious country cooking, great views from the outdoor terrace and home-made cakes. *Piazza della Torre 1, 53017; 0577 735602; www.labottegadivolpaia.it; closed Tue*

DAY TRIP OPTIONS
There's plenty to do in this area, from a bird-watching picnic to a food and wine tour, and a historical trip looking at ancient and modern life.

Walk on the wild side
Starting from Greve in Chianti ❹ drive over to the Val d'Arno visiting the villages of the Via Sette Ponti ❸ and picking up some local produce along the way. Stop at Ponte Buriano ❶ and pick up a map from the visitor centre to follow a trail through the Regional Nature Reserve, stopping for a picnic along the way.

Follow the drive directions in reverse, then retrace the route at the end of the day.

Red, red wine
It's impossible to avoid wine here. In Castellina in Chianti ❺, visit Enoteca Poggio Amorelli for a quick brush-up on the local wines, then buy some snacks in the deli. Visit Radda in Chianti ❽, then it's off to Volpaia ❾ to explore its ancient wine cellars and see its wine-production methods. Finally, drive back to Castello di Brolio ❼, to visit the castle and vineyard owned by the famous Ricasoli family.

From Castellina, take SR22, then SR429 to Radda in Chianti, then through Radda turn left on SP2bis, right on SP114c, SP112 to Volpaia. Return to Radda, down SP2bis, SR429, SP114a, left up SP408 and right on SP484 to Brolio.

Ancient history, modern art
From Greve in Chianti ❹, explore the medieval market town, then drive to Radda in Chianti ❽, to see the architecture of a once powerful city. Then drive across to Castellina in Chianti ❺ for a look at evidence of ancient Etruscan. Stay for lunch and a glass of wine, then head to the Chianti Sculpture Park ❻, for a walk around the outside modern art sculptures in a natural setting.

From Greve in Chianti, take SR222 south then SP114c to Radda in Chianti. Take the Via Strada del Chianti to Castellina in Chianti, then SR222 and SP102 to the Chianti Sculpture Park. Retrace the journey to get home.

Eat and Drink: inexpensive, under €25; moderate, €25–€45; expensive, over €45

Sacred Paths
San Miniato to San Galgano

Highlights

- **The pilgrim way**
  Follow in the footsteps of the pilgrims who travelled the Via Francigena from Northern Europe to Rome

- **Etruscan heritage**
  Visit Volterra, city of the ancient Etruscans, and discover the exquisite art and culture of this civilization

- **Ancient abbeys**
  Experience the solitude and majesty of the pilgrim monasteries – Monte Oliveto Maggiore and San Galgano

- **City of culture**
  Explore beautiful Siena and marvel at the medieval city's masterful pre-Renaissance art and architecture

- **Rural idyll**
  Relax in the unspoilt countryside of the Val di Merse, dotted with sleepy agricultural hamlets

Inside the dramatic roofless nave of the Abbey of San Galgano

Sacred Paths

A thousand years ago pilgrims travelled across these lands on their way to the holy city of Rome, bringing wealth to the churches, abbeys and towns along the routes. This drive starts with the spires of San Miniato, then meanders down the Roman Via Cassia to the monastery of San Vivaldo and magnificent Volterra. The route leads to San Gimignano, famed for its soaring towers and Vernaccia wine, and on to Siena, with its spectacular cathedral and pilgrim hospital. Further south lie the abbey of Monte Oliveto Maggiore, the woods of the Val di Merse and the soaring buttresses of San Galgano.

Above Rennaisance-style bust in an alabaster workshop in Volterra, *see p183*

ACTIVITIES

Attend a summer concert at the monastery of San Vivaldo

Visit an alabaster workshop in Volterra – maybe even take a class

Climb to the top of San Gimignano's Torre Grosso for spectacular views

Witness the Palio horse race in Siena with all its pomp and ceremony

Listen to atmospheric Gregorian chant at Monte Oliveto Maggiore

Ride a steam train from Buonconvento through the local countryside

Cycle through the Val di Merse's pleasant woods and sleepy villages

Above View over the surrounding countryside from Torre Grosso, San Gimignano, *see p184*

KEY

Drive route

0 kilometres   8

0 miles   8

útoli

Vagliagli

222   102

no

Quercegrossa   Pievasciata

Corsignano

Pianella

408

8 11

SIENA   Montaperti

674

715   715

Taverne   Fiorentine

Sant'Andrea   d'Arbia

a Montecchio   Colle

Ghetto   Malamerenda

223

Isola

d'Arbia

agnaia   **GRANCIA**

Radi   **11 DI CUNA**

Grotti   Monteroni d'Arbia

Lucignano   **11**

d'Arbia

Palazzina   Curiano

Casanova   Ponte d'Arbia

Serravalle

Ponte

Macereto   Castelnuovo

Tancredi

Campopalazzi   Bibbiano

Guistrigona

7

Torre a

Castillo

715

438   Vescona

Fontanelle

Pievina

438

Asciano   Pozzuolo

451

Montecontieri

Saltalfabbro   la Canònica

Chiusure

11 9

MONTE OLIVETO

MAGGIORE

10 BUONCONVENTO

451

PLAN YOUR DRIVE

Start/finish: San Miniato to San Galgano.

Number of days: 4–5, allowing for half days in Volterra and Siena.

Distance: Approx 254 km (158 miles).

Road conditions: Generally well signposted and well paved roads.

When to go: The area has good conditions all year round. In spring the landscape is lush; summer is more crowded and hot, but also has many festivals; autumn has truffle festivals.

Opening times: Most shops are open 9am–1pm, then 4–8pm and closed Sun and Mon mornings. In bigger cities, shops are often open over lunch. Most museums are closed Mon. Churches tend to open 7am–12:30pm and 4–7pm, but hours may vary.

Main market days: San Miniato and Monteroni d'Arbia: Tue; Castelfiorentino, Volterra and Buonconvento: Sat Chiusdino: Thu; Colle di Val d'Elsa and Siena: Fri.

Shopping: Volterra has shops selling hand-carved alabaster. Colle di Val d'Elsa is famous for fine crystal. San Gimignano is a good spot to stock up on local Vernaccia DOP white wine.

Major festivals: San Miniato: Truffle Fair, last 3 weekends of Nov; La Luna è Azzurra (children's puppet festival) Jun; Kite Festival, 1st Sun after Easter; **Monteriggioni:** Medieval Festival, 1st two weekends of Jul; **Siena:** Palio (medieval horse race), 2nd Jul & 16th Aug; **Buonconvento:** Crete d'Autunno (food festival) late Oct; **Torri:** Medieval Festival, May/Jun.

DAY TRIP OPTIONS

Families will enjoy a day trip from Volterra, clambering up **towers** and over a **castle** and well preserved **city walls**. Culture buffs will love Siena and the **art** of its **Duomo** and **museums**, as well as Monte Oliveto Maggiore's **abbey** and Buonconvento's **religious art**. For a country trip, head to the Val di Merse from Siena for a **hike/cycle ride**, then see an **abbey** and end at a **hill town**. For full details, *see p187*.

Above Road winding through Volterra's fertile countryside

VISITING SAN MINIATO

Parking
There is parking in Piazza del Popolo and Piazza della Repubblica. For long stays, park in Piazza Dante Alghieri.

Tourist Information
Piazza del Popolo 56027; 0571 42745; www.sanminiatopromozione.it

Buying and tasting truffles
The main street through San Miniato has several *alimentari* (delicatessens) that sell white truffles. The butcher **Macelleria Falaschi Sergio** *(Via Augusto Conti 18)* specializes in truffle salami.

WHERE TO STAY

SAN MINIATO

Miravalle *inexpensive*
An inviting hotel in the historic centre with a restaurant serving Tuscan cuisine. *Piazzetta Del Castello 3, 56028; 0571 419 904; www.albergomiravalle.com*

AROUND CASTELFIORENTINO

Le Boscarecce Country Inn *inexpensive*
A pleasant restored farmhouse with rustic rooms, a garden with a pool and a terrace (3 km/2 miles on the SP4). *Via Renai 19, 50051 (3 km/2 miles north on SP4); 0571 61280; www.leboscarecce.com*

VOLTERRA

Hotel Villa Porta all'Arco *inexpensive*
This pleasant, converted 20th-century villa is a short walk from the historic centre, with friendly, helpful owners. *Via Mazzini 2, 56048; 0588 81487; www.villaportallarco.it*

La Locanda *moderate*
This small hotel, handily located in the historic centre, has comfortable rooms. *Via Guarnacci 24/28, 56048; 058 881 547; www.hotel-lalocanda.com*

Top left Porta all'Arco, an ancient entrance to Volterra **Top right** Fresco at Collegiata di Santa Verdiana, Castelfiorentino **Right** The tower of Frederick rising above San Miniato

① San Miniato
Pisa, Tuscany; 56027
Like a sentinel guarding the Via Francigena, San Miniato's 13th-century **Tower of Frederick** *(open daily)* still dominates the Arno valley. The German Emperor Otto I built a castle in San Miniato in AD 962, and the town became the seat of imperial viceroys with jurisdiction over all of Tuscany. The **Duomo** *(open daily)* is dedicated to the Virgin Mary and San Genesio. A mixture of Gothic and Romanesque architecture, it has majolica plates embedded in its façade. The town is also famous for its highly prized white truffles.

🚗 *From Piazza Buonaparte follow signs to Via Fiancigena, then left into Via Castelfiorentino. Fork right into Via Meleto to a large roundabout. Just before Castelfiorentino take first exit right then left and over the bridge. Park in Piazza John Fitzgerald Kennedy.*

② Castelfiorentino
Florence, Tuscany; 50051
Named after the castle that was built here on the Via Francigena (*see p185*), Castelfiorentino is laid out like a fan below the now crumbling **fortress** and the **Chiesa di SS Ippolito and Biagio** (1195). The **Collegiata di Santa Verdiana** in the lower town has a small museum celebrating the 12th-century contemporary of St Francis who

visited here. It's also worth exploring the modern art museum **BeGo** *(Via Testaferrata; www.museobenozzogozzoli. it)*, which has frescoes by the 15th-century artist Benozzo Gozzoli.

🚗 *Head south on SS429, left towards Volterra, then right on the overpass (SP4). Go straight over the roundabout, and on through Gambassi Terme. At Spillocchi turn right for Montaione, then left at Via Pozzolo and left again at Via Tre Ponti and into San Vivaldo.*

③ The Holy Mount of San Vivaldo
Montaione, Florence, Tuscany; 50050
This extremely beautiful and rarely visited monastery *(Apr–Oct 3–7pm daily, Sun from 10am; Nov–Mar 2–5pm daily; www.sanvivaldointoscana.com)* is where the 14th-century hermit monk Vivaldo lived in a chestnut tree in the forest. Fra' Tommaso da Firenze, on his return from the Holy Land, replicated the holy sites in Jerusalem in 25 stunning chapels (1500–16). The 18 that remain contain large polychrome terracotta sculptures from the workshops of Giovanni della Robbia and Benedetto Buglioni. Concerts are staged here in summer *(Sun)* – check monastery website.

🚗 *Head south on SP65, following signs to Volterra. Drive most of the way through town, then turn sharp left up Viale dei Ponti, then right for covered parking at Piazza Martiri della Libertà.*

④ Volterra

Pisa, Tuscany; 56048

One of the 12 city-states of the Etruscan League, Volterra had well-built walls and portals, and later, a Roman theatre. During the medieval period the town built its Duomo and fine civic buildings and in the Renaissance the ruling Medici built a fort. Volterra is famous for its tradition of alabaster carving – look for the artist's workshops.

A two-hour walking tour

From the car park, head southwest and through **Porta all'Arco** ①, an Etruscan gate from the 3rd or 2nd century BC. Continue up Via Porta all'Arco and turn left at Via del Marchesi to **Piazza dei Priori** ②. To the left is the **Palazzo dei Priori** ③ (1254), the oldest town hall in Tuscany with tera-cotta shields of the Florentine rulers of the 15th century. Turn down Via Turazza to Piazza San Giovanni and the **Duomo** ④, dedicated to Santa Maria. Founded in the 9th century, and reconstructed after an earthquake in the 12th century, the church has a Romanesque façade by Nicola Pisano. Directly in front of the Duomo is the eight-sided **Baptistry** ⑤, built on the site of a pagan temple. Pass the loggia of the founding hospital and turn right into Via Roma and Via Buonparenti. In Via dei Sarti, the **Pinacoteca and Museo Civico** ⑥ (open daily) is worth a visit to see Fiorentino's Mannerist masterpiece, *The Deposition* (1521). Turn into Passo del Gralduccio in Plazza Minucci, then right for excellent view of the 1st-century **Teatro**

Rondel in the style of Luca della Robbia

Romano ⑦. Retrace steps to Via dei Sarti, proceed downhill, turning right into Via Matteotti, a vibrant shopping street, and left into Via Gramsci, which becomes Via Don Minzoni. The **Museo Etrusco Guarnacci** ⑧, one of Tuscany's most important museums, has superb examples of Etruscan ala-baster work. Don't miss the *Funeral Urn of the Married Couple* and the modern-looking statu-ette *Evening Shadow*. At the street end is the 16th-century **Porta a Selci** ⑨. Retrace steps and turn left up Via di Castello. Immediately ahead is the **Fortezza Medicea** ⑩, in two parts. The later building was added by Medici ruler Lorenzo il Magnifico to house criminals, and it is still used as a prison. Continue to the **Parco Archeologico Enrico Fiumi** ⑪ (summer: 8:30am–8pm; winter: 8:30am–5pm), the site of the ancient acropolis. Descend the stairs to the northwest into Via dei Marchesi and head left, back to Piazza Martiri della Libertà.

🚗 **Leave on SS68 east. Turn left at SP47. At the roundabout, take the 3rd exit onto SP1, go around Piazzale Martiri Montemaggio and park in Via dei Foss.**

VISITING VOLTERRA

Tourist Information
Piazza dei Priori 20, 56048; 058 887 257; www.volterratur.it

Alabaster workshops
Visits to Volterra's workshops can be arranged at the tourist office. The **Artists' Co-operative** (5 Piazza dei Priori) has an excellent showroom, and the **Alabaster EcoMuseum** (Piazza Minucci) has interesting displays of tools, techniques and alabaster sculptures.

EAT AND DRINK

SAN MINIATO

Pepenero *expensive*
Chef Gilberto Rossi serves innovative cuisine amid casual-chic décor under brick arches in the centre of town.
Via IV Novembre 13, 56028; 0571 419 523; www.pepenerocucina.it; closed Tue & lunch Sat

AROUND CASTELFIORENTINO

Il Cigliere Del Rustico *expensive*
This family-friendly restaurant serves good Tuscan home cooking – 6 km (4 miles) from town, just off the road.
Via Onofrio Di Paolo 24, 50051; 0571 582 154; www.ciglieredelrustico.it; open Sat eve Jul–Aug, Sun lunch Sep–Dec & Mar–Jun

VOLTERRA

Del Duca *moderate*
A refined restaurant where guests are made to feel very welcome. Great food, excellent wines and superb ambience.
Via Di Castello 2, 56048; 0588 81510; www.enoteca-delduca-ristorante.it; closed Tue

Osteria La Pace *moderate*
This is a small but lively restaurant in the historic centre. Try the home-made tagliatelle with truffle, or grilled meats.
Via Don Minzoni 49, 56048; 0588 86511; www.osterialapace.com

Eat and Drink: inexpensive, under €25; moderate €25–€45; expensive over €45

Right The Romanesque Church of Santa Maria Assunta, Monteriggioni **Centre right** Brightly coloured ceramic wares for sale in Siena **Far right** The multi-towered medieval town of San Gimignano **Below** The Chiostro Grande in the Monte Oliveto Maggiore Abbey

WHERE TO STAY

SAN GIMIGNANO

Hotel Relais Santa Chiara *moderate*
This modern and comfortable hotel is within easy walking distance of the town, with parking, pool and gardens.
Via Matteotti 15, 53037; 0577 940 701; www.rsc.it

Hotel Leon Bianco *moderate*
Right in the centre of San Gimignano, this good-value three-star hotel has elegant rooms and a breakfast terrace.
Piazza Cisterna, 53037; 0577 941 294; www.leonbianco.com

La Collegiata *expensive*
This stunning 17th-century converted monastery offers stylish luxury less than 2 km (1 mile) from the historic centre.
Localitá Strada 27, 53037; 0577 943 201; www.lacollegiata.it

COLLE DI VAL D'ELSA

Relais Della Rovere *expensive*
Pope Julius II built this villa just outside the town next to the monastery. Well-restored, it has elegant rooms.
Via Piemonte 10, 53034; 0577 924 696; www.relaisdellarovere.it

MONTERIGGIONI

La Canonica di San Michele *moderate*
This restored 13th-century villa has retained many original features and is set in an area of pristine natural beauty.
Strada di Fungaia 11, 53035; 0577 317 514; www.lacanonicadisanmichele.com

SIENA AND AROUND

La Grotta di Montecchino *inexpensive*
These self-catering farmhouse apartments, 2 km (1 mile) west of Siena, offer simple, rustic comfort with a barbeque and pool – good for families.
Strada Grossetana 87, Sant'Andrea a Montecchio, 53010; 0577 394 250; www.montecchino.it

Palazzo Fani Mignanelli *moderate*
Superbly located in the historic centre, this swish residence offers spacious, good-value junior suites.
Via Banchi di Sopra 15, 53100; 0577 283 566; www.residenzadepoca.it

Certosa di Maggiano *expensive*
The epitome of luxury, this 14th-century converted Carthusian monastery, on the southeast edge of town, has everything – including a helipad.
Strada di Certosa 82, 53100; 0577 288 180; www.certosadimaggiano.com

⑤ San Gimignano
Siena, Tuscany; 53037

From far away, San Gimignano's medieval towers – 14 of the original 72 remain – are a visible sign of the prosperity brought by the Via Francigena *(see box)*. Don't miss the **Collegiata di Santa Maria Assunta** *(open daily; closed Feb)*, consecrated in 1148, with an interior decorated in the 15th century by artists such as Benozzo Gozzoli. Climb the 218 steps to view the splendid panorama from the tallest tower, **Torre Grosso** *(open daily)*. The **San Gimignano1300** *(Via Berignano 23; open daily)* is a museum whose main exhibit is a scale model of the town in the year 1300.

🚗 *Follow signs to Colle di Val d'Elsa. At the 2nd roundabout, turn left into Via Armando Diaz/SS541. Follow signs for "P-ascensore" in Via di Fontibona. Use the free parking and lift.*

⑥ Colle di Val d'Elsa
Siena, Tuscany; 53034

This historic town is split into two sections, with Colle "alta" overlooking the lively Colle "bassa". The town's location on the River Elsa enabled a

papermaking industry to flourish, but it was glassmaking, particularly fine crystal, that gave it wider fame. From Colle "bassa", take the elevator up to the **castello**, the oldest part of the town, near the tower-house where 13th-century sculptor and architect Arnolfo di Cambio was born. From here, it's a pleasant walk to the west and the impressive twin bulwarks of the **Porta Nova**.

🚗 *Exit the car park turning right and continue until left turn at Via XXV Aprile. Continue onto SP5, over the autostrada, then right on SR2 towards Siena; turn left into Monteriggioni and car park.*

⑦ Monteriggioni
Siena, Tuscany; 53035

A rare example of a garrison town with an intact circle of walls, Monteriggioni safeguarded the Via Francigena and Siena's gateway to the Val d'Elsa. Fourteen towers guard a mere 570 m (1,870 ft) of walls, crowning a gentle rise in the valley. Enter **Porta Franca o Romea** into Piazza Roma and visit the simple, 13th-century Romanesque **Church of Santa Maria Assunta**, first mentioned in the 7th century.

🚗 *Follow signs for Autostrada Firenze-Siena towards Siena. Take Siena Sud exit. Turn right on SP6, then second left at Via di Tuli. Drive through Park dei Tuli and right into the Via Fontanella car park. Follow signs for Piazza il Campo on foot.*

⑧ Siena
Siena, Tuscany; 53100

Many branches of the Via Francigena converged on Siena and perhaps no other city owes so much of its heritage to the pilgrim way. It is said that in

1288, the city contained as many as 90 hotels. Travellers entered through Porta Camollia to the north and Porta Romana to the south – the latter being especially magnificent to welcome those from the papal city. **Il Campo**, the central square, is one of the most famous in Italy and the location of the dramatic horse race, the Palio. The huge **Torre del Mangia** and the 14th-century **Palazzo Pubblico** (open daily) form the apex of the fan-shaped square, with nine segments of herring-bone paving spreading out in front.

The Duomo, **Santa Maria Assunta** (open daily), completed in 1215, is a masterpiece of Tuscan Gothic. The beautiful interior includes inlaid marble floors, black-and-white banded marble pillars and carvings and sculptures by major medieval and Renaissance artists, including some early works by Michelangelo. One highlight is the 15th-century Piccolomini Library, with paintings by Pinturicchio of episodes from the life of Pope Pius II, founder of Pienza. Opposite, the Museum and Art

Pilgrims' Way

The medieval Church encouraged people to make pilgrimages to holy places such as Rome. It was believed that if you prayed at these shrines, you might be forgiven for your sins and have more chance of going to heaven. Many travelled to Rome from France, so these pilgrim routes were known as the **Via Francigena**. Sigeric the Serious, Archbishop of Canterbury (AD 990–994) kept a diary on his trip, detailing the stages. The work was copied many times and distributed widely, thus becoming one of the first travel guidebooks.

complex of **Santa Maria della Scala** (open daily), dating from 1090, was the biggest pilgrim hospice and was richly endowed by the city of Siena. Today, it is a cultural institute, gallery and underground archaeological museum. Its most important exhibit is the fresco cycle in the Sala del Pellegrinaio, which provides amazing detail of both hospital and pilgrim life in the 14th century.

Return to Tangenziale Siena Ovest. Head south onto the ramp, following signs to Arezzo and merge onto SS223 then right again to Arezzo. Merge onto E78/SS73. Take exit for Taverne D'Arbia onto SS438 to Asciano, then turn right onto SS451 and follow signs to Monte Oliveto Maggiore and car park.

Above Fresco from the Piccolomini Library at Santa Maria Assunta, Siena

Monte Oliveto Maggiore
Siena, Tuscany 53041

Surrounded by a serried array of cypress trees and accessed by a small drawbridge, the Benedictine abbey Monte Oliveto Maggiore (open daily) is still an active monastery. The main church is noted for its intricately carved wooden choir stalls and inlays. The library is of immense historical importance, but access is limited. The Chiostro Grande is the main attraction, illuminated by frescoes about the life of St Benedict created by Luca Signorelli in 1497 and Antonio Bazzi (called "Sodoma") in 1505. Another highlight is the atmospheric Gregorian chant (6:15pm daily).

Exit the monastery, turn left at SS451 to Buonconvento. There is ample parking by the walls.

SIENESE PANFORTE

First recorded in the 1300s, panforte, (strong bread) is a rich, chewy mix of flour, almonds, egg white and honey, with dried fruit and candied oranges. It provided sustenance for pilgrims and has become the signature fare of Siena. It is available in many shops in the city.

EAT AND DRINK

SAN GIMIGNANO

Trattoria Chiribiri inexpensive
Serves traditional Tuscan food. Try the coniglio ripieno (rabbit stuffed with meat and vegetables).
Piazza della Madonna 1, 53037; 0577 941 948; www.ristorantechiribiri.it; closed Wed

MONTERIGGIONI

Il Pozzo moderate–expensive
Dine inside or alfresco at this central Tuscan restaurant – try the steak Fiorentina with porcini mushrooms.
Piazza Roma 2, 53035; 0577 304 127; www.ilpozzo.net; closed Sun eve & Mon

SIENA

Zest inexpensive
A quick and tasty lunch-stop, this bar also offer a good choice of wines.
Costa di Sant' Antonio 13, 53100; 0577 47139; www.zestsiena.com

Antica Trattoria Papei moderate
Just behind the Torre del Mangia. Serves traditional Sienese fare such as pici al cinghiale (pasta with wild boar sauce).
Via del Mercato, 6, 53100; 0577 280 894; www.anticatrattoriapapei.com

MONTE OLIVETO MAGGIORE

Trattoria La Torre inexpensive
Located within the abbey complex, this osteria serves typical Tuscan cuisine. Try the ribollita soup and pecorino cheeses.
Loc. Chiusure, 53041; 0577 707 022; closed Tue

Below Steps leading into Santa Maria Assunta, Siena's stunning cathedral

Eat and Drink: inexpensive, under €25; moderate, €25–€45; expensive, over €45

Right Chiusdino, a beautiful Tuscan hill town overlooking the Val di Merse **Below left** Clock on the medieval town hall, Buonconvento **Below right** Attractive street in Buonconvento

CYCLING IN VAL DI MERSE

Biking holiday

Offering woodland trails and relatively quiet roads, Val di Merse is ideal terrain for biking. The tourism website **Terra di Siena** (*www.terresiena.it/en/bici*) has route maps for the area.

WHERE TO STAY

BUONCONVENTO

Podere Salicotto Country Hotel *moderate*
This farmstay puts the emphasis on luxurious comfort with "Bed and Brunch" (for late risers) and a swimming pool.
Strada Prov. le Pieve a Salti, Loc. Salicotti 73, 53022; 0577 809 087; www.poderesalicotto.com

AROUND GRANCIA DI CUNA

Agriturismo San Giorgio *inexpensive*
This farm stay has four apartments and also offers B&B. Set in a quiet location with comfy rooms and good breakfasts.
Strada provinciale di Radi, Loc. Colle Malamerenda, 53014; 0577 378 147; www.san-giorgio.net

TORRI AND AROUND

Antico Borgo di Torri *inexpensive*
This small, family-run B&B in the centre of Torri offers comfortable rooms decorated in a rustic, country style.
Vicolo delle Cantine 1, Loc. Torri, Sovicille; 0577 345 669; www.borgoditorri.it

Villa Ferraia *expensive*
This superb environmental leisure centre offers simple but stylish rooms as well as an organic vegetable garden, farm and astronomical observatory.
Pod. La Ripa, Loc. Tocchi 53015 Monticiano; 0577 757 102; www.villaferraia.com

AROUND CHIUSDINO

Podere Santa Maria *moderate*
Set in walnut forests and olive groves, this farm stay has apartments and rooms with weekly and nightly rates.
Loc. Cucinato, Ciciano, Chiusdino; 347 193 7052; www.poderedisantamaria.it

⑩ Buonconvento

Siena, Tuscany; 53022

Set on a flat, fertile plain, Buonconvento was always vulnerable to attack. After the Sienese defeated Emperor Henry VII in 1313, they built imposing walls, securing this important stop on the Via Francigena. The pleasant *centro storico* is home to the **Museo d'Arte Sacra** (*closed Wed in summer, weekdays in winter*), which has a fine collection of religious art. Also worth a visit is the **Museo della Mezzadria Senese** (*open 10am–1pm Tue–Sun, also 3–6pm Sat & Sun*), an evocative display of farming history in the region. Steam buffs will enjoy the **Nature Train** (*www.terresiena.it*) that puffs from town to town in the area on special days.

🚗 *Head north on SR2 towards Siena. Take exit Monteroni d'Arbia Nord, turn left at Strada Statale Cassia/SR2 (south) then right onto Via Comunale. Park in Piazza della Grancia.*

⑪ Grancia di Cuna

Siena, Tuscany; 53014

This huge structure close to Monteroni d'Arbia is a medieval *grancia*, or fortified farm. Once a hostel providing shelter for pilgrims, it was taken over in the 13th century by Siena's Santa Maria della Scala Hospital, who, over the years, redeveloped it substantially, turning it into an administrative centre

for their estates. The 14th-century centre of the *grancia* is still intact, with a courtyard and winding internal ramps that enabled mules to carry their loads to the storage rooms above what are now private dwellings. To the left of the entrance is a 1314 church dedicated to James and Christopher, the patron saints of pilgrimage and travel.

🚗 *Return to Via Cassia and turn right. At the roundabout turn right to bypass the town and right at Via 4 Novembre/SP23 signposted Castello di Grotti, then turn left for Bagnaia. Then turn right and left onto SP99 for Torri. Park in Piazza Borgo.*

⑫ Torri

Sovicille, Siena, Tuscany; 53018

The Val di Merse is a wooded area, southwest of Siena, dotted with intriguing medieval villages such as Orgia, Stigliano and Torri, whose old mills and huge granaries attest to the fertility of the land. Next to Torri's church is the impressive 11th-century **Benedictine Abbey** (*open 9am–noon Mon & Fri*), now privately owned. The abbey's beautiful cloister is regarded as one of the finest in Tuscany. It was built around a brick parquet courtyard in three elegant tiers – marble, brick and wood – in the 12th, 14th and 15th centuries respectively. Note

Pope Pius II's (1405–64) family coat of arms – Piccolomini – over the doors.
🚗 *Return to SP99, turn left and left again on SP73bis (Massa Marittima). A little way after passing Frosini turn right on Strada Provinciale di Chiusdino/SP31. Park in Piazza Giacomo Matteotti.*

⑬ Chiusdino
Siena, Tuscany; 53012

The hill town of Chiusdino lies between the Colline Metallifere (Metalliferous Hills) and the gentle Val di Merse, both areas of great natural beauty. The historic centre is a medieval warren of steep, narrow lanes. San Galgano was born here into a noble family in 1148. Instead of following a knight's life, he plunged his sword into a rock and became a hermit. The Chapel of Compagnia has a bas-relief (1466) of the sword in the stone and **San Galgano's house** *(open daily)* is now a chapel with a banded brick façade and a 13th-century relief – a copy – by Giovanni di Agostino. The original is in the **Casa Parrocchiale** along with a *Madonna and Child* by Niccolò di Segna of 1336.
🚗 *Exit on Via Piave/SP31, then fork left on the Strada Comunale di Le Vene. Turn left on Strada Provinciale Massetana/SS441. Turn right into the abbey and follow signs to parking.*

⑭ San Galgano
Siena, Tuscany; 53012

One of the most striking and poignant monuments in Tuscany is the roofless, ruined **Abbey of San Galgano**. It was built by Cistercian monks in the 13th century in a fusion of French-Gothic and Romanesque architectural styles,

with a vaulted chapterhouse. On the hill above is the 12th-century **Hermitage of Montesiepi**. Its simple style is offset by a superb banded brick and stone cupola, and by St Galgano's sword in the stone (thought by some to be the source of elements of Britain's Arthurian legend). Although the abbey flourished for several centuries, it was all but abandoned by 1600, and in 1786 its roof collapsed. In summer, it becomes a magical setting for occasional open-air operas.

Above Inside the peaceful and poignant ruins of the Abbey of San Galgano

Above left Chapel built at the birthplace of San Galgano, Chiusdino **Above right** The sleepy hamlet of Stigliano in the Val di Merse

EAT AND DRINK

SAN GALGANO

Salendo *inexpensive*
This wine bar with a terrace is on the road up to the Hermitage of Montesiepi, and offers typical local produce. *ViaPalazzetto 172, 53012; 0577 756 270; closed Mon*

AROUND GRANCIA DI CUNA

La Galera *inexpensive*
This bar-restaurant specializes in grilled meats, seafood and pizza. *Via Roma 193, 53014; 0577 374 024; www.lagalerapubristorantepizzeria.com; closed Mon*

AROUND TORRI

Dal Cateni a Orgia
A fine restaurant in Orgia, this serves excellent food – try the pasta with wild boar and the pine kernel tart for dessert. *Via dei Pratini 19, CAP 53018, Loc. Orgia; 0577 342 028; www.dalcateniaorgia.it; closed Wed*

CHIUSDINO

La Grotta di Tiburzi *inexpensive*
A classic Tuscan kitchen with generous servings of cheeses, salami and crostini, plus delicious pasta with white truffles. *Via Paolo Mascagni 15, 53012; 0577 752 948; closed Wed*

DAY TRIP OPTIONS

Volterra and Siena are great bases for day trips. Kids will love climbing over walls and towers. Adults will enjoy the art that bridged the gap between medieval and Renaissance Italy. Everyone will enjoy the scenery.

Towers, Castles and Walls
From Volterra ④, drive to the towers of San Gimignano ⑤ and climb up the Torre Grosso's 218 steps. Stop off at the castle at Colle di Val d'Elsa ⑥ for lunch and head on to the garrison town of Monteriggioni ⑦.

Follow the instructions in the drive and return the same way.

Pre-Renaissance art
In Siena ⑧, spend the morning exploring the art and architecture of the great city. Pick up a picnic and head for the frescoes of Monte Oliveto Maggiore ⑨, followed by the religious art of Buonconvento ⑩. Return via Grancia di Cuna ⑪.

Follow the drive instructions to Grancia di Cuna, then head for the SR2 and Via Roma back to Siena.

The Val di Merse
Pick up a picnic in Siena ⑧, then head to Torri ⑫ and the Val di Merse. Enjoy a hike or cycle ride, stopping for lunch. Afterwards, learn about the sword in the stone legend by driving on to San Galgano ⑭. Finish the day with a drink in Chiusdino ⑬, which looks out on the pristine countryside.

Take Via Roma to SR2, then head north on "tangenziale" to take SP73bis. Turn left for Torri at Rosia. Return to SP73bis, then SS441 for San Galgano and Chiusdino. Return the same way.

Eat and Drink: inexpensive, under €25; moderate, €25–€45; expensive, over €45

In the Shadow of a Volcano

Castiglione d'Orcia to San Casciano dei Bagni

Highlights

- **Natural beauty**
  Walk in the pristine chestnut forests that cloak Monte Amiata's hillsides and head up to the clean air at the summit for glorious countryside views

- **Mountain villages**
  Explore the pretty medieval villages that ring the mountain, whose forts and simple stone buildings reflect the tough ancient way of life

- **Mountain spa**
  Relax in a natural hot spring, gushing down a limestone waterfall in a forest glade or soak in a sulphurous, smelly but good-for-you mud pack

Man living in harmony with nature –
a classic view of the Val d'Orcia

In the Shadow of a Volcano

Italy's largest extinct volcano, Monte Amiata, dominates the horizon of much of southern Tuscany. It has been important in other ways, too. The mountain's woods provided lumber for Etruscan ships, its heights were a sanctuary for medieval monks and its depths give up minerals for the modern age. This drive takes in a ring of villages around the foot of the volcano, each with its own culture and appeal. Visitors can enjoy the relaxing properties of ancient thermal springs, hike up slopes cloaked with rich chestnut and oak forests – teeming with game and forest fare – enjoy the respite from the heat Amiata offers in summer, or even indulge in exciting winter sports when it snows.

Above The crumbling remains of the castello, Castiglione d'Orcia, *see p192*

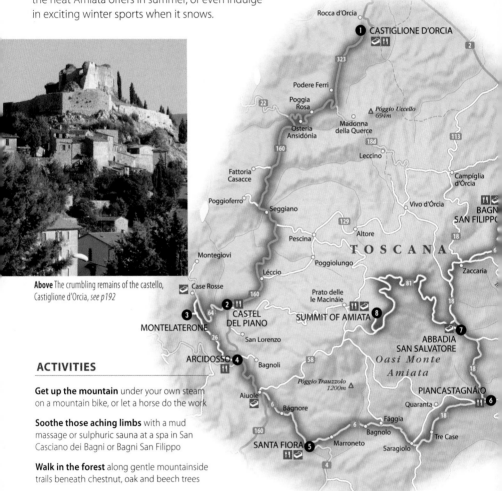

ACTIVITIES

Get up the mountain under your own steam on a mountain bike, or let a horse do the work

Soothe those aching limbs with a mud massage or sulphuric sauna at a spa in San Casciano dei Bagni or Bagni San Filippo

Walk in the forest along gentle mountainside trails beneath chestnut, oak and beech trees

Ski down Monte Amiata at speed in winter on its snow-covered ski slopes

Enjoy a taste of medieval beer with Monte Amiata's local brews

Tour a mining museum on a narrow-gauge train at Abbadia San Salvatore

KEY

— Drive route

Above Pageantry and colour in the medieval heart of Piancastagnaio, *see p193* **Below** Classic Tuscan landscape, seen from Castiglione d'Orcia, *see p192*

PLAN YOUR DRIVE

Start/finish: Castiglione d'Orcia to San Casciano dei Bagni.

Number of days: 2–3 days.

Distance: 117 km (73 miles).

Road conditions: Generally good road surfaces with good signposting. A little isolated in parts. During Dec–Mar, roads can be icy and chains are obligatory in mountain areas.

When to go: Mar–Nov is the best time. Aug is a peak season as holiday-makers escape the heat of the plain.

Opening times: Major museums are open 8:30am–7:30pm and closed Mon. Small museums often only open on weekends outside summer. Churches are generally open 7:30am–noon and 3–7:30pm. Shops open 10am–1pm and 4–8pm and close Sun & Mon mornings.

Main market days: Castiglione d'Orcia: Tue; **Castel del Piano:** Wed; **Arcidosso:** Tue; **Santa Fiora:** 2nd Thu; **Piancastagnaio:** Sat; **Abbadia San Salvatore:** Thu; **Radicofani:** 2nd & 4th Mon; **San Casciano dei Bagni:** 1st & 3rd Thu.

Shopping: Wooden handicrafts from Amiata's forests and organic preserves.

Major festivals: Castiglione d'Orcia: spring market, 1st weekend Apr; **Castel del Piano:** Palio (medieval horse race), Sep; **Montelaterone:** La Festa della Pina (spring festival), Apr; **Arcidosso:** Sagra Della Patata Macchiaiola (potato festival), 3rd weekend Aug; **Santa Fiora & Piancastagnaio:** chestnut festival, late Oct; **Radicofani:** Antichi Mestieri (old traditions), 1st weekend Jun; **San Casciano dei Bagni:** Festa del Ciaffagnone (pancake festival), 2nd & 3rd weekend of Jun.

DAY TRIP OPTIONS

Although the distances aren't great, mountain roads can be winding, so don't try to do too much on a day trip. Gourmets can enjoy the famous Amiata produce – **chestnuts, salami** and locally brewed **beer** – taking in the fine views on the way. Families with young children will find them intrigued by the history behind the area's many **castles**, **forts** and **walled medieval towns**. For full details, *see p195.*

Above The Peschiera, Santa Fiora, built to supply trout to the Aldobrandeschi court

VISITING MONTE AMIATA

Getting to Castiglione d'Orcia
From A1 Autostrada Rome-Florence, exit at Chiusi-Chianciano Terme towards Chianciano. Take SS146, then SP53. Turn left at SR2, then right at SS323. Continue to Castiglione d'Orcia, turning left at SS323, then left up Via Del Fosso.

Tourist Information
Castiglione d'Orcia: *Viale Guglielmo Marconi 13, 53023; 0577 887 363;* Arcidosso: *Piazza Indipendenza, 58031; 0564 968 084.* Santa Fiora: *Piazza Giuseppe Garibaldi 37, 58037; 056 497 7142*

WHERE TO STAY

CASTIGLIONE D'ORCIA

Castiglionae Grossola *inexpensive*
A large stone 16th-century farmstead set in the country – good for walkers. *Via Grossola 4, 53023; 0577 887 537; www.agriturismogrossola.it*

AROUND MONTELATERONE

Agriturismo Sorripe *inexpensive*
This farm stay (with pool), by Mt Amiata's woods, harvests olive oil and chestnuts. *Loc. Case Rosse; 0564 964 186; www.agriturismosorripe.it*

AROUND ARCIDOSSO

Park Hotel Colle degli Angeli *expensive*
This spa resort offers pampered comfort in the clear mountain air: swimming pool, sauna, spa and massage. *Loc. Aiuole, 58031; 0564 967 409*

SANTA FIORA

Hotel Eden *inexpensive*
This simple, rustic hotel offers old-world hospitality. *Via Roma 1, 58037; 0564 97 71 26; www.hoteledensantafiora.it*

① Castiglione d'Orcia
Siena, Toscana; 53023

Only a few ruins on a hill remain of the fortress that once controlled the nearby ancient byway, the Via Cassia. The heart of the town, built on the hillside below the fort, is Piazza il Vecchietta, a sloping cobbled square with a travertine fountain (1618) and the town hall which contains a fresco removed from the original fortress.

From the town centre, take the steep Via della Rocca to the next-door village, **Rocca d'Orcia**, with a much better preserved bastion, **Rocca di Tentennano** (*Apr–Oct: open daily; Nov–Mar: Sat & Sun*), and spectacular views of Mt Amiata and the Val d'Orcia.

🚗 *Drive south along SS323 past Poggia Rosa, then left at SP160, continue past Seggiano to Castel del Piano. Park at Piazza Giuseppe Garibaldi.*

② Castel del Piano
Grosseto, Toscana; 58033

Sitting on the slopes of Mt Amiata, Castel del Piano has been inhabited since the Paleolithic era, but up until the 14th century, it was a stronghold of the Aldobrandeschi family. Spread across the slopes, the modern part of town dwarfs the historic centre, which is best explored from Piazza Giuseppe Garibaldi, an 18th-century attempt to emulate Siena's famous Campo. On Corso Nasini, named after the 17th-century family of painters born here, stands **Chiesa di Madonna delle Grazie** with a beautiful *Madonna col Bambino* by Sano di Pietro (1405–81).

🚗 *Head west on Via della Croce/SP64. Turn left on SP26/Loc. Case Rosse and take a sharp right up Via Nouva to Montelaterone. Park in Via Nouva.*

③ Montelaterone
Grosseto, Toscana; 58031

Founded around AD 1000, this is one of the oldest settlements in the area, with the inner of the two town walls dating from the 11th century. Later, from the early 1200s, the town came under the protection of mighty Siena. Winding streets and vaulted walkways offer an intriguing climb to the ruined 13th-century keep, **Cassero Senese**. The **Palazzo Pretorio** (town hall) from the same period is decorated with the coats of arms of Renaissance-era families. On the road to Arcidosso stands the 9th-century Romanesque church **La Pieve di Lamula**, largely reconstructed in the 12th century.

🚗 *Return to SP26 and head south to Arcidosso. On arrival, turn left up Via Roma to Piazza Indipendenza and park on Corso Toscana.*

Mountain chestnuts

Historically, mountain villagers relied upon the chestnut for survival during hard times. In autumn, they would collect the chestnuts, dry them, then grind them into flour used to make a type of bread. Once poor man's food, the flour is now used to make a rich cake – *castagnaccio* – with walnuts and pine nuts. The Amiata chestnut has a delicious sweet taste when roasted and even has Protected Geographical Indication (PGI).

④ Arcidosso
Grosseto, Toscana; 58031

Just outside Arcidosso, the **Santuario della Madonna delle Grazie** (*open daily*), consecrated in 1348 and expanded in the 16th century, houses works of the 14th-century Sienese school. In 1121,

Above The twin hamlets of Castiglione d'Orcia and Rocca d'Orcia

BIRRA AMIATA

Beer drinkers must try the local brews from Birra Amiata in Montelaterone *(www.birra-amiata.it)*. La Bastarda Rossa is made with Amiata chestnuts and has a rich red colour, while Aldobrandesca is a wheat beer made to a medieval recipe.

---

the town became a stronghold of the Aldobrandeschi family, who built the impressive **Rocca Aldobrandesca** *(open Sat & Sun)* – climb the tower for views. Little of the town's original walls remain, except for two original gates: Porta di Castello and Porta Talassese.

🚗 *From Piazza Indipendenza follow signs to Santa Fiora. Take SP160, then turn left onto SP6 at Aiuole. Park in Via delle Fontane.*

The Prophet of Amiata

In the late 19th century, a man from Arcidosso, David Lazzaretti, founded a church called Giurisdavidismo, which advocated a form of socialism and universal suffrage. Arrested twice by the alarmed authorities of the new Italian state and excommunicated by the pope, he was finally shot dead by the military police in 1878. A museum in Arcidosso's **Palazzo del Comune** *(Piazza Indipendenza; open 9am–1pm Mon–Fri, 5–8pm Sat & Sun)* tells the fascinating story of his life.

❺ Santa Fiora

Grosseto, Toscana; 58037
One of the prettiest Amiata towns, Santa Fiora's castellated centre is entered through the huge Porta al Palazzo into Piazza Garibaldi. Piazza di San Michele is dominated by a statue of the saint in *peperino*, a grey-brown volcanic tufa rock. In Piazza delle Arcipretura, **La Pieve delle Sante Flora e Lucilla** *(open daily)* has blue-and-white glazed terracotta reliefs by Andrea della Robbia from 1465–90. Via della Pescheria leads to a pond, constructed in the 12th century and filled with trout. Santa Fiora makes a good base for hiking through the forests on Mt Amiata's western and southwestern slopes. There's a pleasant signposted walk

through the grove near the Peschiera and the Parco Comunale di San Rocco.

🚗 *Return to SP6. The route is signposted "Roma". Then turn left onto SP18. At Piancastagnaio turn right into Viale Giuseppe Vespa, through the gate and park in Piazza Castello.*

❻ Piancastagnaio

Siena, Toscana; 53025
Its walls and town gates are mostly gone, but Piancastagnaio's medieval townscape endures. The hard stone streets of this mountain town reflect the harshness of life in the medieval era, when poverty was part of the infrastructure. Monumental **Rocca Aldobrandesca** *(Jun–Aug: open daily)* looms over the town. After exploring the tower, head down Via Cavour to the main square, Piazza Matteotti, where the grand Baroque cathedral, **Santa Maria Assunta** *(open daily)*, first recorded in 1188, stands almost hidden behind a crowd of buildings.

🚗 *Head northwest on Viale Giuseppe Vespa and follow SP18 to Abbadia San Salvatore. Fork right at roundabout, then left to park in Via Cavour.*

EAT AND DRINK

CASTIGLIONE D'ORCIA

Il Cassero *inexpensive*
An unpretentious trattoria in the heart of town offering home-made pasta with Amiata mushroom and truffles. *Piazza Cesare Battisti 1, 53023; 0577 888 950; www.trattoriailcassero.com; closed Tue*

La Cisterna nel Borgo *moderate*
Convivial hosts and traditional fare served with an innovative twist. *Via Borgo Maestro 37, Rocca d'Orcia 53023; 0577 887 280; www.cisterna nelborgo.com; closed Mon*

CASTEL DEL PIANO

Taverna Delle Logge *moderate*
This small restaurant serves exceptional local food such as tripe and *peposo*, a mountain stew. Good wine cellar. *V. Della Penna 10, 58033; 0564 973 249; booking advised*

ARCIDOSSO

La Tagliola *inexpensive*
This place in the newer part of town is for confirmed mushroom lovers: enjoy them roasted, fried or raw. *Via di Centro 3, Loc. Bagnoli 58031; 0564 967 351; www.latagliola.it*

Il Bagatto *inexpensive*
This pleasant ice-cream place also serves up quick lunches. *Viale Davide Lazzaretti, 1, 58031; 0564 966 207; closed Wed*

SANTA FIORA

Il Barilotto *inexpensive–moderate*
Generous portions of well-prepared meat and game, traditional but with an innovative twist. Good wine cellar. *Via Carolina 24, 58037; 0564 977 089; closed Wed*

PIANCASTAGNAIO

Enoteca Saxa Cuntaria
This place serves rich mountain food with gusto. Try the Tuscan lamb soup, and the lemon-scented rabbit with porcini mushrooms and olives. *Piazza Giacomo Matteotti 11, 53025; 0577 784 104; www.saxacuntaria.it*

Eat and Drink: inexpensive, under €25; moderate, €25–€45; expensive over €45

Above The typical dark volcanic stone of medieval Abbadia San Salvatore

WHERE TO STAY

ABBADIA SAN SALVATORE

Agriturismo Trefossata *moderate*
This simple farmhouse offers rooms all year round in a tranquil, no frills environment. Good for families.
Trefossata, 53021; 0577 776 204; www.trefossata.it

SUMMIT OF AMIATA

Albergo Sella *inexpensive–moderate*
This chalet operates all year with plenty of snow activities in winter and Nordic walking at other times.
Loc. Vetta Amiata 53021; 0577 789 747; www.albergosella.it

BAGNI SAN FILIPPO

Terme San Filippo *moderate*
This small spa resort in the centre of town, near the natural spring, is the perfect spot to relax in mud baths.
Via San Filippo 23, 53023; 0577 872 982; www.termesanfilippo.com.

AROUND RADICOFANI

Fattoria la Palazzina *moderate*
An elegant 18th-century hunting lodge set on a hill among cypresses and oaks.
Loc. Le Vigne, 53042; 3662718360; www.fattorialapalazzina.com; bikes available

AROUND SAN CASCIANO DEI BAGNI

Il Poggio *expensive*
The Il Poggio farm stay offers riding for experts and beginners. Accommodation is in the farmhouse and 26 apartments in the nearby village.
Celle sul Rigo 53040; 0578 53748; www.ilpoggio.net

Fonteverde *expensive*
This glamorous spa resort offers pampering treatments, massage and highly attentive staff – good restaurant.
Loc. Terme 1, 53040; 0578 57241; www.fonteverdespa.com

Where to Stay: inexpensive, under €100; moderate, €100–€200; expensive, over €200

⑦ Abbadia San Salvatore
Siena, Toscana; 53021
Lombard King Rachis established this abbey, one of the greatest in Tuscany, in AD 743. For centuries it was the most important place in the region and held sway over the valley and the popular pilgrim route the Via Francigena. The magnificent **abbey church** *(open daily)*, in Via del Monastero, has a crypt that dates back to the original building. A town, built from the local volcanic rock, grew around the abbey and expanded due to the mercury mining industry. The mine is now the **Parco Museo Minerario** *(summer: open daily; www.museominerario.it)* with a narrow-gauge train to some of the sights.

🚗 *To exit town, follow signs to the Vetta Amiata on Via Federico Hamman and then onto SP81. On arrival at the large turning circle, there is a car park to the left under the trees.*

⑧ Summit of Amiata
Pianello Vetta, Grosseto, Toscana; 58033
Although usually snow covered from December until March, in summer the peak of Monte Amiata offers pleasant walks with spectacular views of the valley, from a large Crucifix and a statue of the Madonna.

A one-hour walking tour
Follow signs to *Vetta Amiata* (Amiata Summit) to the car park near the Albergo La Croce. Pass through a wood to a wide **grassy slope** ① – in winter this is the ski school slope. The walk up the paved path leads to the **Croce dell'Amiata** ②, a large iron cross. In 1900, for the new century, Pope Leo XIII decreed that the 20 highest peaks in Italy have a cross mounted. It took ten years and the four tons of iron were carried to the 1,730-m (5,676-ft) peak by the people of Abbadia San Salvatore. To the left of the cross is a **viewing platform** ③ looking down on the Val d'Orcia and the town of Abbadia San Salvatore. Due east, in the distance, is the Castello di Radicofani sitting atop a dark pine-clad hill. The path to the right goes past the bar-restaurant La Vetta, where walkers can stop for an aperitif of *vin brulè* (mulled wine). Further along the path to the left is a natural beech thicket **Macchia Faggeta** ④. The forest of Amiata has long been a useful source of lumber – the Etruscans used it to build their boats. In the 8th century, the Abbey took over the jurisdiction of the area, creating towns around the mountain.

After the 18th-century suppression of the monasteries, the cooperative Società Macchia Faggeta was formed, and in 1944 it took over managing the woods, trails, ski runs and lifts.

The mountain path winds through the forest past huge granite boulders. On the largest outcrop is mounted the white **Madonna of the Scouts** ⑤. This second crowning of Mt Amiata was made by the Scouts of Grosseto. The statue was carried to the summit over ten days in 1961. Scouts from all over the world climb the rocks to tie their kerchiefs to the sanctuary. Retrace the route back to the car park.

🚗 *From Abbadia San Salvatore, take SP18 towards Bagni San Filippo. Then fork right on SP61, following direction "Siena" and near the village is located Fosso Bianco.*

ACTIVITIES IN MONTE AMIATA

The ski season runs 20 Dec–14 Mar and there are 60 km (37 miles) of ski runs and trails for cross-country skiers. For lessons, contact **Scuola Sci Amiata West** *www.scuolasciamiataovest.it.*
 To hire a bike to scale the mountain in summer, or a set of skis to slide down in winter, try **Paolo Sport** *(Viale Roma, 4 Abbadia San Salvatore 53021; 0577 778 397).*

EAT AND DRINK

SUMMIT OF AMIATA

La Vetta *inexpensive*
This mountain-top bar/restaurant is useful for a quick hot chocolate, grappa or even a hearty mountain meal, such as polenta with *salsiccia* (sausage). *Loc. Vetta Monte Amiata 2, 53021; 0577 789 803*

BAGNI SAN FILIPPO

Osteria Lo Spugnone *inexpensive*
A pleasant osteria with classic Tuscan dishes such as chunky salami and grilled vegetables drizzled with olive oil. *Via delle Terme 4/6; 0577 872 030; www. lospugnone.it; booking recommended*

SAN CASCIANO DEI BAGNI

La Fornarina *inexpensive*
Smart, modern bar good for a quick snack with a nice glass of wine. *Via San Cassiano 18, 53040; 0578 59022*

⑨ Bagni San Filippo
Siena, Toscana; 53023

The white limestone waterfall Fosso Bianco is an extraordinary natural phenomenon with hot mountain springs steaming with sulphurous vapours. In 1271, a Florentine monk and candidate for pontiff, Filippo Benizi, fled here to dwell in a nearby cave and discovered the spring. The Fosso Bianco and hot springs are accessed from a marked trail off Via del Bollore. The curative effects of the water can be enjoyed at the spa **Terme San Filippo** *(www.termesanfilippo.com).*
🚗 *Follow road down to SP61 and turn right. Take a right turn onto SR2, then left onto SS478. Park by the city walls.*

⑩ Radicofani
Siena, Toscana; 53040

Visible for miles around, hilltop Radicofani dominated the Roman Via Cassia and became a control point on the road between Rome and northern Europe. Etruscan in origin, the town came under the sway of the 8th-century Lombard king Desiderius. The tight cluster of houses are built of Amiata stone and the **Chiesa di San Pietro** has two works by the studio of Andrea della Robbia and

an interesting 14th-century polychrome *Madonna and Child.* Walk up Via della Fortezza to the **castello** *(Apr–Sep: open daily; Oct–Mar: open Thu–Sun)* for spectacular views of the Val d'Orcia. The tower's history includes the time when it was occupied by a local gentleman bandit, Ghino di Tacco, in the 13th century.
🚗 *Head east on SP di Sarteano/SS478. Take a sharp right onto SP54 and turn left onto SS321, then turn right to Can Casciano and park by the city walls.*

⑪ San Casciano dei Bagni
Siena, Toscana; 53040

The Etruscans and Romans enjoyed the hot springs in this area – Augustus himself is said to have visited – and built baths here. By the Middle Ages, a town and castle had been established in the tranquil landscape.
 The turret of the **castello** (built in 1911, despite appearances) and the bell tower of the Collegiata Church dominate the town. Enter through **Porta di Sopra** (Upper Gate) and notice how the medieval structure of the town remains unchanged. Piazza Matteotti, just below the old town, forms a natural terrace with great views over southern Tuscany.

DAY TRIP OPTIONS

Eating local food, such as chestnuts, salami and beer, is a good way to get a feel for a place. Young kids may not like old buildings but they all love castles.

Gourmet day
Start the day at Santa Fiora ❺ and buy freshly roasted chestnuts in season or the rich *castagnaccio* cake. At Piancastagnaio ❻ buy

home-made salami from a butcher *(macelleria).* Drive up to the Summit of Amiata ❽ for a walk and a picnic with a view. Then it's back down to Arcidosso ❹ for a taste of local beer.

From Santa Fiora, follow the drive's instructions to Piancastagnaio, then go past Abbadia San Salvatore and up to Summit of Abbadia. From there, take SP81/SP35/SP58 then SP160 to Arcidosso.

Conquer a castle or two
Castiglione d'Orcia ❶ is a good place to start as it has two castles with great views. There's no fort at Castel del Piano ❷, but it's a fine medieval town. Montelaterone ❸ has everything – ancient walls, a historic centre and a ruined keep.

Follow the driving instructions to Montelarone and back.

Eat and Drink: inexpensive, under €25; moderate, €25–€45; expensive over €45

Umbrian Hills, Tuscan Valleys

Orvieto to Arezzo

Highlights

- **Renaissance masterpieces**
  Marvel at heaven and hell in Orvieto's Duomo by Luca Signorelli and Piero della Francesca's frescoes in Arezzo

- **Noble wine**
  Taste one of the great Italian red wines in the rustic wine cellars and restaurants of Montepulciano

- **Walled towns**
  Meander through the beautiful walled towns of Cetona, Lucignano and Cortona

- **Etruscan sites**
  Discover the ancient treasures of Orvieto, Sarteano and Cortona, showcased in magnificent museums

Classic landscape showing the grey-brown soil of the Crete Sienesi

Umbrian Hills, Tuscan Valleys

This drive follows the Umbrian part of the important route between Rome and northern Europe, now the Strada Statale 71 (SS71), from Orvieto through the hilly hinterland to the north. This was once an Etruscan stronghold, where later, in the Middle Ages, villages passed from one feudal lord to another. The drive then crosses into Tuscany, passing through the pretty towns and vineyards of the Val di Chiana and Montepulciano, on to Val d'Orcia and Renaissance Pienza, through the rolling clay hills of the Crete Senesi. Finally, via the walls of Lucignano, the drive swings back to the SS71 at Cortona and Castiglion Fiorentino, before finishing at the provincial capital, Arezzo.

Above The Giostra del Saraceno, a colourful medieval spectacle held in Arezzo *see p205*

ACTIVITIES

Ride a horse through the hills and nature reserves around Orvieto

Relive 1960s Italian style with a day's touring on a classic Vespa from Cetona

Learn traditional skills and **throw a terracotta pot** at a pottery near Ficulle

Enjoy a glass or two of celebrated DOC wine at Montepulciano

Sample the famous Pecorino di Pienza cheese in the heart of the Val d'Orcia

Photograph your own picture postcards of the rolling hills of the Crete Senesi

Sip prosecco in a hot-air balloon, soaring over the glorious Tuscan countryside

Above Cypresses in the Val d'Orcia near Pienza, *see p202*

KEY

🚗 Drive route

Below Arezzo's Piazza Grande, home to one of the largest antiques market in Europe, *see p205*

PLAN YOUR DRIVE

Start/finish: Orvieto to Arezzo.

Number of days: 3–4 days.

Distance: 204 km (127 miles).

Road conditions: Generally good throughout and well signed.

When to go: This drive is good all year round. Festivals take place throughout the year, but the most important ones are in spring and summer.

Opening times: Major museums are open 8:30am–7:30pm, and closed Mon. Small museums are often only open on weekends outside the summer months. Churches are usually open 7:30am–noon and 3–7:30pm. Shops open 10am–1pm and 4–8pm and close Sun & Mon am.

Main market days: Orvieto & Montepulciano: Thu; Ficulle: 1st Sun of month; Pienza & Castiglion Fiorentino: Fri; Città della Pieve, Cetona & Cortona: Sat; Arezzo: Piazza Sant'Agostino, Mon–Fri; Via Giotto, Sat; antiques, 1st weekend of month.

Shopping: Look for Pecorino cheese and Cinta Senese salami. Orvieto is known for its ceramics, while Arezzo is one of the gold jewellery capitals of Europe, and has some fine antiques.

Major festivals: Ficulle: bread and olive oil festival, late Oct. Città della Pieve: Palio Dei Terzieri (medieval pageant), Aug; Sarteano: food festival, May. Montepulciano: Bravio delle Botti (medieval spectacular), 3rd and 4th Sun in Aug; Cortona: Tuscan Sun Festival (international arts festival), late Jul–early Aug; Arezzo: Giostra del Saraceno (medieval joust), 2nd last Sat in Jun, 1st Sun in Sep.

DAY TRIP OPTIONS

There are three tempting day trips. Families will love Orvieto's **Etruscan museum** and **tunnels**, Roman Ficulle's **castello** and Sarteano's **Etruscan treasures**. For art buffs, Cortona has **religious masterpieces**, Lucignano a **sacred reliquary**, while Arezzo has the finest **Renaissance fresco cycle** there is. Food and wine lovers can take things easy with a **wine tour** with **tastings** at Montepulciano and Pienza's **pecorino**. For full details, *see p205*.

Above Colourful flower-filled balcony in Sarteano **Above centre** View straight out of a Renaissance painting, near Città della Pieve **Above right** Perugino's *Adoration of the Magi*, Città della Pieve

GETTING TO ORVIETO

From A1 Autostrada Rome–Florence, take the Orvieto exit, keeping right to stay on SS205. At roundabout, take 2nd exit onto Via Angelo Costanzi, then fork left onto Strada della Stazione. Park in Piazza Cavour.

WHERE TO STAY

ORVIETO

Hotel Corso Orvieto *inexpensive*
Value-for-money hotel in the historic centre with nice rooms and helpful staff.
Corso Cavour 339, 05018; 0763 342 020; www.hotelcorso.net

Palazzo Piccolomini *moderate*
This fine, centrally located 16th-century renovated palazzo was once the home of the papal Piccolomini family.
Piazza Ranieri 36, 05018; 0763 341 743; www.palazzopiccolomini.it

MONTELEONE D'ORVIETO

Agriturismo I Gergoni *inexpensive*
These self-catering houses have plenty for the sporting minded: bike hire and archery, horse-riding, canoeing and golf.
Vocabolo Gergone 3, 05017; 0763 617 317; www.igergoni.it

CITTÀ DELLA PIEVE

Campogrande *inexpensive*
A pleasant country B&B on the road to Città della Pieve with three stylish suites, one with disabled access.
Campogrande 1, 06062; 0578 298 989

CETONA

La Locanda di Cetona *moderate*
This charming inn has the advantages of being on the central piazza, with friendly hosts and comfortable rooms.
Piazza Balestrieri 4/5/6, 53040; 0578 237 075; www.locandadicetona.com

① Orvieto
Terni, Umbria; 05018
Set on a huge slab of tufa, Orvieto was colonized nine centuries before Christ and flourished in the Etruscan period as Velzna. After the Romans destroyed it in 264 BC, the town didn't revive until the medieval period, when it became the residence of popes. Etruscan finds and medieval and Renaissance art and architecture make Orvieto a compelling place to visit. The startling travertine-and-basalt striped Duomo, **Cattedrale dell'Assunta**, has an Italian-Gothic façade with a large rose window, exquisite reliefs, gold tiles and bronzes. Begun in 1290 from plans by Arnolfo di Cambio, the building took 300 years to finish. Inside is Luca Signorelli's (c.1445–1523) *The Last Judgement* in the **Cappella di San Brizio** *(open daily)*, the finest fresco cycle of the Renaissance. The superb **Faina Archaeological and Civic Museum** *(open daily)*, opposite the Duomo, has a fine collection of Etruscan art. Nearby, explore Orvieto's **underground city** *(0763 344891; www.orvietounderground.it; Mar–Jan: open daily; Feb: weekends only)*, first excavated by the Etruscans.

🚗 *Descend from the rock (rupe) to Via Angelo Costanzi at Orvieto Scalo, taking third exit at roundabout onto SS71. At Ficulle, park to right of the main road.*

② Ficulle
Terni, Umbria; 05016
Strung along a ridge between two citadels, this tiny village dates back to when the Romans established the outpost Castrum Ficulensis (from the Latin *figulus*, or potter). Craftsmen still inhabit the village – near its southern entrance, Porta del Sole, is the family-run pottery of **Fabio Fattorini** *(Via Roma 50)*, started in 1834, and nearby **Vetro In** *(Corso della Rinascita 14)* is the stained-glass workshop of Michela Marilena. The medieval complex of **Castel Maggiore** is explored via a labyrinth of staircases and alleys.

🚗 *Head north on SS71 to Monteleone d'Orvieto. Take a slight left at Via Roma and park in Piazzale Marconi.*

③ Monteleone d'Orvieto
Terni, Umbria; 05017
Founded in 1052 as a feudal castle to defend the northern boundaries of Orvieto, this quiet castellated village has superb views from its medieval walls. Enter it through the medieval **Porta Nord**, rebuilt in 1848, and take Corso Vittorio Emanuele II to the village centre and Piazza Pietro Bilancini, home to the handsome 1888 Torre dell'Orologio (clock tower) and the medieval town well. Via della Ripa, above the western wall, gives views across the Val di Chiana and Monte Cetona.

🚗 *Head north on Via Crocifisso, then left at SS/SP71 to Città della Pieve. Turn right at Via Beato Giacomo Villa, then right and park on the road.*

4 Città della Pieve

Perugia, Umbria; 06062

Almost completely built of brick, this Renaissance town is most famous as the birthplace of the painter Pietro Vannucci, or Perugino (c.1450), who put the home landscape into many of his works. Enter town via the solid **Fortezza** (open daily), built in 1326 and now home to the tourist office. It is a short walk to Piazza Plebiscito with **Perugino's house** (not open), on the left, and the **Cattedrale di SS Gervasio e Protasio** – originally an 8th-century parish church, it was enlarged in the 13th century. Heading north on Via Pietro Vannucci leads to the **Confraternita Santa Maris dei Bianchi**, housing a single painting – Perugino's glorious *Adoration of the Magi*, finished in a few weeks in 1504 using his trademark strong colours. On the left of the Well of the Casaline, is Via Baciadonne (Kiss the Women Street), one of the narrowest streets in Italy.

🚗 *Turn into Viale Marconi and take SS71 towards Chiusi, left on SP146. At the roundabout turn back and then right towards Chiusi on SP49 and left at SS321. Park on the way into town.*

5 Cetona

Siena, Toscana; 53040

The first impression of Cetona is of the large rectangular square, **Piazza Garibaldi**, which seems too large and too modern for a medieval village. But it was the vision of one man, Gian Luigi Vitelli, who was made Marquis of Cetona in 1556 by Cosimo I de Medici, Grand Duke of Tuscany.

Below left View from the pretty terraces of Cetona **Below** Etruscan fresco in the Museo Civico Archeologico, Sarteano

The old town and its narrow streets straggle up the hill to the fortress, **La Rocca**, which Vitelli turned into a residence. Palazzo Vitelli, his family home, is on the main square.

🚗 *Continue west on Via Martiri della Libertà/SP21. On arrival in Sarteano, at the roundabout, take the 3rd exit onto Viale Beato Alberto/SS478 and park in Piazza Duccio Barbagli.*

6 Sarteano

Siena, Toscana; 53047

This charming village has an impressive **castle** (summer: open daily till late; restricted hours in winter) that provides a historical focal point as well as great countryside views. The streets and houses behind the main square still retain their medieval form and atmosphere, and parts of the village walls have been imaginatively incorporated into private housing.

Southern Tuscany was heavily populated by the Etruscans and the **Museo Civico Archeologico** (Via Roma 24; open daily) has some extraordinary and beautifully presented finds.

🚗 *Head north on SP19 onto SS146 to Montepulciano. Turn right on SP17 and immediately left into Via di San Pietro and park in the dedicated parking areas.*

Alternative travel

Enjoy a touch of nostalgia with a drive around the gentle hills of Umbria and Tuscany in true Italian style in a Fiat 500, or on a classic Vespa hired from **Slow Hills** (Via XXV 33, Cetona, 53040; 340 354 1996; www.slowhills.com).

Or leave the wheels behind and explore the gorgeous countryside on a horse with **Wild Horse** (Strada delle Piane, Fraz. San Lorenzo, Monteleone d'Orvieto 05017; 3485 286169; www.maneggiowildhorse.it), who can organize treks and lessons for riders of all abilities.

Above left The beautiful countryside surrounding Cetona **Above** The magnificent façade of Orvieto's Duomo

POTTERY CLASSES

Take a pottery course in a lovely rustic setting on an old farm with potter **Paola Biancalana** (La Badia 8, Ficulle 05016; 0763 891 035; www.paola biancalana.it) who works with a range of ceramics, including terracotta, and likes to use a wood-fired kiln.

EAT AND DRINK

ORVIETO

Trattoria del Moro Aronne *moderate*
This central family-run trattoria offers home-style dishes. Try the *carbonara di fave e baffo*, an outstanding pasta dish with a sauce of pureed fava beans.
Via S. Leonardo 7, 05018; 0763 342 763; www.trattoriadelmoro.info

FICULLE

Le Fontane *inexpensive–moderate*
An unpretentious pizzeria and modest country trattoria that offers crisp pizzas and large plates of traditional food.
Strada Fontane 11, Ficulle 05016; 0763 86512; www.hotelrilarosi.it; closed Mon

MONTELEONE D'ORVIETO

La Tana del Gufo *moderate*
Enjoy wood-fired pizza and *carne alla brace* (meat cooked on the open fire) in a modest, homely atmosphere.
Via Sandro Pertini 47, 05017; 0763 834 756; www.latanadelgufo.com

CITTÀ DELLA PIEVE

Ristorante Zafferano *expensive*
Part of Hotel Vannucci, this elegant restaurant serves superb traditional cuisine with a contemporary twist.
Via Vanni 1, 06062; 0578 298 063; www.hotel-vannucci.com; closed Wed & Oct–Apr

SARTEANO

Osteria da Gagliano *inexpensive*
A delightful small, cosy tavern with a seasonal menu with local produce.
Via Roma 5, 53047; 0578 268 022; closed Tue, booking advised

Eat and Drink: inexpensive, under €25; moderate, €25–€45; expensive over €45

Right (all) Montisi, a pretty town set among beautiful natural scenery that has attracted a thriving community of artists

VISITING MONTEPULCIANO

Tourist Information
Piazza Don Minzoni 1, 53045; 0578 757 341; www.prolocomontepulciano.it

WHERE TO STAY

MONTEPULCIANO

Il Borghetto *inexpensive–moderate*
This value-for-money hotel near the entrance to the historic centre offers a warm welcome. Car parking available.
Via Borgo Buio 7, 53045; 0578 757 535; www.ilborghetto.it

Locanda di San Francesco *expensive*
This central family-run hotel has large rooms and stunning country views.
Piazza San Francesco 5, 53045; 0578 758 725

PIENZA

Podere Spedalone *moderate*
This tranquil farm experience with good rooms and a pool also offers dinner with Giancarlo, the farmer, and his friends.
Podere Spedalone 11, 53026; 338 705 2912; www.poderespedalone.it

MONTISI

La Romita *inexpensive–moderate*
The Bindi family have run this relaxing hotel since 1633. It also has apartments.
Via Umberto I 144, 53020; 0577 845186; www.laromita.net

LUCIGNANO

I Girasoli *inexpensive*
Hotel and apartments with two pools and a tennis court. Great for families.
Selve di Sotto, 52046; 057 581 9020; www.igirasoli.ar.it

Below The early Renaissance façade of the Duomo in Piazza Pio II, Pienza

⑦ Montepulciano
Siena, Toscana; 53045

Set in a commanding position at 600 m (1,970 ft), Montepulciano affords spectacular views of the surrounding landscape. Located on a major crossroads, it became an important conquest of Florence in 1511. The 1.5-km (1-mile) walk uphill into town, from Porta al Prato to Piazza Grande, the centre of the town, with the **Duomo** and the **Palazzo Communale**, is challenging, but worth it for the splendid views and charm of the old civic buildings.

Most visitors will know the name of the town from its high-quality red wine, the prestigious Vino Nobile di Montepulciano, the first in Italy to receive the Denominazione di Origine Controllata e Garantita (DOCG). It can, of course, be sampled in any of the cantinas around Piazza Grande.

Leave Montepulciano west along Via di San Biagio to see **Tempio di San Biagio** *(open daily)*, the Renaissance masterpiece of a church designed by Antonio da Sangallo The Elder in 1529.
🚗 *Return downhill to crossroad with SP146. Turn left on Via San Biagio to Tempio di San Biagio. Head south on Viale della Rimembranza, then turn right at SS146. At Pienza, park in Via degli Archi.*

⑧ Pienza
Siena, Toscana; 53026

This is one of the few places in the world where visitors can be in two Unesco World Heritage sites at once: Pienza and the Val d'Orcia, over which the town has a stunning view. The town was remodelled in 1458–62 by Pope Pius II, who left his symbol, a crescent moon, on every available surface. Pienza is an architectural marvel with an exquisite **Duomo** (1459) on Piazza Pio II – a landmark in Renaissance architecture. Zeffirelli's *Romeo and Juliet* (1968) and *The English Patient* (1996) were both filmed here. Visit **Palazzo Piccolomini** *(closed Mon)*, the pope's former residence and now a museum of opulent interiors. Pienza is also famous for its Pecorino cheese – visit **Zazzeri** *(Il Rossellino 6)* to taste and buy.
🚗 *Turn left at Via San Gregorio/SS146 around to the right. Slight right at SP di Cosona/SP71, then carry on to Castelmuzio. Park in Via della Trove.*

Where to Stay: inexpensive, under €100; moderate, €100–€200; expensive, over €200

⑨ Castelmuzio

Siena, Toscana; 53020

A living museum, this well-preserved medieval village, called "il Castello" by the locals, retains the typical structure of a fortified castle encircled by walls and bastions. There are a few shops inside the main gate and a single bar/pizzeria under the bell tower in the central piazza.

🚗 *Leave northwest on Viale della Rimembranza. At the stop, turn left on Via di Circonvallazione and then right on Via Umberto I. Park on the right.*

⑩ Montisi

Siena, Toscana; 53020

This vibrant village, coiled around an ancient castle keep, dates back to the Etruscans, although much of what's visible was built during the height of the Sienese Republic (14th–16th century). Montisi has attracted a lively creative community over the years, and many artists offer drawing or painting classes. The 13th-century **Castello di Montisi**, at the top of the village, houses a small music academy which puts on summer concerts.

🚗 *Exit town and take SP38 left to Trequanda. Park in Piazzale Cacciaconti.*

The sheep's cheese of Pienza

The wild herbs of the Val d'Orcia are said to give the distinct flavour to the cheese made from Sardinian sheep's milk: **Pecorino di Pienza**. It's lovely with slices of crisp pear and can be aged in hazelnut leaves or straw and flavoured with truffle. *Fresco* (fresh) cheese is slightly soft; *semi stagionato* (part-aged) and *stagionato* (aged) are richer in colour and flavour.

⑪ Trequanda

Siena, Toscana; 53020

This sleepy village is even quieter when the central bar, **La Torre**, is closed *(Tue in winter)*, but it is a pleasant stop and home to the extraordinary **Chiesa SS Pietro e Andrea**. Founded in 1327, this single-naved Romanesque-Gothic church has a bizarre chequerboard façade of travertine marble and local tufa, and contains a fresco, *The Ascension*, said to be by Sodoma.

🚗 *Head east to SP38 and turn left to Sinalunga. At the stop on SS326 follow indications to Siena Sinalunga, then turn right to Lucignano on SP11c. Park off Via di Circonvallazione.*

⑫ Lucignano

Arezzo, Toscana; 52045

This pretty place is a fine example of medieval town planning, with walls and roads in concentric circles. Enter through **Porta di San Giusto** and the road to the north, now Via Roma, was where the poor lived; noble families built their homes along the sunnier road to the south. Up against the walls stands the solid **Torre del Cassero**. At the heart of town, the **Collegiata di San Michele Arcangelo** (1582), the 13th-century **Chiesa di San Francisco** with its striped Gothic façade and the 12th-century **Palazzo Pretorio**, seat of the town council, formed a nucleus of religious and political power. The Palazzo Pretorio houses the **Museo Civico** *(closed Tue)* containing the 14th-century silver, gilded copper and enamel reliquary, the *Albero di Lucignano* (Tree of Life).

🚗 *Head east on Via Procacci/SP28 through Foiano and take a slight right at SP31 (over the motorway), following the signs to Cortona. On SS71, pass through Camjocia centre, then go uphill on SP34. Park off Via Mura del Mercato.*

Above left Cycling in the countryside around Pienza **Above** The chequerboard façade of the Chiesa SS Pietro e Andrea, Trequanda **Below left** Narrow street in the medieval centre of Montisi

---

ACTIVITIES IN MONTISI

It is hard to beat floating over the scenic fields and towns of the Crete Senesi in a hot-air balloon while sipping a glass of chilled prosecco. To have a go at this pleasurable activity, contact **Ballooning in Tuscany** *(338 146 2994; www.ballooningintuscany. com)*. Flights leave from Montisi.

EAT AND DRINK

MONTEPULCIANO

Osteria Acquacheta *moderate*
This plain vaulted room offers simple food in a great Tuscan dining experience.
Via del Teatro 22, 53045; 0578 717 086; www.acquacheta.eu; book ahead

PIENZA

La Buca delle Fate *moderate*
A busy trattoria serving home-made pasta and ragù, wild boar, Tuscan steaks and delicious cakes.
Corso il Rossellino 38/a, 53026; 0578 748 448; closed Mon

MONTISI

da Roberto
This delightful friendly restaurant with a garden serves food prepared with care in a relaxed, unfussy atmosphere.
Via Umberto 3, 53020; 0577 845 159; www.tavernamontisi.com

TREQUANDA

Conte Matto *moderate–expensive*
Enjoy the terrace and excellent food – try the gourmet taster menu with wild boar with chocolate and duck ragù.
Via Taverne 40, 53020; 0577 662 079; www.contematto.it; closed Tue

LUCIGNANO

Il Goccino *moderate*
Intimate, traditional restaurant with good wines and a terrace with a view.
Via Matteotti 90, 52046; 0575 836 707; www.ilgoccino.it; closed Mon

Eat and Drink: inexpensive, under €25; moderate, €25–€45; expensive over €45

Above Restaurant in Piazza della Repubblica, in the heart of Cortona

WHERE TO STAY

CORTONA

Il Sole del Sodo *inexpensive–moderate*
This central B&B is a luxury Tuscan experience offering rooms or suites.
Loc. Il Sodo 5/6, 52044; 0575 612 692; www.ilsoledelsodo.com

Villa Marsili *moderate–expensive*
This elegant hotel is at the busy end of town, but the private villa garden and terrace allows for relaxation in peace.
Viale C. Battisti 13, 52044; 0575 605 252; www.villamarsili.net

CASTIGLION FIORENTINO

Villa Schiatti *inexpensive*
This huge 19th-century villa, near the Castello di Montecchio, has pleasant rooms and a pool. Close to walking trails.
Loc. Montecchio 131, 52043; 0575 651 440; www.villaschiatti.it

AREZZO

Graziella Patio Hotel *moderate*
A chic central boutique hotel, inspired by the writings of Bruce Chatwin.
Via Cavour 23, 52100; 0575 401 962; www.hotelpatio.it; no elevator

⑬ Cortona
Arezzo, Toscana; 52044

One of the jewels of Tuscany, Cortona sits on a mountain spur facing south towards Lago Trasimeno and dominating the Val di Chiana, below. This walk takes in the major sights as well as visiting a few places off the beaten track to see a different side of this hill town.

A two-hour walking tour

Piazza Garibaldi ① at the eastern edge of town is the bus arrival point and a pleasant leafy terrace with wonderful views. Porta Garibaldi, the gateway to the town, leads to **Via Nazionale** ②, Cortona's main shopping street and home to the Tourist Information Office *(open daily)*. Via Nazionale opens out into beautiful Piazza della Repubblica. Dominated by the stone bulk of the **Palazzo del Comune** ③, the square is a mix of shops, wine bars and restaurants. Just off the piazza, at No. 4, is the **Palazzo Cristofanello-Laporelli** ④, now a bank. Built in 1533, the building is a striking architectural confection whose third floor of columns and pilasters looks like a Roman temple high above the square. Via Roma leads straight to the northwest gate, Porta Santa Maria. Around the right-hand side of the staircase, take a few steps into another square, Piazza Signorelli, named for Cortona's famous Renaissance painter, Luca Signorelli.

Gourmet olive oil on sale in Cortona

It is dominated by the 16th-century façade of the **Palazzo Casali** ⑤ to the left, and the loggia of the 19th-century Teatro Signorelli to the right. The palazzo houses the excellent Museo dell'Accademia Etrusca e della Città di Cortona *(closed Mon Nov–Mar; www. cortonamaec.org)*, full of Etruscan finds.

Between the Palazzo and the Theatre, Via Casali leads down to the **Piazza del Duomo** ⑥. The Chiesa di Santa Maria Assunta here has been rebuilt many times in its long history from its origins as a pagan temple. Little remains of interest except some Romanesque elements in the façade. Opposite the Duomo is the Museo Diocesano *(open daily; closed Mon in winter)*, which holds work by Signorelli, Fra Angelico (1395–1455) and Pietro Lorenzetti (1280–1348).

From the museum, return to Piazza Signorelli and the Teatro, often a venue for summer concerts in the Tuscan Sun Festival. Continue uphill to the piazzetta **Croce del Travaglio** ⑦. The road ahead, Via Dardano,

Where to Stay: inexpensive, under €100; moderate, €100–€200; expensive, over €200

Far left The 12th-century Romanesque Santa Maria della Pieve, Arezzo **Left** View of Castiglion Fiorentino and the Val Chiana **Below** Beautiful frescoes inside the Basilica di San Francesco, Arezzo

EAT AND DRINK

CORTONA

La Bucaccia *moderate*
In ancient cellars in the heart of town, this serves traditional cuisine – chestnut ravioli, wild boar – with good wines, too.
Via Ghibellina 17, 52044; 0575 606 039; www.labucaccia.it; closed Mon

Preludio *expensive*
Centrally located restaurant set in a grand palazzo serving elegant and innovative Tuscan dishes.
Via Guelfa 11, 52044; 0575 630 104; www.ilpreludio.net; book ahead

AREZZO

Il Saraceno *moderate*
A cosy restaurant, famous for its rich and hearty food – thick Tuscan soups, steaks and roast meats and tiramisù.
Via Giuseppe Mazzini 6, 52100; 0575 27644; www.ilsaraceno.com

Trattoria La Lancia d'Oro *moderate*
Marzia and Maurizio host a bustling and happy restaurant with excellent mains and desserts. Outdoor tables are best on the day of the antique market.
Piazza Grande 19 (Logge Vasari), 52100; 0575 21033; www.loggevasari.it

leads to Porta Colonia and the car park beyond. Turn right into Via Maffei, a steep street lined with old residences and with only light pedestrian traffic. The road runs up to the Church of San Francesco *(open daily)*, built in 1245 by Brother Elias, St Francis' right-hand man. The simple façade reflects the Franciscan rejection of wealth. Inside there is a painting by local master Pietro Berrettini (1596–1669).

Follow Via Maffei downhill to **Porta Berarda ⑧**. From here, turn right, and return down to Piazza Garibaldi.

🚗 *Follow signs to Arezzo, on SS71, turn right to Castiglion Fiorentino. Follow signs to the centre and park in the big park at the end of the ascending street.*

⑭ Castiglion Fiorentino
Arezzo, Toscana; 52043

Porta Fiorentina, well above the modern town and train station, leads to the historic centre and the **Piazza del Municipio** with its 16th century nine-arched loggia designed by Vasari over a balcony with excellent views. Up past the Palazzo Comunale are the ruins of the fortress, **Il Cassero** (1347). The town's youth gather around Piazza Garibaldi on summer nights. To the south of town stands

the romantic-looking 10th-century **Castello di Monticchio** *(not open)*.

🚗 *Head west on SP40, then right on SS71, then SS73 to the centre. At the next roundabout take the 3rd exit on Viale don Minzoni and carry on toward Bibbiena. On Via Amendola turn right at the roundabout on Via Sette Ponti and follow signs to Pietri park. Take escalator to historic centre.*

⑮ Arezzo
Arezzo, Toscana; 52100

A wealthy, bustling town, Arezzo has been an important commercial centre since Roman times. It has a beautiful medieval heart, whose highlight is Piero della Francesca's 15th-century frescoes, *Legend of the True Cross*, in the apse of the **Basilica di San Francesco** *(open daily; tickets: 0575 352727)*. The Gothic Duomo houses a lovely fresco of Mary Magdalene (left of the main altar) also by Piero. The main pedestrian street, **Corso Italia** runs directly down the hill to the Romanesque **Santa Maria della Pieve** and **campanile** with double mullion windows. Behind this is the beautiful Piazza Grande, venue of the medieval pageant of the Giostra del Saraceno and a monthly antiques market.

DAY TRIP OPTIONS

Obvious themes here are Etruscans, which will appeal to families, Renaissance art and cheese and wine.

Etruscan treasures
Orvieto ❶ has a superb Etruscan museum and ancient tunnels. Pretty Ficulle ❷, a Roman village, has a good castle to explore. Enjoy pizza in walled Monteleone d'Orvieto ❸, then on to Sarteano ❻ for more Etruscan finds.

From Orvieto, take SS71 to Ficulle and Monteleone d'Orvieto. At Chiusi, take SS146, then SS476 to Sarteano. Return via A1 if in a hurry, or retrace route.

Renaissance genius
At Cortona ⑬, see Museo Diocesano's religious art and explore the town. Drive to Lucignano ⑫ for lunch and to see the *Tree of Life*. Then it's off to Arezzo for Piero della Francesca's sublime frescoes (book in advance).

From Cortona, take SP31 and SP28 to Lucignano, take SS25 to SP327, then SS73 to Arezzo. Return to start on SS71.

A rich palate
Using Montepulciano ❼ as a base, arrange a wine tour with the tourist office, then set off to Pienza ❽ to taste the best of its famous Pecorino cheese. Return for a Chianina steak, more fine wine and a semifreddo.

Take SS146 Montepulciano to Pienza.

Umbria's Verdant Valleys

Perugia to Arrone

Highlights

- **Fortified hill towns**
  Explore the medieval walled towns and fortifications of Trevi, Campello, Spoleto, Ferentillo and Arrone

- **Spiritual journey**
  See Assisi, the home of St Francis, and experience the same calm and solitude in his grotto at the hermitage

- **Roman era remains**
  Travel back in time to witness the power and glory of ancient Rome at Perugia, Spello, Campello and Spoleto.

- **Wild beauty**
  Enjoy the diverse natural features of the valleys, from woods and gentle rivers to steep gorges and rocky cliffs

The medieval hill town of Trevi, overlooking the valley of Clitunno

Umbria's Verdant Valleys

Slicing through the green heart of Umbria are the Valle Umbra and the Valnerina valleys. The former was created by a river system from the Fonte di Clitunno, that eventually joins the River Tiber near Perugia. The latter was carved out by the River Nera, rising high in the Monti Sibillini to the east. This drive follows the Valle Umbra from ancient Perugia to the holy city of Assisi, home of St Francis, and passes Roman ruins and medieval villages on the way to the great Lombard city of Spoleto. From here, it joins the neighbouring valley and follows the River Nera, past ancient abbeys and once mighty fortresses.

Above The medieval heart of Spoleto, *see p214*

0 kilometres   8

0 miles   8

ACTIVITIES

Indulge in some of Perugia's famous chocolate

Walk in the footsteps of Saint Francis in the woods around the Eremo delle Carceri

Sample the fresh and fruity olive oil in Trevi

Try your hand at medieval crafts in a workshop in Bevagna's museum

Ride a bike along the mountain paths of the Valnerina

Head for the hills and try free-climbing at Ferentillo

Ride the rapids by white-water rafting on the River Nera

Above Olive groves below Trevi, known for its olive oil production, *see p213*
Below The frescoed Chiesa di San Giovanni Battista, Arrone, *see p215*

KEY

Drive route

PLAN YOUR DRIVE

Start/finish: Perugia to Arrone.

Number of days: 3–4, allowing half a day to explore Perugia.

Distance: Approx 150 km (93 miles).

Road conditions: Generally good but take the alternative route between Eremo delle Carceri and Spello in winter if the road over Mt Subasio is closed.

When to go: The valleys offer activities and interest all year round. Summer is best for sports and festivals. In autumn, the first pressing of olive oil is available.

Opening times: Major museums are open 8:30am–7:30pm, and closed Mon. Small museums are often only open on weekends outside summer. Churches vary but are generally open 7:30am–noon and 3–7:30pm. Shops in Perugia and Assisi have extended trading hours, but others often open 10–1pm and 4–8pm and close Sun and Mon mornings.

Main market days: Perugia & Assisi: Sat; **Spello:** Wed; **Trevi, Arrone:** Thu; **Campello sul Clitunno:** 3rd Mon of month; **Spoleto:** Fri. **Ferentillo:** Tue.

Major festivals: Perugia: Umbria Jazz, Jul; Euro Chocolate exhibition, Oct; **Assisi:** Calendimaggio (May day festival) 1st Thu, Fri, Sat after 1 May; **Bevagna:** Mercato delle Gaite (medieval market), Jun; **Spoleto:** Festival dei Due Mondi (music and dance), Jun–Jul; **Scheggiano:** Trout Festival, Aug.

Shopping: Perugia has high fashion as well as chocolate. Assisi has all kinds of religious souvenirs. The area between Bevagna and Spoleto produces the excellent Sagrantino di Montefalco wine. Bevagna is also famous for medieval crafts: textiles, candles, parchment and hand-made paper.

DAY TRIP OPTIONS

History buffs will enjoy the Roman sights – from **arches** and **theatres**, to **temples** and **villas**. Those interested in spiritual paths, can follow in the steps of St Francis, from his **basilica** to the **grotto** where he prayed. Art lovers will enjoy the **frescoes** and **paintings** in the **churches** and **palazzos** of Perugia and beyond. For full details, *see p215*.

Above The Tempio di Sant'Angelo, Perugia, reputedly built over a pagan site

VISITING PERUGIA

Parking
Exit the motorway at Perugia Madonna Alta, taking the direction "stadio" to Porta Nova car park (3,000 spaces).

Transport
A shuttle train – *minimetrò* – runs from the car park at Porta Nova station to the historic centre at Pincetto.

WHERE TO STAY

PERUGIA

Arte Hotel *inexpensive*
A bright, modern hotel, just off the main road, with a contemporary art theme.
Strada Trasimeno Ovest 159, 06132; 075 517 9247; www.artehotelperugia.com

Montecorneo Country House
inexpensive–moderate
These apartments are in three cottages in the grounds of an 18th-century villa.
Strada dei Loggi 136, 06126; 075 388 230; www.montecorneo.com

Castello di Monterone
Residenza d'Epoca *expensive*
A chance to stay in a real 13th-century castle – but in luxury – with frescoes and other original architectural details.
Strada Monteville 3, 06126; 075 572 4214; www.castellomonterone.it

ASSISI

Hotel La Fortezza *inexpensive*
Value-for-money hotel in the historic centre, with terrace views and free wi-fi.
Vicolo della Fortezza 19/B, 06081; 075 812 418; www.lafortezzahotel.com

Le Dimore di San Crispino *expensive*
A historic residence with elegant and refined apartments and good views.
Via Sant'Agnese 11, 06081; 075 804 3257; www.assisibenessere.it

① Perugia
Umbria; 06100

The capital of Umbria, this ancient Etruscan city grew into a mighty presence in the medieval period. From the 14th century it was ruled by a papal legate and, after violent feuding, went to war with the pope over the price of salt. This walk takes in the full history of Perugia.

A three-hour walking tour
From the Porta Nova car park, take the *minimetrò* shuttle to Pincetto station and emerge at Via Rupe. Turn into Via G Oberdan, then **Piazza Matteotti** ①. Walk straight up Via Giuseppe Mazzini, then right into wide Corso Vannucci to **La Pasticceria Sandri** ②, a historic café and pastry shop specializing in chocolate. Opposite is the **Collegio del Cambio** ③ *(Mar–Oct: open daily; Sep–Feb: closed Mon & pm)*, two exquisite rooms of the Money Exchange Guild (built 1452–57) with frescoes completed in 1500 by Pietro Vannucci (Perugino). Further along is the **Galleria Nazionale dell' Umbria** ④ *(closed Mon)*, one of the finest museums in Central Italy with works by Perugino, Pinturicchio and Piero della Francesca. The museum is in the huge **Palazzo dei Priori** ⑤, a civic building built in the 13th–15th centuries. The entrance in Piazza 4 Novembre, up a semi-circular staircase, leads into the Sala dei Notari *(open daily; Oct–May: closed Mon)*. Its Gothic portal is surmounted by a griffin and a lion, the city's symbols, and the hall is supported by eight massive arches, fully painted in the late 1200s with biblical scenes. In the centre of the piazza is the **Fontana Maggiore** ⑥, a majestic 25-sided fountain sculpted by father and son Nicola and Giovanni Pisano

in 1278. The **Cattedrale di San Lorenzo** ⑦ *(open daily)* flanks the piazza with the Loggia di Braccio (1423) and a statue of Pope Julius III (1555). Passing the façade of the cathedral, turn left, then right into Via Ulisse Rocchi, at the end of which is the huge **Arco Etrusco** ⑧ in Piazza Fortebraccio. This imposing structure, once the main gate into the city, was built in the 3rd century BC. Proceed up Via Garibaldi, then turn right into Via Tempio to the round early Christian **Tempio di Sant'Angelo** ⑨ *(open daily)*, with its 16 columns, built in the 5th–6th centuries. Return to Via Garibaldi, turn right into Via Rondine, left into Via Benedetta, then into Via Fagiano, which turns into **Via Acquedotto** ⑩, an aqueduct (now a footway) built in 1254 to bring water into the city from Monte Paciano. At the end, turn right into Piazza Cavallotti, then up Via Maestà delle Volte and back into Piazza 4 Novembre. Stroll down Corso Vannucci to **Piazza Italia** ⑪ for views over the abbey of San Pietro to Assisi in the distance. In 1540, the ruling papacy sought to quell the rebellious populace by building a huge fortress over their houses. On the unification of Italy in 1860, Umbrians, free of papal rule, tore down the building and erected their provincial offices instead. On the west side of this building, an escalator

Below View of Rocca Maggiore, set on the hill above Assisi decends into Via Baglioni, where shells of houses still remain in the foundations of the **Rocca Paolina** ⑫. Keeping to the left on the way down, exit the underground maze through Porta Marzia and turn left into Via Marzia to Via Guglielmo Oberdan and the entrance to the *minimetrò*. For those with a sweet tooth, the Perugina Museo *(Viale San Sisto, San Sisto 06132; open Mon–Fri; www.perugina.it)*, just outside town, reveals the processes involved in making the city's delicious chocolates, including the famous Baci.

🚗 *Turn left on Autostradale Perugia-A1 towards Roma-Assisi, take Foligno exit onto SS75 to Assisi, exit Ospedalicchio. Follow signs to Assisi on SS147. Piazza Matteotti has an underground car park.*

St Francis of Assisi

Born around 1181 in Assisi, this high-spirited son of a wealthy cloth merchant had a vision that called him to a spiritual path and a life of poverty. He wandered far and wide, inspiring followers and founding the order of Friars Minor in 1210. His visions and profound faith changed the course of Christian history and he was canonized only two years after his death in 1226. St Francis (San Francesco) is the patron saint of Italy.

② Assisi

Perugia, Umbria; 06081
With an average of 4–5 million visitors every year, Assisi is one of the most important pilgrim sites in Italy. It is a small town that displays its artistic and religious patrimony well, but its back streets and alleyways still merit exploration. The central Piazza del Comune was the original Roman forum and the splendid columns of the 1st-century BC Temple of Minerva have been retained in the façade of the church **Santa Maria sopra Minerva**. The German writer Goethe (1749–1832) thought it was the most beautiful building in Italy.

The town's most visited site, the **Basilica di San Francesco**, was commenced immediately after St Francis' canonization in 1228. In two parts, the lower and upper, the church contains frescoes by Cimabue, Giotto, Simone Martini and Pietro Lorenzetti that are the cornerstone of pre-Renaissance art. The **Basilica di Santa Chiara** – St Clare was a contemporary of St Francis – is a fascinating Gothic extravagance. Nearby, the 12th-century Romanesque **Cattedrale di San Rufino** is where both Francis and Clare were baptized.

🚗 *Turn right out of car park and take a slight right at Via Santuario delle Carceri/SP251, following brown signs for Eremo delle Carceri. Park after the left curve on the road.*

Above The Romanesque-Gothic Basilica di San Francesco, Assisi

EAT AND DRINK

PERUGIA

La Pasticceria Sandri *inexpensive*
A Perugian institution, this splendid café has been serving the finest chocolates and aperitifs since 1947. *Corso Vannucci 32, 06123; 075 572 4112*

Da Cesarino *moderate*
By the Fontana Maggiore, enjoy typical Umbrian delights such as *penne alla norcina* (creamy sausage pasta). *Piazza 4 Novembre 5, 06123; 075 572 8974; closed Wed*

Trattoria del Borgo *expensive*
This antique trattoria in the centre of Perugia is one of the finest in Umbria. Try *cappellacci di capriolo* (venison pasta) or Chianina beef with porcini. *Via Sposa 23/A, 06123; 075 572 0390; www.trattoriadelborgoperugia.it*

ASSISI

Al Camino Vecchio *inexpensive*
Expect large portions of freshly prepared food in this good-value trattoria. *Via San Giacomo 7, 06081; 075 812 936; www.bellaumbria.net/trattoria-Alcaminovecchio*

Trattoria Pallotta *moderate*
Enjoy the rustic atmosphere and Umbrian cuisine – thick *strangozzi* pasta drizzled with olive oil and truffles. *Vicolo della Volta Pinta 3, 06081; 075 812649; www.pallottaassisi.it*

Osteria Pozzo della Mensa *moderate*
This fine restaurant near San Rufino serves excellent dishes such as baked radicchio with pecorino and walnuts. *Via del Pozzo della Mensa; 075 815 5236; www.osteriapozzodellamensa.it*

[Map showing Perugia city centre with numbered locations: 9 Tempio di Sant'Angelo, 10 Via Acquedotto, 8 Arco Etrusco, 7 Cattedrale di San Lorenzo, 6 Fontana Maggiore, 5 Palazzo dei Priori, 4 Galleria Nazionale dell'Umbria, 3 Collegio del Cambio, 2 La Pasticceria Sandri, 1 Piazza Matteotti, 11 Piazza Italia, 12 Rocca Paolina. Scale: 0 metres 250, 0 yards 250]

Eat and Drink: inexpensive, under €25; moderate, €25–€45; expensive over €45

Above View of Trevi, topped by the spire of the Duomo San Emiliano **Above right** Entrance to the secluded and peaceful Eremo delle Carceri **Below** Pathway through the forest, Eremo delle Carceri

WHERE TO STAY

SPELLO

La Corte del Conte *inexpensive*
This minimalist boutique hotel has been recently renovated and has a superb cocktail bar and restaurant..
Piazza Vallegloria 13, 06038; 0742 301 135; www.lacortedelconte.com

Hotel Palazzo Bocci *moderate*
Lavish palazzo in the historic centre with frescoed ceilings and large rooms. Outdoor terrace in the summer.
Via Cavour 17, 06038; 0742 301 021; www.palazzobocci.com

BEVAGNA

Il Chiostro di Bevagna *inexpensive*
Great value for money in the historic centre: enter through the frescoed cloister almost opposite the Duomo.
Corso Matteottti 107, 06031; 0742 361 987; www.ilchiostrodibevagna.com; private parking included

Hotel Palazzo Brunamonti *inexpensive*
In the town centre, this lavish historic residence has excellent-size rooms and attentive staff – a good-value hotel.
Corso Matteotti 79, 06031; 0742 361 932; www.brunamonti.com; secure parking

TREVI

Natalini *moderate*
This farm stay, at the foot of Trevi's hill, has well-restored studio apartments and rooms. There is a restaurant on-site and bicycles for hire.
Via Casa Bozzi 4, 06039 San Lorenzo di Trevi; 0742 399 472; www. agriturismonatalini.it

③ Eremo delle Carceri
Perugia, Umbria; 06081
Clinging onto the steep slope of Monte Subasio, this is a 14th-century religious sanctuary where silence is required. Wander through medieval passageways and under low archways to reach, at the heart of the ancient hermitage, the **Grotto of St Francis** who prayed here in the 13th century. Outside, cross over a bridge into the forest to see the **Tree of the Birds**, a holm oak where the saint is said to have preached to the birds. Look for the sign of the cross scratched on boulders along the path by pilgrims. The tranquil hermitage is an ideal spot for a walk in the woods.

🚗 *Continue uphill on SP251 to go over Mt Subasio towards San Silvestro (faster route: SS75 towards Foligno and exit Spello). Turn sharp right at Via Subasio/ SP249 towards Spello centre. At the stop take SS75, then turn right at Via Martin Luther King for parking.*

④ Spello
Perugia, Umbria; 06038
Called Hispellum in the 1st century BC, this delightful town, draped around a low ridge, still has some important Roman monuments. The entry gate Porta Consolare, the Piazza della Repubblica, originally the forum, and the magnificent Gate of Venus on the western side, date from the Augustan era. The highest part of the town is a knot of medieval lanes and houses. The cathedral, the 13th-century **Chiesa di Santa Maria Maggiore** *(open daily)*, has a Romanesque portal and frescoes by Perugino, but the highlight is the superb Cappella Bella, painted by Umbrian artist Pinturicchio in 1500.

🚗 *From car park, turn right, then left at Via Roma, then right at roundabout onto SS75 towards Foligno. Turn right into SS316 to Bevagna. Turn right to park off Via Alcide De Gasperi.*

⑤ Bevagna
Perugia, Umbria; 06031
Once the important Roman city of Mevania, Bevagna today has a more medieval air about it. The central Piazza Silvestri is flanked by the Gothic **Palazzo dei Consoli** and the 12th-century Romanesque **Church of San Michele Arcangelo** *(both open daily)*, notable for the bas-reliefs and mosaics on its portal. Mosaics of fabulous sea creatures, once the floor of the Roman baths, are visible from outside Via Porta Guelfa. The **Museo Comunale di Bevagna** *(closed Mon)* displays Roman funerary urns and tells the history of medieval guilds. It is also possible to book classes in paper, making, candle-making and weaving.

🚗 *Take SS316 south and after the bridge turn left to Montefalco. From there follow signs for Trevi, onto SP447 and over the motorway. Follow signs for Trevi "centro" and park in Piazza Garibaldi.*

Where to Stay: inexpensive, under €100; moderate, €100–€200; expensive, over €200

⑥ Trevi

Perugia, Umbria; 06039

Like a conical snail shell of medieval buildings, Trevi coils around a spur in the Valle Umbra. The town is enclosed by two circuits of walls and entered through Porta di Lago into Piazza Mazzini. At its centre, the highest point, stands the **Duomo San Emiliano** with its 11th-century façade. St Emiliano was thrown to the lions, but they licked his feet and face – look for the carvings. The **Museo Civiltà dell' Ulivo** *(Largo Don Bosco; open daily)*, set in a former Franciscan convent, reveals the history of local olive cultivation.

🚗 *Head south on SP425 and turn left after 5 km (3 miles) for Campello sul Clitunno. The Tempietto is on the right, not well marked and with little parking.*

Above Clocktower and Palazzo Comunale, Piazza Mazzini, Trevi

⑦ Campello sul Clitunno

Perugia, Umbria; 06042

A popular holiday destination in the Roman era, this area's later strategic importance is evident in the medieval castles and forts dotted over its hills.

Just outside Campello sul Clitunno, the **Tempietto del Clitunno**, decorated with Byzantine frescoes, is a gem of a late-Roman or early Christian church, whose perfect proportions and lavish Corinthian column screens inspired 16th-century architect Andrea Palladio.

At the **Fonti del Clitunno**, another 500 m (1,500 ft) further along the SS3, crystal clear water gushes from the hillside into a series of lakes and ponds, creating an ambience of rare beauty that has inspired poets and painters

from Virgil (70–19 BC) to Lord Byron (1788–1804) and from Poussin (1594–1665) to Corot (1796–1875). The park, now privately owned, is ideal for children to explore and feed the ducks. The area is known for its olive oil and there are several *frantoio* (olive mills) around town worth visiting.

The SP458 leads southeast from the centre of Campello sul Clitunno, turn left again and follow signs to the tiny fortified village of **Castello di Campello Alto**. Founded in the 10th century by the Baron of Burgundy, the village passed to Federico Barbarossa, Holy Roman Emperor, 200 years later. Set amid slopes cloaked in olive groves, it has well-preserved 13th-century walls.

🚗 *Return down the hill and turn left into exSS3/Via Flaminia to Spoleto. Turn right at Viale Giacomo Matteotti (signed Spoleto), and left for car park.*

The Via Francigena di San Francesco

This pilgrim trail follows the paths that wayfarers used on the journey from Austria to Umbria and on to Lazio, to visit the places where St Francis lived and worked. After the fall of Rome in the 5th century AD, roads were no longer maintained and were unsafe. Wheeled traffic was less viable so travellers went on foot and mule, resting at pilgrim stops along the way. This drive roughly follows the trail from Assisi to Arrone, part of the Via Francigena di San Francesco. Religious and non-religious pilgrims still walk the Via Francigena, which is fairly well marked.

EAT AND DRINK

SPELLO

Porto Venere *moderate*
This charming restaurant serves good food, including asparagus, porcini and truffles with home-made pasta.
Via Torri di Properzio 37; 0742 301 896; www.ristoranteportavenere.it

La Bastiglia *moderate*
This highly acclaimed restaurant offers innovative Umbrian cuisine and has an impressive wine cellar. Also has rooms.
Via Salnitraria 15, 06038; 0742 651 277; www.labastiglia.com; closed Tue

BEVAGNA

Osteria Il Podesta *moderate*
Traditional central *osteria* with a cosy atmosphere and vaulted dining room.
Corso Matteotti 67, 06031; 0742 361 832; closed Wed

TREVI

Cantina Del Bartoccio *inexpensive*
On a small piazza, this simple restaurant offers typical Umbrian dishes and a good house wine.
Piazza Giuseppe Mazzini, 5A, 06039; 345 040 3513

CAMPELLO SUL CLITUNNO

Parco del Clitunno Trattoria *moderate*
Surrounded by the lake and trees, with a play area for kids – fish is the speciality.
Loc. Fonti del Clitunno, 06042 Campello; 0743 521 052; closed Wed

Ristorante Fonti del Clitunno *moderate*
Right by the springs, this traditional *osteria* provides good Umbrian food.
Via Flaminia 7, 06042 Campello; 0743 275 057; www.fontidelclitunno.it

Below left The fortified hamlet of Castello di Campello Alto **Below right** The Tempietto del Clitunno, an inspiration for Neo-Classical design

Above The Teatro Romano, Spoleto, still used for cultural events

WHERE TO STAY

SPOLETO

Palazzo Leti Residenza d'Epoca
moderate
This former aristocratic residence has a magnificent Italian-style garden.
Via Filippo Brignone 13, 06049; 0743 224 930; www.palazzoleti.com

Gattapone *expensive*
Just below the Rocca, in a quiet location, it is popular with celebrities at Festivals.
Via del Ponte 6, 06049; 0743 223 447; www.hotelgattapone.it

SCHEGGINO

Le Vaie *inexpensive*
Experience a traditional farm stay with four simple rooms in a rustic setting.
Loc. Vaglie, Sant'Anatolia Di Narco, 06040; 0743 613 269; www.agriturismolevaie.com

ABBAZIA DI SAN PIETRO IN VALLE

Abbazia San Pietro in Valle *expensive*
Stay in the 8th-century monastery in a superbly restored and tranquil hotel.
Via Case Sparse di Macenano, 05034; 0744780129; www.sanpietroinvalle.com

FERENTILLO

Il Borgo *inexpensive*
This country house B&B has a pleasant, rustic feel and comfortable rooms.
Vicolo S Anselmo 1, 05034; 3292 287 075; www.ilborgo-agriturismo.it

ARRONE

Fiocchi Residence *inexpensive*
Unfussy self-catering apartments near an adventure park, with access to pool.
Via Piè d'Arrone 1, 05031; 0744 389 961; www.residencefiocchi.com

Right top View of Spoleto, a strategically important city **Right bottom left** The River Nera, once Scheggino's first line of defence **Right bottom right** Fresco of San Sebastian in Arrone's Chiesa di San Giovanni Battista

⑧ Spoleto
Perugia, Umbria; 06049
Important since Etruscan times – and famous today for its summer arts festival, this delightful city has some interesting Roman ruins. The splendid **Teatro Romano e Museo Archeologico** *(open daily)* is near Piazza della Libertà. Other Roman highlights to look out for are the **Arco di Drusus**, the triumphal arch into Roman Spoleto, and **Casa Romana** *(open daily)*, a villa with mosaics from the 1st century AD.

After the fall of Rome, Spoleto was the capital of the Lombard Duchy of Spoleto for over 600 years (570–1201), before falling to the papacy. At it's heart is the **Duomo di Spoleto** (1175–1227) *(open daily)*. The Romanesque façade is outstanding, with rose windows, a huge bell tower and a Renaissance portico. Inside is just as impressive, with frescoes by Pinturicchio (1454–1513), and Fra Filippo Lippi (1406–69). The city is crowned by the **Rocca Albornoziana** *(closed Mon)*. Built by the militant Cardinal Albornoz to secure the papal dominions in the 14th century, this garrison fortress is divided into two large and elegant courtyards and was used as a prison until 1982. Highlights include the 15th-century frescoes in the *camera pinto* (painted room) and superb views. To the southwest is the spectacular **Ponte delle Torri**, a road and aqueduct with ten perfect arches.
🚗 *Exit car park right, then left, and left again on SS3 north. Take Cassia/Norcia exit for SS685. After tunnel, take SR209 right, towards Roma. Turn left at Piazza del Mercato and park at Scheggino.*

⑨ Scheggino
Perugia, Umbria; 06040
This medieval hamlet built by the Duchy of Spoleto to defend a bridge over the River Nera is now easily accessed by a footbridge. The 12th-century walls form a classic triangle – with a watchtower at the apex – and managed to withstand a sustained siege in 1522. In the village centre is the 13th-century **Chiesa di San Nicolò**, with a Paleochristian chapel and fine frescoes attributed to Lo Spagna (died c.1529).
🚗 *Continue south on SR209. Turn right at Via dell'Abbazia following signs to the car park.*

⑩ Abbazia di San Pietro in Valle

Ferentillo, Terni, Umbria; 05034

This abbey (now a luxury hotel) was founded in the 8th century by the Lombard Duke of Spoleto. The duke had a vision of St Peter and built a church on the site of a 4th-century hermitage. He took monastic vows

and is buried in an exquisite tomb in the **church** (open Apr–Sep: 10am–1pm and 3–5pm Sat & Sun, 3–5pm Mon–Fri; Oct–Mar by appointment: www. sanpietroinvalle.com). The church also has frescoes by the Umbrian School, which preceded Giotto by 150 years.
🚗 *Return to SR209 and head south. At Ferentillo Precetto, turn left on SP74, then 2nd left onto Via della Circonvallazione. Park in Piazza Mazzini.*

⑪ Ferentillo

Terni, Umbria; 05034

Two castles, Matterella and Precetto, guard the Val di Nera at Ferentillo, where the valley narrows. They were constructed in the 12th century to protect the Abbazzia di San Pietro in Valle. The 16th-century **Church of**

Santo Stefano, in Precetto, was built over an older crypt where bodies were naturally mummified. It makes a fascinating, if ghoulish, display: **Museo delle Mummie** (open daily). Ferentillo's cliffs make it a centre for the sport of falesia (free-climbing) – climbing without equipment; contact **Il Viaggiotto** (0744 58741; www.ditt.it).
🚗 *Return to SR209 and turn left. At Fontechiaruccia, turn left at the roundabout for Arrone on SP4. Park in Piazza Garibaldi.*

Mountain Adventures

The combination of mountains and rivers makes for exciting sports such as white-water rafting. Contact **Val Nerina Adventure** (348 771 1170; www.pangea-italia.it) or **Rafting Marmore** (330 753 420; www. raftingmarmore.com). Or try a thrilling, guided mountain-bike tour. Contact **Umbrian Mountain Bike** (0744 287 686; www.umbriainmountainbike.it).

---

⑫ Arrone

Terni, Umbria; 05031

Perched on a rocky precipice, Arrone defended the Valnerina Pass between Abruzzo and the Duchy of Spoleto. In the lower town is the 16th-century **Chiesa di Santa Maria Assunta** (open daily) with fine frescoes. The walk up to the medieval upper town is tough but rewarding. Built as a 10th-century fortification, the houses nestle around the piazza with its **Torre degli Olivi** (Tower of Olives). The 12th-century Gothic **Chiesa di San Giovanni Battista** (the key holder lives next door) contains colourful frescoes depicting the martyr San Sebastian, the patron saint of plague victims, wounded by arrows.

Above Narrow medieval street in the heart of Spoleto **Left** The fortified town of Ferentillo at the mouth of the Val di Nera

---

EAT AND DRINK

SPOLETO

La Lanterna *inexpensive*
A homely, central trattoria; try *strangozzi* pasta with courgettes and saffron. *Via della Trattoria 6, 06049; 0743 49815; closed Wed*

Pentagramma *expensive*
Celebrated restaurant serving top regional cooking with great wines. *Piazza della Libertà, 06049; 0743 223 141; www.ristorantepentagramma. com; closed Mon; booking essential*

ABBAZIA DI SAN PIETRO IN VALLE

Hora Media *moderate*
Dine in the refectory on quality fare, well cooked – pheasant, trout and truffles. *Via Case Sparse 4, 05034; 0744 780 950; closed Tue & lunch*

ARRONE

Trattoria Rossi *moderate*
Expect classic Umbrian cuisine at this popular family restaurant specializing in river crayfish, truffle and steak. *Voc. Isola, 705031; 0744 388372; www.rossihotelristorante.it*

DAY TRIP OPTIONS

These valley towns were strongholds in Roman times, hence their many architectural sights and works of art.

Roman holiday

Enjoy the sights at the Roman town of Spello ④, then head for Bevagna ⑤ to see the artifacts in the town museum. Lunch at Campello ⑦, with its Classical church and lovely scenery, before stopping at Spoleto ⑧, with its collection of fascinating Roman architecture.

Follow the drive's instructions, but don't stop at Trevi. Return the same way.

In St Francis' footsteps

Spend a day in the shoes of St Francis. Start at Assisi ②, to view the town where the young man grew up. Buy food supplies, then head for the Eremo delle Carceri ③, where he spent some time. Have a picnic on a walk through the beautiful forest.

Follow the drive's instructions from Assisi to the hermitage and back.

Medieval art

Start from Perugia ①, exploring its famous art gallery and palazzos. Next stop is Assisi ②, for its Gothic frescoes in the Basilica di San Francesco. Spello ④ also has some glorious 15th–16th century frescoes by Perugino and Pinturicchio, as does Spoleto ⑧.

Follow the drive instructions from Perugia to Assisi. Take the SS147 and SS75 to Spello. Take the SS75 from Spello and then SS3 to Spoleto.

Eat and Drink: inexpensive, under €25; moderate, €25–€45; expensive over €45

Lands of Myth and Legend

Rieti to Lago di Corbara

Highlights

- **Marvellous mountains**
  Head for the hills beyond Rome, once home to the Sabines, for good skiing in winter and enjoyable hikes in summer

- **Languor by the lake**
  Unwind by the calm waters of Lago di Piediluco, surrounded by painterly landscapes of hills and mountains

- **Roman town**
  Explore the atmospheric remnants of Carsulae, once a thriving Roman provincial settlement

- **Historic hill town**
  Visit splendid Todi, with its medieval squares, great cathedral and spectacular domed church

Narni, perched on a hillside with the Abbazia di San Cassiano opposite

Lands of Myth and Legend

Northeast of Rome, the land of the Sabines stretches into the Apennine mountains, where, according to the Roman imagination, fortune-telling sibyls and all manner of mythical creatures dwelt. Nowadays, mountain areas such as Terminillo are holiday resorts for modern Romans, along with dreamy lakeside Piediluco and the waterfalls at Marmore – both on the Grand Tour itineraries of the Romantic poets and painters in the 18th and 19th centuries. This drive also follows the ancient Via Flaminia for a short way north through the well-preserved but little-known remains of Roman Carsulae.

ACTIVITIES

Go skiing or snowboarding at Terminillo or Leonessa

Follow in the footsteps of the ancient Romans along the time-worn stones of the Via Flaminia

Shoot the rapids on the River Nera near the Cascata da Marmore

Take to the water gently by going boating on Lago di Piediluco

Picnic by the Tiber near Todi, just like the ancient Umbrians

KEY

▬▬▬ Drive route

Above The pretty and peaceful lakeside resort of Piediluco, *see p221*

PLAN YOUR DRIVE

Start/finish: Rieti to Lago di Corbara.

Number of days: 3–4 days.

Distance: About 200 km (124 miles).

Road conditions: Generally good, except for Terminillo to Leonessa, which is often impassable in winter.

When to go: Apr–Oct, especially May and Sep. In winter, skiing is popular in Terminillo and Leonessa, but snow chains must be carried.

Opening times: Most museums open 10am–6pm, with small museums often only open on weekends outside the summer months. Churches are usually open 7:30am–noon and 3–7:30pm.

Main market days: Rieti: Mon, Fri and Sat; **Leonessa:** Fri; **Narni:** Fri; **San Gémini:** Tue; **Massa Martana:** Fri; **Todi:** Sat.

Shopping: Look out for truffles and truffle products, such as small jars of truffle butter, in Rieti and Leonessa. Todi has a linen and textile shop in Piazza del Popolo, and there are antique shops behind the Duomo.

Major festivals: Leonessa: Sagra della Patata (potato festival), 2nd weekend Oct; **Piediluco:** Festa delle Acque (water-based fun), last week Jun; **Narni:** Black Festival of Jazz, Aug; **Todi:** Festival of the Arts, last week Aug, 1st week Sep; **Massa Martana:** Gelato Festa (ice-cream festival), 2nd week Aug; **San Gémini:** Giostra delle Arme (medieval joust), last week Sep.

DAY TRIP OPTIONS

Rieti in the land of the Sabines, on the slopes of the Apennines, is a good place from which to explore the **hills** and **mountains** of the region. **Water-sports** in abundance are available on the **lake** at Piediluco and the **River Nera** at the base of Marmore **waterfalls**. Brush up your **history** by following the footsteps of the **Roman legions** from Narni to San Gémini and Carsulae. For full details, *see p225*.

Above Fountain in Rieti, once a prominent Sabine town **Right** Cascata da Marmore, a spectacular man-made waterfall

WATERSPORTS ADVENTURES

The **Centro Canoa e Rafting "Le Marmore"** (Via Carlo Neri 28, 05037, Papigno Terni; 330 753 420; www. raftingmarmore.com) organizes rafting and inner-tube river descents.

WHERE TO STAY

RIETI

Grande Albergo Quattro Stagioni inexpensive–moderate
This grand old-style hotel in the historic centre offers a wide range of facilities. Piazza Cesare Battisti 14, 02100; 0746 271 071; www.hotelquattrostagioni.com

Hotel Miramonti moderate–expensive
Set in one of the oldest buildings in Rieti, this four-star hotel has moderately priced rooms and more expensive suites. Piazza Oberdan 5, 02100; 0746 201 333; www.hotelmiramonti.rieti.it; parking can be difficult.

Park Hotel Villa Potenziani expensive
On a hill outside town, this villa enjoys all the benefits of a country location – silence, fresh air and top views (note: it's often used for weddings on weekends). Via Colle San Mauro 6, 02100; 0746 202 765; www.villapotenziani.it

LEONESSA

Hotel La Torre inexpensive
This chalet-style hotel is handy for the old town and the ski fields. Full- or half-board accommodation is available as it has its own restaurant. Largo Bixio Cherubini 1, 02016; 074 692 2166; www.hotellatorreleonessa.it

Right Fortified Labro, founded on a steep hill in the 10th or 11th century **Far right** Porta Spolentina, one of the main gates of Leonessa

❶ Rieti
Rieti, Lazio; 02100
Before the Romans established their Empire, Central Italy was occupied by a number of warlike tribes. The Sabines lived on the slopes of the Apennines and fought often with their neighbour, Rome, before eventually being defeated in 295 BC. Rieti was one of the Sabines' largest settlements and its medieval city walls are still standing around this bustling provincial capital, which is regarded as the geographical centre of Italy today, as marked in Piazza San Rufo. Unusually, the city centre has three linked piazzas, one of which (Piazza Vittorio Emanuele) was the old Roman forum. The beautiful Romanesque arches of the crypt of the Papal Palace in Via Cintia are worth a visit. The **Basilica di Santa Maria Assunta** (open daily) has an impressive exterior and bell tower (1252), linked by a fine loggia.

🚗 *There are many brown signs to Terminillo. Head for Via del Terminillo, SS4bis, uphill for 20 km (12 miles). Turn left into the car park at the village.*

❷ Terminillo
Rieti, Lazio; 02017
This accessible and modern ski resort is a winter playground for modern-day Romans. In warmer months the village and its surroundings provide welcome relief from the heat of the plains below. The area was first established as a resort in the 1930s and now has all the facilities of an alpine ski village. A pleasant 15-minute circular walk at Campoforogna

provides spectacular views and a number of the original mountain huts (now abandoned) can be seen.

🚗 *Follow SS4bis uphill, at the end of Piazzale Campoforogna, turn left for Leonessa, on SP10. The road circles the mountain down to Leonessa with amazing views. Turn left into SS471, and then left again at town gate to parking area. In winter, return to Rieti and take SS79 north to Leonessa.*

❸ Leonessa
Rieti, Lazio; 02016
Virtually hidden among the Monti Reatini, this lovely old town is a surprising find. Enter through the northern gate, the impressive Porta Spoletina, into the narrow Corso San Giuseppe, the main street by virtue of its shops, bars and 15th-century **Chiesa di Santa Maria del Popolo**. It suddenly opens out into the large Piazza VII Aprile, the scene of most of the town's social activity. The square is larger than in most towns this size as many of its public buildings were destroyed in an earthquake in 1703.

Left The pleasant lake resort of Piediluco, a good place for watersports **Below** Fountain in Piazza VII Aprile, Leonessa

🚗 *Return to SS471 north, then turn left (west) at the large junction. Drive on SP521 to the crossroad with SS79 and follow signs on the right to Labro on SP5. Park near the town entrance.*

④ Labro
Rieti, Lazio; 02010
This beautifully restored little town, clinging tightly to its steep conical hill, still keeps watch over the road below, which it was built to control. One of many fortified settlements in the area established in the 10th and 11th centuries, Labro was the seat of the Nobili family, who controlled much of the region and built the castle. The town's narrow alleys and stairways are paved with rough stone, and the castle is inhabited by the Nobili-Vitelleschi, descendants of its original occupants *(open for visits or tours: 0746 636 020).*

🚗 *Head back to SP5, turn right into SS79 towards Piediluco. Follow signs into town to the parking.*

> #### The Legend of the Falls
> According to legend, the beautiful nymph Nera, from the valley, fell in love with the shepherd Velino, from the plains above. But the all-powerful goddess Juno disapproved and turned her into a river, now called the Nera. The distraught Velino threw himself off the cliffs and turned into a waterfall to join his love in an eternal watery union.

⑤ Piediluco
Terni, Umbria; 05100
Like a coastal resort, Piediluco is strung out along the shore of a lake with the same name. Even though it is only two streets the town has a large church, **St Francis** *(open daily),* built in the 13th century and decorated with

15th-century frescoes. There's no real piazza, but footpaths and small parks provide good vantage points. Excellent climatic conditions – the absence of wind and currents – make the lake an ideal spot for watersports and it is home to the **National Rowing Centre** *(www.canottaggio.org).*

On the east side of town, there is a lido, where small boats and canoes can be hired. Or, opposite the Trattoria di Marilù, there is a kiosk where visitors can take a scenic lake tour or hire a boat *(0744 369 085; www.piediluco.eu).*

🚗 *Return to SS79 and carry on to marmore and Papigno, then turn right for Cascate Inferiore, then right again on SR209. Stop by the road or enter the park a short distance further on.*

⑥ Cascata delle Marmore
Terni, Umbria; 05100
The Roman consul Manlius Curius Dentatus created this astonishing man-made cataract more than 2,000 years ago. As a way of draining the malarial plain of Rieti, in 271 BC a channel was cut through the rock to allow the River Velino to flow down to the River Nera, in three distinct stages, creating the highest waterfall in Europe (165 m/541 ft). Its rampant energy is now harnessed to provide electricity, and the falls are turned on and off twice a day. Marmore is little more than a railway siding, but the steep path to the summit of the falls affords great views of the cascade (alternatively, drive to the top via Terni).

🚗 *For Narni, head towards Terni, skirting the edge of town to the south to get on the Via Flaminia Ternana SS3 (follow signs to Narni at the many roundabouts). The road runs straight into Narni. There is large parking area to the right, and a lift into the town.*

EAT AND DRINK

RIETI
Bistrot *moderate*
Book ahead for this small and stylish, classic "Slow Food" restaurant.
Piazza San Rufo 25, 02100; 0746 498 798; closed Oct, Sun & Mon

Trattoria Tito *moderate*
Typical trattoria serving home-made pastas and hearty meals, with a comprehensive wine list.
Via San Rufo 5, 02100; 0746 201 202; www.trattoriatito.com

TERMINILLO
Sfizi di Vini *moderate*
Bright and busy little wine bar/trattoria on the main square of the village. Best to book during summer.
Piazzale Pian de Valli 39, 02017; 334 307 3575; www.terminillo.org/ristorantesfizidivini

LEONESSA
Trattoria Alesse *inexpensive*
Small, family-run eatery on main street serving traditional local foods.
Corso San Giuseppe 61, 02016; 0746 922 130; closed Thu

Leon d'Oro *moderate*
Right on the central piazza, this offers a classic menu with a Roman influence.
Corso San Giuseppe 120, 02016; 0746 923 320; closed Mon

PIEDILUCO
Trattoria da Marilù *moderate*
Enjoy freshwater salmon from the lake on the terrace – unforgettable.
Corso Raniero Salvati 3, 05038; 0744 368 559; www.trattoriadamarilu.com; closed Wed

Eat and Drink: inexpensive, under €25; moderate, €25–€45; expensive, over €45

Above The Benedictine Abbazia di San Cassiano, Narni **Bottom left** Stretch of the Via Flaminia in Roman Carsulae **Bottom right** Piazza Garibaldi, the square at the heart of modern-day Narni

WHERE TO STAY

NARNI AND AROUND

Hotel dei Priori *inexpensive*
Convenient and pleasant little hotel in the oldest part of town with helpful staff. It's popular, so book early.
Vicolo del Comune 4, 05035; 0744 726 843; www.loggiadeipriori.it

Torre Palombaro *moderate*
Sumptuous accommodation at a reasonable price only a ten-minute drive east from Narni. Expect a warm welcome in this tranquil, rural retreat.
Strada della Cantinetta 3, 05035; 0744 744 617; www.torrepalombara.com

SAN GÉMINI

Locanda di Carsulae *inexpensive*
Near the springs that provide the famous San Gémini mineral waters, this pleasant, small hotel offers rooms that have been refurbished in a traditional Umbrian style.
Via Tiberina 2, Località Fonte 05029; 0744 630 163; www.gruppobacus.com

7 Narni
Terni, Umbria; 05035

Despite being close to some of Umbria's most industrialized areas, Narni is a very beautiful town. The Romans conquered it in 299 BC and established a settlement called Narnia, but its history goes back much further. Its simple main square, Piazza dei Priori, is graced by the elegant **Loggia dei Priori** by Gattapone (1300–83). There are some delightful medieval bas-reliefs and the tiny pulpit used by St Bernadino. In Via Mazzini, by the square, the beautifully proportioned **Chiesa di Santa Maria Impensole** *(open daily)* has hardly been altered since 1175.

On the wooded hillside west of town sits the 10th-century **Abbazia di San Cassiano** *(only open for services)*, built on the Via Flaminia to watch over the corridor between Rome and Ravenna – it's a lovely walk to the abbey.

🚗 *Take Via Roma out of town and head for Narni Scalo. Take Strada dei Tre Ponti/SP1 downhill, turn right at SS3ter and cross the bridge. The Roman bridge is on the right. At San Gémini, park to the left of the entrance gate.*

8 San Gémini
Terni, Umbria; 05029

Door carving from San Gémini

This town sits on the Roman road, the Via Flaminia, which still forms its main street (called Via Roma). The main piazza is home to the **Chiesa di San Francesco**, which has some fine carvings on its portal. To one side of the Palazzo Municipio, the medieval **Porta Tuderte** leads to the oldest part of the town, where the **Palazzo Vecchio** is a fine example of early medieval architecture.

🚗 *Return to SS3 and head northeast. Turn right at the Fonte di San Gémini and on Via Carsulae follow signs to the car park at the archaeological site.*

9 Carsulae
Terni, Umbria; 05100

The Via Flaminia, which runs from Rome to Fano on the Adriatic *(see Drive 24)*, kept the ancient capital supplied with supplies from Northern Italy and abroad. The *municipium* of Carsulae grew up on this important road and its remains provide an insight into Roman life. It is thought that the city was abandoned after it was damaged by an earthquake.

A one-hour walking tour

On the road from San Gémini, the car park for the Carsulae Archeological site is clearly marked. From the **car park** ①, steps lead to a subway beneath the road and along a path to the **ticket office** ②. There is also a small museum here, and although most of the larger items from the site have ended up elsewhere, there are still some good terracotta pieces from the 1st century AD. From the entry gate, the path winds downhill towards the main site. Cross a section

The Chronicles of Narnia

This hugely popular series of books (1949–54) by CS Lewis is based in part on the Classically educated author's detailed knowledge of ancient myths and legends. Some literary scholars believe that a map of early Rome in the author's possession is proof that he used the name of the Roman city for his series, as Narnia had been underlined. For the Romans, Narnia was an outpost on the edge of the known world, beyond which lurked all manner of mythical creatures, strange beasts and weird peoples.

of field to an unmistakable stretch of the **Via Flaminia** ③, made of large grey stones and rutted by the passage of countless carts and chariots. Standing in the middle of this historic road, it's easy to imagine the passing traffic through this once important provincial town.

Slightly ahead and on the right-hand side of the road stands the only intact building on the site, the **Church of Saints Cosma and Damian** ④. This dates from the 11th century, when a pre-existing building was converted to religious usage. The solid columns at the front come from the nearby Roman basilica and have been used to good effect to create a stylish loggia and entrance. Inside the church there are damaged frescoes of saints.

Opposite the church, the remains of a tight cluster of buildings and shops at road level show how the

prime commercial space in a city centre was as much sought after in Roman times as it is today. Nearby, the **twin temples** ⑤, next to **the forum** ⑥ indicate the traditional layout of the settlement. Proceed along the Via Flaminia in a northerly direction to the **Arco di San Damiano** ⑦ – also known as Arco di Traiano. This is an archway from the Augustan era (1st century BC), built as a symbolic northern entrance to the city. Just beyond the gate – and outside the walls – there are three large funerary monuments, similar to those found outside Rome along the Via Appia. These ruins give an indication of the importance of Carsulae.

Heading back along the well-worn Via Flaminia to the arch near the forum, turn left through scattered remnants of buildings. This is believed to be the site of the city basilica, which was not a church but an administrative centre and tribunal. Only bits of the foundations remain.

Beyond the basilica and a little further east are the **amphitheatre** and **theatre** ⑧, constructed in a natural valley in the terrain. These two buildings played an important part in the life of any Roman town and reflect sporting obsessions still current today. The elliptical-shaped amphitheatre was the scene of gladiatorial games and entertainments, ranging from athletic competitions to brutal fights to the death. The theatre, which predates the amphitheatre, was for more cultural events and both buildings reflect the Roman ability to build functional, safe and efficient buildings for large numbers of people.

From the theatre, head back to the car park.

🚗 *From the car park, return to SP113 and then turn right. Continue as SP113 becomes SP420. At the end of the street turn onto SP316, then turn right on SP416 and continue into Colpetrazzo town.*

Above The Arco di San Damiano, Carsulae, the northern entrance to the Roman city

EAT AND DRINK

NARNI

La Gallina Liberata *inexpensive*
A simple restaurant offering home cooking with no menu and no prices on display. Dishes vary daily.
Vicolo Belvedere 13, 05035; 349 254 3515; www.lagallinaliberata.weebly.com

La Loggia *moderate*
This excellent little restaurant specializes in southern Umbrian dishes. Try the *manfricoli* pasta with fava beans, Pecorino cheese and pancetta.
Vicolo del Comune 4, 05035; 0744 726 843; www.loggiadeipriori.it; booking advised

Il Gattamelata *moderate*
This old-fashioned restaurant overlooking the square and Duomo serves traditional food at reasonable prices. Worth it for a window seat.
Via Pozzo della Communità 4, 05035; 0744 717 245; www.ristoranteilgatta melatanarni.com; closed Mon

SAN GÉMINI

La Pecora Nera *inexpensive*
Bright and breezy osteria where the emphasis is on food and fun.
Piazza San Francesco 2, 05029; 334 882 4346

Below Via Garibaldi, a cobbled main street in the town of Narni

Funeral Monuments
⑦ Arco di San Damiano
0 metres 150
0 yards 150
The Forum ⑥
Twin Temples ⑤
⑧ Amphitheatre and Theatre
④ Church of Saints Cosma and Damian
Via Flaminia ③
Car Park ① ② Ticket Office
🅿

Above Network of passageways, part of Colpetrazzo's original structure as a castle

---

WHERE TO STAY IN TODI

Hotel Fonte Cesia *moderate*
Situated in the heart of Todi, this old building has been nicely renovated but some rooms are quite small. There is a good restaurant and helpful staff.
Via Lorenzo Leonj 3, 06059; 075 894 3737; www.fontecesia.it; free parking

Relais Todini *moderate*
A little Umbrian luxury in picture-postcard countryside, ten minutes from Todi. Gorgeous views and well-appointed rooms and apartments.
Frazione Collevalenza, 06050; 075 887 521; www.relaistodini.com

Hotel Tuder *moderate*
Clean and comfortable mid-class hotel just outside the historic centre, a short walk into town.
Via Maestat del Lombardi 13, 06050; 075 894 2184; www.hoteltuder.com

---

⑩ Colpetrazzo
Perugia, Umbria; 06056
A former castle, this delightful little medieval town sits in an area of remote countryside. With one bar, one church and one small square, there is not a lot to see, but its simple layout, solid stone houses and arched alleyways give it a pleasant, close-knit atmosphere. A good place to stop and get a feel for the pace in an Umbrian farming community.

🚗 *From Colpetrazzo, continue north on SP416 to rejoin the main road/SP316. Turn right, and a little further on stands the Church of Santa Maria in Pantano. Park on either side of the road in front of the church. After seeing the church, carry on to Massa Martana.*

⑪ Massa Martana
Perugia, Umbria; 06056
The small religious complex of the **Church of Santa Maria in Pantano** *(open Sun)* has a slightly unorthodox appearance. Its large square façade, with a central rose window and doorway, leans out over the road and the chunky bell tower looks like it is part of a fortress. Dating back to the end of the Roman Empire, the church was built on the site of a temple next to the Via Flaminia. The structure contains building materials from the Roman era to the Renaissance. Note the pagan bas-relief under the window to the left of the door. Ask at the nearby bar for access to the church.

Ancient Massa Martana is not so much a walled town as a town within a fort – it has now been totally restored since it was damaged in the earthquake of 1997. There is an inscription that has been embedded in the medieval town gate, which records that Emperor Hadrian repaired the Via Flaminia in AD 124.

🚗 *From Massa Martana, take SP414 to Todi – following signs. The road goes through Collevalenza, with its modern religious shrine, and across the plains to Todi. There are car parks around town and paid parking in the centre.*

⑫ Todi
Perugia, Umbria; 06059
One of the best known and most interesting hill towns in Umbria, Todi combines art, history and architecture in a thriving cultural scene. With Etruscan origins and later Roman reinforcement, the town enjoys a

Top right Elegant lakeside residences beside Lago di Corbara **Right** Piazza del Popolo, Todi, once the Roman forum in the centre of town **Far right** Pretty cyclamens in the medieval town of Colpetrazzo

---

EAT AND DRINK

TODI

La Mulinella *inexpensive*
Eat with the locals at this friendly trattoria near Todi. Home-made pasta, especially lasagne, is worth trying.
Loc. Ponte Naia 29, 06050; 075 894 4779; closed Wed

Vineria San Fortunato *moderate*
Found right on the main piazza, this *enoteca* serves good local dishes. Excellent wine list.
Piazza Umberto 1, 506059; 392 371 4140; closed Mon

Cavour *moderate*
The alfresco dining area makes this a great venue on warm summer evenings – not to mention the excellent food and wine. Try pizza with black truffles and porcini or pasta with wild asparagus.
Corso Cavour 23, 06050; 075 894 3730; closed Thu

Pane e Vino *moderate*
Cosy and interesting restaurant with an emphasis on local seasonal food and a good selection of local wines.
Via A Ciuffellii 33, 06050; 075 894 5448; www.panevinotodi.com; closed Wed

Top left Todi (left) and the Church of Santa Maria della Consolazione (right) **Below** Vines growing beside man-made Lago Corbara

vantage point high above the Tiber, evolving to its present state in the late Middle Ages and Renaissance. The magnificent main square, **Piazza del Popolo**, was the Roman Forum and is now the site of splendid public buildings including the 12th-century cathedral, the **Duomo di Santa Maria Annunziata** *(open daily)*. The grand façade (the top half is unfinished) of **San Fortunato** *(open daily)* looms over an imposing set of marble steps. Its huge, airy Gothic interior contains an exquisitely carved walnut choir (1590) – engraved with the town symbol, an eagle – and high pulpits which enabled the Franciscans to preach to a large congregation. Beside the church, a pleasant park with panoramic views stretches across a space once occupied by a fortress. **Santa Maria della Consolazione** *(open daily)*, on the edge of town, echoes the style of the great churches of Rome and Florence. In the shape of a Greek cross, with a large dome and four apses, the church (built 1508–1607) is an impressive architectural confection.
🔲 *Follow signs out of town west towards Orvieto. The road runs downhill and joins the SS448, following the course of the Tiber to Lago di Corbara.*

The Eagle of Todi
Legend has it that an eagle revealed where Todi should be built. Long ago a tribe of Umbri, led by Tudero, were feasting near the river when an eagle swooped down and seized the red cloth their meat was arrayed upon. It flew off and dropped the cloth high on top of a hill. This was interpreted as a sign from the gods to found a town there. The eagle clutching the cloth is still the symbol of Todi and can be found on the wall of the Palazzo dei Priori.

⑬ Lago di Corbara
Orvieto, Terni, Umbria; 05018
When the south-flowing Tiber reaches Todi, it turns sharply to the west towards Orvieto. It flows through verdant, undeveloped countryside and scenic valleys. The road runs beside the river, providing picnic spots and photo opportunities. The artificial Lago di Corbara and a huge area of the surrounding land are part of the regional **Parco Fluviale del Tevere** *(www.parks.it)*. The area is also famous for its wine.

DAY TRIP OPTIONS
Easy day trips can be planned around activities such as skiing, walking or watersports. Evidence of the Romans abounds for history buffs.

Land of the Sabines
From a base in the Sabine town of Rieti ❶ it is an easy drive to either Terminillo ❷ or Leonessa ❸ for summer walks and, in winter, for snow sports. Access is good, as the roads are kept ploughed in winter.

Follow the drive instructions.
Lakes and waterfalls
Staying near Narni ❼ provides many choices for watersports enthusiasts. Pottering around in a motor boat on the lake at Piediluco ❺ is always a relaxing way to spend an afternoon. For more thrills, Cascata da Marmore ❻ and the Nera River offers exciting rafting, canyoning and kayaking.

Follow the drive instructions in reverse from Narni to Cascata da

Marmore and on to Piediluco and back.

Following the Roman legions
From Narni ❼, follow the ancient Via Flaminia. From here the road is almost dead straight to San Gémini ❽, another Roman outpost. Next, drive onto the ruins of Carsulae ❾, where the paving stones carry the marks of ancient Roman chariots.

Follow the drive instructions and then back again to return to Narni.

Eat and Drink: inexpensive, under €25; moderate, €25–€45; expensive, over €45

The Stone of the Apennines

Città di Castello to Jesi

Highlights

- **Ancient landscapes**
  Enjoy the countryside around Città
  di Castello, virtually unchanged
  since Roman times

- **Underground marvels**
  Explore the subterranean world at
  Frasassi, whose cathedral-size caves
  are filled with fabulous rock formations

- **Castelli di Jesi**
  The collection of ancient hilltop
  castles around Jesi are easy to
  visit and perfect for sampling the
  delicious local white wine

- **Secluded retreat**
  Breathe the pure air of the hills at the
  Eremo di Fonte Avellana, far from the
  everyday, industrial world

Sweeping hairpin bends on the approach
to Castelbellino

The Stone of the Apennines

Running the length of the Italian Peninsula, the Apennine mountains have long formed an important barrier, fiercely protected by forts and castles in the struggle for the fertile lands of Central Italy. In medieval times, the mountains also provided sanctuary for religious communities. Life here was harsh, and place names reflect the tough terrain – "Sassoferrato" (iron stone), "Frasassi" (between rocks) and "Pietralunga" (long stone). This drive starts in the Roman towns of Northern Umbria, passes over unspoilt terrain, and finally meanders through the gentle wine country of Le Marche.

KEY

- Drive route

Above The ancient town of Gubbio, built on a steep hill, *see p230*

ACTIVITIES

Go truffle hunting and taste local delicacies in Città di Castello

Become a native of Gubbio by running around its fountain three times – keeping an elbow in the water

Learn how to watermark handmade paper at the paper museum in Fabriano

Go on an underground adventure at the caves in Frasassi – all equipment supplied

Sample some delicious Verdicchio wine from the hill towns around Jesi

Above Maiolati Spontini, one of the Castelli di Jesi near Cupramontana, *see p234*

Below The 17th-century façade of the Duomo di San Florido, Città di Castello, *see p230*

PLAN YOUR DRIVE

Start/finish: Città di Castello to Jesi.

Number of days: 3 days.

Distance: 240 km (150 miles).

Road conditions: Good to excellent all year except in winter, when ice and snow are common and higher sections must be negotiated with care. Snow chains should be carried.

When to go: Spring and early summer bring clear days and wildflowers. Autumn is best for festivals and the grape harvest. Summer is pleasant in the hills but the beaches get busy.

Opening times: Most museums open 9am–7pm Tue–Sat (closed 1–3pm). Shorter hours in winter. Churches are usually open 8am–12pm and 4–7pm.

Main market days: Città di Castello: Thu & Sat; **Gubbio:** Tue; **Cagli:** Wed; **Fabriano:** Sat (Piazza Garibaldi); **Cupramontana:** Mon; **Jesi:** Wed & Sat.

Major festivals: Città di Castello: Festival of Nations (music), last week in Aug, 1st week in Sep; Truffle and Mushroom Festival, 1st weekend in Nov; **Gubbio:** Festival of the Ceri *(see p231)*, 15 May; **Cagli:** Distini Salumi (charcuterie), last week in Apr; **Serra de Conti:** Festa della Cicerchia, (food festival) last weekend in Nov; **Cupramontana:** Wine Festival, 1st Sun in Oct; **Jesi** Opera Season, end Sep–Nov *(www.fondazionepergolesispontini.com)*.

Shopping: Truffle products (sauces, butters) are common in Città di Castello. In Gubbio, the ceramics and leather goods are of high quality. Fabriano is known for its handmade paper. The white Verdicchio wine of the Castelli di Jesi is crisp and clean on the palate and a good local buy.

DAY TRIP OPTIONS

From Città di Castello, explore the Roman townships – from Gubbio, with its **theatre** and **gate**, to Sassoferrato, site of a **historic victory**. Visit the **quiet hermitage** at Avellana for a **walk** and a **picnic**, then explore the **caves** of Frasassi. Tour the **wine castles** of Jesi, sampling the delicious **white wine**, **local foods** and **Wine Label Museum**. For full details, *see p235*.

Above Roman Amphitheatre in front of Gubbio's Palazzo dei Consoli **Below** Pretty Pietralunga seen from the road into town

WHERE TO STAY

CITTÀ DI CASTELLO

Residenza Antica Canonica *moderate*
Beautifully converted former presbytery in the town centre. All rooms and suites are former monks' cells. There are self-catering facilities and free parking.
Via San Florido 23, 06012; 075 852 3298; www.anticacanonica.it

Hotel Le Mura *moderate*
Built into the town walls, La Mura is a small, comfy hotel that is conveniently located. Good staff and a pleasant restaurant serving Umbrian cuisine.
Via Borgo Farinario 24, 06012; 075 852 1070; www.hotellemura.it; guest parking

GUBBIO

Bosone Palace *moderate*
This is a lovely central 14th-century palazzo – Dante and Petrarch once stayed here. It also has a fine restaurant.
Via XX Settembre, 06024; 075 922 0688; www.hotelbosone.com

Tre Ceri *moderate*
Just inside the old walls and handy for car parks, this comfortable residence is easy walking to Gubbio's main sights.
Via Benamati 6/8, 06024; 075 922 109; www.treceri.it

❶ Città di Castello
Perugia, Umbria; 06012
The Roman historian Pliny the Younger had a villa near Città di Castello, then called Tifernum, and wrote in AD 96 of "this welcoming plain surrounded by mountains crowned with wild forests". Little has changed to this day. Ringed by medieval walls, this is a quiet and prosperous country town with elegant shops, good restaurants and some fine public architecture, such as the solid **Palazzo Comunale** (1322–38), built by Angelo da Orvieto.

Another local, Alberto Burri (1915–95) was internationally renowned as a sculptor and abstract artist who pioneered the use of unusual materials such as burlap, pumice and tar. His work can be seen in the **Palazzo Albizzini** *(open daily)* and **ex-Seccatoio Tabacco** *(www.fondazioneburri.org)*.

Autumn and spring are good times to hunt for truffles. Search for the elusive tubers with Saverio Bianconi *(075 851 1591; www.tartufibianconi.it)*, then eat your finds back at his farm.

🚗 *Take Viale V Veneto southwest, turn left under railway, then right on SP106 to Pietralunga. Park near main square.*

❷ Pietralunga
Perugia, Umbria; 06026
Surrounded by the Apennines, this small mountain town has an old fortress that dates back to Roman times, but its most significant feature is the pentagonal 8th-century **Rocco Longobardo**, which dominates the central piazza. The **Santa Maria** church nearby was also built in the 8th-century, and restored in the 18th century. The narrow medieval streets winding around behind the church offer occasional views down the Carpinella Valley.

🚗 *Descend from town and take SP201 south, then turn left onto SP204. At the roundabout, turn left onto SS219 for Gubbio. Follow signs for "Centro" and park in Viale del Teatro Romano.*

❸ Gubbio
Perugia, Umbria; 06024
An unspoilt medieval citadel with an impressive Roman theatre, Gubbio's earlier heritage is revealed by its Eugubine Tablets. These spell out observances and rituals in Latin, Etruscan and Umbrian and are the only decipherable record of the original Umbrians.

A two-hour walking tour
The **Roman theatre** ① was built at the end of the 1st century BC and is still used for summer concerts. From here, cross Viale del Teatro Romano and walk through a covered passage. Turn left into Via Cavour to **Piazza G Bruno** ②, lined with houses built from pale Gubbio stone. Turn right into Via dei Consoli, over a small bridge across the Carmignano – just a stream at this point. Then it's a short walk up to Lago del Vescovado and the simple 16th-century **Fontana dei Matti** ③ (Fountain of the Madmen). It is said that true citizens of Gubbio must run around the fountain three times – with an elbow in the water. Walk up the gentle slope of Via dei Consoli, past stylish leather goods and ceramic shops, to the splendid **Piazza Grande** ④. This beautiful square, at the heart of Gubbio is flanked on three sides by historic architecture and has great views of the valley below.

The Romanesque-Gothic Palazzo dei Consoli is home to the Museo Civico *(open daily)* and the seven bronze Eugubine Tablets (3rd century BC).

Just past the main square, the road becomes Via XX Settembre. On the left there is a sign for *"La ascensori"* (lift), up to the **Museo Diocesano** ⑤ *(open daily)*, with a modest collection

CITTÀ DI CASTELLO

Vineria del Vasaio *moderate*
Cosy underground restaurant in a restored pottery. The wine plays an important part in the menu and there is wine sampling by the glass with snacks.
Via della Cacioppa 4, 06012; 075 852 3281

Preludio *moderate*
Enjoy classic Italian fine dining, including *gnocchetti* with truffles, swordfish tartare and beef fillet in Barolo sauce with caramelized pears.
Corso V Emanuele 42, 06012; 075 855 6469; www.ristorantepreludio.it; closed Tue

Le Logge *moderate–expensive*
This offers sophisticated variations on well-known local specialities including truffles. Try the *tagliatelle di castagne* (chestnut flour). Extensive wine list.
P Matteotti, Logge Bufalini, 06012; 075 864 2304; www.ristorantelelogge.com

GUBBIO

Ristorante Picchio Verde *moderate*
This family-run restaurant has served typical Umbrian dishes for generations.
Via Savelli Della Porta 65, 06024 ; 075 927 6649 ; www.ristorantepicchio verde.com; closed Tue

Alla Balestra *moderate*
Good-value, central restaurant serving Gubbian delicacies – try *Umbricelli alla norcina con tartufo* (truffle pasta).
Via della Republica 41, 06012; 075 927 3810; www.ristoranteallabalestra.it

All'Antico Frantoio *moderate*
Popular eatery on the walkway to the Roman amphitheatre specializing in wood-fired pizza and home-made pasta.
Via del Teatro Romano, 06012; 075 922 1780; www.allanticofrantoio.it

Below left The crenellated Palazzo dei Consoli, Gubbio *Below right* View of the thickly wooded hills around Gubbio

of religious art, and Gubbio's Duomo, perhaps the only one in Italy without a piazza. Next to the cathedral is the splendid Palazzo Ducale *(closed Mon)*, built in 1480 by the Duke of Urbino, Federico da Montefeltro. Its elegant courtyard echoes the one in the Ducal Palace in Urbino *(see p243)* – enjoy the Giardini Pensili (Hanging Gardens), where a small bar provides drinks and snacks and stunning views.

Amble down the narrow lanes back to Via XX Settembre, and carry on to the towering **Porta Romana** ⑥. Outside the walls is the Chiesa di San Agostino (Saint Augustine), with 15th-century frescoes in its apse.

Just uphill from the church is the **cable car station** ⑦, which takes passengers to the top of the hill and the **Basilica di Sant Ubaldo** ⑧, where the 12th-century patron of Gubbio still lies in state above the altar.

Return to the Porta Romana and take Corso Garibaldi to Via della

Repubblica. Turn left towards Piazza Quaranta Martiri (Piazza of the 40 Martyrs) a grim reminder of a World War II atrocity in which the Nazis executed 40 people to avenge partisan actions. The piazza includes a public garden and the impressive two-storey **Loggia dei Tiratori** ⑨, home of the Woollen Workers' Guild and a medieval hospital. These days it often hosts an artisan market and displays of art. The piazza is the site for Gubbio's weekly market *(Tue)*.

From here it is a short walk back to Via Cavour and the car park.

🚗 *From Viale del Teatro Romano, follow signs to Scheggia. Exit town via a medieval gate with traffic lights onto SS298. At Scheggia, take Via Flaminia/ SP3 left to Cagli. Park in main square.*

Festival of the Ceri
On May 15 each year, St Ubaldo's day, Gubbio goes a little crazy. *Ceri* is Italian for candles, and the large wooden totems carried around town look like candles. (Some say they echo the phallic symbols used to worship Ceres, the Roman god of the harvest.) Each "candle" represents a saint and teams of enthusiastic men take it in turns to carry them up to the Basilica di Sant Ubaldo in a sort of race.

Above Rugged and wild landscape near Sassoferrato

⑤ Eremo di Fonte Avellana
Pesaro, Le Marche; 61040

Nestled among remote hills, this beautiful monastery (open 9:30am–noon, 3–6pm daily) is home to a small group of Camoldesi monks and offers a perfect spot for contemplation. The grounds are open and there is a bar, a shop and picnic tables. There are hourly guided tours (in simple Italian) for a small donation. Of particular interest is the Scriptorum, which is beautifully illuminated with natural light. Below the monastery is a botanical garden devoted to plants of the region.

🚗 *Return to SP106/SP52, then turn left towards Sassoferrato. Follow signs for "Centro" and Cabernardi. Ascend via Martiri della Libertà. At the roundabout, turn back, take Via Cardinal Albornoz and park near the Rocca.*

④ Cagli
Pesaro, Le Marche; 61043

Cagli was one of the towns that sprang up along the Roman Via Flaminia. The impressive **Palazzo Pubblico** in the main square, Piazza Matteoti, indicates Cagli's importance in the late Middle Ages when it was a flourishing Comune. The square's fountain adds a touch of Renaissance style and there's a popular bar, too. The **Torrione**, or round tower, at the end of town is now a modern sculpture museum. Cagli's decline started as the Via Flaminia's importance diminished and was completed when the railway line was destroyed in World War II. The town is now a remote and relaxed place with a few Roman remains, some impressive Renaissance architecture, good restaurants and bars – and virtually no tourists.

🚗 *Take SP424 towards Pergola, then right on SP121 to Frontone. Pass through Frontone on SP121; after the town centre, turn left on SP106, following signs to Foce Avellana. After 1 km (half a mile), turn left for the monastery.*

⑥ Sassoferrato
Ancona, Le Marche; 60041

This attractive little town is famous as the place where Rome defeated the Samnites and the Gauls in 295 BC. At the Battle of Sentinum – which took place just south of town – the Romans won control of the whole of Central Italy. There are a few Roman artifacts at the **Palazzo dei Priori** (closed Mon).

Above the town, the square 14th-century **Rocca Albornoz** guards a small cluster of Renaissance buildings, squares and narrow streets. The park below the rocca has views of the countryside and mountains beyond.

🚗 *Take SP360 southwest, then on to SP16. After about 4 km (2 miles) take the smaller left fork to Fabriano. Follow signs to "Centro", and park on the street.*

WHERE TO STAY IN SASSOFERRATO

Country House Federico I *inexpensive*
This impressive hotel is on the edge of town with country views. All the rooms are brightly painted.
Largo San Cristoforo 1, 60041; 0732 958 056; www.countryhousefederico.it

Vicolo Santa Chiara *inexpensive*
This B&B offers two bright, clean self-contained apartments overlooking the main square. The entrance in a charming medieval lane reflects the atmosphere in this part of town.
Vicolo Santa Chiara 1, 60041; 328 205 1370; www.vicolosantachiara.it

---

Below left Stream in a limestone ravine near the Grotte di Frasassi **Below centre** The 13th-century Palazzo del Podestà, Fabriano **Below right** The Eremo di Fonte Avellana, in the hills of Le Marche

Visiting the Grotte di Frasassi
To visit the caves, buy a ticket from the ticket office *(0732 90080; www. frasassi.com)* in the car park in Largo Leone XII, as access to the caves is via a ravine that can only be reached by bus. The bus runs every 12 minutes and the fare is included in the cost of the entry ticket. Tours take just over one hour, and cover a walk of 1.5 km (1 mile). Enthusiasts can take the longer three-hour tour. It is pretty chilly inside the caves and a light jacket and sensible shoes are recommended for visitors.

in the fascinating **Museo della Carta** or the Paper Museum *(closed Mon)* in the San Domenico complex.

🚗 *Take Via Dante, which joins SS76 towards Ancona. Exit for Sassoferrato Grotte Frasassi/Genga after 10 km (6 miles). Park in Largo Leone XII's car park.*

⑧ Grotte di Frasassi
Ancona, Le Marche; 60040
Speleologists regard the limestone caves at Frasassi as among the best in Europe. They are a vast complex of caverns, some the size of cathedrals, with amazing formations of stalagmites and stalactites, crystalline lakes and gleaming alabaster arabesques.

The caves were only discovered after World War II, when speleologists abseiled into the vast empty space of the Ancona Abyss. They were opened to the public in 1974 and the complex can now be entered from ground level. If caving does not appeal, then just along the road there is a Roman bridge with a small medieval tower and gate. This leads to the beautiful Romanesque abbey of **San Vittore delle Chiuse**. Built in the 10th century, this simple but supremely elegant building is an architectural delight.

The road to the caves runs through a ravine from where visitors can drive on to the town of **Genga**, which sits perfectly preserved, as though in a time capsule. Note how the houses have been built into the bedrock.

🚗 *From Genga, follow directions to Arcevia on SP15. Turn right onto SP360. Near Arcevia, on Viale Martiri della Resistenza, take the left fork to "Centro" and park outside the walls in Via Mazzini.*

Above View of the unspoilt verdant hills of Le Marche

EAT AND DRINK

SASSOFERRATO
La Taverna di Bartolo *inexpensive*
Enjoy hearty rustic food such as *strozzapreti taleggio e radicchio* (homemade pasta with taleggio and red chicory) in the main square.
Piazza Matteoti 7, 60041; 0732 958 067; closed Mon

La Rocca *moderate*
The garden terrace is a popular spot in summer, offering classical regional cooking and pizzas in the evening.
Via Cardinal Albornoz 3, 60041; 0732 95444; closed Tue

FABRIANO
Nonna Rina Ristorantino *moderate*
This simple restaurant has a quiet ambiance and offers traditional local dishes served with a modern twist. It also features vegetarian and vegan menu options.
Piazza Garibaldi 25, 60044 ; 0732 040 930; closed Mon

Da Lucignolo
This restaurant offers home cooking – especially grilled meats – handily close to the main square.
Via Filippo Corridoni 22, 60044; 0732 628 227; closed Wed

Below Palazzo del Podestà and the Fontana Maggiore, Fabriano

Above Series of brick-built arched alleyways, Sassoferrato

⑦ Fabriano
Ancona, Le Marche; 60041
Its origins possibly go back to Roman times, but Fabriano only came to prominence in the Middle Ages. The magnificent **Palazzo del Podestà** (1255) and **Fontana Maggiore** (1285) in Piazza del Comune testify to its coming of age. Behind the altar in the Baroque **Cattedrale di San Venanzio** *(open daily)* are some wonderful 12th-century frescoes of the *Martyrdom of St Lawrence*. One of the most important painters of the early Renaissance, Gentile da Fabriano (1370–1427), was born here and his spectacular masterpiece, *Adoration of the Magi*, now in the Uffizi, Florence, is considered the high point of International Gothic.

Fabriano earned a reputation as one of the first places to make high-quality paper and the town is still known for its fine watermarked paper. The ancient processes of making paper by hand from rags are demonstrated

Above Fields and vineyards on the hills around Cupramontana **Above right** The pretty central piazza, Cupramontana **Below** The Porta della Croce, the main entrance to Serra de' Conti

WHERE TO STAY IN JESI

Hotel Federico II *moderate*
This modern hotel may lack character but it is on the edge of town and has plenty of facilities such as parking, pools, gym, sauna and a restaurant.
Via Ancona 100, 60035; 073 121 1079; www.hotelfederico2.it

Hotel dei Nani *moderate*
Another modern hotel with plenty of facilities on the edge of the old town.
Viale del Lavoro 34, 60035; 073 148 46; www.hoteldeinani.it

Notti sulle Mura
This tiny B&B offers colourful and smallish rooms in a characterful building close to the historic centre.
Via Spaldi 16, 60035; 329 764 55 33; www.nottisullemura.it

9 Arcevia
Ancona, Le Marche; 60011
The old fortress, or rocca, of Arcevia at the top of the town was destroyed long ago and only a few fragments remain in what is now a pleasant park. From here, the main street (Via Mazzini) leads through the town, past grand palazzos to the main square, Piazza Garibaldi. Further along, the **Collegiata di San Medaro** *(open daily)* has two fine paintings by Signorelli and a ceramic altarpiece by Giovanni della Robbia (1469–1529), whose fluency exceeded that achieved by previous artists.

Descend from Arcevia toward Senigallia on to SP360. Follow signs to Serra de' Conti. Park below the city walls at Porta della Croce.

10 Serra de' Conti
Ancona, Le Marche; 60030
One of the few brick-walled towns in the area, Serra de' Conti faces west across the Misa valley. Entry to the

historic centre of medieval and Renaissance buildings is through the Porta della Croce. The **Chiesa di San Michele** is a fine Romanesque-Gothic building that is both simple and beautiful. The nearby church of **Santa Maria Maddalena** provides a stunning Baroque contrast inspired by the 15th-century architect Borromini.

Leave on SP11 past Montecarrotto, and Moie. At Moie, take SS76 toward Ancona. Exit toward Castelbellino/ Monte Roberto and follow signs to Castelbellino on SP11. Head for "Centro" and park in Via Giacomo Leopardi, just under the town walls.

Castelli di Jesi
In the hinterland west of Jesi, nearly every hilltop is fortified in some way. Known as Castelli di Jesi, these strongholds, which include Cupramontana, Staffolo, Monte Roberto, Castelbellino and Maiolati Spontini, are synonymous with the vineyards that produce Verdicchio, the famous white wine of the area. This is a light, dry, straw-coloured wine that is often served in fish-shaped bottles.

11 Cupramontana
Ancona, Le Marche; 60034
A town within a town, Cupramontana's old town is tightly clustered around its main piazza and church, while the rest of the town sits comfortably spaced around the old walls. The town has Roman origins (Cupra was a goddess of fertility), but its architecture is mostly Neo-Classical. The capital of the Castelli di Jesi area, Cupramontana is also the centre of the wine-producing area. It is surrounded by vineyards, and serious

wine buffs might like to visit the **Wine Label Museum** (hours variable).

🚗 *Head northeast on SP9, under the SS76, then cross the Esino on SP502. Join SP76 into Jesi. Park on the street.*

Local Musicians

Giovanni Battista Pergolesi (1710–36) was a celebrated musician who was born in Jesi. For someone who died at 26, he made an enormous contribution to music, virtually inventing *opera buffa* (comic opera). He also wrote serious secular and sacred music – his haunting hymn *Stabat Mater* is the best known. Gaspare Spontini (1774–1851), born in Maiolati Spontini, was successful during his lifetime, but his fame was relatively short-lived and his music is rarely performed today.

🔟 Jesi

Ancona, Le Marche; 60035

Jesi's main claim to fame is as the birthplace of Frederick II, Emperor of the Holy Roman Empire (1194), and

Below The River Esino, which runs from the hills of Le Marche into the Adriatic

Above Looking down Jesi's Corso Matteotti to the Arch of Clementine

the influential musician Pergolesi. The entrance to the town is through the Arch of Clementine (1734) to Corso Matteotti, the main shopping street. To the right is the **Pinoteca Comunale** in Palazzo Pianetti, a wonderful Rococo building featuring many works by Renaissance artists including Lorenzo Lotto (1480–1557). A little further along is the Piazza della Repubblica and the grand Teatro Pergolesi. Continue straight on into the oldest part of town and the 15th-century **Palazzo della Signoria**, which now houses an important library of 115,000 books. The medieval reading room, the Sala Maggiore, still has its original wooden shelving. Further along still is Piazza Federico II, site of the Roman forum and where, according to legend, Frederick II was born in a tent in 1194, much to the amazement of the locals. The **Cattedrale di San Settimio** (open daily) was rebuilt in Neo-Classical style in 1732 and retains only elements of its earlier form. The **Museo Diocesano** (open am and late pm on weekends) next door holds some interesting carved wood pieces from the old churches of Jesi.

EAT AND DRINK

CUPRAMONTANA

Trattoria Anita *inexpensive*
A traditional, family-run trattoria serving honest home-made food such as pasta, and lamb and rabbit dishes. Like everything else, the house wine is their own – and good. *Via F Filzi 5, 60034; 0731 780 311; closed Tue in winter*

JESI

Pasticceria Bardi *inexpensive*
This makes a good stop for morning coffee and a well-made pastry. *Corso Matteoti 27, 60034*

L'Intreccio *moderate*
This contemporary restaurant specializes in fish dishes. *Via Rinaldi 15, 60035; 073 121 5018; closed lunch & Tue*

Osteria I Spiazzi *moderate*
Enjoy excellent modern Marche food in a medieval streetscape – try *involtini con carciofi* (pork rolls with artichoke), *insalata di pollo con frutta* (fruity chicken salad) and heavenly ice creams. *Piazza Nova 8, 60034; 073 121 5961; www.osteriaispiazzi.com; closed Mon–Sat lunch*

DAY TRIP OPTIONS

The drive divides into three sections – for history buffs, for those looking for peace and quiet and wine lovers.

Roman exploration
Start at Città di Castello ①, once Pliny the Younger's home town, then head to Pietralunga ②, with its Roman fortress. Travel on to Gubbio ③ with its Roman Theatre and Gate, then enjoy lunch. Finally, head to historic Sassoferrato ⑥, where the Romans won control over Central Italy.

Follow the drive's instructions from Città to Gubbio, then take SS298, SS360, SP360 to Sassoferrato, and back.

Woods and caves
Stock up on food in Cagli ④, then drive to Eremo di Fonte Avellana ⑤. Tour the monastery, then go for a walk and a picnic. Drive through Sassoferrato ⑥ to the Grotte di Frasassi ⑧ for a tour. Return home.

Follow drive's instructions from Cagli to Sassoferrato, then SP360 to Filipponi.

Turn right to caves. Return the same way.

The wine castles of Jesi
Start at Serra de' Conti ⑩, with its fine churches. Head to Cupramontana ⑪, via the Castelli di Jesi of Monte Roberto, Maiolati Spontini and Castellbino, sampling the wine along the way. At Cupramontana, visit the Wine Label Museum and lunch there, then head to Jesi ⑫, with its fine palazzos and churches.

Follow the drive's instructions and back.

DRIVE **24**

Montefeltro Mountains

Rimini to Fano

Highlights

- **Coastal resorts for every taste**
  Splash about at glamorous lidos around Rimini, quieter beaches below the cliffs at Castel di Mezzo, and the family resort of Fano

- **Pristine wilderness**
  Get away from it all in the wild mountains above Pennabilli and the rock-filled Parco Naturale Sasso Simone e Simoncello

- **A Renaissance jewel**
  Enjoy the relaxed pace of Urbino, a beautiful town filled with some of the Italy's finest art and architecture

- **Impregnable fortresses**
  Discover the fortresses of San Leo, Sassocorvaro and Gradara still in much the same condition as when they were built over 500 years ago

Sassocorvaro and Mercatale, located beside a man-made lake

Montefeltro Mountains

This drive starts on the Adriatic coast with its buzzing seaside towns, beaches and bars, then heads inland to the fairytale republic of San Marino, guarded by forbidding towers. Further inland lies Montefeltro, a region of unspoilt highlands, dotted with sleepy hill towns that are steeped in history. The atmosphere is quiet and peaceful and the air is pure – if it wasn't for the walls and forts guarding every town, it would be easy to forget that constant struggle shaped and defined the area. Even the beautiful Renaissance centre of culture and learning, Urbino, was paid for from the profits of war. Finally, head back to the coast and the spectacular cliffs at Gradara and Fano for more beach fun and the freshest seafood there is.

Above The impressive fortress at San Leo, *see p242*

ACTIVITIES

Act like a Roman in Rimini – cross the Ponte di Tiberio, march through the Arco di Augusto and speak in the former Roman forum

Clamber up the heights of San Marino and look hang gliders and eagles in the eye

Hike among the rocks of the Parco Naturale Sasso Simone e Simoncello

Walk along the crenellated walls of the castle at Gradara

Ride a horse in the foothills around Carpegna

Swim in the Adriatic Sea from the beach at Fano

0 kilometres   6

0 miles   6

KEY

 Drive route

PLAN YOUR DRIVE

Start/finish: Rimini to Fano.

Number of days: Approx 3–4.

Distance: Approx 230 km (143 miles).

Road conditions: Good, but often steep ascents/descents. Snow chains must be carried in winter months.

When to go: All year, though winter is not recommended. In spring and late autumn there may be some snow and ice on higher sections of road. In August, all the beach resorts are busy but the inland areas are not.

Opening times: Close to the coast, and in San Marino and Gradara, many attractions stay open late as visitors return from the beach. In summer, many bars and restaurants are open all week. Churches usually open 8am–12:30pm and 3:30–7:00pm.

Main market days: Rimini: Wed & Sat; Santarcangelo: Mon & Fri; Urbino: Sat; book fair, 4th Sun of month; Gradara: Sun; Fano: Wed & Sat; antique market, 2nd Sun of month.

Major festivals: San Leo: medieval jesters festival, last weekend in Jun; Pennabilli: antiquarian festival, mid-Jul; buskers festival 3rd week Jun; Carpegna: Festa del Prosciutto, mid-Jul; Urbino: kite festival, 1st weekend in Sep; Fano: Jazz by the Sea, last week in Jul; Mardi Gras, 3 weekends in Jan–Feb.

Shopping: San Marino offers duty-free shopping on electronic goods, cameras and alcohol. In Urbino, try the soft and crumbly *casciotta d'Urbino* cheese. Fano is known for the local speciality *moretta di Fano* – coffee with a shot of liqueur and citrus peel.

DAY TRIP OPTIONS

There are distinct day trips to be enjoyed here. Visit **Roman ruins** and splendid **beaches**, then **towers** with **vertiginous views** and a **fort-cum-prison**. Tour a **palace**, rich in **art**, then visit a sturdy **castle** before going for a **hike** among huge rocks. From a **beach resort**, head to **clifftop villages** for **walks** and a **swim**, then round the day off with a drink in a **castle**. For full details, *see p245*.

Above The twin rocky outcrops of Simone and Simoncello near Carpegna, *see p242*

Below Quaint street in the clifftop town of Fiorenzuola di Focara, *see p245*

Above Picturesque countryside enroute to San Merino **Below** Torre dell'Orologico in Piazza Tre Martiri, Rimini

WHERE TO STAY

RIMINI

Savoia Hotel Rimini *moderate*
This contemporary hotel is right on the beach and has great views. Good for a swim and evening promenade.
Viale Lungomare Murri 13, 47921; 0541 396 600; www.starwoodhotels.com

Grand Hotel Rimini *expensive*
Splendid "beau monde" hotel made famous by Fellini. Enjoy *la dolce vita* at the beach in luxury and elegance.
Parco Federico Fellini 1, 47921; 0541 560 000; www.grandhotelrimini.com

THE REPUBLIC OF SAN MARINO

Hotel Cesare *moderate*
Small modern hotel in a good central position with easy access to town.
Salita alla Rocca 7, 47890; 0549 992 355; www.hotelcesare.com

Hotel Titano *moderate*
With great views from the top floors, this central hotel is a good base to explore town. Ask about parking when booking.
Contrada del Collegio 31, 47890; 0549 991 007; www.hoteltitano.com

❶ Rimini
Emilia-Romagna; 47921
A busy seaside town, Rimini is the most popular resort on the Adriatic. But alongside the nightclubs, there is an interesting mix of Roman and Renaissance architecture. The **Piazza Tre Martiri** is the former Roman forum, where Julius Caesar addressed his troops before advancing on Rome in 49 BC. Nearby, in Via IV Novembre, is the beautiful **Tempio Malatestiana** *(open daily)*, with its unfinished façade. This was commissioned in 1450 by the tyrant Sigismondo Malatesta, who had his and his wife Isotta's initials carved in the roundels.

North and south of the old town lie two impressive Roman remains. The **Ponte di Tiberio** (AD 14–21), built from Istrian stone, is a fine example of Roman engineering. On the southern side of town, the **Arco di Augusto** (AD 27) shows Rimini's importance of in Roman times. (The battlements were added in the Middle Ages.) Piazza Cavour is the Renaissance hub of Rimini, with its palazzos, fountain and statue of Pope Paul V. The

rough-hewn Castel Sismondo, started by Sigismondo in 1437, stands in Piazza Malatesta and provides a striking space for summer art exhibitions.
🚗 *Head inland on Via Marecchiese, turn right on SS16 and left on SS9 to Santarcangelo. Park in Via Federico Montevecchi.*

❷ Santarcangelo di Romagna
Rimini, Emilia-Romagna; 47822
Set on a small hill in the coastal plain, Santarcangelo offers a pleasant break from the beach culture of Rimini. Dominated by the **Rocca Malatestiana and Monastery**, this medieval town sits on a mass of catacombs dating back to early Christian times. Visit the Tourist Centre *(Via C Battisti 5; www. iatsantarcangelo.com)* for tickets to the catacombs. Wear something warm, as it is chilly underground. Many of the town's pleasant buildings are adorned by plaques bearing poems, a custom initiated by poet, screen writer and local, Tonnino Guerra.
🚗 *Take SP14 west to Ponte Verucchio. Cross River Marecchia, then follow signs to Verucchio. There is plenty of parking.*

❸ Verucchio
Rimini, Emilia-Romagna; 47826
A key defensive post in pre-Roman times, Verucchio was the site of Iron-age settlements in the 8th century BC. Locally discovered artifacts can be seen in the **Museo Civico Archeologico**. The town is topped by an imposing *rocca* built by Malatesta in the 13th century.
🚗 *Take SP 32 to San Marino "Centro". Use top car park P7, Cava degli Umbri.*

❹ The Republic of San Marino
Repubblica di San Marino (RSM); 47890
The world's oldest republic is perched on top of the cliffs of Monte Titano and maintains its own army, mint and parliament. With a population of 32,000, it is effectively a part of Italy despite its independent status. The United Nations gave San Marino World Heritage Status in 2008.

A two-hour walking tour
From the car park, walk past tennis courts to Via della Fratta. On the right is a stone path (Salita alla Cesta) up to the **Second Tower** ❶ *(entry fee – covers all towers)*. To the right is the pleasant Parco Naturals and the Third Tower (Montale), a former prison and lookout, is visible to the south. The

Second Tower (Cesta) was built in the 13th century on the remains of a Roman fortress. It is at the highest point of Monte Titano and houses an armoury museum with exhilarating views – not recommended for vertigo sufferers. It's a testament to their skills that the medieval masons managed to create such elegant stonework on this sheer precipice. Returning down Salita alla Cesta, there is a path to the right, Passo delle Streghe (Witches Way), through parkland to the **First Tower (Guaita)** ②. This slightly larger castle shares the views of its twin. It was used as a prison as recently as 1975 and still has prisoners' graffiti in some rooms. Continue down Salita della Rocca, past the trinket sellers. As the path sweeps around to the left, continue straight on into what looks like a restaurant, signed "Ingresso Giardino". This is a public right of way. Enter, then go down some steps into the Bishop's Garden. From here another stone staircase leads to narrow Contrada Magazzini, then into **Piazza Domus Plebis** ③. The Basilica di San Marino was built here at the beginning of the 19th century over a Roman church. It is grand but a bit empty. The sweet little church next door, the Chiesa di San Pietro, contains two

Statue of Liberty, Palazzo Pubblico

beds carved into the rock. Believed to be those of St Marino and his companion St Leo, they are said by many to have healing powers.

Below the square to the right, **Contrada Omagnano** ④ leads to the northernmost point on the cliff, and the cable car (down to Borgo Maggiore, every 12 miutes). A sharp left into narrow Contrada di Pianello leads to **Piazza della Libertà** ⑤ and San Marino's Palazzo Pubblico – a mini palace for a mini republic. There is a Changing of the Guard *(May–Sep)* every hour on the half hour. Continue along Contrada del Collegio, but at the next junction take a slight left uphill along Contrada della Croce. At the city wall, turn right, down to Viale Donna Felicissima and **Piazza Garibaldi** ⑥. The porticoed loggia of San Francesco graces this busy little square. The church itself is now a small museum and picture gallery (included in the ticket for the towers). A few steps downhill is the Piazza del Titano and the state museum, the **Palazzo Pergami-Belluzzi** ⑦ *(open daily)*, which has some archeological finds and minor artworks.

Exit right from the museum and walk beside the Chiesa di San Francesco – look for the Templar symbol in the stonework at the base of the church. Continue along to Piazza Sant'Agata, then follow the city wall left, up to Via della Fratta and the car park.

🔲 *Zig-zag down to Borgo Maggiore, turn left at the roundabout for San Leo and on to SP 258 left to San Leo. Drive into town and park in the main square.*

Left San Marino's elegant Palazzo Pubblico, built in 1884 **Below** Peaceful Santarcangelo di Romagna, a change of pace from Rimini

EAT AND DRINK

SANTARCANGELO DI ROMAGNA

Lazaroun *moderate*
Enjoy classic Romagnolo cooking, with well-presented dishes such as rabbit salad, pheasant with prunes and chestnuts, and amaretti semifreddo. *Via del Platano 21, 47822; 0541 624 417; www.lazaroun.it*

VERUCCHIO

Ristorante La Rocca *moderate*
Stop in on the walk up to the rocca – the quality of the food is almost as spectacular as the views. *Via Rocca 34, 47826; 0541 679 850; www.ristorantelaroccaverucchio.com; closed Wed eve & Mon–Thu lunch*

THE REPUBLIC OF SAN MARINO

Cantina di Bacco *inexpensive*
Refreshingly old-fashioned place in the middle of town selling local specialities. *Contrada Santa Croce 35, 47822; 0549 992 840; www.cantinadibacco.net*

Ristorante Bolognese *inexpensive*
Typically hearty Bolognese food. Try the *stringhetti al sugo di verdure* (pasta with vegetable sauce). *Via Basilicus 28, 47890; 0549 991 299*

Eat and Drink: inexpensive, under €25; moderate, €25–€45; expensive, over €45

VISITING URBINO

Tourist Information
Located just inside the main city gate.
Via Vittorio Veneto, 4, 61029; 0541 964 115; www.gradara.org

WHERE TO STAY IN URBINO

Hotel Raffaello *moderate*
In the very old part of town (ask for parking directions when booking), this old seminary has been transformed into a convenient, modern hotel.
Vicolino Santa Margherita 40, 61029; 0722 4784; www.albergoraffaello.com

Albergo Italia *moderate*
With smart modern interiors and a central location close to the lift and car park in Piazza Mercatale, this hotel makes a convenient city stopover.
Corso Garibaldi 32, 61029; 0722 2701; www.albergo-italia-urbino.it

Albergo San Domenico *moderate*
Beautifully restored monastery opposite the Palazzo Ducale, complete with cloister and Roman cistern, but all modern conveniences as well.
Piazza Rinascimento 3, 61029; 0722 2626; www.viphotels.it

Top right Rocky outcrops of Simone and Simoncello **Below left** Fountain in Piazza Dante Aligheri, San Leo **Below right** Façade of the Chiesa di Sant'Antonio Abate, Pennabilli **Bottom** Countryside around Pietrarubbia, looking towards San Marino

⑤ San Leo
Rimini, Emilia-Romagna; 61018
This spectacular town enjoys the reputation of being the most impregnable fortress in Italy, built as it is on a near vertical cliff. Settlement began in the 8th century and its buildings are variously Longobard, Romanesque and from the Renaissance. For many years it was part of the Papal States, and its impressive **castle** became a prison for miscreants such as Count Cagliostro, an infamous charlatan and necromancer. It is now a lovely little place with two simple but beautiful Romanesque churches.

🚗 *From San Leo turn right towards Carpegna. Turn right onto SP6 towards Novafeltria/Maiolo – great views – do not take right turn to Novafeltria but head down to the Marecchia Valley and SP285. The turn left to Pennabilli is on a dangerous corner so carry on to the roundabout and return. Park in town.*

⑥ Pennabilli
Rimini, Emilia-Romagna; 61016
The two fortresses of Penna and Billi were joined into one in the 14th century and the remains of the castles are visible above the still united town. The main square, Piazza Vittorio

Emanuele II, with its red-brick Chiesa di Sant'Antonio Abate, sits between the two forts. It is a charming town of medieval streets and squares brightened up in summer by crimson geraniums in terracotta pots.

🚗 *Take SP1 to exit from town, then turn left on SP84 towards Carpegna.*

⑦ Carpegna
Pésaro, Le Marche; 61021
A brief heyday in the late Middle Ages gave Carpegna just one impressive building. Planned, but not built until 1675, Palazzo dei Principi di Carpegna's main claim to fame is that it was used to hide much of Italy's art collection during World War II. Carpegna is also the headquarters of the **Parco Naturale Sasso Simone e Simoncello**. Sasso means "rock" or "stone" in Italian, and the two rocky outcrops or "sassi" are visible to the west on the road into Carpegna. For information on walking or trekking, pop into the Visitor Centre *(Via Rio Maggio, Carpegna; 0722 75350; www.parcosimone.it).*

🚗 *Take SP1 east and follow signs to Pietrarubbia. On a hairpin bend on the right, a white road signed "Petrelle" leads to the rock. Either drive or walk.*

⑧ Pietrarubbia
Pésaro, Le Marche; 61023
A monumental outcrop suddenly emerges on the road from Carpegna to Pietrarubbia like a huge thumb raised to the heavens – locals call it the "Giant's Finger". Pietrarubbia itself is a good place to survey the Montefeltro region, from San Marino in the north-east and the Adriatic to the Apennines. The ruins of the medieval town and castle on the hill above town can be seen and visited from Pietrorubbia.

Far left Well-defended Sassocorvaro, set high on a hill **Left** The turrets and towers of Urbino, a centre of learning during the Renaissance **Below** The "Giant's Finger" rock formation on the road to Pietrarubbia

ACTIVITIES IN MONTEFELTRO

For horse-riding, try the **Centro Ippico Montefeltro** *(Via Provinciale, Carpegna; 0722 77696)*. For details of organized treks, contact **Sistema Turistico Urbino e Montefeltro** *(Via Pucinotti 33, Urbino; 0722 320 437; www.urbinoeilmontefeltro.it)*.

EAT AND DRINK

SAN LEO

Osteria Belvedere *moderate*
This cosy restaurant offers fine alfresco eating – try *prosciutto di Carpegna* and local cheeses with *marmellata* (fruit jelly). *Via Tosselli 19, 61018; 0541 916 361; www.belvederesanleo.it*

Hotel Ristorante Castello *moderate*
With tables on the main square, this is the spot for a coffee, an aperitif, a light snack and a bit of people watching. *Piazza Dante 11/12, 61018; 0541 916 214;www.hotelristorantecastellosanleo. com; closed Thu in winter*

URBINO

Il Cortegiano *inexpensive*
Close to the Palazzo Ducale, this restaurant provides quick snacks or proper dining in the courtyard. *Via Pucinotti 13, 61029; 072237307; www.ilcortegiano.it; closed Sun–Tue eve*

La Trattoria del Leone *moderate*
This popular place in the historic centre is fairly small so booking is recommended. *Via Cesare Battisti 5, 61018; 0722 329 894; www.latrattoriadelleone.it*

Vecchia Urbino *moderate*
This restaurant serves delicacies such as truffles and porcini, as well as more adventurous dishes – *testina di agnello alla brace* (chargrilled lamb's head). *Via dei Vasari 5, 61029; 0722 4447; www.vecchiaurbino.it; closed Tue*

🚗 *From the "Giant's Finger" take SP1 towards Pietrarubbia. SP1 becomes the SP6 near Sassocorvaro, then SP3bis and SP37/SP67. There is plenty of parking.*

Piadina

The *piada* or *piadina* is the perfect gastronomic symbol for the area and has been rather overlooked in favour of the pizza. Pellegrino Artusi (1820–1911) – the first writer to gather together recipes from all over Italy in one cookbook – didn't deem it worth an entry. But, properly made, the warm, round flatbread, filled with *prosciutto crudo* and *stracchino* cheese is paradise on a plate.

⑨ Sassocorvaro

Pésaro, Le Marche; 61028
The road to Sassocorvaro passes first through the pretty market district of Mercatale with views of the castle above and the lovely artificial lake. In the heart of Sassocorvaro, the chunky fortress **La Rocca Ubaldinesca** *(open daily)* is a fine piece of 15th-century defensive architecture. Its remote location and solid design meant it was never breached in earlier centuries, and during World War II it was used to hide many of Italy's art works – it is now a museum. At the other end of the street there are pleasant views over the Fiume Fóglia lake, below.
🚗 *Head out of town on Via Roma SP 67. Follow signs to Urbino on SS73bis. Follow the road around town to Piazza Mercatale, for underground parking.*

⑩ Urbino

Le Marche; 61029
This enchanting city flourished under the patronage of Duke Federico da Montefeltro (1422–82). His university

attracted painters, architects and mathematicians from far and wide.

The huge Palazzo Ducale, which houses the **Galleria Nazionale delle Marche** *(closed Tue pm)*, dominates the approach to Urbino from the south. The fairytale quality of the turrets that frame the duke's private quarters belies the strength of an undefeated military power. The courtyard is a masterpiece of the Greek and Roman humanist ideals that would become hallmarks of the Renaissance. In its day, the palace was the largest building in Europe.

The gallery's most famous works are Piero della Francesca's enigmatic *The Flagellation* (c.1460), often cited as the world's greatest small painting; *The Ideal City*, a perspective study attributed to Piero or his students; and the gorgeous *La Muta* (1507) by Raphael. The duke's private study is lined with finely worked wood panels and the servants' quarters and kitchens below stairs are worth seeing to understand how the other half lived.

Across the square from the palace is the **Cattedrale di Urbino**. Founded in 1062 but often rebuilt, it has an 18th-century Neo-Classical façade.

Near the Piazza della Repubblica, **Casa Natale di Raffaello** *(open daily)* has been preserved since the 19th century as a monument to the painter Raphael and retains its evocative atmosphere. Nearby the **Oratories of San Giovanni and San Giuseppe** *(open daily)* have frescoes by the Salimbeni brothers (c.1416). Blending International Gothic with a more natural approach, they are an exciting foretaste of the Renaissance.

🚗 *Follow signs to Perugia/Pésaro on SP423; drive toward Pésaro to Montecchio, then turn left on SP 38 towards Gradara. Park in front of castle.*

Above Colourful geraniums in terracotta pots are a feature of the towns on this drive

Where is Montefeltro?
Stretching from the Marecchia Valley in the north to Pésaro and Urbino, Montefeltro is today a loosely defined area. It was originally a diocese under Charlemagne, the first Holy Roman emperor – its first bishop was appointed in AD 826. The family known as the Montefeltros began their reign in Urbino in 1267, often clashing with the Malatesta family, who rose to power in Verucchio in 1239 and held the Rimini-Pésaro seaboard for the next 300 years.

⑪ Gradara
Pésaro, Le Marche; 61012
This spectacular fortified town dates back to the 12th century and was gradually encased in a double line of medieval walls. The castle is now the **Museo Nazionale della Rocca** *(closed Mon pm)*. Superbly preserved, it is a fantasy fortress of crisp crenellations, towers and bastions (it is also said to be the location of the love story in Dante's *Divine Comedy*). Gradara buzzes with daytrippers and events in summer. In the early evening, once the coach parties have gone, taking a walk around the castellated walls is a great way to admire the sunset.

🚗 *Exit following signs to Cattolica/ Gabbicce Mare – under the A14 – take a dogleg, then follow signs for Gabbicce Mare/Centro. Follow Viale della Vittoria to the sea, then turn right into Via Panoramica uphill to Gabbicce Monte, then Castel di Mezzo and the Parco Naturale Monte San Bartolo.*

⑫ Castel di Mezzo
Pésaro, Le Marche; 61100
This is a tiny town in the centre of the 10-km (6-mile) strip of greenery, known as the **Parco Naturale Monte San Bartolo** *(www.parcosanbartolo.it)*. The green clifftops between Gabbicce Mare and Pésaro are a welcome relief from the long strips of organized lidos to the north, stretching as far as Trieste. The Parco Naturale Monte San Bartolo offers numerous walking trails and leisure activities. Castel di Mezzo itself is little more than a church, a restaurant and a few houses, but the town is certainly worth a quick stop for a short clifftop walk or a leisurely meal looking out to sea.

🚗 *Carry along the Strada Panoramica Adriatica to Fiorenzuloa di Focara. Parking can be difficult but there are generally spaces along the road.*

WHERE TO STAY

GRADARA
La Loggia di Gradara Relais *moderate*
Combining the ultra modern and the ancient, this tiny hotel is both unusual and interesting. As parking is outside the walls, guests are driven to the hotel in an electric car. Try for a balcony room.
Via Dante Alighieri 2, 61012; 0541 964 154; www.laloggiagradara.it

FANO
Hotel Orfeo *inexpensive*
The Orfeo is a small family-run hotel near the historic centre and makes a good base for exploring the city. They also have an excellent restaurant.
Corso Matteoti 5, 61032; 0721 803 522; www.hotelorfeo-fano.it

Siri Hotel *moderate*
On the main road into town, this ultra-chic modern hotel is well situated for both the beach and the historic centre. There's a shuttle to the private beach.
Viale Buozzi 69, 61032; 0721 802 593; www.sirihotelfano.it

Above Countryside around the fortified city of Gradara **Bottom left** Gradara's pretty town centre, popular with daytrippers **Bottom right** Bas reliefs above the doorway of the Chiesa di San Michele, Fano

to Fano on SS16 along the seafront. At
Fano, the road bends to the right and
becomes Via Bruno Buozzi. Park here.

⑭ Fano

Pésaro, Le Marche; 61032
Although Fano has plenty to offer as
a beach resort, it is also a working
town with a history going back to the
Roman era. That said, the impressive
Arco di Augusto is virtually all that
remains from ancient times. Close by
the arch is the **Porta Maggiore**, built
in 1227, but equally ravaged by time.
Down the same street – once the
Roman main road – is the **Cattedrale
Santa Maria Assunta** (open daily). It has
been restored many times, but retains
its plain Romanesque exterior and
contains medieval sculptures and
other works of art by Renaissance
artists. The small **Chiesa di San Michele**
was built in 1494, and the bas-reliefs
above the doorway date to 1511.

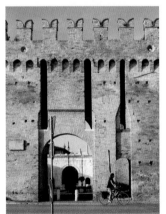

⑬ Fiorenzuola di Focara

Pésaro, Le Marche; 61100
On a sunny day, this tiny fortress town
can get crowded as it is a starting
point for the trek to the stunning
beach below. It still has the classic
elements of a hill town and the old
entrance gate and walls remain.
Fiorenzuola was originally part of a
defensive coastal network and a
primitive lighthouse in medieval times.
🚗 *Continue along Strada Panoramica
Adriatica to Pésaro, then follow signs*

EAT AND DRINK

GRADARA

Il Bacio *moderate*
Dine under the shady mulberry tree
in warm weather, and enjoy this
restaurant's delicious specialities.
*Via Roma 8; 0541 964 620;
www.ilbacioristorante.it*

Mastin Vecchio *moderate–expensive*
Just off the main street, Mastin Vecchio
has a lovely courtyard for summer
dining and offers cheaper (osteria) or
more traditional (ristorante) options.
*Via Alighieri 5, 61012; 0541 964 024;
www.mastinvecchio.com*

AROUND CASTEL DI MEZZO

Bar Panoramic *inexpensive*
On the road just beyond Gabicce
Monte, this friendly bar has superb
views and cheap drinks.
Via Panoramica 47, 61011; 0541 830 439

Taverna del Pescatore *moderate*
This excellent fish restaurant has
a perfect clifftop position.
*Castel di Mezzo 23, 61100; 0721 208
116; www.tavernadelpescatore.it;
closed lunch Tue & Wed*

FANO

Casa Nolfi Ristorante *moderate*
Inside the Hotel Augustus, this is one
of Fano's best seafood restaurants.
Casa Nolfi specializes in *brodetto
Fanese*, the excellent local fish soup.
*Via Gasparoli 59, 61032; 0721 809 781;
evenings only, closed Sun*

Osteria Mocambo *moderate*
This popular local fish restaurant near
the port has a top reputation and serves
great paella, which is unusual in Italy.
*Viale Carioli 135, 61032; 0721 170
6171; closed Wed, booking advised*

Top left The unspoiled clifftop reserve of Parco
Naturale Monte San Bartolo **Left** The medieval
Porta Maggiore, Fano

DAY TRIP OPTIONS

There are some great days out to be
enjoyed in Montefeltro, for families,
art lovers, activity enthusiasts and
those looking for a relaxing time.

A family day from Rimini
The resort of Rimini ❶ – with its
Roman remains – is a great starting
point for a tour inland to San Marino
❹. Take a walk up the tiny republic's
steep streets with stunning views.
Next stop is San Leo ❺ and its
formidable clifftop fortress. Return to
Rimini for some relaxing beach time
and a cooling dip in the sea.

Take SS72 from Rimini to San Marino to
the top car park. Return the same way.

Renaissance and rocks
Spend the morning touring the
Palazzo Ducale at Urbino ❿, the city
was the birthplace of Raphael and, in
its heyday it was a centre for the best
minds of the time. Enjoy lunch before
heading to Sassocorvaro ❾ to see
its sturdy castle, then drive to the
"Giant's Finger" at Pietrarubbia ❽ for
a walk in the beautiful countryside.

*Retrace the drive's instructions from
Urbino to Pietrarubbia, and back.*

Take a break from blue to green
From the lively beach resort of Fano
⑭, enjoy a change of pace by driving
to the peaceful, green, clifftop oasis
of the *Parco Naturale Monte San
Bartolo*. Stop for strolls at pretty
Fiorenzuola di Focara ⑬ and Castel
di Mezzo ⑫, climbing down the
cliff to the lovely beach for a swim.
Visit romantic Gradara ⑪ and stay
for a drink as the sun sets.

*Follow the drive's instructions in reverse,
from Fano to Gradara. If time is of the
essence, return via the A14. If not, take
SP47 back to the coastal road to Fano.*

The Heart of Le Marche

Loreto to Grottammare

Highlights

- **Pilgrimage destination**
  Visit the historic house from the Holy Land in Loreto's grand cathedral and see some exceptional art inspired by strong religious devotion

- **Majestic peaks**
  See the spectacular Monti Sibillini from viewpoints in quaint old towns along the way

- **Mostly marble**
  Enjoy a drink in one of Italy's most beautiful piazzas, the main square of delightful Ascoli Piceno – a town built almost entirely of travertine

- **Beachside fun**
  Wander along Grottammare's palm-lined promenade, relax on the hot sand or enjoy a meal of fresh seafood served with excellent local wine

View from Acquaviva Picena towards the Monti Sibillini

The Heart of Le Marche

Although not well-known to foreign visitors, the beach resorts of Le Marche buzz with activity all summer. But the region's inland treasures remain almost undiscovered. Starting at the holy city of Loreto, this drive sweeps over the Conero Peninsula and into the historic towns between the coast and the mountains. The famous opera town of Macerata, the serene abbey at Fiastra and the Roman ruins of Urbs Salvia are key stops. Next, the road climbs into the foothills of the Monti Sibillini, with spectacular views from the medieval towns of San Ginesio, Montefortino and Montemonaco.

Above The ancient fortress town of Grottammare, keeping watch over the modern coastline, *see p255*

KEY

Drive route

ACTIVITIES

Go for a swim at any of the beaches near Sirolo

Explore the underground cave system at Osimo, which dates back to pre-Christian times

Enjoy an outdoor opera at the world-famous Sferisterio in Macerata

Choose climbing, walking or skiing on a visit to the Parco Nazionale dei Monti Sibillini

Taste some great wines in the province of Ascoli Piceno

Promenade at Grottammare, under palms imported from the Canary Islands

0 kilometres 10

0 miles 10

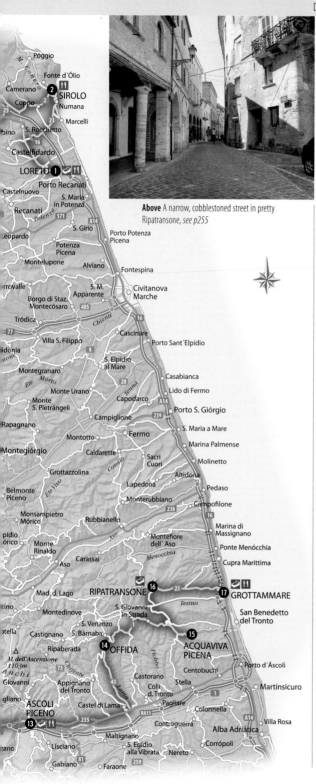

Above A narrow, cobblestoned street in pretty Ripatransone, *see p255*

PLAN YOUR DRIVE

Start/finish: Loreto to Grottammare.

Number of days: 3–4 days.

Distance: Approx 240 km (149 miles).

Road conditions: Good-quality roads with one or two steep ascents.

When to go: All year round but best in spring and autumn. August is very crowded on the coast but quiet inland.

Opening times: Churches open 8am–12:30pm and 3:30–6:30pm. Shops in inland towns within driving distance of the coast stay open late in summer to cater for those returning from the beach.

Main market days: Loreto: Tue; Osimo: Thu; Macerata: Wed; San Ginesio: Sun; Sarnano: Thu; Ascoli Piceno: Wed.

Specialized markets: Macerata: Il Barattolo flea market, 2nd Sunday of month; Ascoli Piceno: antiques market, 3rd weekend of month.

Major festivals: Macerata: Sferisterio (opera festival), Jul–Aug; San Ginesio: Palio (medieval festival) 15 Aug; Ascoli Piceno: Quintana (medieval festival) 1st Sun in Aug; Carnivale, late Feb–early Mar; Offida: Carnivale, Feb–Mar.

Shopping: In Macerata, look for Varnelli – an aniseed-flavour liqueur. Ascoli Province is known for its hand-made shoes. Offida is regarded as one of the best lace-making centres in Italy. In Grottammare, pick up handmade ceramics from Argyla (www.argyla.it), next to the fortress.

DAY TRIP OPTIONS

From the High Renaissance **architecture** of Loreto, it's a short drive to the **catacombs** in Osimo, where early Christians sheltered from perse-cution. The towns in the foothills of the Monti Sibillini provide ready access to the **national park**, where **churches** perch on cliff tops, **castles** keep watch for invaders and **vineyards** stretch as far as the eye can see. The marble town of Ascoli Piceno is rich in **art**, **architec-ture** and **history**; beyond it lies perfect **picnic** country and Grottammare's **sea-side** delights. For full details, *see p255.*

Above Secluded sandy beach on the Conero Peninsula near Sirolo

WHERE TO STAY

LORETO

Hotel Loreto *inexpensive*
Central, modern location with great countryside views from its terrace.
Corso Boccalini 60, 60025; 071 750 0106; www.loretohotel.it

MACERATA

Arcadia Hotel *inexpensive*
Within the old walls and close to the main attractions, this modest hotel offers parking, a good breakfast and professional staff.
V P Matteo Ricci 134, 62100; 0733 230063; www.arcadiahotelmacerata.it

Below Arco Gotico, the main shopping street in clifftop Sirolo **Below right** Typical Le Marche vineyard on the road to Macerata **Bottom** The tower of Castello di Montefiore, visible from a distance

① Loreto
Ancona, Le Marche; 60025

This small hill town is one of Italy's holiest sites and often throngs with pilgrims. It is also a place where Renaissance popes invested heavily in fine art and architecture. In the huge **Basilica della Santa Casa** *(open daily)* sits a small and very old building. Pilgrims come here to see where the Virgin Mary received the news that she was to become the Mother of God (The Annunciation). They believe that this is her actual house, carried by angels to Italy in 1294 from Nazareth in the Holy Land. Many famous 14th- and 15th-century architects, such as Bramante, Sangallo and Martini, worked on the basilica's decoration and the soldier pope, Julius II, gave it a military exterior. Of special interest is the large marble screen, designed by Bramante – one of many great works of art in the complex. The town's piazza, fountain and the quadrangle of buildings surrounding it all have a High Renaissance feel, which makes it like a mini Rome away from Rome.

🚗 *From Loreto, take SP77 east. At the roundabout, head north towards Sirolo, then turn right onto SP23 to Sirolo and follow signs for "Centro". Park near Piazzale Marino.*

② Sirolo
Ancona, Le Marche; 60020

Perched on a clifftop overlooking the Adriatic, Sirolo is a beachside town some distance from the beach. In a sense, this adds to its attraction – it gets a cooling sea breeze in summer and combines the ambience of a hilltown with ocean views. The main square, Piazzale Marino, offers the best views of the beaches of the Conero Peninsula, and the tiny medieval streets behind it buzz with activity in summer.

🚗 *From Sirolo, drive west downhill on to SP2. Drive straight over roundabout, then turn left under the autostrada on SP25. Then follow signs to Osimo. There are parking meters all around town.*

The Santa Casa at Loreto
In 1291, Acre, the last bastion of the Christian crusaders, fell to the Turks, leaving the Holy Land under the control of Muslims. To protect their Christian heritage, a crusader family arranged to remove "Mary's house" to safety. That same year, the house arrived in Croatia, and in 1294 in Loreto. The stonework is similar to examples from Nazareth from around the time of the birth of Christ. Gradually the myth grew that angels had carried the *Santa Casa*, or Holy House, to Italy.

③ Osimo
Ancona, Le Marche; 60027

The ancient Greeks, who colonized nearby Ancona in the 3rd century BC, founded Osimo. In 174 BC, the Romans took possession and some elements from this time still remain – great rectangular blocks in the town walls, and a Roman fountain. The town's age shows in many of its public buildings, particularly the intricate Romanesque carvings around the doors of the **Cattedrale di San Leopardo** *(open daily)* and the official buildings in the main square, **Piazza del Comune**. Below the town is a labyrinth of catacombs, **Le Grotte** *(open Tue–Sun)*, dating back to pre-Roman times. The tourist information office *(www.osimoturismo.it)* is in Via Fonte Magna, near the Roman walls.

🚗 *Take Via C Colombo/SP361 following signs to Macerata. The Castello di Montefiore, with ample parking, is just before town.*

Where to Stay: inexpensive, under €100; moderate, €100–€200; expensive, over €200

Above Piazza Mazzini, Macerata, home of the weekly market

④ Montefano
Macerata, Le Marche; 62010

The imposing tower of the **Castello di Montefiore** is visible long before reaching Montefano. Little remains of the original polygonal castle built in the 14th century, except some of the walls and the keep. The tower withstood the artillery onslaught of six centuries of wars, but was damaged in World War II. Now restored, it is used as a summer concert venue and can be explored. Nearby Montefano is a pretty little town very typical of this part of Le Marche.

🚗 *Take SP361 to Montecassiano. Turn right onto ring road, Viale Giovanni XXIII. Park near one of the town gates.*

Rosso Conero
Red wines from the Monte Conero region have been highly regarded in Italy since ancient times; illustrious Roman authors Pliny the Elder (AD 23–79) and his nephew Pliny the Younger (AD 61–112) both praised the wines of this area to the south of Ancona. Today's "Rosso Conero" wines are strong, full-bodied reds. The main grape is Montepulciano, to which a small percentage of Sangiovese can be added. This inexpensive, readily available wine benefits from ageing.

⑤ Montecassiano
Macerata, Le Marche; 62010

With medieval walls and three robust gateways, Montecassiano is a set-piece historic village. The swallow-tail battlements of the **Palazzo dei Priori**, the loggia below, and the spire of the **Collegiata di Santa Maria Assunta** *(open daily)* behind the

archway, make the main square, **Piazza Leopardi**, look like it should be the setting for an opera. During festivals held here in October, they make *sughitti*, a sweet polenta cake made from wine *mosto* (must), maize flour and local walnuts.

🚗 *Continue on SP361. At a major junction, there's a sharp left on to SP77, past Roman ruins at Helvia Recina. Stay on SP77 to Villa Potenza, then SP37 to Macerata. Park in Piazza Mazzini (except Wed market day).*

⑥ Macerata
Macerata, Le Marche; 62100

When the Visigoths destroyed the Roman town of Helvia Recina in AD 408, the people moved to the hill above. By the 12th century, Macerata had established itself and eventually became the provincial capital. Famous today for open-air opera at the **Sferisterio**, the town has a lively historic centre. Along Corso Matteotti, there are a number of Renaissance palazzos, the most striking being the **Palazzo dei Diamanti**. The street leads into the architecturally jumbled Piazza della Libertà. Its jewel is the small but perfectly formed **Loggia dei Mercanti** (1505), a fine example of Renaissance harmony. The tenor Beniamino Gigli (1890–1957) once serenaded the town from the loggia's balcony after a performance at the Sferisterio in 1930.

🚗 *From the parking on Piazza Mazzini turn right on Sferisterio and take Corso Carioli south from roundabout. Then turn right around the city walls towards Via Roma/SP77 and continue on SP77. At Sforzacosta, follow brown signs to abbey on SP78; ample parking.*

Below left Passageway in the catacombs beneath Osimo **Below** Porta Amando Diaz on the west side of Montecassiano

Above The cloisters at the Cistercian Abbadia di Fiastra **Above centre** The pleasant wooded nature reserve of the abbey **Far right** Elegant façade of the Collegiata della SS Annunziata, San Ginesio

WHERE TO STAY

URBISAGLIA

Locanda Le Logge *inexpensive*
Very chic, small B&B with three nice rooms and a restaurant – book ahead.
Corso Gianelli 34, 62010; 0733 506788; www.locandalelogge.it

AROUND SAN GINESIO

Il Casolare *inexpensive*
Views of the Monti Sibillini and food fresh from its own farm make this an authentic and enjoyable experience.
Contrada Vallimestra 44, San Ginesio 62026 (on SP45 west of town); 0733 656 688; www.agriturismocasolare.it

MONTEMONACO

Hotel Monti Azzurri *inexpensive*
Based in the centre of town, this hotel makes a good base for touring and has comfortable rooms and home cooking.
Via Roma 18, 63048; 0736 856 127; www.hotelmontiazzurri.com

⑦ Abbadia di Fiastra
Macerata, Le Marche; 62029
A Cistercian abbey, Fiastra has an extreme simplicity and a distinct lack of adornment that seems to add to its calming and spiritual atmosphere. The original population of monks came here from Milan in the 12th century and used the nearby Roman ruins for much of their building material. The beautiful and impressive Romanesque church, monastery and exquisite cloister now form a lively cultural centre in a large, thickly wooded **nature reserve** *(www. abbadiafiastra.net)*. This park is known as "La Selva" and is ideal for walking and activities such as bird-watching.

🚗 *Take SP78 south from the abbey, ignore a signed right turn to Urbisaglia. The ruins of Urbs Salvia appear on the left of car park. To get to Urbisaglia, return to the signed turn off, turn left and follow the road uphill to the town.*

Below The small hill town of Montefortino, dating back to Roman times

⑧ Urbisaglia
Macerata, Le Marche; 62010
The scattered remains of **Urbs Salvia** *(Jun–Sep: open daily; Oct–May: weekends only)* indicate that this ancient town occupied a significant position in the Roman Empire. The road runs right past the Archaeological Park and its well-preserved town walls, amphitheatre, sanctuary complex and fresco-covered cryptoportico (underground passageway).

Urbisaglia, on the hillside above, emerged in the Middle Ages. The town has a typical medieval layout and its impressive, squat-bastioned 16th-century **Rocca** stands in architectural contrast with the more delicate Baroque **Chiesa di San Lorenzo** just next door.

🚗 *Return to SP78 south, turning right uphill to San Ginesio as signed. There is plenty of parking available in town.*

⑨ San Ginesio
Macerata, Le Marche; 62026
At 700 m (2,300 ft) above sea level, San Ginesio nestles into the foothills of the Monti Sibillini. Entrance to the town is through the **Porta Picena**. To the right is the loggia of the **Ospedale dei Pelligrini**, established in 1295. To the left is a large church, **Santa Maria in Vepretis** *(closed)*, and the small park nearby has a sensational view towards the south. In the town's central square, Piazza A Gentili, the **Collegiata della SS Anunziata** *(open daily)* has a lovely ornate terracotta façade. The public gardens also have wonderful views to the mountains.

🚗 *Return to SP78 and carry on to Sarnano. Park near main square.*

Where to Stay: inexpensive, under €100; moderate, €100–€200; expensive, over €200

Cistercian Architecture

The Cistercians were a monastic order that evolved in France in the 12th century. They believed that people of faith should live simple lives of hard work and prayer, and saw decoration as a diversion from spiritual matters. As a result, they built large, plain and elegant buildings. The Cistercians were great conservationists who built in remote locations, and after the drastic deforestation of the 10th and 11th centuries, developed systems of managed agronomy.

⑩ Sarnano
Macerata, Le Marche; 62028
Built almost entirely from brick, Sarnano still retains its medieval streetscape and ambience. From Piazza Alta, at the top of the town, the view of the terracotta roof tiles and the valley spread out below is enchanting. The square, eerily quiet for Italy, is sometimes called "the silent square" as there are no bars or restaurants. The town's main public buildings, the **Palazzo del Popolo**, the **Palazzo dei Priori**, the **Palazzo dei Podestà** and the **Chiesa di Santa Maria Assunta** (open daily) all date from the late 13th century. The tiny ski resort of **Sassotetto** (www.sarnanoneve.it) is a 20-minute drive away, offering Alpine and cross-country skiing.
🚗 *Continue south on SP78 through Amándola, turning right on SP83 to Montefortino. Park just outside town.*

Below View from San Ginesio, in the foothills of the Monte Sibillini

⑪ Montefortino
Ascoli Piceno, Le Marche; 63044
Dating back to the Roman era, this town gave its name to a type of helmet worn by the Roman legions. **Porta Santa Lucia** is the main entrance to the narrow streets of the town. **Palazzo Leopardi** (Jul–Aug: open daily; winter: Sat pm & Sun) is a small museum known as the Little Louvre of the Sibillini. It contains a fine collection of Renaissance art, including works by Perugino, Carracci and others.
🚗 *Return to SP83, heading south to Montemonaco. Turn right at the sign for the town and park in Piazza Roma.*

⑫ Montemonaco
Ascoli Piceno, Le Marche; 63048
At 1,080 m (3,540 ft), Montemonaco has clear, sharp air, fantastic views and even a few medieval corners to explore. To the east, the view extends across a large swathe of Le Marche to the Adriatic. Walk uphill along Via Italia, and past the small 13th-century Palazzo Comunale. Continue to the **Chiesa di San Benedetto** (open daily), which holds a relic of the right arm of the saint encased in silver and a polychrome wooden crucifix from the late 15th century. Walk along the path to the **Parco Monteguarnieri**, with breathtaking mountain views.
🚗 *Retrace route on SP83 and follow signs to Ascoli Piceno, turning right on SP74, left on SP86, then right on SP237 to the Via Salaria SS4. Exit to Ascoli Piceno and follow signs to "Centro". Turn right at Via Adriatica and sharp left at Via Porta Torricella for car park.*

Above left Montefortino, set among towering peaks **Above** Brick-built Sarnano, a good base for exploring the Sibillini Mountains

EAT AND DRINK

URBISAGLIA
Locanda Le Logge *inexpensive*
This restaurant is highly regarded by the locals and offers a fixed-price gourmet menu of Marchegiana specialities. Booking advised.
Corso Gianelli 34, 62010; 0733 506788; www.locandalelogge.it

SAN GINESIO
Terra Nostra *inexpensive*
Home-made pasta and desserts make this cosy central eatery a good choice for local specialities such as wild boar and porcini. The menu also offers Argentinian dishes.
Piazza Gentili 3, 62026; 0733 656 957; www.terranostrasanginesio.it

MONTEMONACO
Bottega della Cuccagna *inexpensive*
This place offers a mouthwatering selection of cheeses, salamis, wines and other local delicacies. Just buy a picnic lunch to eat outside. The adventurous might want to stay at their refuge on the mountainside.
Via San Lorenzo, 63048; 0338 469 5073; www.bottegadellacuccagna.it; closed Wed

Eat and Drink: inexpensive, under €25; moderate, €25–€45; expensive, over €45

Above The medieval festival of Quintana, held in Ascoli Piceno's Piazza del Popolo in August

WHERE TO STAY

ASCOLI PICENO

Palazzo Guiderocchi *moderate*
This central, venerable building offers elegant rooms, Wi-Fi and a restaurant The annexe also has good-value rooms.
Via Cesere Battisti 3, 63100; 0736 259 710; www.palazzoguiderocchi.com

RIPATRANSONE

Hotel Piceno *inexpensive*
This friendly hotel run by the Picceri family represents good value for money.
Via G Leopardi 12, 63038; 0735 9418; www.hotelpiceno.eu

GROTTAMMARE

La Torretta sul Borgo *inexpensive*
This friendly B&B in the old part of town is a modern amenity with a historic feel.
Via Camilla Peretti 2, 63013; 0735 736 864; www.latorrettasulborgo.it

Below Ripatransone, viewed through a Gothic gateway into town

13 Ascoli Piceno
Le Marche 63100

Originally a defensive site at the confluence of two rivers, Ascoli grew to prominence in the Middle Ages. Although it is often said to have the most beautiful piazza in Italy, what gives Ascoli its elegant charm is the fact that virtually every building is made of travertine marble.

A three-hour walking tour

From the **car park** ①, walk across the wooden bridge and take the lift to the city level. To the left there is a narrow lane into **Piazza Arringo** ②, the scene of many political speeches. At the eastern end is the Duomo di Saint Emidio *(open daily)*, home to a polyptych by the 15th-century artist Carlo Crivelli. Beside the Duomo stands the Battistero di San Giovanni *(open daily)*. Built in the 12th century, over a Roman temple, this beautiful building has a square base and an octagonal upper storey. The Palazzo Vescovile on the other side of the Duomo houses the Museo Diocesano *(open Mon–Fri am, Sat & Sun pm)* with a fine collection of religious art. In the Palazzo Comunale, with its Baroque exterior, is the Pinacoteca Civica with 15th- and 16th-century works by artists such as Crivelli, Titian, Reni, Guercino and other masters.

Exit the piazza by Via XX Settembre to **Piazza Roma** ③, a formal square with palms and an imposing bronze statue commemorating the city's war-dead. Turn right and cross the square to either Via Panichi or Via Macello. Both lead to **Piazza del Popolo** ④,

hailed by many as the most beautiful piazza in Italy. One side is lined by Caffè Meletti, an elegant Liberty-style bar, and the other by a fine arcade topped by swallow-tailed battlements. Also on the square is the Gothic Chiesa di San Francesco, notable for its ribbed vaulting, a statue of Pope Julius II over the door and the Loggia dei Mercanti, a 15th-century addition. Also of interest is the 13th-century Palazzo dei Capitani, whose central clocktower and façade are decorated with reliefs and statues.

Head west along Corso Mazzini to **Piazza Sant Agostino** ⑤ and its 13th-century Romanesque church. Across the square, Palazzo Merli's twin towers recall a time when Ascoli bristled with over 100 of them. Continue along Corso Mazzini. At the back of Sant'Agostino, the cloisters of the old convent house the **Galleria D'Arte Contemporanea** ⑥, with a large collection of modern Italian art. Turn right from the gallery, then left into Corso Mazzini to Piazza San Tomaso and the **Museo dell'Arte Ceramica** ⑦. Cross the square to Via del Pozzetto, turn left (back to Corso Mazzini) and finish at the 1st-century Porta Romana.

Where to Stay: inexpensive, under €100; moderate, €100–€200; expensive, over €200

Turn right into Corso di Sotto, which leads into Via dei Soderini. This part of town has a medieval feel. Continue to Via Dei Lombardi and one of Ascoli's oldest towers, **Torre Ercolani** ⑧. The road leads to Via delle Stelle, along the city walls above the River Tronto. A bit further on is one of the ancient bridges into Ascoli, **Ponte Solestà** ⑨ built in the 1st century. The gateway and towers were built in the 13th century. Turning away from the river, walk up Via Solestà, then left into Via delle Donne, which opens into **Piazza V Basso** ⑩. Here, the Romanesque Chiesa dei SS Vincenzo e Anastasio has a façade divided into sections that once held frescoes of biblical scenes – it was called "La Bibbia dei Poveri" (the Bible of the Poor). Continue along Via Cairoli and turn right into Via del Trivio. On the right and behind San Francesco is the old cloister, now used for markets and performances. Turn right into Corso Mazzini and retrace steps back to the car park.

🚗 *Viale Indipendenza is the main road east, becoming SP235 to the coast. Turn left to Offida on SP43. Park in square.*

⑭ Offida
Ascoli Piceno, Le Marche; 63035
On the approach to Offida, the **Chiesa di Santa Maria della Rocca** appears as though floating on the cliff face. The church has an impressive Romanesque façade. The **crypt** *(open daily)* runs the full length of the church and contains 14th-century frescoes attributed to the Maestro di Offida. The centre of town is Piazza Vittorio Emmanuele II, given an elegant air by the arcades of 14th-century **Palazzo Communale**, a handsome building with a clock tower.

🚗 *Head east on SP1, follow signs for Acquaviva Picena. Park near town walls.*

⑮ Acquaviva Picena
Ascoli Piceno, Le Marche; 63030
The medieval fortress that still forms the heart of this town dominates the hillside to the west. Known as La Rocca, it houses an ancient weapons museum – the **Museo delle Armi Antiche** *(summer: open Tue–Sun)*. The walk through its ancient corridors and the view from its battlements are worth the price of entry.

🚗 *Return along SP1 north, then turn right on SP32. Park in town.*

⑯ Ripatransone
Ascoli Piceno, Le Marche; 63038
On the highest point between the sea and the mountains, Ripatransone had an advantage over its rivals. This is what generated the wealth that built the **Palazzo del Podestà** (1304) and the **Palazzo Comunale**, which holds documents in its archive dating back to 1216. Both buildings are in the main square, Piazza XX Settembre, known as the Belvedere del Piceno because of its excellent views in all directions.

🚗 *Take SP23 to Grottammare. At the fourth hairpin bend, turn left into Via Cagliata. Park on the edge of town.*

⑰ Grottammare
Ascoli Piceno, Le Marche; 63013
Originally built as a defensive bastion against raids from the sea, this tiny medieval fortress town now keeps watch over legions of holiday-makers on the beach below. The town has two churches, a ruined fort with curvy corbels and an excellent vantage point over the coast below. The **Chiesa di Santa Lucia** *(open daily)* is at the northernmost tip of the old town. The Chiesa di San Giovanni Battista now houses the **Museo Sisto di Grottammare** *(summer: open Mon–Sun)*.

Above The tiled roof of the Chiesa di Santa Lucia, Grottammare, looking out to sea

EAT AND DRINK

ASCOLI PICENO
Migliori *inexpensive*
This lively venue on Piazza Arringo serves all the local delicacies, including *olive Ascolane* – olives stuffed with meat, coated in breadcrumbs and fried – as a takeaway snack.
Piazza Arringo 2, 63100; 0736 250 042

Cafe Lorenz *moderate*
Like Florian's in Venice but not as costly. Attentive service, and a great location. Open late. Good for a drink or a meal.
Piazza del Popolo 5, 63100; 0736 259 959; www.ristorantelorenzcafe.it

GROTTAMMARE
Osteria dell'Arancio *moderate*
This well-regarded restaurant caters for discerning diners with good fish and meat dishes and excellent wines.
Piazza Peretti 1; 0735 631 059; evenings only; closed Wed

DAY TRIP OPTIONS
There are three distinct sections to this drive: the lowlands, the mountains and the coast.

The lowlands around Loreto
From Renaissance Loreto ①, it is a short drive for history buffs to Osimo ③ with its Roman fountain and walls and labyrinth of catacombs. A visit to the tower of Montefano ④ will intrigue budding military historians.

Take SP16 to Osimo, then SP361 to Montefano. SP82, then SP77 to Loreto.

Parco Nazionale dei Monti Sibillini
San Ginesio ⑨ is a good base from which to explore the national park. Drive to Sarnano ⑩ to visit the ski resort Sassotetto, either for skiing in winter or walking in summer. Head on to Montefortino ⑪ for Renaissance art, then on to Montemonaco ⑫ for a short climb and great views.

Follow the drive's instructions.

Ascoli Piceno to the sea
Spend the morning touring Ascoli Piceno ⑬, pick up some food and follow the drive to Ripatransone ⑯ – stopping for a scenic picnic along the way. Head on to for Grottammare ⑰ for some time on the beach.

Follow the drive's instructions, missing out Acquaviva Picena. Return via A14 and RA11, if pressed for time.

Eat and Drink: inexpensive, under €25; moderate, €25–€45; expensive, over €45

General Index

Acknowledgments

Dorling Kindersley would like to thank the many people whose help and assistance contributed to the preparation of this book.

Contributors

Gillian Arthur has been living in Friuli-Venezia Giulia, running wine and walking tours for almost a decade. She works as a wine educator when she is not leading walking tours in Italy and France.

Kate Hughes loves travel, the arts and food and wine, so has found her perfect metier in writing and contributing to guides (including Rough Guides and Fodor's) on Italy, where she returns as often as possible.

Gillian Price, based in glorious Venice, is a travel writer and outdoor enthusiast. Besides authoring walking guides, she has been writing for magazines and Dorling Kindersley guides to Italy for many years.

Lucy Ratcliffe has been writing about the Italian Lakes for over a decade. She lived in Milan for three years and now shares her time between Bergamo and Barcelona.

Christine Webb, a former art director, designer and magazine designer, has worked in Sydney and Bangkok. She left her native Australia in 2000 for Italy, where she works as a freelance journalist, photographer and artist.

Marius Webb is a former radio broadcaster and producer based in Tuscany. With Christine, he has contributed to a number of travel guides as a freelance writer including *Best of Tuscany 2008* and *Time Out Italy 2008*.

Celia Woolfrey is a journalist living in London. Besides writing for *The Guardian*, *Time Out* and Rough Guides, she has also authored several Eyewitness Travel guides to Italy for Dorling Kindersley.

Fact checker Janice Jones

Proofreader Indira Chowfin

Indexer Helen Peters

Design and Editorial
Publishing Director Clare Currie
Publisher Vivien Antwi
List Manager Christine Stroyan
Senior Managing Art Editor Mabel Chan
Senior Cartographic Editor Casper Morris
Project Editors Alexandra Whittleton, Rada Radojicic
Project Art Editor Shahid Mahmood
Senior Editors Michelle Crane, Georgina Palffy
Production Controller Linda Dare
Picture Researcher Ellen Root
Senior DTP Designer Jason Little

Special Assistance
Rosie Whitehouse, Maria Pevere

Editorial Assistance
Chris Barstow, Hugh Thompson, Debra Wolter

Revisions Team
Umesh Aggarwal, Avanika, Subhashree Bharati, Cristina Dainotto, Federico Damonte, Sarah Fraser, Bharti Karakoti, Sumita Khatwani, Priyanka Kumar, Suresh Kumar, Bhavika Mathur, Alison McGill, George Nimmo, Kenan Özyurt, Sands Publishing Solutions, Marcella Simoni, Solveig Steinhardt, Jo-Ann Titmarsh, Ajay Verma, Penny Walker

Photographers
Anna Mockford and Nick Bonetti, James Tye, Christine Webb

Additional Photography
Dan Bannister, Demetrio Carrasco, Steve Gorton, John Heseltine, Paul Harris and Anne Heslope, Roger Moss, Kim Sayer, Helena Smith, Rough Guides: James McConnachie

Maps
Cartographic Production
Lovell Johns Ltd, www.lovelljohns.com

Source Data
Base mapping supplied by Kartographie Huber, www.kartographie.de

Elevation Data
SRTM data courtesy of ESRI

Picture Credits
The Publishers would like to thank the following for their kind permission to reproduce their photographs:

(Key: a-above; b-below/bottom; c-centre; f-far; l-left; r-right; t-top)

akg-images: 26-7. **Alamy Images**: Garry Gay 13tl; Hackenberg-Photo-Cologne 110tl; LOOK Die Bildagentur der Fotografen GmbH 111br; MARKA 14tr; Neil Setchfield 13br; Stock Italia 240bl. **Corbis**: Alfredo Dagli Orti 119tr; Douglas Pearson 231br. **Dreamstime**: Adogslifephoto 22tr; Leonid Andronov 135br; Olga Buiacova 13tc; Piero Cruciatti 51tc; Horst Lieber 7tr; Rinofelino 11bl; Andrey Salamchev 18tl; Sfocato 137tc; Webwizards 148-149. **Hotel Greif**: Annette Fischer 23tr. **Photolibrary**: Peter Adams 2-3; Age fotostock/Alberto Paredes 13tr; Alamy/Hackenberg-Photo-Cologne 109tl; imagebroker 10br, 95tr; Fresh Food Images/John Sims 38-9; Giuglio Gil 27c; imagebroker 109bc, /Dr Wilfried Bahnmueller 95tc; Lonely Planet Images/Andrew Bain 95cl, /Mark Daffey 18bl; Mauritius/Torino Torino 112tr; PhotoEquipe153 10bl; Radius Images 94tl; Robert Harding Travel/James Emmerson 91br, /Tony Gervis 90tr; The Travel Library/H G Schmidt 94b; Westend61 86-87, 92tl.

Jacket
Front: **Corbis**: Frank Lukasseck; Back: **Dorling Kindersley**: Anna Mockford and Nick Bonetti c, James Tye cr, Christine Webb cl; Spine: **Corbis**: Frank Lukasseck.

All other images © Dorling Kindersley
For further information see: www.dkimages.com

Phrase Book

IN AN EMERGENCY

Help!	**Aiuto!**	*eye-yoo-toh*
Stop!	**Fermate!**	*fair-mah-teh*
Call a	**Chiama un**	*kee-ah-mah oon*
doctor.	**medico**	*meh-dee-koh*
Call an	**Chiama un'**	*kee-ah-mah oon*
ambulance.	**ambulanza**	*am-boo-lan-tsa*
Call the	**Chiama la**	*kee-ah-mah lah*
police.	**polizia**	*pol-ee-tsee-ah*
Call the fire	**Chiama i**	*kee-ah-mah ee*
brigade.	**pompieri**	*pom-pee-air-ee*
Where is the	**Dov'è il telefono?**	*dov-eh eel teh-leh-*
telephone?		*foh-noh?*
The nearest	**L'ospedale**	*loss-peh-dah-leh-pee-*
hospital?	**più vicino?**	*oo vee-chee-noh?*

COMMUNICATION ESSENTIALS

Yes/No	**Si/No**	*see/noh*
Please	**Per favore**	*pair fah-vor-eh*
Thank you	**Grazie**	*grah-tsee-eh*
It's a pleasure	**Prego**	*preh-goh*
Excuse me	**Mi scusi**	*mee skoo-zee*
Hello	**Buon giorno**	*bwon jor-noh*
Goodbye	**Arrivederci**	*ah-ree-veh-dair-chee*
Good evening	**Buona sera**	*bwon-ah sair-ah*
morning	**la mattina**	*lah mah-tee-nah*
afternoon	**il pomeriggio**	*eel poh-meh-ree-joh*
Evening	**la sera**	*lah sair-ah*
yesterday	**ieri**	*ee-air-ee*
today	**oggi**	*oh-jee*
tomorrow	**domani**	*doh-mah-nee*
here	**qui**	*kwee*
there	**la**	*lah*
What?	**Quale?**	*kwah-leh?*
When?	**Quando?**	*kwan-doh?*
Why?	**Perchè?**	*pair-keh?*
Where?	**Dove?**	*doh-veh?*

USEFUL PHRASES

How are you?	**Come sta?**	*koh-meh stah?*
Very well,	**Molto bene,**	*moll-toh beh-neh*
thank you.	**grazie.**	*grah-tsee-eh*
Pleased to	**Piacere di**	*pee-ah-chair-eh dee*
meet you.	**conoscerla.**	*coh-noh-shair-lah*
See you later.	**A più tardi.**	*ah pee-oo tar-dee*
That's fine.	**Va bene.**	*va beh-neh*
Where is/are …?	**Dov'è/Dove sono …?**	*dov-eh/doveh soh-noh?*
How long does	**Quanto tempo ci**	*kwan-toh tem-poh*
it take to get to …?	**vuole per**	*chee voo-oh-leh pair*
	andare a …?	*an-dar-eh ah …?*
How do I	**Come faccio per**	*koh-meh fah-choh*
get to …?	**arrivare a …?**	*pair arri-var-eh ah …?*
Do you speak English?	**Parla inglese?**	*par-lah een-gleh-zeh?*
I don't understand.	**Non capisco.**	*non ka-pee-skoh*
Could you speak	**Può parlare**	*pwoh par-lah-reh*
more slowly,	**più lentamente,**	*pee-oo len-ta-men-teh*
please?	**per favore?**	*pair fah-vor-eh?*
I'm sorry.	**Mi dispiace.**	*mee dee-spee-ah-cheh*

USEFUL WORDS

big	**grande**	*gran-deh*
small	**piccolo**	*pee-koh-loh*
hot	**caldo**	*kal-doh*
cold	**freddo**	*fred-doh*
good	**buono**	*bwoh-noh*
bad	**cattivo**	*kat-tee-voh*
enough	**basta**	*bas-tah*
well	**bene**	*beh-neh*
open	**aperto**	*ah-pair-toh*
closed	**chiuso**	*kee-oo-zoh*
left	**a sinistra**	*ah see-nee-strah*
right	**a destra**	*ah dess-trah*
straight on	**sempre dritto**	*sem-preh dree-toh*
near	**vicino**	*vee-chee-noh*
far	**lontano**	*lon-tah-noh*
up	**su**	*soo*
down	**giù**	*joo*
early	**presto**	*press-toh*
late	**tardi**	*tar-dee*
entrance	**entrata**	*en-trah-tah*
exit	**uscita**	*oo-shee-ta*
toilet	**il gabinetto**	*eel gab-bee-net-toh*
free, unoccupied	**libero**	*lee-bair-oh*
free, no charge	**gratuito**	*grah-too-ee-toh*

MAKING A TELEPHONE CALL

I'd like to place a	**Vorrei fare**	*vor-ray far-eh oona*
long-distance call.	**una interurbana.**	*in-tair-oor-bah-nah*
I'd like to make	**Vorrei fare una**	*vor-ray far-eh oona*
a reverse-charge	**telefonata a carico**	*teh-leh-fon-ah-tah ah*
call.	**del destinatario.**	*kar-ee-koh dell dess-*
		tee-nah-tar-ree-oh
I'll try again later.	**Ritelefono più**	*ree-teh-teh-foh-noh*
	tardi.	*pee-oo tar-dee*
Can I leave a	**Posso lasciare**	*poss-oh lash-ah-rch*
message?	**un messaggio?**	*oon mess-sah-joh?*
Hold on.	**Un attimo,**	*oon ah-tee-moh,*
	per favore	*pair fah-vor-eh*
Could you speak	**Può parlare più**	*pwoh par-lah-reh*
up a little please?	**forte, per favore?**	*pee-oo for-teh, pair*
		fah-vor-eh?
local call	**telefonata locale**	*te-leh-fon-ah-tah*
		loh-cah-leh

SHOPPING

How much	**Quant'è,**	*kwan-teh*
does this cost?	**per favore?**	*pair fah-vor-eh?*
I would like …	**Vorrei …**	*vor-ray*
Do you have …?	**Avete …?**	*ah-veh-teh …?*
I'm just looking.	**Sto soltanto**	*stoh sol-tan-toh*
	guardando.	*gwar-dan-doh*
Do you take	**Accettate**	*ah-chet-tah -teh kar-teh*
credit cards?	**carte di credito?**	*dee creh-dee-toh?*
What time do	**A che ora apre/**	*ah keh or-ah*
you open/close?	**chiude?**	*ah-preh/kee-oo-deh?*
this one	**questo**	*kweh-stoh*
that one	**quello**	*kwell-oh*
expensive	**caro**	*kar-oh*
cheap	**a buon prezzo**	*ah bwon pret-soh*
size, clothes	**la taglia**	*lah tah-lee-ah*
size, shoes	**il numero**	*eel noo-mair-oh*
white	**bianco**	*bee-ang-koh*
black	**nero**	*neh-roh*
red	**rosso**	*ross-oh*
yellow	**giallo**	*jal-loh*
green	**verde**	*vair-deh*
blue	**blu**	*bloo*

TYPES OF SHOP

antique dealer	**l'antiquario**	*lan-tee-kwah-ree-oh*
bakery	**il forno**	*eel forn-oh*
	/il panificio	*/eel pan-ee-fee-choh*
bank	**la banca**	*lah bang-kah*
bookshop	**la libreria**	*lah lee-breh-ree-ah*
butcher	**la macelleria**	*lah mah-chell-eh-ree-ah*
cake shop	**la pasticceria**	*lah pas-tee-chair-ee-ah*
chemist	**la farmacia**	*lah far-mah-chee-ah*
delicatessen	**la salumeria**	*lah sah-loo-meh-ree-ah*
department store	**il grande**	*eel gran-deh*
	magazzino	*mag-gad-zee-noh*
fishmonger	**il pescivendolo**	*eel pesh-ee-ven-doh-loh*
greengrocer	**il fruttivendolo**	*eel froo-tee-ven-doh-loh*
grocery	**alimentari**	*ah-lee-men-tah-ree*
hairdresser	**il parrucchiere**	*eel par-oo-kee-air-eh*
ice-cream parlour	**la gelateria**	*lah jel-lah-tair-ee-ah*
market	**il mercato**	*eel mair-kah-toh*
newsstand	**l'edicola**	*leh-dee-koh-lah*
post office	**l'ufficio postale**	*loo-fee-choh pos-tah-leh*
shoe shop	**il negozio di**	*eel neh-goh-tsioh dee*
	scarpe	*skar-peh*
supermarket	**il supermercato**	*eel su-pair-mair-kah-toh*
tobacconist	**il tabaccaio**	*eel tah-bak-eye-oh*
travel agency	**l'agenzia di viaggi**	*lah-jen-tsee-ah dee*
		vee-ad-jee

SIGHTSEEING

art gallery	**la pinacoteca**	*lah peena-koh-teh-kah*
bus stop	**la fermata**	*lah fair-mah-tah*
	dell'autobus	*dell ow-toh-booss*
church	**la chiesa**	*lah kee-eh-zah*
	la basilica	*lah bah-seel-i-kah*
closed for	**chiuso per le**	*kee-oo-zoh pair leh*
holidays	**ferie**	*fair-ee-eh*
garden	**il giardino**	*eel jar-dee-no*
library	**la biblioteca**	*lah beeb-lee-oh-teh-kah*
museum	**il museo**	*eel moo-zeh-oh*
railway station	**la stazione**	*lah stah-tsee-oh-neh*
tourist	**l'ufficio**	*loo-fee-choh*
information	**di turismo**	*dee too-ree-smoh*

STAYING IN A HOTEL

Do you have any vacant rooms?	**Avete camere libere?**	ah-veh-teh kah-mair-eh lee-bair-eh?
double room	**una camera doppia**	oona kah-mair-ah doh-pee-ah
with double bed	**con letto matrimoniale**	kon let-toh mah-tree-moh-nee-ah-leh
twin room	**una camera con due letti**	oona kah-mair-ah kon doo-eh let-tee
single room	**una camera singola**	oona kah-mair-ah sing-goh-lah
room with a bath, shower	**una camera con bagno, con doccia**	oona kah-mair-ah kon ban-yoh, kon dot-chah
porter	**il facchino**	eel fah-kee-noh
key	**la chiave**	lah kee-ah-veh
I have a reservation.	**Ho fatto una prenotazione.**	oh fat-toh oona preh-noh-tah-tsee-oh-neh

EATING OUT

Have you got a table for…?	**Avete una tavola per … ?**	ah-veh-teh oona tah-voh-lah pair …?
I'd like to reserve a table.	**Vorrei riservare una tavola.**	vor-ray ree-sair-vah-reh oona tah-voh-lah
breakfast	**colazione**	koh-lah-tsee-oh-neh
lunch	**pranzo**	pran-tsoh
dinner	**cena**	cheh-nah
The bill, please.	**Il conto, per favore.**	eel kon-toh pair fah-vor-eh
I am a vegetarian.	**Sono vegetariano/a.**	soh-noh veh-jeh-tar-ee-ah-noh/nah
waitress	**cameriera**	kah-mair-ee-air-ah
waiter	**cameriere**	kah-mair-ee-air-eh
fixed price menu	**il menù a prezzo fisso**	eel meh-noo ah pret-soh fee-soh
dish of the day	**piatto del giorno**	pee-ah-toh dell jor-no
starter	**antipasto**	an-tee-pass-toh
first course	**il primo**	eel pree-moh
main course	**il secondo**	eel seh-kon-doh
vegetables	**il contorno**	eel kon-tor-noh
dessert	**il dolce**	eel doll-cheh
cover charge	**il coperto**	eel koh-pair-toh
wine list	**la lista dei vini**	lah lee-stah day vee-nee
rare	**al sangue**	al sang-gweh
medium	**al puntino**	al poon-tee-noh
well done	**ben cotto**	ben kot-toh
glass	**il bicchiere**	eel bee-kee-air-eh
bottle	**la bottiglia**	lah bot-teel-yah
knife	**il coltello**	eel kol-tell-oh
fork	**la forchetta**	lah for-ket-tah
spoon	**il cucchiaio**	eel koo-kee-eye-oh

MENU DECODER

l'acqua minerale gassata/ naturale	lah-kwah mee-nair-ah-leh gah-zah-tah/ nah-too-rah-leh	mineral water fizzy/ still
agnello	ah-niell-oh	lamb
aceto	ah-cheh-toh	vinegar
aglio	al-ee-oh	garlic
al forno	al for-noh	baked
alla griglia	ah-lah greel-yah	grilled
l'aragosta	lah-rah-goss-tah	lobster
arrosto	ar-ross-toh	roast
la birra	lah beer-rah	beer
la bistecca	lah bee-stek-kah	steak
il brodo	eel broh-doh	broth
il burro	eel boor-oh	butter
il caffè	eel kah-feh	coffee
i calamari	ee kah-lah-mah-ree	squid
i carciofi	ee kar-choff-ee	artichokes
la carne	la kar-neh	meat
carne di maiale	kar-neh dee mah-yah-leh	pork
la cipolla	la chip-oh-lah	onion
i contorni	ee kon-tor-nee	vegetables
i fagioli	ee fah-joh-lee	beans
il fegato	eel fay-gah-toh	liver
il finocchio	eel fee-nok-ee-oh	fennel
il formaggio	eel for-mad-joh	cheese
le fragole	leh frah-goh-leh	strawberries
il fritto misto	eel free-toh mees-toh	mixed fried dish
la frutta	la froot-tah	fruit
frutti di mare	froo-tee dee mah-reh	seafood
i funghi	ee foon-ghee	mushrooms
i gamberi	ee gam-bair-ee	prawns
il gelato	eel jel-lah-toh	ice cream

l'insalata	leen-sah-lah-tah	salad
il latte	eel laht-teh	milk
lesso	less-oh	boiled
il manzo	eel man-tsoh	beef
la melanzana	lah meh-lan-tsah-nah	aubergine
la minestra	lah mee-ness-trah	soup
l'olio	loh-lee-oh	oil
il pane	eel pah-neh	bread
le patate	leh pah-tah-teh	potatoes
le patatine fritte	leh pah-tah-teen-eh free-teh	chips
il pepe	eel peh-peh	pepper
la pesca	lah pess-kah	peach
il pesce	eel pesh-eh	fish
il pollo	eel poll-oh	chicken
il pomodoro	eel poh-moh-dor-oh	tomato
il prosciutto cotto/crudo	eel pro-shoo-toh kot-toh/kroo-doh	ham cooked/cured
il riso	eel ree-zoh	rice
il sale	eel sah-leh	salt
la salsiccia	lah sal-see-chah	sausage
le seppie	leh sep-pee-eh	cuttlefish
secco	sek-koh	dry
la sogliola	lah soll-yoh-lah	sole
gli spinaci	lyee spee-nah-chee	spinach
succo d'arancia/ di limone	soo-koh dah-ran-chah/ dee lee-moh-neh	orange/ lemon juice
il tè	eel teh	tea
la tisana	lah tee-zah-nah	herbal tea
il tonno	eel ton-noh	tuna
la torta	lah tor-tah	cake/tart
l'uovo	loo-oh-voh	egg
vino bianco	vee-noh bee-ang-koh	white wine
vino rosso	vee-noh ross-oh	red wine
il vitello	eel vee-tell-oh	veal
le vongole	leh von-goh-leh	clams
lo zucchero	loh zoo-kair-oh	sugar
gli zucchini	lyee dzu-kee-nee	courgettes
la zuppa	lah dzu-pah	soup

NUMBERS

1	**uno**	oo-noh
2	**due**	doo-eh
3	**tre**	treh
4	**quattro**	kwat-roh
5	**cinque**	ching-kweh
6	**sei**	say-ee
7	**sette**	set-teh
8	**otto**	ot-toh
9	**nove**	noh-veh
10	**dieci**	dee-eh-chee
11	**undici**	oon-dee-chee
12	**dodici**	doh-dee-chee
13	**tredici**	tray-dee-chee
14	**quattordici**	kwat-tor-dee-chee
15	**quindici**	kwin-dee-chee
16	**sedici**	say-dee-chee
17	**diciassette**	dee-chah-set-teh
18	**diciotto**	dee-chot-toh
19	**diciannove**	dee-chah-noh-veh
20	**venti**	ven-tee
30	**trenta**	tren-tah
40	**quaranta**	kwah-ran-tah
50	**cinquanta**	ching-kwan-tah
60	**sessanta**	sess-an-tah
70	**settanta**	set-tan-tah
80	**ottanta**	ot-tan-tah
90	**novanta**	noh-van-tah
100	**cento**	chen-toh
1,000	**mille**	mee-leh
2,000	**duemila**	doo-eh mee-lah
5,000	**cinquemila**	ching-kweh mee-lah
1,000,000	**un milione**	oon meel-yoh-neh

TIME

one minute	**un minuto**	oon mee-noo-toh
one hour	**un'ora**	oon or-ah
half an hour	**mezz'ora**	medz-or-ah
a day	**un giorno**	oon jor-noh
a week	**una settimana**	oona set-tee-mah-nah
Monday	**lunedì**	loo-neh-dee
Tuesday	**martedì**	mar-teh-dee
Wednesday	**mercoledì**	mair-koh-leh-dee
Thursday	**giovedì**	joh-veh-dee
Friday	**venerdì**	ven-air-dee
Saturday	**sabato**	sah-bah-toh
Sunday	**domenica**	doh-meh-nee-kah

Driver's Phrase Book

SOME COMMON ROAD SIGNS

accendere i fari	headlights on
attenzione	watch out, caution
autostrada	motorway (with toll)
banchina non transitabile	soft verge
caduta massi	falling rocks
centro	town centre
code	traffic ahead
controllo automatico della velocità	automatic speed monitor
cunetta o dosso	ditch
deviazione	diversion
disporsi su due file	two-lane traffic
divieto di accesso	no entry
divieto di fermata	no stopping
divieto di transito	no thoroughfare
dogana	customs
escluso residenti	residents only
fine del tratto autostradale	end of motorway
ghiaccio	ice
incrocio	junction
incrocio pericoloso	dangerous junction/ crossroads
informazioni turistiche	tourist information
lavori in corso	roadworks
nebbia	fog
non oltrepassare	no access
pagare qui	pay here
parcheggio a giorni alterni	parking on alternate days
parcheggio a pagamento	paying car park
parcheggio custodito	car park with attendant
parcheggio incustodito	unattended car park
pedaggio	toll
pedoni	pedestrians
pericolo	danger
pista ciclabile	bicycle trail
rallentare	reduce speed
scuola	school
senso unico	one way
sosta vietata	no parking
sottopassaggio	subway
strada a fondo cieco	dead end
strada camionabile	route for heavy vehicles
strada ghiacciata	ice on road
strada statale	main road
strada sdrucciolevole	slippery road
strada secondaria	secondary road
uscita camion	works exit
veicoli lenti	slow lane
zona a traffico limitato	restricted traffic area
zona pedonale	shopping centre

DIRECTIONS YOU MAY BE GIVEN

a destra	right
a sinistra	left
dritto	straight on
giri a destra	turn right
giri a sinistra	turn left
il primo/la prima a destra	first on the right
il secondo/la seconda a sinistra	second on the left
vada oltre …	go past the …

THINGS YOU'LL SEE

acqua	water
area di servizio	service area
aspirapolvere	vacuum cleaner
autolavaggio	car wash
autorimessa	garage (for repairs)
benzina	petrol
benzina senza piombo	unleaded petrol
benzina super	4-star petrol
casello autostradale	motorway toll booth
cera per auto	car wax
code	traffic queue
deviazione	diversion
gasolio	diesel oil
gommista	tyre repairs
guidare a passo d'uomo	drive at walking speed
liquido tergicristallo	windscreen washer liquid
olio	oil
raccordo autostradale	motorway junction
spegnere il motore	turn off engine
spingere	push
stazione di servizio	service station
tirare	pull
uscita	exit
vietato fumare	no smoking

THINGS YOU'LL HEAR

Vuole una macchina con il cambio automatico o manuale?
Would you like an automatic or a manual?

Esibisca la patente, per favore?
May I see your licence, please?

Mi fa vedere il passaporto, per favore?
May I see your passport, please?

USEFUL PHRASES

Could you check the oil/water level, please?
Potrebbe controllare il livello dell'olio/dell'acqua, per favore?
potreb-be kontrol-lare eel leevel-lo del ol-yo/del akwa pair fah-vor-eh

Fill it up, please!
Faccia il pieno, per favore!
facha eel p-yeno pair fah-vor-eh

I'd like 35 litres of 4-star petrol, please.
Mi dia trentacinque litri di super, per favore.
mee dee-a trentacheenkwe leetree dee soopair pair fah-vor-eh

Do you do repairs?
Effettua riparazioni?
ef-fet-too-a reeparatz-yonee

Can you repair the clutch?
Può ripararmi la frizione?
pwo reepararmee la freetz-yone

There is something wrong with the engine.
C'è qualcosa che non va nel motore.
cheh kwalkoza ke non va nel motore

The engine is overheating.
Il motore si surriscalda.
eel motore see soor-reeskalda

I need a new tyre.
Ho bisogno di una gomma nuova.
o beezon-yo dee oona gom-ma nwova

Can you replace this?
Può sostituirlo?
pwo sosteetoo-eerlo

The indicator is not working.
La freccia non funziona.
la frech-cha non foontz-yona

How long will it take?
Quanto tempo ci vorrà?
kwanto tempo chee vor-ra

Where can I park?
Dove posso parcheggiare?
dove pos-so parkej-jare

I'd like to hire a car.
Vorrei noleggiare una macchina.
vor-ray nolej-jare oona mak-keena

I'd like an automatic/a manual.
Vorrei una macchina con il cambio automatico/manuale.
vor-ray oona mak-keena kon eel kam-bee-o owtomateeko/manwale

How much is it for one day?
Quanto costa per un giorno?
kwanto kosta pair oon jorno

Is there a mileage charge?
C'è un supplemento per il chilometraggio?
cheh oon soop-plemento pair eel keelometraj-jo

When do I have to return it?
Quando devo riportarla?
kwando devo reeportarla

Where is the nearest petrol station?
Dov'è la stazione di servizio più vicina?
doveh la statz-yone dee sairveetz-yo p-yoo veecheena

How do I get to …?
Come faccio per arrivare a …?
koh-meh fah-choh pair arri-var-eh ah

Is this the road to …?
È questa la strada per …?
eh kwesta la strada pair

Which is the quickest way to …?
Qual'è la strada più breve per …?
kwal eh la strada p-yoo breve pair

USEFUL WORDS

automatic	con il cambio automatico	kon eel kam-bee-o owtomateeko
bonnet	il cofano	kofano
boot	il portabagagli	portabagal-yee
brake	il freno	freh-no
breakdown	il guasto	gwa-sto
car	l'automobile, la macchina	ow-toh-moh-beeleh, mak-keena
car ferry	il traghetto	traget-to
car park	il parcheggio	parkej-jo
clutch	la frizione	freetz-yone
crossroads	l'incrocio	een-kro-cho
drive	guidare	gwee-dar-eh
engine	il motore	mo-tor-eh
exhaust	lo scappamento	skap-pamento
fanbelt	la cinghia della ventola	cheeng-ya del-la ven-to-la
garage (for repairs)	l'autorimessa	ow-toh-ree-mes-sa
gear	il cambio, la marcia	kam-bee-o, mar-cha
gears	le marce	mar-cheh
headlights	i fari	far-ee
indicator	la freccia	frech-cha
junction	l'incrocio	een-kro-cho
licence	la patente	pa-ten-teh
lorry	il camion, l'autocarro	kam-yon, ow-toh-kar-ro
manual	con il cambio manuale	kon eel kam-bee-o man-wah-leh
mirror	lo specchietto	spekk-yet-to
motorcycle	la motocicletta	moto-chee-klet-ta
motorway	l'autostrada	ow-toh-strada
motorway entry	raccordo di entrata	rak-kor-do dee en-tra-ta
motorway exit	raccordo di uscita	rak-kor-do dee oo-shee-ta
number plate	la targa	tar-ga
petrol	la benzina	bendz-eena
petrol station	la stazione di servizio	statz-yone dee sair-veetz-yo
rear lights	i fari posteriori	far-ee post-airy-oree
ring road	raccordo anulare	rak-kordo anoolareh
road	la strada	stra-da
spare parts	i pezzi di ricambio	petzee dee ree-kam-bee-o
spark plug	la candela	kan-deh-la
speed	la velocità	ve-loh-chee-ta
speed limit	il limite di velocità	lee-mee-teh dee ve-loh-chee-ta
speedometer	il tachimetro	tak-ee-me-tro
steering wheel	il volante	vo-lan-teh
traffic lights	il semaforo	seh-ma-foro
trailer	il rimorchio, la roulotte	ree-mork-yo, roo-lot
transmission	la scatola del cambio	ska-toh-la del kam-bee-o
tyre	la gomma	gom-ma
van	il furgone	foor-gon-eh
warning sign	il triangolo	tree-angolo
wheel	la ruota	rw-oh-ta
windscreen	il parabrezza	para-bretza
windscreen wiper	il tergicristallo	tairjee-kreestal-lo

Road Signs

SPEED LIMITS AND GENERAL DRIVING INDICATIONS

Give way

Compulsory stop

Your route has priority

Your route no longer has priority

You have priority at the next junction

Junction gives priority to traffic from the right

Give way to oncoming traffic

No overtaking

Roundabout

No access for vehicles over 3.5 m in height

Speed limit

End of speed limit

Obligatory minimum distance of 70 m

Minimum speed limit

Residential area with special speed limit

WARNING SIGNS

Unspecified danger

Succession of bends

Slippery road

Risk of strong crosswinds

Risk of rockfalls

Speed bumps

Road narrows

Road narrows on the left

Level crossing with barrier

Level crossing with no barrier

Steep descent

Wild animals

Children crossing, or school

Pedestrian crossing

Road works